JIM BOEHEIM
and
Syracuse Basketball

JIM BOEHEIM
and
Syracuse
Basketball

IN THE ZONE

DONALD F. STAFFO
FOREWORD BY DAVE BING

SPORTS
PUBLISHING

Sports Publishing books may be purchased in bulk at special discounts for sales promotion, corporate gifts, fund-raising, or educational purposes. Special editions can also be created to specifications. For details, contact the Special Sales Department, Skyhorse Publishing, 307 West 36th Street, 11th Floor, New York, NY 10018 or info@skyhorsepublishing.com.

Sports Publishing® is a registered trademark of Skyhorse Publishing, Inc.®, a Delaware corporation.

Visit our website at www.skyhorsepublishing.com.

10 9 8 7 6 5 4 3 2 1

Library of Congress Cataloging-in-Publication Data is available on file.

Cover design by Tom Lau
Cover photography by Associated Press

Print ISBN: 978-1-6835-8248-9
eBook ISBN: 978-1-6835-8250-2

Printed in the United States of America

CONTENTS

FOREWORD

I have fond memories of Jimmy Boeheim during our years at Syracuse University. Our friendship has lasted fifty-six years, and the life lessons learned together at Syracuse have lasted a lifetime. My experiences there provided me with the knowledge and value system that has guided me throughout my professional and personal life.

In the Zone is an outstanding book. It captures the essence of what it's like to live and bleed Orange. And it tells in vivid detail how Jim became the face of Syracuse basketball. This book provides an up close and personal look at the inner workings of a basketball program that went from being good to being a powerhouse under Jim's leadership.

Donald Staffo has a unique writing style that makes the book enjoyable to read. He states in the Preface that he "tried to paint a picture" that will enable Syracuse fans to relive their memories. The detailed descriptions of Syracuse's biggest games and key events and the mini-profiles of the Orange's top players certainly do that. Mission accomplished!

Jim is one of the greatest college basketball coaches of all time. For anyone who is a fan of Syracuse basketball—or simply loves college basketball in general—this book offers an insider's look into the talent and motivation of a legendary Hall of Fame coach and his huge influence on the SU program.

Staffo provides an extremely detailed account of how Jim's love for the game propelled him to more than 1,000 wins in a remarkable run as Syracuse's head coach. This book offers a thorough telling of how Jim has led Syracuse to success year after year, while also navigating challenges and scandals that sometimes arose during his career. Additionally, Staffo offers a peek into Jim Boeheim, the person. The caring man who made it his mission to raise awareness and money in the fight against cancer and to support many other charitable causes.

This is the most comprehensive book on Syracuse and Jim Boeheim that I am aware of. I, and I'm sure my teammates, appreciate the time, incredible amount of research, and the work that the author put in to share the Syracuse basketball story with not only the Orange Nation but with fans and followers of college basketball. I give the book my stamp of approval.

I loved Syracuse when I was a student there. And I still love Syracuse. The years I spent at SU had a tremendous impact on my life and career. So has my friendship with Jim.

And, without a doubt, Jimmy Boeheim's imprint will remain on Syracuse basketball, now and far into the future.

I hope you enjoy *Jim Boeheim and Syracuse Basketball: In the Zone.*

—Dave Bing
NBA All-Star and Hall of Famer, former mayor of Detroit, and
founder of Bing Youth Institute,
Detroit, Michigan

PREFACE

A native of Central New York, I have followed Syracuse basketball closely for about sixty years and very closely when Jim Boeheim played for and later was an assistant and head coach of the Orangemen. In the early 1980s, I covered basketball for a number of national publications, including seven years for *Basketball Times*. I periodically interviewed Boeheim and occasionally contributed features on Syracuse to several other national publications. I wrote at the time what probably is one of the longest articles ever written about Boeheim, which appeared in serial fashion in four very lengthy segments in what was then known as *The Big Orange*. I began working on this book in 2010 with the intent of publishing the book when Boeheim retired, but then in 2017, he decided to continue coaching, so I decided to release the book now.

This book is based on lengthy interviews, hundreds of conversations and email exchanges with dozens of people, and extensive research. The Syracuse basketball alumni is an extended family going all the way back to Boeheim's teammates, with the players and people who I contacted providing me with ways to reach other people who might have something to contribute to this project. Intensive interviews with the people who knew Boeheim the best at various junctures of his life are the core of the book. Covering Alabama football and basketball for the Associated Press and other media outlets for thirty years helped me gain access to all of these people.

Other information is from following and studying Syracuse basketball daily and by accessing almost all of Boeheim's press conferences and the information I accumulated over nearly forty years from a variety of places. References and sources are appropriately credited in the text, except in instances when I could not locate or identify them properly. In those instances, I apologize. It must be recognized that opinions vary and memories can be faulty and selective. The result is that people may have different recollections of those involved and the events themselves. Furthermore, almost everyone close to the SU program has an opinion on Boeheim or a Boeheim story. The reader may wonder why someone in particular wasn't contacted or included. That's because the information they provided was perhaps similar to what others said, especially those who knew him best.

The book begins with highlights from Boeheim's career and then more or less progresses chronologically through his coaching career. Some seasons are detailed while others are skimmed; some of Syracuse's important or memorable games are highlighted, and some of the Orange's legendary players are profiled. Noted are several "Syracuse moments," which are instances and occurrences that are unique to the program and ingrained in the minds of Orange fans as putting the spotlight on Syracuse and, in some ways, set the program apart from others.

Boeheim has enjoyed a very successful Hall-of-Fame career, but to some, his achievements will be tainted due to off-the-court indiscretions that happened under his watch. Boeheim's basketball expertise and philanthropy cannot be questioned. However, some of his decisions, whether right or wrong, will be. His amazing accomplishments will remain a matter of record, but some of them will be accompanied by an asterisk. What he has achieved and the charitable work he has done through the Jim and Juli Boeheim Foundation far outweighs any issues that became a part of his story. The book recognizes Boeheim's on-the-court achievements, with the understanding that, officially, the

NCAA vacated 101 wins from 2004–07 and 2010–12, the nine regular season games he missed in 2015–16 due to an NCAA-imposed suspension, and the Big East conference records for 1979–2013 and the Atlantic Coast Conference records from 2013–16. These and other adjustments are reflected in the Appendix and in other places in the text.

The book is about the Syracuse basketball program as much as its coach. An attempt is made in various places to "paint a picture" to allow readers to "relive" events and relate to certain players. What follows is an attempt to provide an accurate, balanced, and fair portrayal of Boeheim and his program. With Boeheim a polarizing figure, there is little chance the contents will please or even satisfy everyone. Boeheim was offered opportunities to participate in this project but declined. Therefore, this is an unauthorized work based on the people who know him best.

1

AT THE TOP OF HIS PROFESSION

The 2003 NCAA Championship

Jim Boeheim always had the numbers, right from the very beginning when he jump-started his coaching career by winning 100 games in his first four years, faster by season than any other coach in history. By number of seasons, he is tied for second quickest to reach 400, 600, and 700 wins, the third to reach 800, and one of only three coaches and the second fastest to notch 900 victories. Boeheim is the second-winningest men's college basketball coach of all time, behind his good friend Mike Krzyzewski, who has accumulated 1,100 victories. Over 42 years, Boeheim has compiled an on-the-court win-loss mark of 1,027–371, although after sanctions, the official record is 926–371.

Once the all-time leader with 38 20-win seasons, he is now second with 33. At one point, he had 17 straight 20-win seasons, which has since been adjusted to 14. Prior to the sanctions, Boeheim won at least

26 games in a season 20 times while competing in what was at times the best basketball conference in the country. A winner of a record 10 Big East regular season championships, five Big East tournaments, and a league-best 15 advances to the conference championship game, Boeheim has won 60 NCAA tournament games, since reduced to 56, tied for fifth all-time among Division I coaches. His teams have played in a post-season tournament every year except 1993 and 2014 when the Orange was ineligible due to NCAA sanctions. The numbers and accomplishments, very impressive indeed, speak for themselves.

It's the respect that took a long time coming. For most of his career, the nothing-but-a-winner Syracuse basketball coach made Rodney Dangerfield look like a piker. Even though he shot up the coaching win-list and took the Orange to the NCAA Tournament 32 times, the Final Four four times, and into the championship game three times, few electronic and print journalists considered Boeheim among the nation's best coaches until Syracuse made its remarkable run to the NCAA championship in 2003. More members of the media began to publicly acknowledge that Boeheim just might know a little something about round-ball when he was inducted into the Naismith Memorial Basketball Hall of Fame in 2005. A few more jumped on board the Boeheim bandwagon when Krzyzewski appointed him an assistant coach for the United States Olympic basketball team in 2008 and then again in 2012 and 2016.

Some, however, were still reluctant to include Boeheim in the upper echelon of coaches, always putting him in a small group just below those designated as elite coaches, despite the fact that Boeheim had a head-to-head winning record against some of those very same coaches. The Johnny-come-latelies who finally began to give Boeheim his due did so grudgingly and only after trotting out the same old tired criticisms about his whining sideline demeanor, vanilla personality, poor bench coaching, playground offense, junk defense, and soft schedules. They found fault with his cranky behavior. They didn't like the way he dressed, but Juli, his wife, improved that. Sometimes they harped on his personal mannerisms. When it snowed too much in Syracuse, the longtime, hardcore critics blamed Boeheim.

On April 7, 2003, in New Orleans, when Hakim Warrick blocked Michael Lee's shot as the game clock was winding down, enabling Syracuse to hang on and beat Kansas to win the national championship, Jim Boeheim finally got the 27-year-old, 800-pound gorilla off his back. Then he slammed that gorilla on the Superdome floor and stomped on it. With the sounds of "One Shining Moment" reverberated throughout the arena, highlights of the tournament being shown on the big video display board, and all of it was being shown on television in hundreds of countries, Boeheim, like a two-bit character actor who finally won an Academy Award for a leading role, felt like he was on top of the world. It was like the globe was a basketball, and he was holding it in the palm of his hand. On that night when Boeheim left the building, he took a deep breath and exhaled, gave a sigh of relief, and looked up. In his view, the sky over the Mississippi River and Lake Pontchartrain had a distinct orange hue.

A magnet for critics who throughout most of his career continually said that he couldn't win "the big one," he, at last, didn't have to pay attention to the talking heads and couch-potato coaches who always belittled his coaching ability. After all the grief he'd taken over the years and the nonsense he had to listen to as detractors took potshots at him, Jim Boeheim finally got the last laugh. At least until the NCAA pulled the rug out from underneath him in 2014.

Boeheim almost won the national championship in 1987, when the chimpanzee on his back was eleven years old and only weighed 100 pounds, but Indiana's Keith Smart made that shot from the corner with five seconds left to beat the Orange, and the chimp held on. In 1995, when the monkey was 19 years old and 400 pounds, Boeheim was almost rid of it when the Cuse came within two points of Kentucky with four minutes to go, but SU couldn't catch the Wildcats, and the monkey tightened its grip around Boeheim's neck.

A week after April Fools' Day in 2003, with a big lift from Carmelo

Anthony, his superstar freshman, Boeheim finally felt a lot lighter, like he was walking on air. The smile on his face told the whole story. Relieved and grinning from ear to ear, he was a happy man that night. Walking down Bourbon Street wearing beads and with a big, floppy, oversize orange cowboy hat with white trim that someone gave him, with his wife Juli by his side, his feet never hit the ground. On that cool evening in The Big Easy, life just didn't get any better for a man who, despite all the wins, never seemed to be able to enjoy them.

Oh, some of his critics still came out of the woodwork and made noises when Syracuse slipped up, which it did from time to time in the following years, but Boeheim had finally become secure in his own skin and their droning didn't bother him anymore, at least not like it did when he had that gorilla on his back. They could find fault with him all they wanted to because it didn't matter anymore. Boeheim had validated his career, whether it needed validating or not. The real pressure was off, and Jim Boeheim continued to do what he did best—win basketball games almost every time his team took the floor. The Boeheim-bashers still existed, but their complaints rang hollow, because Boeheim held all the trump cards—he'd cut down the nets, had the ring, was enshrined in Springfield, Massachusetts, was named national coach of the year, and three times was a part of a championship coaching staff that successfully represented the United States of America on the world stage that is the Olympic Games. One by one he had jumped all the hurdles, overcame all the obstacles, conquered all the challenges, and outlived many of the critics that were a part of his profession. It took over four decades, but Jim Boeheim finally earned the respect that he deserved. Not from everybody, of course, but at least from everybody that mattered.

"Jim has been one of the top coaches for a long time. He is one of the brilliant coaches in the history of our game," stated Duke coach Mike Krzyzewski, the all-time winningest college basketball coach who is recognized by his peers and the general public as a giant in the coaching profession. "The recognition that he is getting is long overdue."

Roy Williams, who has won three national championships at North Carolina stated, "Jimmy is one of the best coaches in the game ever." Jay Wright, who coached Villanova to the 2015–16 and 2017–18 national championships, stated, "I believe [Boeheim] is the smartest basketball mind around." Former Louisville coach Rick Pitino, once considered by most as among the best in the business, called Boeheim a Hall of Fame coach ten years before Boeheim was actually inducted. Many other top-tier coaches said similar things.

As Boeheim's Syracuse teammate Chuck Richards said, "I live in North Carolina now, which is in ACC country, and when I wear my Syracuse hat, people stop me and say, 'Syracuse … Jim Boeheim.' They immediately associate Syracuse with Jim and ask about him. When I tell them he was my teammate, they'd ask 'Do you ever see him? Do you talk to him?'

"Any way you cut it, Jim is an icon. He's an institution. He's done wonderful things for Syracuse University. People don't know the chancellor's name, but they know about Jim. He's the face of Syracuse University. There may not be another one like him. I'm very proud of what he has done for my alma mater."

Dave Bing, Syracuse's best-ever basketball player and the former mayor of Detroit, put it more succinctly when he stated, "Jim Boeheim *is* Syracuse University basketball. The players come and go, but the one constant over these past [four-plus] decades has been Jim Boeheim." Famed SU-trained sportscaster Bob Costas stated, "Even considering the cavalcade of bold-faced names that are a part of the history of Syracuse sports, Jim Boeheim is at, or near, the top of the list. His combination of endurance and excellence have made him iconic, both in his sport and at his University." Roosevelt Bouie, the star of Boeheim's first recruiting class, said that Syracuse is unique because all the players that came through the program in the last forty-plus years all played for the same coach. "Whenever we get together and start telling Boeheim stories, someone will say to me, 'Well, how did you know that?' And I tell them because it all started with us."

In college basketball, things change from year to year and almost completely every five or ten years. Everything, that is, except Jim Boeheim. Through 2018, Syracuse University has played 2,882 basketball games, and Jim Boeheim, as a player, graduate assistant, assistant coach, or head coach, has been associated with 1,625 of them, counting the year freshmen couldn't play on the varsity squad. Of the school's 1,988 victories, Boeheim has been involved with almost 1,600 of them. He has coached 1,398 Division I games, second among active coaches. Plus, there was the year he spent at his alma mater as the freshman coach when his team won 18 of 20 games. Coaching that long at one place, Boeheim is a dinosaur, a throwback to another era.

Syracuse and Jim Boeheim. Jim Boeheim and Syracuse. The coach and the college fit together like links in a chain, perfectly content to be wrapped up in one another. Most people alive can't think of one without the other, the place without the person, the person without the place. It's like cheese and crackers. In some ways, the two are inseparable, so perhaps the union is more like toasted cheese or more apropos Orange marmalade, with the only thing able to pry the two apart being Boeheim's retirement.

Inducted into the Naismith Memorial Basketball Hall of Fame

Triggered by the national championship, respect for Boeheim as a coach soared, reaching its apex when he was accorded the highest honor in his profession. On September 9, 2005, Boeheim was inducted into the Naismith Memorial Basketball Hall of Fame in Springfield, Massachusetts. Presented by his former teammate, roommate, and fellow Hall of Famer Dave Bing, and supported by more than a dozen of his former players who were in attendance, Boeheim joined the hallowed halls occupied only by icons—people who were the best at playing the game such as Bob Cousy, Oscar Robertson, Wilt Chamberlain, Bill Russell, and Michael Jordan and the best at coaching the game such as Red Auerbach, Adolph Rupp, John Wooden, Dean Smith, Bobby Knight, Mike Krzyzewski, Rick Pitino, and John Calipari. For anyone associated with the game of basketball, it doesn't get any higher or any better than that.

"Jim is very deserving of being in the Hall of Fame," said his long-time friend and colleague Rick Pitino, who was the first assistant that Boeheim hired after becoming head coach. "I respect him as a coach. To stay at one place that long and to continue to be extremely successful is an exceptional accomplishment because familiarity breeds contempt."

Roosevelt Bouie, the star of Boeheim's first recruiting class, was at the induction and said, "I saw what he did the first four years. He followed his plan. He just kept on winning, so it made perfect sense to me. I wasn't surprised at all that Coach got into the Hall of Fame." Dale Shackleford, who also played on Boeheim's first team, said, "He's worked hard. He put in the time and effort, and he deserves the recognition. I'm just glad that I was a part of it when he was starting out his career."

Louis Orr is unique in that he played for, coached under, and coached against Boeheim. He had been a head coach at Siena, Seton Hall, and Bowling Green. He understood better than most the magnitude of the achievement. "The longevity is amazing, considering how tough it is to win that many games and be that successful for such a long time," he stated. "It's an exceptional accomplishment, especially to do it at one school. I feel blessed and honored to have been there in the beginning. Coach has been a big part of my life. He has helped build my confidence and self-esteem as a man, from where I was to where I am now. He helped take my basketball career to another level. Anytime I need to talk with him, he has always been there for me. I'm very thankful."

That evening Boeheim thanked everyone at every level who had helped him climb to the top of the mountain and enter basketball heaven. He credited his parents, family, his players, and assistant coaches through the years. He acknowledged his role models and how they inspired him to ascend to a level of achievement that as a kid and young man seemed so distant that he only dreamed about it. Similar to just about everyone else, Boeheim thought the only way he was ever going to get into a Hall of Fame was to buy a ticket.

During his acceptance speech, Boeheim tried to put into words his feelings and gratitude, saying: "People always ask me what it means to be in the Basketball Hall of Fame. When you start out at five years old and all you want to do is play basketball and then, when you can't play anymore, you want to coach the game of basketball, it's almost impossible (to express how I feel) … But to be with the (people already enshrined) is an unbelievable feeling for me. I've never been so grateful for any award …I'm just privileged to be in this building, and to actually have my picture up there is something beyond anything I could ever imagine."

Krzyzewski thinks Boeheim's installation among the greats made Boeheim better. "I don't think Jim's desire to win changed. As you accomplish or you're recognized, you have to be careful that it doesn't diminish your desire to do future things," he said. "Jim didn't lose the hunger to do more."

A Three-Time Olympic Gold Medal Coach

2008 Olympic Games

Boeheim achieved another highlight in a career filled with them when he served as an assistant coach under Krzyzewski in the 2008 Olympic Games in Beijing, China, where the United States won its first gold medal in men's basketball since 2000. On Team USA, Boeheim coached NBA all-stars LeBron James, Kobe Bryant, Dwyane Wade, and former Syracuse superstar Carmelo Anthony. Krzyzewski said he handpicked Boeheim because he respected Boeheim's overall knowledge, coaching ability, and his relationships with people. "I could make one choice on my own for the USA staff, and I picked Jim right away. The bottom line is there was not another guy I wanted more than Jim to sit next to me when we had to make decisions that had to be made to win a gold medal. He knew the game well. He understands people. I trust him," explained Krzyzewski. "The main reason I picked Jim is because he analyzes things, and then when he says something, he's pretty much always right. Jim has been a career friend to me. Because of our relationship, he's not reluctant to say something."

It didn't hurt that Boeheim was also the maestro of the 2–3 zone defense and could teach his patented defense to the coaches and the US Olympians. To teach the dogs new tricks—in this case, the dogs were among the best basketball players in the world—you have to know more than the dogs. "It speaks volumes that someone like 'Coach K' would pick Jim to be on his staff," stated Dick Ableman, another teammate of Boeheim's at Syracuse. "I don't think Jim ever got the recognition that he deserved, so it's good to see he's finally getting it."

2012 Olympic Games

Boeheim and Krzyzewski returned for an encore in the 2012 London Olympic Games and guided the United States to another gold medal, again defeating Spain in a fight to the finish in the championship game. When the clock ran out on the Spaniards, Bruce Springsteen's "Born in the U.S.A." rocked the arena. Although many might disagree, Kobe Bryant, a member of the team that again starred LeBron James and many of the 2008 Olympians, proclaimed the 2012 group better than the 1992 "Dream Team" that featured Michael Jordan, Magic Johnson, Larry Bird, Patrick Ewing, and Charles Barkley. From an Orange standpoint, Carmelo Anthony set an American Olympic single-game scoring record, firing in 37 points. He buried 10 of 12 three-point shots and made 13 of 16 field goal attempts in an 83-point victory (156–73) over completely outclassed Nigeria.

The 2012 Olympic Games was the most watched event in US television history, according to NBC and based on ratings data from Nielsen. Men's basketball played a significant part in attracting viewers, and

Boeheim played a role in the historical extravaganza. Krzyzewski and Boeheim both announced that they were retiring from Olympic coaching. But lo and behold, Krzyzewski and Boeheim changed their minds.

2016 Olympic Games

Krzyzewski and Boeheim added another chapter to their Olympic odyssey by winning their third gold medal during the 2016 Olympic Games in Rio de Janeiro. With only Anthony and Kevin Durant returning from the 2012 team, the US team still proved too much for the rest of the basketball world. Anthony, the first four-time American men's basketball Olympian and first American men's basketball three-time gold medalist, became the most prolific scorer in US men's basketball history with 336 points. Anthony also holds the US record for rebounds (125), field goals made (113), free throws made (53), and games played (31). With three gold medals and one bronze, Anthony became the most decorated male in Olympic basketball history.

Boeheim called coaching in the Olympics a great life experience. After the 2012 Olympics, he told the *Syracuse Post-Standard*, "It can't get much better than this." However, in his final column in a series that he submitted to the same newspaper following the 2016 Olympics, Boeheim wrote, "The national championship for Syracuse in 2003 will always be the high-water mark for me. That was my alma mater, my team, my players, and our fans. That remains the top experience of my basketball life. But this is a pretty neat one, too. To represent your country and be a part of this is pretty good."

Boeheim Stayed the Course

Boeheim's national and international experience began in 1982. He first hitched up with Krzyzewski on the 1990 USA team that picked up the bronze medal at the World Championships in Argentina. Including the Olympics, Boeheim served as an assistant coach or a head coach on fourteen different international teams that represented the United States. Jim Boeheim had done extensive globetrotting. Despite his coaching resume, Boeheim, for much of his early years, was always in the background when talk of good coaches came up. That's where he remained for most of his career. But Boeheim hung in there, stayed the course, paid his dues, and methodically collected victories as the years turned into decades. Like a fine wine, Boeheim aged. As good as he was when he was young, Boeheim got better as he got older. Finally, after earlier legends like Dean Smith, Lute Olson, Eddie Sutton, Denny Crum, Bobby Knight, and Jim Calhoun retired, Boeheim found himself as one of the patriarchs of the coaching profession. He was among the handful of coaches that ESPN and the other networks regularly called on for comments regarding any situation involving college basketball. He became a reoccurring guest on national radio and television talk shows. He was recognized as one of the relatively few resident experts of his profession. Like cream, Jim Boeheim had risen to the top of the coaching totem pole. It just took a while.

Boeheim eventually became a household name among sports fans around the country and in some parts of the world. His face was recognizable, and not just during basketball games and interviews but nationally due to being in a Nike Jordan advertisement with Carmelo Anthony. He was even in a couple of Hollywood movies: *Blue Chips* (1994) and *He Got Game* (1998), in which he made cameo appearances. He routinely hobnobbed with celebrities. In September of 2010, Boeheim was featured on *Man v. Food* with host Adam Richman on the Travel Channel, with the program filmed in Liverpool, New York, at Heid's, famous for its hot dogs. During 2011 March Madness, Boeheim even popped up on *Late Show with David Letterman* as the brunt of one of Letterman's jokes. With the almost nonstop coverage of the NCAA Tournament games taking place on four networks, under the topic "10 indicators of whether viewers had been watching too much college basketball," number two was: "You've spent thousands of dollars on plastic surgery to look like Jim Boeheim." Boeheim was recognized at Yankee Stadium. He was interviewed on CNN after the National Fathers' Day Committee selected him one of six "Fathers of the Year." In the Syracuse area, he was in commercials and on Christopher's clothing store billboards. He was here. He was there. It seemed like Jim Boeheim was everywhere. Everybody knew Jim Boeheim.

But none of that just occurred, and it didn't happen overnight. To better understand Jim Boeheim and how much he has achieved, it helps to know where he and the Syracuse program came from.

2

GROWING UP IN LYONS, NEW YORK

James Arthur Boeheim was born on November 17, 1944, in Lyons, New York, a small village about ten miles north of the New York State Thruway and halfway between Rochester and Syracuse. A little, quaint rural community of about 5,000 people, Lyons is a few long basketball passes south of Lake Ontario. Like a lot of places, things in Lyons have changed. The town is not thriving the way it did a half-century ago. "In the 1960s, it had a big manufacturing base, but that has disappeared," explained Tony Santelli, Boeheim's best friend growing up and a longtime resident. "Now it's a poor little town compared to what it was back then." One thing that hasn't changed is that Lyons remains proud of its favorite son. The town can be approached from four directions: north and south on Route 14, and east and west on Route 31. People approaching the town from each direction are greeted with a large orange sign:

WELCOME TO LYONS, NY
HOMETOWN OF LEGENDARY COACH
JIM BOEHEIM
OF THE SYRACUSE ORANGEMEN
NCAA
BASKETBALL CHAMPIONS 2003

The Boeheim family lived in a nondescript colonial brick house on 77 Williams Street, across from an elementary school, and where Jim's father operated a funeral home. The family consisted of Boeheim's father, Jim Sr., his mother Janet, and his younger sister Barbara. By all accounts, Janet was a charming and pleasant woman, but Boeheim and his father at times had difficulty getting along. The father and son had what could be called a contentious relationship. They played all kinds of games together, but the activities always turned competitive and frequently included or ended in disagreements, with Janet sometimes having to calm down her husband and son when the arguments got too heated.

Even when Jim was a youngster, the old man tried his hardest to best the kid. Boeheim told Jack McCallum of *Sports Illustrated*, "It didn't matter if it was ping-pong, golf, cards, or pool. He tried to beat me every way he could, every time he could. When I could finally beat him, he didn't take it very well. He's definitely the person who taught me how to compete. My father had a good side, but he kept it pretty well hidden." Jim got to where he could best his father in everything but cards, and that made matters worse.

Boeheim was even more specific, telling television sports reporter Graham Bensinger, "Every game we ever played was to the blood. We never played for fun. When we started playing ping-pong, he'd beat me 21–2, 21–1, 21–3. Eventually, it was 21–10. Then when I finally beat him, he put the racket down and that was it. We never played again. That's the way it was for every sport. I [ended up] beating him in everything, but it took a long time."

Santelli witnessed the relationship up close and provided some insight: "I saw the whole thing. One time we were playing golf and Jim was beating his father. By the fourth hole, his father quit and went home, telling Jim, 'I'm not playing golf with you anymore.' We never made it through nine holes. The best way to describe it was that it was a love-hate relationship," said Santelli. In terms of competitiveness and the desire to win, Santelli put it this way, "Jim's father wasn't a whole lot different than his son is today."

The tumultuous times with his father notwithstanding, Boeheim years later said that his parents always supported him. "My father never pushed me. He just was competitive," Boeheim explained.

"Jim's father was hard, but his mother balanced that out," said Santelli. "His parents always attended Jim's basketball games in high school and in college. Jim's father always wanted Jim to excel, just not at his expense." Still, even when watching his son play, no matter how well Jim did, apparently the young Boeheim couldn't satisfy the old man. "Even if he had a good game, Jim told me that, after the game, he would get a lecture from his father," Santelli related. Asked if that relationship bothered Jim, Santelli said, "No, nothing bothered Jim. That's how confident he was with himself."

Like father, like son. The future coach picked up his fiercely competitive spirit from his dad, a characteristic that benefited him right from the get-go as an athlete and later as a coach. "The one obsession I have is to win," he would say years later. "Whether it's on the court, or playing golf, or racquetball. If you get in my way, I'll run over you. I want to win. I hate losing more than I like winning." Boeheim's attitude and drive to be successful cannot be stated any more succinctly. Add to that his stated fear of failure and the result is a man with a pit bull temperament trained to compete.

A string bean kid with a bookworm appearance and looking like the "before" picture in those bodybuilding advertisements, it was by sheer determination that Boeheim overcame any physical deficiencies he had to become an outstanding athlete. That explains why down the road Boeheim wouldn't back down or be intimidated by big John Thompson, such as when Boeheim unleashed a fury in a tirade in the Big East Tournament postgame press conference when he felt the referees had taken a game away from Syracuse against Thompson's Georgetown Hoyas, angrily flipping a chair as he exited the room. The ferocious will to win was ingrained in him, going all the way back to his battles with his father. Instead of being beaten down by an overbearing father, Boeheim parlayed that experience to help himself not just succeed but become one of the very best in a very competitive business.

As the son of a mortician, Boeheim was raised around coffins and corpses, but even in elementary school, he knew that he wanted to dribble and toss balls in baskets rather than embalm people and put them in boxes. There was a basketball goal in the driveway to the house Boeheim grew up in, where a young Jim Boeheim spent hours shooting baskets and working on his skills. "He did that every day. That's all he did," said Santelli, who is a couple of years younger than Boeheim and has been friends with him since grade school. "I used to play there with him, but I wasn't in his league. He played even in the winter. I know, because I helped him shovel snow."

Jim Weeks, Boeheim's next-door neighbor, remembers young Jim being a skilled shooter at eight or nine years old. "We played one-on-one, PIG, 21 [and other individual competitions]. I don't think I ever won a game, and I most likely failed to score in numerous outings," he said in an email. "I was a year older, and I still couldn't beat him."

Many times Boeheim played late into the evening. It was his sister Barbara's job to let him know when it was time to quit. "I was the one Dad sent to turn out the lights on the court when he decided the neighborhood had had enough of the bouncing ball," she wrote in an email. The long hours of practice shooting at the goal in Jim's driveway during the heat of summer and cold of winter, as well as the disciplined tutelage he received from Lyons High School coach Dick

Blackwell through his formative years, paid big dividends. It was his basketball ability that took him away from his hometown.

Kids, including many of his future high school teammates, congregated at Boeheim's court to play hoops. It was during those pickup games that Boeheim, who had a penchant for calling fouls on the other players, was tagged with the moniker "Sid," after former NBA referee Sid Borgia. Some wonder if it's why, when he became a coach, Boeheim always thought the officials were calling more fouls on his players.

A couple of Boeheim's classmates, who wished to remain anonymous, said that throughout his high school years Boeheim was just consumed by basketball. A loner, he was content with playing hoops and golf whenever he got a chance. "Jim didn't have a lot of close friends because all he did was play basketball," said Santelli. Asked if Boeheim had girlfriends in high school, Santelli, who was best man in Boeheim's first wedding and was also in Boeheim's second wedding, responded: "Not really. He wasn't one to socialize. I don't think he went to the prom. His only real friends were his basketball friends. I was his best friend. We went fishing. He taught me how to shoot woodchucks. We went out to Sodus Point. We did things like that."

Considered by those who knew him as pretty much more or less a one-trick pony, in truth, if the sport involved competition and a ball, Boeheim played it as a kid. Though he concentrated on basketball and golf, Boeheim, because of his hand-eye coordination and athletic ability, was a Little League baseball all-star as a pitcher and shortstop and played quarterback and wide receiver in sandlot football. He was also a sports fan, pulling for the Brooklyn Dodgers in baseball, the Boston Celtics and nearby Syracuse Nats in basketball, and the Cleveland Browns in football. However, it was basketball that he loved, and Boeheim was being schooled in the game at an early age. Coach Blackwell ran a feeder program on Saturday mornings for the town's youngsters, with the practice sessions sometimes lasting several hours. Beginning in grade school, Boeheim was a regular participant in the programs, developing his skills and soaking up as much knowledge as he could about the game he loved. With his roots dug deep in Lyons, all the practice and dedication paid off in his future endeavors.

Appreciating the opportunities and the facilities that were available to him as a youth, Boeheim wanted to provide similar opportunities for inner-city kids in Syracuse. In 2009, Carmelo Anthony and Boeheim, as a part of their Courts 4 Kids initiative to refurbish and build basketball courts on playgrounds, dedicated their first basketball court at Wilson Park near the Carrier Dome. After redoing Schiller Park on Syracuse's north side in 2010, Boeheim told those in attendance that he spent hours at such a place in his hometown. "I went to our neighborhood court every day, and if I hadn't, I never would have played at Syracuse," he said. "It was the only place to play." In 2011, Boeheim refurbished Skiddy Park, stating, "I'd like to do a court a year and keep doing this project until we get every park in the city redone." In 2012, Boeheim restored two courts at Leavenworth Park on the corner of Wilkinson Street and Barker Avenue. A month later, his program overhauled Lewis Park. Boeheim then turned to renovating the courts at the Syracuse Boys and Girls Clubs. Boeheim also put in new courts at the Booker T. Washington Community Center in Auburn. In 2015, Boeheim renovated Comfort Tyler Park on the corner of Colvin Street and Comstock Avenue near Manley Field House and across the street from his office in the Melo Center. Two more courts were renovated in Utica. Supporting another of his passions, Boeheim's foundation in 2016 renovated The First Tee Golf Complex at Butternut Creek near Jamesville, which also became the home for the Boeheims' foundation.

Boeheim played three years of varsity basketball for Blackwell, a legendary coach in Lyons who compiled a 210–80 record and won nine Wayne-Finger Lakes League Championships in 16 years at the school. When Boeheim was a junior and senior, the Lyons Lions posted back-to-back records of 15–1 and 14–0 and won the league championship, with Boeheim earning All-State honors. In the 1962 New York State Class AA Finals, in front of a then-record 9,871 people at the

Rochester War Memorial, Lyons lost to undefeated East Rochester, 58–57, in double overtime, despite an 18-point performance from Boeheim. They finished with an overall 20–1 record. All the excruciating losses he suffered in big games notwithstanding, Boeheim to this day says the one to East Rochester still haunts him and remains, along with the loss to Indiana in the national championship game, the most disappointing of his career.

Boeheim, then 6-foot-3 and 150 pounds, played on Lyons teams that went 48–10. He scored 1,012 points during his high school career, including 520 points his senior season when he fired in 24.9 points per game to lead the Wayne-Finger Lakes League. In his junior year, he was league runner-up in scoring, with 19.3 points per game. Over the course of his high school career, Boeheim averaged 17.8 points per game.

Lyons had the same starting team during Boeheim's junior and senior years. Along with Boeheim, who was the two-guard, there was 6-foot-5 center Don Oakleaf, Joe Holly, David Fratangelo, and Gary Tunnison. "They were an outstanding team," said Santelli, who noted that around the time Boeheim played, Lyons had a four-year period when they only lost six games. "I remember one game at the end of the first quarter they had a 40–8 lead over Canandaigua, the second-best team in our league, and Jim had 21 points in the first quarter. But Coach Blackwell never wanted to embarrass an opponent, so he would always pull his starters when games got out of hand." Boeheim finished with 33 points, after being taken out in the third quarter, as Lyons cakewalked to an 85–44 victory. Other teammates on the 1962 team included Mike DeCola, Joe Arnitz, Jim DeVito, David Barnes, David Maine, and Jerry Sellenne. The pride of Lyons, the townspeople packed the school gymnasium to see the team play.

Boeheim credited much of his development, work ethic, and success to Blackwell. "I had a great high school coach, an unbelievable coach, who was very successful and pushed us very hard and disciplined every player on the team," Boeheim told Kevin Newell of *Coach and Athletic Director* magazine. "He taught me that there was only one way to play basketball. He was a stickler for fundamentals and details and doing things the right way. He taught me that at an early age, and it carried over."

Santelli recalled Boeheim being slow, but he "played smart. He had the best basketball mind. He understood all aspects of the game, even back then." According to Santelli, Boeheim became acquainted with the zone defense in high school. Boeheim said Lyons played a lot of 1–2–2 zone. Boeheim was also influenced by former Penn State coach John Egli, whose Nittany Lions used a 2–3 zone against the Orangemen when Boeheim was in college. Boeheim's teammates at Syracuse said that he also picked up some of his zone philosophy from their coach, Fred Lewis, who they pointed out also played a lot of zone. Later, when Boeheim was an assistant, Syracuse coach Roy Danforth added the 2–3 to SU's system. Boeheim said that he used various forms of the 2–3 zone throughout his tenure as SU's head coach, tweaking and modifying it from time to time, depending upon the situation. Therefore, a hybrid is perhaps the most accurate way to describe the zone that became synonymous with Boeheim.

Jim was also a very good golfer, twice winning the National Association of Basketball Coaches Tournament and with it the title "Best Golfer in College Basketball." He apparently got his golfing gene from his mother. "Janet was a great golfer," stated Santelli. "She would shoot in the 80s from the men's tee. She and her husband were also master bridge players. They would go all over and play."

Boeheim played three years of varsity golf under Blackwell, who also moonlighted as the golf pro at the Wayne Hills Country Club, where Jim and his father frequently played, or more accurately, competed and argued. Blackwell passed away in 2008, but his son Matt recalls his father talking about Boeheim. "My dad said that Jim was very tenacious, and he had a very high, competitive spirit," Matt Blackwell said. "My dad said that Jim loved the game, and when he was playing, he was in his element. He loved the competition. He described Jim as a tall, gangly, bony guy with a long reach. His defensive game was as good as his offensive game. He was pretty fearless. He really liked to mix it up. He was a player who played way beyond himself and got more out of his ability than anybody could expect."

The way Coach Blackwell depicted the young Boeheim is in some ways what the older Boeheim looked for in the players he recruited—tall, thin kids with a wide wingspan who aggressively played defense and were not afraid to crash the boards. This includes guys like Louis Orr, Rafael Addison, Erich Santifer, Damone Brown, Herman Harried, Wendell Alexis, Hakim Warrick, Kueth Duany, Wes Johnson, and C. J. Fair right on through Jerami Grant, Chris McCullough, Tyler Roberson, Tyler Lydon, Oshae Brissett, and Marek Dolezaj. Players who, despite there slight stature, battled with the big boys to get the ball. Players who fought hard and never gave up, no matter what the situation or odds.

"My dad was not the type of person that would overpraise anybody, but I think in Jim, my dad met the student-athlete who matched my father's own drive," said Blackwell. "One of my father's favorite expressions was, 'To grow, reach beyond your grasp.' My dad wanted to see other people achieve. I know my dad was intensely proud of Jim and his accomplishments. My dad held Jim in his highest regard. I'm sure my father knew that he had coached someone special. I think my dad considered Jim a part of his own legacy." In the *Lyons Tale*, the school yearbook, under Boeheim's senior picture, it says, "Call him Sid or call him Heimer, at basketball there's no one finer."

Further linked with his high school mentor, Boeheim and Blackwell were part of the first classes inducted, in 2003, into the Lyons Central School District Hall of Fame and the New York State Section V Hall of Fame. Both Blackwell and his protégé were also enshrined in the New York State Basketball Hall of Fame.

Like everyone else who knew Boeheim in high school and college, Santelli never envisioned his grade school and high school friend becoming famous and going on to be inducted into the Naismith Basketball Hall of Fame and be part of the coaching staff of the US Olympic Team. "Probably not," he said when asked. "But once he became Roy Danforth's assistant at Syracuse, we knew he had a shot at becoming a head coach somewhere, maybe at Syracuse. Jim was always fabulous with the X's and O's. Everyone knew that he knew basketball. We didn't know, though, that he could recruit as well as he did. But he's taught a rotation of assistant coaches how to recruit. He's outstanding in recognizing players that other people didn't think would be good. He's made some very good teams with what others might call second- and third-team players."

Santelli, who for years went on annual golfing trips with Boeheim and who still sees Boeheim periodically, said, "Jim hasn't changed a bit. He always was a competitor in everything he did. He has a good sense of humor. He's got a steel-trap memory. He's probably misunderstood by people who don't know him very well. He's a great guy to be around. I used to see him a lot more. We keep in touch."

From talking to people who knew him, Boeheim was a small-town person who grew into a big-time personality, but he was uncomfortable doing so. He was a guy who at one time would have been content coaching Lyons High School, like his mentor Blackwell, or the University of Rochester, where he once applied, as long as his teams were winning. He would have been happy without the spotlight or the glamour and definitely without having to deal with the press. However, once he became a celebrity, despite all the pressure and criticism he absorbed and put up with media he disdained, he wouldn't trade any of it. After experiencing everything that he had, once he saw Paris, he wouldn't have been satisfied if had he stayed in Lyons or Rochester.

Boeheim Becomes Involved in the Fight against Cancer

Both of Boeheim's parents died from cancer. Janet succumbed to leukemia at the age of 58 in 1976, not long after her son took the Syracuse job and before he really became successful. Jim Sr. passed away from prostate cancer at the age of 68 in 1986, a year before his son made it to his first national championship game as a head coach. Decades later at the age Jim Sr. died, his son recorded his 900th victory. Boeheim himself was diagnosed with prostate cancer in December 2001. Looking back on when he found out he had the dreaded disease, he told Graham Bensinger, "You remember the moment, trust me; it straightens you right up." Boeheim underwent surgery at the Barnes-Jewish Hospital in St. Louis. During the 2001–02 season, after missing only three games, he returned to the sidelines after his team lost to North Carolina State and Georgia Tech while he was recuperating. The three contests were the only games he missed in 39 years—that is until the NCAA suspended him for the first nine ACC games of the 2014–15 season.

Jim Calhoun, Boeheim's coaching colleague at Connecticut, also developed prostate cancer not long after Boeheim. When Calhoun was diagnosed with squamous cell carcinoma—a form of skin cancer—Boeheim was among the first to call his friend to offer support. Boeheim's college teammate, Chuck Richards, who played center when Boeheim was a freshman and sophomore, also contracted prostate cancer and confided in Boeheim. "Jimmy was the first person I called," related Richards. "He recommended Dr. William Catalona, who is one of the best surgeons in the country and who had done numerous operations, including surgeries on celebrities." Boeheim also lost one of his closest friends, Bill Rapp Jr., to esophageal cancer at the age of 65, as well as fellow coaching colleagues Jack Bruen from nearby Colgate University to pancreatic cancer at age 48 and Jim Valvano, who took North Carolina State to the national championship, to leukemia before the age of 50. "This cause is very important to me because of the personal experience I've had with family members, friends, and coaches dying from cancer," Boeheim said. "It's a very devastating disease."

Consequently, Boeheim became a very strong advocate of cancer research. Always the competitor on the basketball court, he was taking on an opponent much tougher than Georgetown and Connecticut combined. Boeheim stated, "Prostate cancer is definitely one of the biggest challenges I've faced. I'm looking forward to working with a strong team of people in the fight against cancer." Boeheim became increasingly involved on several fronts in the fight against the "Big C," serving for many years as one of the leaders of the Coaches Against Cancer campaign, a cooperative fundraising program of the American Cancer Society and the National Association of Basketball Coaches that has raised more than $100 million since its inception. Following Missouri coach Norm Stewart's lead, Boeheim was one of the first coaches to raise money for Coaches vs. Cancer. In 2005, Boeheim received the James P. Wilmot Cancer Center's Inspiration Award. Boeheim served as the 2009 national spokesman for the "Know Your Score: Fight Prostate Cancer" campaign. In 2015, Boeheim was honored for his coaching and charitable work at the Dick Vitale Gala, which generated more than $2 million to fight cancer and pushed Vitale's own cancer fundraising efforts to $14 million. In June 2016, the American Cancer Society presented Boeheim with the Circle of Honor Award. Raising money for cancer is "really the best thing that I've ever done in my life," stated Boeheim.

Boeheim has been involved in several other charitable endeavors, including serving as the honorary chairman of the Kidney Foundation and working with organizations for multiple sclerosis, cystic fibrosis, Children's Miracle Network, Make-a-Wish, Pioneer Center for Human Services, Lighthouse, People in Wheelchairs, Easter Seals, the Special Olympics, Rescue Mission, Children's Miracle Network, Eldercare Foundation, Syracuse Community Health Center, SUNY Upstate Medical University, Boys & Girls Club of Syracuse, Jack Bruen Fund, and Casey's Place.

Boeheim and his wife Juli started their own foundation in 2009: The Jim and Juli Boeheim Foundation. They have annually hosted their charity "Basket Ball" in Syracuse that each year generates between $500,000 and $700,000, and in 19 years, they have raised over $7 million. Jim has some input, but Juli essentially runs the foundation, pretty much deciding where the donations go. "Jim's foundation that he has with Juli, that's not about his ego. He's very humble. There's not one once of narcissism in his body," stated Richie Duffy, a former teammate of Boeheim's at Syracuse. "He defers the Foundation to Juli."

Gerry McNamara, who played on Syracuse's national championship team, told the *Rochester Democrat and Chronicle*, "What (Boeheim) and his wife have done, beyond the sport of basketball, is probably more impressive than anything he's done on the basketball court." In 2011, Boeheim was the recipient of the Father of the Year Award that was given in New York City. Four months later, Boeheim and Juli were honored as Distinguished Mentors by the Mary Nelson Youth Center in Syracuse. In 2014, Boeheim received the Jimmy V Award and became the fifth recipient of the Wayman Tisdale Humanitarian of the Year Award. They are "probably two of the best awards I've ever gotten," he stated. "They're very meaningful."

3

===

PLAYING WITH BING AT SYRACUSE

The year was 1962. John F. Kennedy was president of the United States. A first-class postage stamp cost four cents. John Glenn Jr. became the first American to orbit the Earth. *West Side Story* won the Academy Award for Best Picture. Johnny Carson had just begun his long run as host of *The Tonight Show*. Marilyn Monroe died. The NBA Nats were still playing in Syracuse. And 17-year-old Jim Boeheim enrolled at Syracuse University.

A small-town high school hotshot, Boeheim had considered going to Colgate, but he spurred the Red Raiders to walk-on at Syracuse. Featuring Bob Duffy, Richie Duffy's older brother, Colgate back then had a stronger basketball program than Syracuse. At the time, Syracuse was a national power in football after winning the 1959 national championship, but they were a perennial loser in basketball. While halfback Ernie Davis helped the Orangemen beat Texas in the 1960 Cotton Bowl and two years later became the first African

American to win the Heisman Trophy, the Syracuse basketball team in 1961–62 had the nation's longest losing streak, dropping 27 games in a row. Attendance at basketball games was usually around a thousand and was "more like several hundred," according to former SU sports information director Larry Kimball. More specifically, when the steep drop in performance began on February 22, 1961, only 939 people attended a game in the Onondaga County War Memorial to watch Syracuse lose to Canisius, 83–78, and on February 28, 1962, a mere 482 showed up to witness Syracuse's 81–68 loss to Niagara, which marked the last game played in the War Memorial. The effort in futility finally ended on March 3, when the Orange squeezed out a 73–72 win at Boston College.

"That was not a lot of fun…" Manny Klutschkowski told Bud Poliquin of the *Syracuse Post-Standard*. "Those were tough times. The freshmen [team] used to kick our tails at every single practice." To put the athletic program at that time into perspective, Manley Field House, where the basketball team was to play its games, was built that year, but it was primarily used as an indoor practice facility for the nationally-ranked football team.

This was at a time when the big names on campus were football stars Floyd Little and Larry Csonka, and Syracuse was producing the best running backs in the country. Before Davis, there was the fabled Jim Brown, an eight-time NFL rushing champion, the league's all-time rushing leader when he retired and the standard by which all running backs are compared. Then came Jim Nance, who finished fifth in the nation in rushing his senior year before moving on to the Boston Patriots of the AFL where he twice led the league in rushing and was named MVP in 1966. Little became a three-time All-American and the 1971 NFL rushing leader while playing for the Denver Broncos. Csonka, the prototype fullback, starred for the undefeated 1972 Miami Dolphins and was named Super Bowl VIII MVP. Along with Davis on the Syracuse national championship team was John Mackey, who played for the 1971 Super Bowl V winning Baltimore Colts and is the namesake of the Mackey Award that is given to the best tight end in college football. Brown, Little, Csonka, and Mackey all became Pro Football Hall of Famers. Davis, potentially the best of them all, died from leukemia before ever playing a game for the Cleveland Browns. The Browns retired Davis's jersey, making Davis the only player in NFL history to have his jersey retired without ever playing a game. Into this scene at Syracuse came Boeheim, along with Dave Bing, a high school All-American basketball player from Washington, DC. It was the football team that was in large part responsible for upgrading the basketball program.

"Ernie and John Mackey had an awful lot to do with it," explained Bing, telling why he decided to attend Syracuse over UCLA, Maryland, Michigan, and other basketball powers that had targeted him. "I thought that if they were the type of people who went to Syracuse, I wanted to go there too. At that time, Syracuse was content with being a football power. It didn't have a basketball program with a 'name.' I wanted to help change that," said Bing, who became the best basketball player in Syracuse history and the school's all-time leading scorer until being surpassed by Sherman Douglas in 1989.

Change it he did. Bing was the shining star and the magnet that attracted talented teammates to Syracuse. They included Chuck Richards, Rick Dean, George Hicker, Sam Penceal, Rex Trobridge, Dick Ableman, and Frank Nicoletti, all highly recruited players targeted by SU head coach Fred Lewis. Lewis invited Boeheim to try out for the team as a walk-on. Richie Duffy, a returning point guard, was picked to show Boeheim around campus. "I tried to convince Jim to come to Syracuse even though Colgate and Cornell were offering half-scholarships and Syracuse was not because I thought I was a better player than Jim and therefore Jim wouldn't be a threat, which turned out not to be true."

Bing was so talented that Boeheim initially questioned his decision about going to Syracuse. "I took a chance that I could play at Syracuse," he said, "but my first week, when I first saw Dave Bing play, I had second thoughts. He was the best player that I had ever seen by far." When Boeheim told his mother how overwhelmed he was with Bing, she said, "Don't worry about Bing; just be better than the other players." When Boeheim started out second string on the freshmen team, he realized it was going to be very difficult to get a scholarship. "I gambled, but I wouldn't advise anybody to take that risk," said Boeheim, who credited freshman coach Morris Osborne with helping him get the last available scholarship.

Bing and Nicoletti, a second-team high school All-American, visited Syracuse on the same day. Ernie Davis showed them around campus. Bing and Nicoletti roomed together as freshmen, with Nicoletti being the first white athlete at Syracuse to room with a black athlete. "I think our coach wanted me to make sure that Dave didn't get into any trouble," he joked. Bing was unimpressed when he first saw Boeheim, a gawky-looking string bean. "I couldn't believe Boeheim was actually a basketball player," he said. Bing and Boeheim roomed together their sophomore and junior years. Many on the team lived on the seventh floor of DellPlain Hall. The group grew pretty close and remains so today. They were happy to share their recollections of Boeheim and, in separate and lengthy interviews, pretty consistent in their analysis of Jim as a player and person, as well as the teams they played on. Boeheim is not hard to figure out, because, in several instances, they uncannily used the same or similar words and phrases to describe him. Furthermore, what they said is also in line with what people who knew Boeheim when he was growing up said, as well as how his coaching colleagues like Mike Krzyzewski and Rick Pitino described him years later. Except for sides of Boeheim's personality that he only reveals to his closest friends, for the most part, what you see is what and who Jim is.

Back to the Bing effect. Richards, a 6-foot-9 center who transferred from Army, came to Syracuse in the Bing–Boeheim class. The first person at West Point over 6-foot-6 back when the academy had a height-restriction rule, Richards was recruited to help Syracuse elevate a basketball team that had, as he called it, been "putrid." Like most of his classmates, Richards had several scholarship offers but chose Syracuse because of Bing.

"My coach at West Point told me that Fred Lewis was hired at Syracuse and he was bringing in six or seven 'super-dupers.' When I found out that Dave Bing was coming to Syracuse, I said, 'I'm hooking onto that train.' When we got there, as a group, we wanted to bring Syracuse basketball up to the level of SU football. We wanted to be part of the group that would do that."

Hicker was offered more than seventy scholarships but quickly decided on Syracuse. "When I practiced with Bing on my recruiting visit, I said, 'Wow, I want to go there and play with him." Ableman and Trobridge were high school teammates at Bethlehem Central High School, just outside of Albany. Ableman referred to the basketball team that Syracuse had the year before his group arrived as "horrible," apropos for a rag-tag outfit that won just two of 24 games and mostly floundered around in frustration. Ableman said football obviously was the main attraction at SU, and "we were the secondary act in town, no question." He credits his recruiting class with helping the Orange basketball program get back on track. "Our freshmen class had some really great players," Ableman stated. "I don't mean to put the varsity down, but people would come to our freshmen games, and then leave before the varsity game."

Richards, a captain in his junior and senior years, recalled that during the fall, the guys on the basketball team would get together for informal 5-on-5 scrimmages at old Archbold Gymnasium. "Dave Bing stood out, but the other players were all very good, highly recruited players too. In 1964–65, we had a great team and were ranked No. 7 in the preseason.

"And then there was Jimmy, a skinny guy with funny-looking glasses who was not on scholarship but was more of a 'throw-in.' The rest of us were recruited from all over, and we wondered, 'Who is this guy? What's he doing here?' Jimmy was 6-foot-4, but he only weighed about 140 pounds. He couldn't pass the 'look-test,'" said Richards. "I mean, if you were a real player and you saw him, you'd say, 'Ah, come on.'

"But it didn't take long. You could tell that Jimmy was a good basketball player. He could compete. Jimmy was going up against some really good competition, and he worked and worked and really proved himself. Freshmen couldn't play on the varsity then, but by his sophomore year, Jimmy got playing time. Jimmy was a real 'heady-type' player who tried to get the other guys involved. He was an excellent teammate," continued Richards, who in his junior year averaged 22 points per game while Bing as a sophomore accounted for 22.2 points, the only time two SU players averaged more than 20 points per game. "Sometimes Jimmy would take a shot and you'd wonder and son of a gun it went in."

Duffy provided this visual description for those old enough to remember early television. "Jim was fairly tall, but he looked like a bag of bones with everything going in an unathletic way. In practice, when Jim came dribbling down the court with those funny glasses, he reminded me of 'Mr. Peepers,'" referring to the name of a comic character played by Wally Cox in the TV program *Mr. Peepers*, which ran in the early 1950s. "He looked awful, but he could play. He knew the game. You turn your head to the side and the next thing you know, he's burying a 22-foot shot."

Ableman said Lewis recruited guys "who could jump, rebound, and run, and Jim couldn't do any of those things. From a talent standpoint, Jim was way down the list. If you looked at him, it was unlikely that you would think he was a basketball player. He was lanky and skinny. He wasn't short, but he had no size. Jim could shoot, and if you asked him, he would probably say he had a jump shot, but it really was a one-hand push shot. Oh, he might have gotten off the floor an inch or two. We were pretty proud of our warm-up routine where we would have eight or nine guys in a row dunk because it was exciting for the fans, but I don't remember Jim dunking. Not once," said Ableman. "But Jim was like a gym rat. He just kind of hung around. He was a smart, scrappy player. In practice, he and I got into it many times because he would hold, push, or give you a little shove. I suspect that he felt he needed to do those things in order to compensate for his deficiencies. But Jim would not be intimidated."

Nicoletti described Boeheim as "a garbage player and a pain in the ass, and I say that as a compliment. He was so skinny that people just knocked him all over the place, but he was so persistent." An example of Boeheim's mental toughness and no-quit attitude occurred during a practice session when Boeheim's glasses were broken. He went into the locker room and a few minutes later, with his glasses taped up, returned ready and willing to mix it up some more. What Boeheim lacked in physicality, he made up for with determination. He was not a "front-runner" like some who only played well when things were going their way. Boeheim was a "gamer" the team could count on when the going got tough. "That's why he became a good player by the time he was a senior," stated Nicoletti.

Dean joked, "As far as basketball ability, Jimmy wasn't a very physical player, but he was the kind of teammate that I would like to have with me in every situation, except a fight." Maybe Boeheim wouldn't start a fight, but he certainly wasn't afraid, and if fisticuffs flared up, he wasn't going to back off. Rex Trobridge recalled a game against Pittsburgh where the Panthers' Brian Generalovich, also a Pitt football player who was drafted into the NFL by the Steelers, broke away on a fast break with only Boeheim standing between Generalovich and the basket. "Generalovich decided to go right through Boeheim, and he put Boeheim right into the bleachers," detailed Trobridge. "Jim was black-and-blue all over the next day, but he stood right there and took the charge. He was a hard-nosed basketball player who wouldn't shy away from contact. He was a very fiery competitor. He took basketball very seriously. It was very much his life." Hicker reinforced that by stating, "Jimmy hated to lose. He was extremely competitive, as competitive as anyone I've ever played with, and he still is."

Ableman mentioned a postseason all-star game in 1966 played in Albany. "I'm from the area, and a lot of people came out to see me, but Jim beat me out for the MVP in my hometown," he related. "He played a good game and deserved the award." All said unequivocally that Boeheim overcame physical limitations to make important contributions to the success of the team. "Jimmy got 100 percent out of his ability," stated Dean, who played with Boeheim for three years.

"Jimmy was a solid, steady player. He was always willing to do what he was supposed to do. He would lull the opposition into a false sense of security. The minute the guy guarding Jimmy would slouch off on him to try to overplay and stop Bing, Jimmy would kill them. I remember several games when Jimmy just went off. He always managed to get the job done."

Hicker, who averaged 15.9 points a game and was the second-leading scorer behind Bing and ahead of Boeheim, said, "Obviously Dave Bing was the scorer, but Jim was probably the smartest guy I played with. Jim had a high basketball IQ. He just always, always was a very smart player," repeated Hicker, himself a deadeye shooter with his shot tagged "The Hicker Flicker" that enabled him to finish as the fourth all-time scorer in school history, behind Bing, Billy Gabor, and Vinnie Cohen. "Jim also had a nose for the basketball. He had an uncanny ability to know where the ball was going when it came off the rim." Others said the same thing, with slightly different phrasing. Dean described Boeheim as "more of a cerebral player. He was probably the smartest player we had. Jimmy just had a sense of where the basketball was going. Somebody would take a shot and the ball would take a crazy bounce. There would be ten guys on the court. Somehow Jimmy would know where the ball was going and the other nine wouldn't."

Penceal put it this way. "Boeheim could not jump but always seemed to be in the right place at the right time. We would all be jumping over the rim to get the ball, and he would be right there when it came down." Duffy simply stated, "Jim got more rebounds off the floor than anybody I know."

Trobridge said Boeheim was a good basketball player, but lacked athleticism. "He wasn't as gifted as some other players. He couldn't run like a deer or jump over the rim, but instinctively, he knew where to be at the right time. He might claim to have dunked once, but I'm not sure any of us saw it," he said. Penceal believed "the difference between Boeheim and some of us was cultural. Some of us were urban players who came from big inner-city high schools. We were used to doing a lot of improvising, but Boeheim came from a small, rural high school. Boeheim's basketball mind-set was to stick to the script. He was a player who did exactly what the coach said every time. That's why I'm not surprised that he became a successful coach." Or as Ableman clarified, "We were pretty sophisticated in what we did, and Jim learned the plays. He took advantage of his moments, and when he got in the games, it was damn hard to get him out. He earned his playing time. Once he got in, you knew he really belonged in there. We had some really good athletes who were on scholarship, but he earned our respect." Boeheim's coach, Fred Lewis, passed away in 1994, but assistant Roy Danforth recalled Boeheim being a "very good all-around player who understood the game and saw the floor well. He was a real good passer, and he could shoot."

Surrounded by the outstanding recruits brought in by Lewis, at first sight, Boeheim looked to be a thorn among roses and violets. But when given a chance to show his stuff, Boeheim blossomed like a wilted flower when given water and exposed to sunlight. Whereas first impressions indicated that he be discarded with the other weeds that walked on, Boeheim proved that he belonged in the good-looking garden that Lewis was grooming.

The Syracuse teams that Boeheim played on were more similar to the teams he coached early in his career rather than later. "We were helter-skelter with a plan," was the way Dean, the 6-foot-6, 225-pound center/forward who averaged 18 points and 9.1 rebounds per game as a senior, described the mid-1960s Orangemen. "Everybody on our team could shoot, and we were allowed to shoot if we were within our range. Our style was, when the ball goes up, go to the boards, rebound, and run. We were always looking to fast break. We full-court pressed 40-minutes a game." Ableman agreed, saying, "We pressured and ran from the beginning to the end of the game." More specifically Trobridge said Syracuse ran drills every practice where "we rebounded the ball, fired the ball to the corner, who quickly passed it to half court. We definitely pushed the ball up the court and definitely played a transition game. We played pressure defense." Penceal explained that Syracuse could play up-tempo because "we were in top shape. That enabled us to come back and win games when we were behind by 20 or more points."

In the 1963–64 season, Syracuse finished 17–8. That December, the Orangemen won the Hurricane Classic, beating Bill Bradley-led Princeton, 76–71, one night and host Miami the next, with All-American Rick Barry, 86–85, in overtime. Bradley and Barry were two of the biggest names in college basketball at the time, with Bradley averaging 30.1 points and 12.1 rebounds a game and Barry 29.8 and 16.5. The SU teams during the Bing era were tournament-good two out of the three years. Syracuse was invited to the National Invitational Tournament (NIT) in New York City, which at the time was a highly respected eight-team tournament.

"Back then, the NCAA and the NIT were almost on equal footing," stated Richards. "It was really an honor to play in the old Madison Square Garden. Playing there was one of the thrills of my life. It was a fabulous place to play." C. M. Newton, the former coach at Alabama, athletic director at Kentucky, and chairman of the NCAA's NIT Selection Committee, stated, "I had come through an era when the NIT was more prestigious than the NCAA." Danforth said the NIT still had a lot of esteem as late as the early 1970s. "If my recollection is correct, St. John's, in 1971, turned down the NCAA to go to the NIT." Mike Krzyzewski, in John Feinstein's book *Last Dance*, stated, "When I played at Army for Bob Knight in the late 1960s, the National Invitational Tournament was as big a deal in our minds as the NCAAs … In 1968, we were 20–4 and invited to the NCAAs. We knew we weren't going to beat UCLA with [Lew] Alcindor, but we honestly thought we could win the NIT. So Coach Knight decided to take the NIT bid. The next year we went back to the NIT and shocked South Carolina, which had been ranked No. 2 in the national polls for a lot of the season."

In the NIT, Syracuse lost to NYU, 77–68, despite a 31-point performance from Bing. A sophomore, Bing was the leading scorer on the team with 22.2 points per game, and Richards was the top rebounder with 9.1 per game. Boeheim, who had been awarded a scholarship by that time, averaged 5.1 points per game. The following season, 1964–65, Syracuse crushed American University in their first game, 127–67. Out of the gate, it looked liked the makings of another pretty good team and another pretty good year. However, the Orangemen promptly lost their next six games and eight out of the next nine. "We lost a lot of seniors off that NIT team, so the next year, it took a little while for the team to jell with all the new talent coming in," explained Penceal. "We were inexperienced, and that's why we had that drop-off." As team captain, Richards thought it was a little more than that. "We had a great team. We had size, speed, and some talented players who could shoot, but we had some disgruntled players on the bench who became upset when they were put in a game and then yanked when they made a mistake," he related. "In looking back on it, as a captain, I probably should have sat down with the coaches and talked about it. About halfway through the season, we started to click, but it was too late." The Orangemen did bounce back to win five in a row, but the damage to the season had already been done. Syracuse dipped to 13–10. Bing led SU in both scoring, with 23.2 points a game, and rebounding, with 12 boards a game. Boeheim averaged 8.9 points per game. Despite its mediocre record in 1964–65, Syracuse was a prolific scoring team in Bing and Boeheim's junior year. "We averaged 83 points a game," said Richards, who categorized the SU squads he played on as "run-and-gun." "We practiced defense and picked up opponents about three-quarters court, and we got the ball off the boards and got it out and down the court in a hurry. We played pretty much inside-out, with Bing being the penetrator."

Things really came together the following year when Bing and Boeheim were seniors. Syracuse won its first seven games and climbed to No. 7 in the national polls. The Orangemen ventured across the country to play in the Los Angeles Classic where, despite Bing pouring in a school-record 46 points, No. 2-ranked Vanderbilt derailed SU, 113–98. Syracuse picked up a couple more wins on the West Coast, beating Northwestern, 105–75, and St. John's, 113–97, with

Bing lighting up the Johnnies for 38 points en route to winning the tournament's Most Valuable Player Award. Syracuse went 12–4 the rest of the way to complete the regular season 21–5, earning the school's first NCAA Tournament invitation since 1956–57. In 1966, the NCAA Tournament consisted of sixteen teams. In what was then the Elite Eight, Syracuse was shipped to Raleigh, where they defeated Davidson in the East Regional, 94–78, before being beaten in the regional final, 91–81, by a Duke team that finished 26–4. Duke was No. 2 in the country and sent its entire starting team to either the NBA or ABA. The Bing–Boeheim team recorded the second 20-win season in Syracuse history.

Years later, when Boeheim became Syracuse's coach, ESPN color commentator Dick Vitale, when announcing Syracuse games, frequently mentioned that Bing and Boeheim were teammates in college. Vitale deservedly praised the play of Hall of Famer Bing and liked to say that all Boeheim had to do was bring the ball up the court, pass it to Bing, and then get out of the way. Although it sounded cute, that was not accurate. As a senior, Bing did average 28.4 points a game and made first-team All-American, but Boeheim, the "other guard" who had walked on but by his senior year had worked his way up to team captain, was no slouch. Boeheim averaged nearly 15 points per game and was an integral part of a high-octane offense that averaged a national-best 99.9 points per contest during the regular season. The Orangemen, with four double-figure scorers, barely missed becoming the first NCAA Division I team to average 100 points a game during the regular season, a feat later accomplished by the 1969–70 Artis Gilmore-led Jacksonville University Dolphins. Syracuse would have needed to score 124 points in its season finale against Colgate to average 100 points, but they came up just short in a 122–88 victory over the Red Raiders. "We missed it by one basket," stated Penceal. "I had the ball at the end and could have shot it, but I passed it off, and the clock ran out." Regardless, Syracuse established an NCAA regular-season average per game scoring record, something all the players on the team were proud of.

The 1965–66 NCAA team was led by All-American Dave Bing, with Dean and Hicker, nicknamed 'The Blond Bomber" for his long-range shooting skills, named United Press International (UPI) Honorable Mention All-Americans. Bing, Boeheim, and company concluded their careers with the Orangemen ranked 16th in the final UPI poll. The Syracuse basketball turnaround was complete. With Bing leading the way and Boeheim along with the other supporting players making contributions while fulfilling their roles, the heralded recruiting class took a program that had only won 14 games in the three seasons prior to their arrival to winning 52 games during their three varsity seasons.

Boeheim finished his career with 745 points and became the 10th player in Syracuse history to score more than 400 points in a season. A good shooter, he made slightly more than half of the shots he took (.519) and just shy of 70 percent of his free throws (.695). In 2016, sportswriter Seth Davis asked Boeheim if, after walking on, he ever dreamed his college experience would turn out as well as it did. Boeheim candidly responded, "I believed I was a good player, so I was not surprised at the success that I had as a player."

Don Lowe, who later became the longtime athletic trainer at Syracuse, was a student at Kent State when the Orangemen played the team during Boeheim's senior year. Lowe said he went to the game specifically to see Bing play. Years later, he told Boeheim that he didn't remember Jim playing in that game at all. "I told Jim that, and he just looked at me and smiled," said Lowe.

Dave Bing

As a senior, Bing finished fifth in the nation in scoring. SU's first consensus All-American in thirty-nine years, Bing became the school's all-time top scorer with 1,883 points, a mark that held up until 1989 when Sherman Douglas surpassed it by pouring in 2,060 points. But Bing played when freshmen were ineligible for the varsity, whereas others who later topped his scoring total played four years and played far more games. Bing put an exclamation point on his SU career by becoming the first basketball player in school history to be named Athlete of the Year. Bing was the second person selected in his NBA draft class in 1966, going to the Detroit Pistons. He was named NBA Rookie of the Year for the 1966–67 season. In his second season, he averaged 27.1 points per game to lead the league in scoring. Bing scored 18,322 points and averaged 20.3 points, six assists, and 3.8 rebounds a game over the course of his 12-year NBA career. He made the NBA All-Star team seven times and was named All-Star MVP in 1976. On December 19, 1981, Bing's No. 22 and No. 8 worn by Vic Hanson, a three-time All-American at SU from 1925 to 1927 and the only person inducted into the College Football and Naismith Memorial Basketball Hall of Fame, were the first jersey numbers to be retired by Syracuse University. In 1996, Bing was named one of the fifty greatest NBA players of all time. That same year he was inducted into the Naismith Memorial Basketball Hall of Fame, a ceremony attended by a number of his Syracuse teammates, including Boeheim, Penceal, Harper, and Richards. After a successful career as a business tycoon and noted philanthropist, Bing, on May 11, 2009, was elected mayor of Detroit, a position he held through December 31, 2013.

Boeheim the Student, the Person

Boeheim's teammates reminisced about Boeheim the college student. Trobridge thought Boeheim was more of a loner when he was in college. "He was not a social butterfly, and he was not a party-goer. He kind of stuck to himself," he said. "He was single-minded, with basketball for Boeheim pretty much it. I wouldn't say that Jim was really close friends with other people on the team, except for maybe Dave Bing, who became his roommate."

Dean, however, said the team was close, and Boeheim was just "one of the guys," describing him as quiet, easy-going, laid-back, and not at all pushy. "We would play cards or [shoot] pool for quarters or, if we had some money, for a dollar. Jim would just take our money. He was the best bridge player, the best card player, the best whist player, pretty close to a scratch golfer. Jimmy was a very talented, smart individual. He was one of the best academic students. He didn't always have to go to class because school came easy for him." Bing clarified that and was able to shed some light on Boeheim's study habits, specifically his penchant for taking naps and pulling all-nighters. "Jim liked to sleep, and he didn't like going to class," Bing said. "He studied for exams all night and did well on the tests. Then he'd sleep for the next two days."

Hicker, who hung around with Boeheim when the team traveled and as a sophomore, looked up to him and remembered Boeheim as introverted. "When we went on road trips, we spent a lot of time together," related Hicker. "Jim was more relaxed. We would go out to dinner, go to the movies, and do things like that."

Duffy referred to Boeheim as being shy, but Boeheim apparently was not timid. "He liked to argue, and it didn't matter about what," he said. "He never turned away a chance to disagree. He wasn't a part of the fun group." According to Danforth, that trait sometimes annoyed the head coach. "Fred Lewis always considered Jim Boeheim a pain in the butt because he always had an opinion, and Boeheim always stuck to his guns in what he said, regardless of whether he was right or wrong." Rick Pitino, not one of Boeheim's teammates but a member of Boeheim's first Syracuse coaching staff, clarified that characteristic with this example: "Jim likes to talk politics, and he will argue his point, but then at the end of the day, he will take the opposite point of view and still argue. It just depended upon what part of the day it was. We called him 'The Contrarian.'" Many people believe that Boeheim maintained that trait throughout his coaching career, with members of the media and discontented fans describing Boeheim as stubborn when he steadfastly refused to change whatever he was doing if it wasn't working, such as not switching to a man defense when the zone was getting carved up or losing games because he repeatedly went into a semi-stall with too much time remaining on the clock.

A couple of people said Boeheim had at least one girlfriend while in college, with Dean recalling Boeheim involved in a somewhat serious relationship his senior year. "I think he fell for this girl, and it was pretty passionate," he laughed. Boeheim's high school buddy, Tony Santelli, remembered that romance as well. "She was Jewish, and she dumped him because the family was against the relationship," he recalled. "Jim was hurt pretty bad by that."

To understand Boeheim's personality, you need to know the backstory. As a player, Boeheim occasionally was the butt of jokes. Because of his rural roots, he was sometimes called "Farmer," which Penceal said Boeheim didn't like. Bing said Boeheim was ridiculed because of his appearance. "People made fun of [Jim]," said Bing, who counseled Boeheim not to fret over the criticism. "Just try to be a nice person, and you'll be fine," Bing told his friend and teammate. Boeheim was teased for his penchant for wearing Hush Puppies shoes when others were wearing Clark Desert Boots, the style of the day. "We would get on his case about those Hush Puppies, but he was proud of it," related Trobridge. "He certainly dresses better today than he did then, and I credit his wife Juli for that. Today he's a lot more polished, but he has the same personality." Because of his pencil-thin legs, Boeheim's socks always fell down when he played, causing Penceal to laugh and say, "Boeheim had floppy socks before Pete Maravich made floppy socks famous." Dean laughingly said, "Boeheim was a nerd before nerds were nerds."

Brian McLane was a student statistician for Syracuse basketball during the Bing–Boeheim years and heard a lot of that. "When you're young and you're on the receiving end of stuff, why would people expect you when you got older to forget all that? From my fifty years of observation, I think Boeheim is now more comfortable with his players than with the people he played with," opined McLane, who has attended over three-quarters of all the games that Boeheim has either played in or coached and has remained friends with Boeheim and very good friends with many of the players from that era. "Jimmy doesn't let people into his inner circle. Juli gave Jim his personality.

She was a gift to him. Jim the father is a whole different personality from his public persona. As a father, Jim is not good; he is a great father!"

Bill Brodsky was a basketball team manager from 1961 through 1966 and saw things from a little different perspective. Besides doing the typical things that a manager does, such as recording team statistics, making financial arrangements for road trips, and picking up after the players, Brodsky also was responsible for keeping the players in line. "I was often the babysitter for the guys. I had to do the bed checks to see if they were in," he stated. "I never had any bed check problems or any problems with Jim like I had with some of the other guys. Jim was a pretty serious fellow who had a mature outlook on life. He had his head screwed on straight. He was a good student and more intellectual than some of the others. He was not a clown like some of them were. But he was somewhat anti-social, and I don't mean that in any negative way." Nicoletti agreed, saying, "A lot of us guys went out and did crazy things. Jim never did."

McLane said many players on the team had "jock mentalities." "They worked hard, and they played hard. Many spent a lot of time at the Tecumseh Club, a bar close to campus. The only one that wasn't like that was Jimmy. Jimmy was serious all the time." McLane recalled when the basketball team went to California to play in the Los Angles Classic that the players were given tickets for the Rose Bowl football game. "Everybody on the team chose to go to Tijuana and party," stated McLane. "Everyone except Jimmy and the manager."

Except that his once toothpick-thin frame has filled out and he is now more sophisticated, Boeheim's teammates and friends say that Boeheim really hasn't changed all that much through the years. Brodsky, who stayed at Syracuse to earn a law degree, stated, "Jim was Jim. He was just like he is today. He didn't try to impress anybody, and he doesn't now. He's not out there pounding his chest. He's not a publicity hog. Today with Jim, it's not about him. It's about the players, the program, and getting the job done. He really cares and is concerned about the players, their academics, and what they are going to do when they are finished playing basketball."

Duffy said Boeheim was and still is a pretty clean-cut person. "Jimmy doesn't drink. I've never seen him have a glass of wine, not even with a meal," he related. "He always drinks Cokes. A bunch of us guys would get together and everybody is shit-faced, but Jimmy is dead sober and is still the life of the party. And another thing, I'd be surprised if Jimmy has ever danced with a girl in his life. We've been to dinner dances with him, and he never dances."

Pitino, however, said that after Jim met Juli, he would sometimes have a glass of wine. "Before he met Juli, he didn't know a bottle of wine from Ripple. He wouldn't know how to order it. Before Juli, Jim didn't have any social skills whatsoever. One time we were at Dr. [Paul] Fallon's home in Skaneateles, and when it was time to cut the cake, Jim was in Dr. Fallon's office watching the Mets game on television. His social skills were ridiculous. After he met Juli, his life took on a whole new look. He was a terrible dresser. He wore plaid sport jackets. Now he wears Armani. Before he met Juli, Jim thought Armani was a wing player from Buffalo. Juli has really dressed him up. It was a total makeover. It took a Kentucky woman to bring out the real Jim Boeheim. Juli made Jim a man of the world."

Ableman said he sees Boeheim every two or three years. "He is pretty much the same guy I knew in college," he said. "I don't remember Jim being the most popular guy on the team. He was always pretty low-key. I don't think his personality has changed that much. If you are talking basketball, he's very outgoing. But he's a funny guy to figure out. When other topics come up, to get him to talk is like pulling teeth. He's more of a listener. When you're talking about family, children, and jobs, he's not an easy conversation. If the topic changes to basketball, his radar picks right up. My wife and I spent some time with him, and afterwards, she said, 'You know, he hasn't changed a bit.' And she's right."

While Pitino said that before Juli straightened him out that Boeheim thought good dining was eating at Denny's, Duffy noted that now Boeheim loves to go to great restaurants and that his favorite place to eat in New York City was the world-famous Carnegie Deli before it closed in 2016. "But Jim goes to eat, not talk," Duffy said. "To me, dinner is a two-hour social affair. I like to have a couple of drinks and relax and enjoy it. Not Jimmy. Jimmy eats very fast. He wants to eat and not socialize. With Jim, it's thirty minutes."

From talking with those who knew Boeheim as a boy to those who know him as a senior citizen, it is clear that Boeheim is not and never has been interested in winning any personality contests. He's not interested in carrying on small talk or shooting the breeze, except on certain occasions when he's around those he considers his close friends. Then he can be charming. Then, they all agreed, he can be the life of the party.

Dean thought that Boeheim is sometimes misconstrued. "He's quiet and doesn't talk a lot. He's more observant. He watches what's going on. Sometimes, I think people think Jimmy is a little aloof, distant, or hard to get to know," related Dean, who still saw Boeheim periodically before Dean lost his battle against bone cancer. "But if you get to know him, he's not like that at all. Once you get to know Jimmy, he's a pretty sharp guy. He's smart and insightful, and he's got a dry sense of humor." Really very similar to the way that Pitino and Krzyzewski described Boeheim.

Dean reasoned that people didn't perceive Boeheim to be friendly was because they weren't fully aware and didn't understand all the obligations that Boeheim had because of his coaching job and the numerous other things he was involved in. However, Duffy provided a couple of examples to show that Boeheim's public persona is not who he is. "We've been very, very close friends for the last thirty-five years," Duffy said. "One time, I was in Syracuse and stopped by practice unannounced. Jim didn't even know I was coming. After about fifteen or twenty minutes, he strolls over to where I was. I said, 'Let's have dinner tonight.' He said that he couldn't, but then a little while later, he came back and said OK. He rearranged his schedule for me.

That's the kind of friend he is. Another time, Jim came to visit me, and we played golf at one of the clubs that I play at. Now Jim is a competitor but [unlike his father] in a very respectful way. He's very amicable, gentlemanly, and he understands the etiquette and social elements of the game. We have a lot of laughs. The people at the clubs where I play say he's a different guy than who they see on TV. To this day, I always get comments about what a nice guy he is."

Duffy, who served on the Syracuse athletic board from 2007 to 2009, said Boeheim takes his golf seriously. "I remember a time around 1995 when he came down to Vero Beach in Florida when he and Juli were dating. He only had a very short amount of time between when his plane landed and when he was to leave, but he was determined to play golf. He hadn't touched a club since October, and without hitting any balls and without any warmup, we played eighteen holes, and he shoots something like a 74. He's a tremendous athlete."

Hicker and Duffy remain particularly close to Boeheim. When they and Brodsky talk with Boeheim, they all say it is mostly about investments. Duffy remarked, "We talk about everything but basketball. We talk about everything way beyond basketball. We'll talk about investments. Jim goes to people he knows and trusts. He invests his money very conservatively. All his stocks are blue chips." Brodsky said, "Nowadays, basketball doesn't come up in the conversation. We discuss investments and how we can help athletes prepare themselves financially for their future." Trobridge said that when he and his former teammates get together, they rarely talk basketball. When the conversation turns to Boeheim, he laughed and said that it's more like, "How in the hell did he end up with Juli?"

In retrospect, none saw anything in their teammate that would lead them to believe that Boeheim would go on to have a Hall of Fame and Olympic career. "No, I had no idea that he would accomplish what he has," stated Hicker. "Except, as I said, that he had a very high basketball IQ. He was an intelligent player, and he wanted to pursue coaching. But to accomplish what he has, no I didn't see that in his future."

Dean said, "I probably would be lying to you if I said that I was smart enough to know that Jimmy would go on to do what he has. I wasn't that insightful. When you're 20 years old and playing with twenty or twenty-five guys, you can't foresee how any of them are going to turn out. The only one was Dave [Bing], because we all knew that he was going to make it to the NBA." When asked the same question, Richards responded, "Really, to be honest, no. But you could see that down the road he might want to get into the coaching end of it, but to reach the level of success that he has, no there was nothing that I saw that would indicate that."

Penceal stated, "If you asked me back then who amongst us was going to be a coach, I wouldn't have said Boeheim. I would have said Richie Cornwall or Richie Duffy because they were more vocal and because of the way that they handled themselves on the floor and positioned themselves. Boeheim was a bit of an introvert. He was quiet and not as outgoing as Cornwall and Duffy. You could see that in practice. Boeheim was a walk-on, and it took awhile for him to become a part of the team, to become more vocal and assume a leadership role on the team. Even as a junior and senior, his personality was not as outgoing as those other guys."

Duffy didn't foresee Boeheim becoming a big-time coach either, though he noticed something that Boeheim had in common with high-achieving people. "As a businessman, I dealt on a daily basis with some very famous and successful people," he said. "One of the consistent attributes of those varying personalities was that they all were very focused on the mission at hand. And Jimmy is the same way." Harper also didn't see basketball in Boeheim's future. "He was the coach of the golf team and a very good golfer," he said. "If his future was going to be in sports, I would have thought that it was going to be in golf more than basketball." Nicoletti called Boeheim "the ultimate overachiever. I give him so much credit for accomplishing everything that he has."

Something interesting is that while at Syracuse Boeheim was a resident hall advisor. On his floor was Tom Coughlin, a football player from nearby Waterloo who teamed up in the Orange backfield with All-Americans and future Pro Football Hall of Famers Floyd Little and Larry Csonka. Coughlin, like Boeheim, went on to greater fame as a head coach, winning Super Bowls XLII and XLVI with the New York Giants. As Boeheim's teammates didn't have an inkling that Boeheim would go on to have super success as a big-time college coach, Boeheim didn't see anything special that would indicate Coughlin would one day reach the pinnacle of the professional football coaching profession. "When I started hearing stories about what an intense, serious coach he was, I thought someone was putting me on because that was so unlike everything I've known about him," Boeheim said to a writer. "The quietest, most mild-mannered guy I've ever known. The last guy you would think would be a tough football coach. The last guy," he told writer Scott Pitoniak.

Looking at the big scheme of things beyond basketball, Brodsky emphasized that Boeheim is involved in a lot of stuff besides coaching. He stated, "Although I'm not living in Syracuse now, I'm pretty confident in saying that Jim is one of the most prominent guys in the Central New York area."

Boeheim's teammates all return to campus whenever they can, some frequently, some periodically, and some more than others. They all regularly watch the Orange on television and keep tabs on their former teammate, Jimmy, as many called him. They're all very proud that he has lifted their alma mater to basketball heights that they could not have imagined back in the day. Moreover, it seemed they all enjoyed taking a trip down memory lane. Ableman probably summed up everyone's feelings best by stating, "When Syracuse won the national championship, I was pretty damn proud. We were all wearing our Syracuse stuff."

Boeheim graduated from Syracuse in 1966 with a bachelor's degree in social science and then in 1969 with a master's in the same discipline. He has credited his former coach Fred Lewis for teaching him how to recruit the right way. "He showed me how to get out and get great players," said Boeheim, acknowledging an ability that is the bloodline of a basketball program. "He was also a very good practice coach." Boeheim learned well, and that helped him to become the success that he has.

Playing in the Eastern League

While his teammates all went their separate ways, Boeheim never strayed too far from his passions, which is basketball and the nest that is Syracuse. He joined a semipro team based in Binghamton, and he averaged around 35 points a game. Boeheim then played professionally on weekends for six years with the Scranton Miners, who became the Scranton Apollos, in the old Eastern Professional Basketball League, which became the now-defunct Continental Basketball Association. Boeheim was a second-team All-Star and played on two championship teams. In 136 games, he made almost 900 field goals, over 30 three-point shots, nearly 80 percent of his free throw attempts, grabbed 475 rebounds, dished out 563 assists, averaged 17 points a contest, and scored over 2,300 points. He performed well enough to be named "Honorable Mention" on the Eastern League/Continental Basketball Association All-Time Team. The Scranton Miners were owned by Arthur Pachter, coached by ex-Syracuse Nat Paul Seymour, and played in the Scranton CYC building.

"Playing in the Eastern League was a tough situation for anybody," related Richards, who a year before Boeheim also played in Scranton, a blue-collar mill town. "We played games on Saturday and Sunday nights in high school gyms in front of anywhere from a few hundred to maybe 1,500 people. We had to drive to Scranton on weekends to play, or to where ever we were playing if it was an away game, and then we'd drive back home Sunday night so we could go to our jobs on Monday morning."

Besides Scranton, the Eastern League, depending upon the year, had teams in hardscrabble, off-the-beaten-path places such as Harrisburg, Wilkes-Barre, Johnstown, and Allentown in Pennsylvania, Hartford and New Haven in Connecticut, and Trenton, Camden, Asbury Park, and Sunberry in New Jersey, as well as Binghamton, New York, and Wilmington, Delaware. There were some good players in the Eastern League, including many former NBA players such as Paul Arizin, Ray Felix, Woody Sauldsberry, and K. C. Jones, all older guys who had retired from the NBA and were on their way down. There were also other players who went on to make a name for themselves such as John Chaney, Hubie Brown, and Bob Love. "We made some money, but not a lot of money. A guy like Arizin could make $150 a game and $300 on a weekend, which was a lot of money in the mid- to late 1960s," stated Richards. "It was a different time, before players were going to Europe, South America, and other places to play. It was probably like the NBDL [National Basketball Development League, now known as the G-League] is today. The NBA only had about ten teams, so there weren't many openings, so players looked around for opportunities to play." Boeheim told *Syracuse Post-Standard* beat writer Mike Waters that he made $100 a night his first year and $200 a night his second year when some of the Eastern League's top players left to play in the newly formed American Basketball Association. Players had to pay their own travel and lodging expenses. Boeheim stayed at the Hotel Casey in Scranton for $28 a night.

Richards said that there were some "characters" in the Eastern League, and "some great players who had questionable backgrounds." With a lot of players fighting to get to, or get back to, the NBA or ABA, it made for rugged competition. Never one to shy away from physical play, Boeheim was up to the challenge. Boeheim enjoyed his best season in the Eastern League in 1968–69 when he averaged 23.4 points, 4.5 assists, and 3.8 rebounds a game, good enough to make the All-Star team and get him a look-see with the NBA.

Richards said the Chicago Bulls, coached by former Syracuse Nat Johnny Kerr, invited Boeheim to camp. Hicker confirmed that by saying Boeheim had just recently told him that he was the last man cut by the Bulls when Chicago instead opted to keep Dave Schellhase, a consensus All-American out of Purdue. Later, Boeheim got a call from the Detroit Pistons, who were then coached by Paul Seymour, Boeheim's coach at Scranton who had moved up to the NBA. The Pistons wanted to take a look at Boeheim as the fourth guard, behind Bing, former Providence All-American Jimmy Walker, and either Tom Van Arsdale or Howie Komives, who played for Bowling Green and led the NCAA in scoring with a 36.7 average in 1963–64. Boeheim passed on that possibility.

"I definitely knew I was a borderline NBA player," Boeheim said. "I had one opportunity to go up. I had to make a big decision." Though the NBA didn't work out, the coaching gig that Boeheim ended up with didn't turn out too badly.

A Downturn at Syracuse

While he played in the Eastern League, Boeheim had also been a graduate assistant, helping Lewis with basketball while serving as SU's varsity golf coach, producing an 18–13–1 record over six seasons until the program was cut in 1973. However, Syracuse experienced a brief downturn in its basketball program. Soon after Bing and Boeheim departed, SU regressed to 11–14 in 1967–68, 9–16 in 1968–69, and 12–12 in 1969–70. However, let's first backtrack a bit. Syracuse had historically been a very successful basketball program, suffering only twelve losing seasons from 1900 through 1959, the year the football team won the national championship. Beginning in 1911, Edmund Dollard recorded a 151–59 record in 13 years, including his 1917–18 team that was later declared national champions by the Helms Foundation. Lewis Andreas followed Dollard, and in his first season in 1925–26, Andreas won the school's second Helms Foundation national championship. He went 358–135 in 25 years. Marc Guley took over the reins and had some respectable years, going 136–129 from 1950 until 1959.

Guley's 1956–57 team finished with an 18–7 record and reached the Elite Eight before losing, 67–58, to eventual national champion North Carolina, but the team perhaps could have advanced further had it not been for societal norms of the time. Syracuse's top three players were black—Vinnie Cohen, Manny Breland, and Jim Brown—but Brown, an All-American in football and lacrosse, refused to play his senior year because Syracuse had an unwritten rule that said that no more than three black players could be on the floor at any one time, meaning that Brown would not start. "Jim Brown told me the program was racist," stated Don Cronson, who played freshman basketball at SU in 1960–61 at a time when Guley was simultaneously coaching both the freshman and varsity teams. Brown averaged double figures in points as a sophomore and junior and was a beast on the boards. It's conceivable the Orangemen could have competed for the national championship if Brown, arguably the best all-around athlete of all time, played that season. Guley was dismissed after his last two teams finished 4–19 and 2–22.

Fred Lewis, who was the second-leading scorer in the nation in 1944–45 when he played for legendary Clair Bee at Long Island University, was brought in from Southern Mississippi to stop the bleeding. After going 8–13 his first season, Lewis, a former All-Star in the old National Basketball League, turned the program around, compiling a 91–57 mark that included the Bing–Boeheim years. Lewis had another good year after the Bing-led team exited, finishing 20–6 with a squad that went to the NIT but then dropped off to 11–14 in 1967–68, his final year. "I don't know what happened," uttered Harper, who was a senior during that losing season. "We just couldn't win."

Things were different then. When Lewis coached, he had only one assistant coach, Roy Danforth, who had played for him at Southern Mississippi. "In those days, it was only a two-man staff," explained Danforth. "Not only was I the only assistant for awhile, but I taught half a load in the PE Department."

College basketball was also undergoing a lot of changes. The NCAA tournament was expanding, and the game, aided by increased exposure due to television, was gaining in popularity. Some say the modern era of Syracuse basketball began with Lewis, who set the foundation for what was to come by bringing in Bing, who could have gone anywhere. Danforth was elevated to the head position in 1968. After experiencing a losing season in his first year, Danforth got Syracuse started on the steady climb back to basketball respectability. It wasn't easy, and it didn't happen overnight. From the groundwork laid by Lewis, Danforth built a program that advanced to postseason play his last six years, including making the NCAA tournament his final four years.

As an Assistant Coach

Danforth gave Boeheim the added responsibility of coaching the freshmen basketball team while continuing as varsity golf coach. Duffy tells of a recruiting trip that Boeheim made to White Plains when Boeheim stayed at his house. "We were shooting pool, and all he was doing was bitching and moaning about how little money Syracuse was paying him," Duffy related. "Jimmy was the low man on the totem pole, and they were paying him something like $2,500." Regardless of the paltry income, Boeheim was all about business. Perhaps an indication of things to come, Boeheim guided the Orange frosh, tagged "The Tangerines," to a 16–2 record. One of those wins came against a team coached by his former teammate Sam Penceal. "I brought my prep team up from New York to play against Jim's freshmen team, and we lost," recalled Penceal, not only one of the first but one of many coaches who would suffer defeat at the hands of a Boeheim-coached team. As the golf coach, Boeheim exhibited the same competitive spirit he had when playing with his father. "Boeheim was always a better player than most of us," Frank Beyer, a member of Boeheim's golf team, told *Syracuse Post-Standard* columnist Bud Poliquin. "But he couldn't make short putts for money. We'd always have side bets in practice. At Penn State, he three-putted from four feet and lost a quarter. And he didn't talk to me for two days."

In 1972, Boeheim was promoted to the full-time assistant basketball coach. "Jim was a very good assistant coach," related Danforth. "He had a good knowledge of the game, he did a good job of scouting, and he got along well with the players. When he played, he was a thinker, and that's what made him a good coach."

When Syracuse went on road trips, Boeheim roomed with Don Lowe, the athletic trainer. Lowe said Boeheim read constantly. "He was always reading a book, mostly novels, but he also particularly liked history. And he enjoyed watching movies." Lowe said Boeheim also appreciated good food, especially Italian. Lowe told how years later when Syracuse was playing in a tournament in Denver that Boeheim asked him to locate a good restaurant. Lowe gave him the name of an Italian restaurant. "But when I told him, Jim said, 'An Italian restaurant in Denver? Are you kidding me? It can't be any good.'" So Boeheim opted to eat elsewhere while Lowe and a few others went to the Italian restaurant. While eating, Lowe met and talked with the owner of the restaurant and who Lowe found out was an Italian from New York City. Lowe mentioned Boeheim's name and what Boeheim had said. The owner of the restaurant was aware of Boeheim and told Lowe to bring Boeheim to the restaurant. "When I told Jim, he agreed to go, but he said, 'This had better be good.' Jim went to the restaurant to eat, and he enjoyed it so much that he went back to the Italian restaurant to eat the next night too. Jim loves good Italian food."

As the 1970s began, Richard Nixon was in the White House, Abbie Hoffman was in jail, Martin Luther King Jr. and Bobby Kennedy had been assassinated, Woodstock and Berkeley were in the rearview mirror, and the Beatles had broken up. And basketball was about to become big at Syracuse, but not yet. Times were different. NIT invitations for Syracuse were not taken for granted—they were relished! After the Orangemen had been shut out of postseason play for four years, Danforth took SU to the NIT in 1971 and 1972. In the late 1960s to mid-1970s, with local favorites but nationally unknown players such as sharpshooter Greg "Kid" Kohls, "Sweet D" Dennis DuVal, Utica's Dale Shackleford, Mike and Jimmy Lee, Rudy Hackett, Marty Byrnes, Jimmy "Bug" Williams, the "Rocket Man" Chris Sease, and others, Syracuse teams hustled, scrapped, and battled looking for respect. DuVal completed his SU career with 1,504 points, second at the time behind Bing. DuVal, who in 1991 became the chief of police in Syracuse, led the team through a Harlem Globetrotter-like warmup routine that revved up the crowd, with the theme from *Shaft* and "Who's That Lady" blaring in the background. With Mike Lee at 6-foot-4 and the 6-foot-2 Mark Wadach as forwards and 6-foot-6 Bob

Dooms at center, Danforth's 1971 through 1973 teams were tagged "Roy's Runts." The run-and-press Runts at one point fought their way to a No. 13 national ranking.

During this time the "Voice of the Orange" was Joel Mareiniss, a play-by-play announcer who had an instantly recognizable voice and a passion for his alma mater that came through to his radio listeners. He had such catchphrases as "dirty, but good" when a bad-looking SU shot went in; "ice water in his veins" when one of the Orangemen made a free throw in a clutch situation; "up the invisible ladder" when Vaughn Harper, Sease, or someone else skied for a rebound; "No. 22 on his jersey, No. 1 in your heart" when introducing DuVal; "the Bouie boomerang" when describing a block by the big center; "Dale Shackleford is his name, basketball is his game"; "Hickeroo for two" when George Hicker hit a longshot; and on a fast-break layup "[so-and-so] with the snowbird." Mareiniss's energy and enthusiasm endeared him to his fans and added excitement to Syracuse's growing fan base.

In 1974, Syracuse scored over 100 points four times, including putting a 110–53 hurt on an outmanned Bucknell team coached by a young Jim Valvano. Years later, after winning the national championship at North Carolina State, Valvano was told by this writer that he was in attendance at that Orange–Bisons game. Valvano quipped, "Yeah, you had to remind me of that game. At halftime, we were down by eight—eight touchdowns!

"I was trying to get my assistant coaches to help me pump up the team, but they were all too busy updating their resumes."

Boeheim was an assistant when Syracuse broke through a seemingly unattainable barrier to make its first-ever appearance in the Final Four in 1975. An undersized and unheralded group that included Hackett, Jimmy Lee, Sease, Williams, Earnie Seibert, and Ross Kindel led the No. 20 Orangemen to a huge upset of No. 6 North Carolina in the East Regional of the NCAA tournament, which by then had grown to thirty-two teams. After that 78–76 thriller over the Tar Heels, it took another dramatic 95–87 overtime win over No. 17 Kansas State to propel Syracuse to what would eventually be called "The Big Dance." In San Diego, as a Cinderella team ala Gonzaga and Butler of later years, the Orangemen joined traditional basketball powers UCLA, Kentucky, and Louisville. "It was the blue-bloods against the blue-collars," Seibert told writer Bud Poliquin. "People saw us out there and it was like we crashed the party or something."

Syracuse's first appearance in the Final Four was much different than its next three trips. In 1975, SU was a lightly regarded dark-horse team that had hope but no real expectations. The team, the coaches, the school, and its followers were elated just to be in the tournament. After beating North Carolina, Syracuse was playing with house money, and everything thereafter was gravy. Any wins in San Diego would just be frosting on the cake.

Cinderella lost her slipper as SU lost to the Wildcats, 95–79, and then to the Cardinals, 96–88, in overtime. In the process, however, Syracuse proved that it could compete with the big boys. The 6-foot-8 Hackett grabbed 407 rebounds, which was at the time a single-season school record. After a playing career overseas, Hackett went on to become an assistant coach at Southern California.

In 1975–76, Syracuse followed up their Final Four appearance by going 20–9. As ECAC champions, the Orangemen played in the NCAA tournament, where they fell to Texas Tech in the first round, 69–56, in a game played in the Lone Star State. Compiling a 139–55 ledger, Danforth had a nice nine-year coaching run at SU, with the Orangemen most of the time flirting with national recognition. "Back then, we were an Eastern team playing on television once a year," said Boeheim.

Meanwhile, Boeheim, gaining a reputation as an excellent recruiter, was getting antsy to become a head coach. He applied for the opening at the University of Rochester, an NCAA Division III school just west of his hometown. A month after applying for that job, Danforth resigned from Syracuse and took the head basketball job at Tulane. That announcement caused Boeheim, believing he had an inside track, to quickly shift his interest to his alma mater. He applied for the job. Impressed with his assistant, Danforth supported the promotion. Asked if he recommended Boeheim to be his successor, Danforth stated, "Absolutely. I would recommend Jim for any job that he wanted."

When Danforth departed, Syracuse was at a point where it could attract a coach with a national reputation. Les Dye was the athletic director at the time and a four-man search committee was formed, which was chaired by vice-chancellor Cliff Winters. According to John Robert Greene as explained in his book *The Edgers Years*, the committee, which also consisted of trustee W. Carrol Coyne, board chairman David Bennett, and vice president Mel Mounts, was reportedly discussing Rutgers head coach Tom Young, a hot name at the time after he took the Scarlet Knights to the Final Four. Another candidate was Virginia Military University head coach Bill Blair, who had just led his team to the Elite Eight. Bill Frieder, an assistant coach at Michigan, which had just lost to Indiana in the national championship game, was also in the running.

Boeheim wanted the job and tried to abort the search. Using the offer he had to become the head coach at Rochester as leverage, he pressured Winters and the selection committee to make a quick decision by promising to bring in Roosevelt Bouie, a 6-foot-11 center from nearby Kendall who was flying under the national radar. Boeheim had been recruiting Bouie, but with the coaching change, Bouie had a change of heart and was getting ready to commit to St. Bonaventure. Boeheim boldly stated that he could land Bouie if he were named the coach. Ploy or not, the strategy worked, because Boeheim was the only person the committee interviewed.

"The Syracuse people were wavering about who they were going to bring in. I was the assistant coach, and I'd brought in the players. I said, 'Listen, I'm going to Rochester tomorrow,' and I just walked out of the room," Boeheim told sportswriter Graham Bensinger. "I wasn't sure if I was going to get the job, but I felt that I had made my case. The decision had to be made early because of recruiting, and that's why I pressed the issue."

"Jim told me that he gave them twenty-four hours to make their decision," stated Duffy. Apparently impressing the committee, Boeheim, helped by an outpouring of support from current and former Syracuse players, was offered the job about a half-hour after he left the meeting, about twenty-three and a half hours sooner than the deadline he told Duffy that he gave the committee. He immediately accepted. Rochester's loss was Syracuse's gain. And the rest, as they say, is history.

Boeheim became nationally recognized. Few, however, remember the coach that he replaced. It's a good trivia question, and the man that preceded Boeheim has good-naturedly had a little fun with it. Danforth related to Syracuse columnist Bud Poliquin how he would be sitting at a bar when a Syracuse game came on television and that he would make a wager with the guy sitting next to him on who coached Syracuse before Boeheim. "Nobody ever knows. People have short memories," he said. "I'll say Roy Danforth, and the guy buys me a drink. I've won a lot of drinks that way. It doesn't bother me as long as a guy buys me a drink."

4

NAMED SYRACUSE HEAD COACH

The Beginning of the Boeheim Era

On April 1, 1976, Steve Jobs and Steve Wozniak formed the Apple Computer Company. Two days later, Jim Boeheim was named the seventh head basketball coach in Syracuse University history. Thirty-one years old at the time, he jumped at the opportunity that paid him $25,000 a year and $75,000 over three years. "Ever since I came to Syracuse I wanted to be the head coach. Today my dream has come true," expressed Boeheim. Fast-forward for a second. Four decades later, thanks to Jobs and Boeheim, Apple and Syracuse basketball are national name brands.

Boeheim then landed Roosevelt Bouie, who became the key component of Boeheim's first Orange teams. "I liked Jim Satalin, who was the head coach at St. Bonaventure, and Jim Boeheim, who was an assistant coach when he was recruiting me, because they had characteristics like my father," explained Bouie on his decision to choose

Syracuse over the Bonnies, Michigan State, Georgia Tech, and Duke. "They were soft-spoken and tended to listen. I wanted to go to a big-time program with a coach who would make me toe the line, but in a way that I wouldn't become resentful of later. I got a good report on Coach Boeheim from the players. When Jim Boeheim was named head coach, I decided to go to Syracuse."

Ironically, Syracuse weather worked in the Orange's favor in landing Bouie. "When I visited Georgia Tech and Duke, the weather was warm, and all the girls were running around in bikinis," recalled Bouie. "I thought I would flunk out the first semester if I went to a place like that. I wanted to go to a school where I could play basketball and study. My first year at Syracuse we got 210 inches of snow before the end of January, so that's what I did—played basketball and studied."

Boeheim inherited the program from Danforth and, in a way, became the extended third branch of the iconic Clair Bee coaching tree. It was Danforth who got the ball rolling again, but it was Boeheim who took the Cuse to the big time.

As soon as Boeheim got the SU job, he went to New York City and got Rick Pitino to be his first assistant coach. Boeheim had been impressed with Pitino's work at Howard Garfinkel's Five-Star Basketball Camp. Pitino was a freshman basketball player at the University of Massachusetts when Julius "Dr. J" Erving was a senior. He had just finished an assistant coaching stint at Hawaii and was out of work. Young, brash, and unpolished, Pitino possessed the potential to become a successful coach.

In an often repeated story, Pitino and his new bride Joanne had just gotten married and were staying at the old Americana Hotel in New York when Boeheim showed up to offer Pitino a position on his staff. Boeheim called Pitino down to the hotel lobby and a discussion that was initially intended to take a half hour extended to about four hours. "At first, [the interruption] was no problem because I didn't have a job, so it was a good thing," articulated Pitino, "but then the discussion dragged on and on. I kept calling Joanne [to keep her abreast of what was going on], but after about three hours, she was becoming irked." Left alone, Joanne watched television. Pitino listened to Boeheim while his wife stewed. During the discussion, Pitino managed to get Boeheim to up the ante a little, agreeing to a contract for a reported $17,500, which was $4,500 more than he was originally offered. As he had been with the search committee and in his pursuit of Bouie, Boeheim was persistent and got the man he wanted.

"I probably wouldn't do it that way now," Boeheim told George Vecsey of the *New York Times,* regarding the manner in which he crashed Pitino's honeymoon. "I was fired up." Again, at the consternation of Joanne, Boeheim immediately dispatched Rick to Cincinnati to recruit Louis Orr, a skinny, 6-foot-9, 165-pound forward who, along with Bouie, would become the dynamic one-two punch of Boeheim's early Orange teams that won 100 of 118 games. Orr had some lower-level scholarship opportunities, but Boeheim got wind of him through the grapevine and wanted him. "I had a few offers, but not a lot, and it was late in the signing period," recalled Orr. "There were a few phone calls, and that got the ball rolling."

Since Boeheim was keeping Pitino on the go, the newly appointed assistant coach didn't even have time to get an apartment. For two weeks, Joanne stayed with Boeheim and his two roommates, one of which was a waiter and the other a professional harness-racing handicapper. Surprisingly, Pitino said his wife didn't have a problem with the unusual living arrangement. "She really didn't mind it," he said.

Pitino said he was hired to teach man-to-man defense. During the two years he spent with Boeheim, Syracuse played man-to-man defense about 25 to 30 percent of the time. Pitino said Boeheim taught the 2–3 zone, which Danforth had also used. "He taught me the zone," said Pitino.

When they went on recruiting trips, Pitino said Boeheim would read about two novels a week. "Jim is a very smart man," he said. Pitino may have recognized that Boeheim was smart, but *USA Today* columnist Dana O'Neil reported about a time Pitino thought he had a leg up on his boss. Pitino told O'Neil that the two were recruiting

Rich Shrigley and, since Pitino had had the most contact with Shrigley and therefore knew the most about him, that he would do all the talking when the two went to New Hampshire for a home visit.

"I got this. I know everything about this kid. I'll do all the talking," a confident Pitino told O'Neil, emphasizing that he repeated that to Boeheim to let the head coach know that Pitino thought he had an edge in prying Shrigley away from North Carolina State, which was also pursuing the young man. In pushing Syracuse, Pitino pointed out how Shrigley would be a better fit for the Orange than he would be for the Wolfpack when Shrigley's mother interrupted by saying, "Yes, I told Norman that." Surprised that the mother referred to NC State coach Norman Sloan so casually by his first name, Boeheim piped in, "Do you know Coach Sloan?"

"Yes, he's my brother." Taken back by his lack of awareness, Pitino said, "After that, I didn't say a word the rest of the night." Recalling the recruiting trip, and though he lost the recruit, Boeheim, who remained a lifelong friend of Pitino, thought the coincidence was hilarious. "'Yeah, I'll do all the talking,' he kept telling me."

Besides golf, Boeheim also liked to play tennis. As he did when he played basketball with his friends on the court next to his house, Boeheim also tried to officiate the contests. Pitino said, "When I played him in tennis, he would make all the line calls down on my end of the court, about ninety feet away. Of course, they would all go against me. Jim has X-ray vision. When he said it went out, he was right. We called him 'Superman.'"

Another thing Boeheim did upon becoming the head coach was to ask Lowe, who was planning to give up basketball to serve exclusively as the athletic trainer for football, to stay on as basketball athletic trainer. "I decided to stay on as basketball trainer because of Jim. I really liked Jim. He and I had always gotten along great. We respected each other. He liked me and let me do my job," explained Lowe, who served as athletic trainer for SU basketball from 1975 until 2000. "I'm glad I stayed on because we had a great relationship for almost twenty-five years."

1976–77

For perspective, on November 2, 1976, Jimmy Carter defeated incumbent Gerald Ford to become the first candidate from the Deep South since the Civil War to become President of the United States. On November 26, at the age of 32, Boeheim started his college career by beating Harvard, 75–48, in the Tip-Off Classic at Springfield, Massachusetts. The Syracuse starters in that game were Bouie at center, forwards Dale Shackleford and Marty Byrnes, and guards Jimmy Williams and Ross Kindel. On the bench were Orr, Larry Kelley, Bob Parker, Reggie Powell, Hal Cohen, and Cliff Warwell. Boeheim played mostly man-to-man defense in the first half and was barely ahead, 35–33, at intermission. In what would be shades of the future, Boeheim switched to a 2–3 zone in the second half, the move that triggered a 23–4 Orange run that broke the game wide open.

If Boeheim had any thoughts that this was going to be an easy way to make a living, they were quickly dispelled the next evening when Syracuse lost to West Virginia, 83–78. So the coach who would go on to make winning a habit started out 1–1 and, in doing so, had Orange fans scratching their heads and wondering if this guy with no head coaching experience, other than as a golf coach, was the right man for the job. The Syracuse faithful breathed a little easier when the team rattled off seven straight wins before losing to Maryland, 96–85, at the Maryland Invitational. Included was Boeheim's first signature win. In only his fourth game, Boeheim engineered a monumental 76–75 upset of No. 1 Louisville at Freedom Hall. It was a rematch of schools that staged the overtime nail-biter in the 1975 Final Four, won by the Cardinals, 96–88. Following the victory, an excited Boeheim proclaimed, "This has to rank up with the [North Carolina] win as the greatest in Syracuse history!"

"I was from Cincinnati, and that was the first time I was playing close to home," said the lanky Orr, who looked like a splinter in a forest of redwoods but played much bigger. "It was a war. I wore braces then, and I remember getting elbowed in the mouth, and my lip got caught on my braces. It was a great environment. Louisville had Darrell Griffith, Wesley Cox, Ricky Gallon, and Rick Wilson. They had a crew, and I was a freshman, just a pup. I remember thinking, 'This is big-time basketball.'"

Eleven more victories followed before St. Bonaventure beat the Orange. Syracuse closed the regular season with four wins. In ECAC postseason play, SU got a payback victory over the Bonnies and then defeated Old Dominion. In the NCAA Mideast Regional in Baton Rouge, Louisiana, in a Southeastern Conference arena, Syracuse was pitted against Tennessee, with its stars Ernie Grunfeld and Bernard King. No matter, what would become the "Louie and Bouie Show" bested the "Ernie and Bernie Show" as the Orangemen beat the Volunteers, 93–88, in overtime. In doing so, Boeheim bagged his second signature win. With the victory, Syracuse made the statement that, in upstate New York at least, SU was "The Big Orange."

Four days later, however, Syracuse came out flat against the University of North Carolina–Charlotte and was soundly beaten, 81–59. Led by Cedric "Cornbread" Maxwell, perhaps the school's top all-time player and who down the road would have his jersey retired by the Boston Celtics, the 49ers toasted the sixth-ranked Orangemen in the regional semifinals. This was the first of what would be several NCAA tournament games that Boeheim would lose early in his career to so-called mid-major teams. Given the talent at his disposal, Boeheim began to pick up the reputation of being an underachiever. To be fair, though, UNC–Charlotte was a very good team that went on to beat No. 1-ranked Michigan before losing to eventual national champion Marquette in the Final Four. It could be argued, therefore, that maybe the 49ers were underrated, and perhaps that wasn't as big of an upset as many people thought. Regardless, Syracuse's inaugural 26–4 season under rookie coach Jim Boeheim was successful beyond anyone's wildest imagination. In just a matter of months, Boeheim had put his stamp on the program. Little did people know that this was just a sign of things to come and that winning basketball games at Syracuse would become as normal as shoveling snow in the winter.

Asked about his goals when he first took over the program, Boeheim back then said, "At the time, we were coming off a successful season [20–9]. We had a commitment to stay successful. That was easier than trying to build from nothing. We were in a situation where we had to have a good recruiting year. We didn't have a center. We were able to recruit two players who became good players for us—Roosevelt Bouie and Louis Orr. That made that first year very successful." The successful season also increased enthusiasm for basketball at Syracuse, resulting in a $1.1 million expansion of Manley Field House, increasing the capacity of the building from 8,200 to 9,500.

1977–78

Syracuse and Boeheim followed up with a 22–6 campaign that included two big early-season wins. The Orangemen defeated Earvin "Magic" Johnson-led Michigan State, 75–67, in the inaugural Carrier Classic. It was Boeheim's first big home win. Still, Boeheim was livid that Johnson got the tournament Most Valuable Player Award over SU's Marty Byrnes, even though SU beat the Spartans to win the championship. Boeheim angrily stated that the MVP should be awarded to a player from the winning team. Sticking up for his player, Boeheim made his point, but Johnson got his trophy.

Pitino recalled that incident. "Boeheim was incensed," he stated. "He had the stat sheet in his hand, and he rolled it up and threw it at the back of [*Syracuse Post-Standard* writer] Rob Lawin's head. Later, I saw Rob, and I told him not to worry about it, that that was just Jim being Jim."

Honest with his opinions sometimes to a fault and outspoken as if he believed he was always right, this was the first time that Boeheim assertively went against the grain to express his feelings. The explosive behavior was a characteristic that would occur periodically throughout his career, sometimes effectively and sometimes not so much.

After winning its own tournament, Syracuse then got a huge win at New Mexico in the Lobo Classic, 96–91, over a team led by

All-American Michael Cooper that finished the season 24–4 and ranked No. 4 in the country by UPI. Skipping ahead for a moment, in 1998, before SU played and beat New Mexico in the NCAA tournament, Boeheim, despite all the big wins over the years, still said that win in the second season of his coaching career was special. "It was the best game that I've ever been involved in," he stated twenty-one years later. The 1977 game at "The Pit," a unique underground facility that in 1999 was declared the loudest arena in the country and ranked 13th in *Sports Illustrated*'s Top 20 sports venues of any kind, made such an impression on Boeheim that the 2016–17 New Mexico media guide still contained his picture with his quote that the game remains "one of the most exciting games of my career."

"I remember the pace of the game and the number of dunks, especially on their part," stated Orr, a valuable sixth man during his first year and thereafter a three-year starter. "The crowd was crazy." Bouie also mentioned the dunking exhibition that the Lobos put on and that the game was helter-skelter. "They made like five dunks in a matter of seconds, but we ended up winning. Later on, I played with Michael Cooper in Italy, and he told me, 'You guys messed up our season.'"

Beyond the victory, a tradition was born. Thereafter, Syracuse fans at the beginning of each half would remain standing and clapping until the Orange made a basket, something they picked up from the Lobos' rabid fans at The Pit in Albuquerque. Syracuse notched a 22–6 ledger, but the season ended on a sour note as SU lost to St. Bonaventure in the ECAC Upstate-South playoffs and then to Western Kentucky in the NCAA Mideast Regional in Knoxville, Tennessee. Against WKU, the Orange squandered a five-point lead with 54 seconds to go. The contest was tied at the end of regulation and went into overtime. With time winding down in overtime, Marty Byrnes made a basket, but the field goal was discounted because Byrnes was fouled before the shot. Byrnes missed the front end of a one-and-one free throw situation. A make would have tied the game, and two makes could have won the game. Instead, the Hilltoppers escaped with an 87–86 win.

1978–79

Syracuse started the 1978 season ranked ninth in the nation and went into Rupp Arena for the Kentucky Invitational with a 6–0 record, only to leave Lexington with two losses. The Orange was deflated by No. 15 Illinois, 64–61, and then by the No. 11 host Wildcats, 94–87. SU rebounded with 19 consecutive wins, including a victory over St. Bonaventure in the ECAC Upstate Regional. Following a loss to Georgetown in the ECAC Upstate–South Championship game, the Orangemen beat Connecticut in the NCAA East Regional, but their season came to a close with a 26–4 record after being eliminated by Pennsylvania, 84–76.

"We didn't have any superstars or high school All-Americans. We were a bunch of upstate New York guys who all played together and wanted to win," stated Dale Shackleford, a native of nearby Utica who played on Danforth's last team and Boeheim's first three teams. "Nothing was guaranteed. Just because you started the last game didn't mean you were going to start again. We had to compete every day in practice. Coach Boeheim had the will and determination to win, but it was up to us to work hard. We just wanted to work and get the job done."

1979–80

The first season of play in the Big East Conference was in 1979–80. In addition to SU, the charter members were Boston College, Connecticut, Georgetown, Providence, St. Johns, and Seton Hall, making it the best basketball conference in the East and considered by many on a par with the better conferences elsewhere in the country. It was also the senior seasons for Roosevelt Bouie and Louis Orr. The Orange started fast again, winning their first 14 games, including a big win in January at No. 10 Purdue, which featured All-American center Joe Barry Carroll. The Boilermakers later that year made it to the Final Four. The Purdue coach was Lee Rose, who in 1976, as

UNC–Charlotte's coach, utilized his slow-down, control-style offense to mastermind the 49ers' NCAA tournament upset of SU.

Purdue had an elevated court, and Boeheim was so excited after the game that he was jumping around and turned his ankle. He didn't tell anyone, but Don Lowe, SU's basketball trainer, noticed Boeheim limping badly afterward. "The ankle had really swollen up. It was huge," stated Lowe, "but Jim didn't say a word." Bouie said by the time the team got back to Syracuse, Boeheim could hardly walk.

Syracuse then experienced a hiccup at Old Dominion, getting nipped by the Monarchs, 68–67. SU won seven in a row before playing its final game in Manley Field House, the old indoor football building that had a raised court over a dirt floor, wooden bleachers, a wooden balcony, and a track around the outside of the court. Georgetown snapped the Orange's 57-game homecourt winning streak by squeaking out a 52–50 victory on two free throws by Eric "Sleepy" Floyd in the final seconds. Rubbing salt into the wound, Hoyas coach John Thompson Jr. infamously declared, to the chagrin of the Syracuse Nation, "Manley Field House is officially closed!" That statement triggered what would over the course of the next decade become one of the greatest rivalries in college basketball. "That definitely fueled it," stated John Thompson III, big John's son, several years later.

Syracuse then beat St. John's, Niagara, and Boston College to win the first Big East regular-season championship. The Orangemen downed Connecticut in the first round of the Big East tournament but lost again to Georgetown, 87–81. SU got a victory over Villanova in the first round of the NCAA East Regional. In the next round, Syracuse was sent home by Iowa, thus finishing the season with an overall record of 26–4. The "Louie and Bouie Show" ran for four glorious seasons and produced 100 wins, with Boeheim becoming the first coach to reach the century mark in victories in his first four seasons. Bouie, who started from the get-go, averaged 16.1 points and 8.1 rebounds per game. Orr averaged 15.9 points and 8.5 boards. Bouie concluded his career as SU's all-time leader in blocks (327), second in points and third in rebounds. Orr scored 1,487 points, and in 2001, he became the first Big East player to become a head coach in the conference when he took over at Seton Hall. The Louie and Bouie group also put Boeheim's first recruiting class in the books.

"We were a regional team. When the Big East started, Coach Boeheim took us from being an Eastern team to a team with more national notoriety. We were ranked in the Top 10 and as high as No. 2. Coach really elevated the program and took it to another level," stated Orr. He modestly added: "Roosevelt was always the guy. He was the anchor. Roosevelt was the first legitimate big man in the East. I kind of rode on his coattails. He really made my life on the court a lot easier. It was actually the 'Bouie and Louie Show.'"

Reminiscing about his now famous coach's first four years on the job, Bouie said, "Coach Boeheim was very serious. Even then, he was immaculate with the X's and O's. There was never a doubt in your mind that he knew what he wanted to do. As far as preparation for our opponent, we knew exactly what to expect.

"When we practiced, there was not a chair in the gym, so you couldn't sit down in practice. We had 15-second water breaks. There were no distractions. There was no talking except for the coaches calling out things like good pass, good shot, block out, back door, help, and things like that. It was always constructive. There was never anything negative.

"We were the best-conditioned team in the country. We had to run a mile under six minutes. We had a full-court drill where you had to make 120 layups in three minutes. We could do it if we did everything correctly. If we did it, then we had to make 126 layups in three minutes." Wendell Alexis, who played from 1983 through 1986, was more specific regarding Boeheim's conditioning requirements. He said that centers had to run a six-minute mile but that the forwards had to cover the distance in five and a half minutes and the guards in five minutes and fifteen seconds and under. "Coach Boeheim expected us to report in shape," he stated.

Bouie said, "Coach told me exactly what he wanted me to do, and I was like a remote-control toy. I did what I was told. I did anything and everything he asked me to do… Before a game, Coach would get very excited. He was wired."

Orr explained that in the early days, Boeheim had to "fight for respect. He had to fight for everything. He had to establish himself and his program," he stated. "Later, the success that he had, along with his family and children, gave him more perspective. I think his life is very balanced now. From a professional point of view, only a few guys have accomplished what he has, so he has his place in history. He has touched a lot of peoples' lives. I think he's very confident in who he is. I think that he is in a good place in his life."

Bouie credited Boeheim with helping him settle down during his freshman year. "I came from Kendall, New York, a small town of 600 people. There were more people in my dorm than there were in the town where I grew up. Every day was a challenge for me," he said. "One day after practice I was tired and just sitting in the locker room, and Coach came up to me and said, 'Rosie, if you just continue to play like this, as hard as you can, what more can I ask of you? Just keep doing exactly what you're doing.'

"I said, 'Wow, I can do that.' That took a big weight off of my shoulders. What he said at that time was extremely important for my career," related Bouie. Orr also provided what he felt was a possible life-changing situation. Prior to his junior year, major surgery was required after Orr twisted his knee in the preseason. He said a decision by Boeheim and trainer Don Lowe probably saved his career. "It required arthroscopic surgery, and there were only two doctors in the country at that time doing that type of surgery: Frank Jobe in Utah, and someone in California. Don Lowe and I flew to Salt Lake City," confided Orr. "After the surgery, I was practicing in three or four days, and within a week, I was playing. To me, that was a pivotal point in my career. It probably saved my career. I'm thankful to Syracuse for sending me all the way to Utah to have the surgery. I think I might have been the first guy at Syracuse to have arthroscopic surgery." Lowe confirmed that the operative arthroscopic surgery was the first of its kind performed on any Syracuse athlete.

Shackleford, who came to Syracuse a year before Bouie and Orr and who still works at Boeheim's summer camp, said Boeheim was a lot tougher when he first started out then he is now. "It's a different generation, and the players are different," he explained. "Today you have the four- and five-star camps and AAU basketball catering to the kids. Some of them are not developed for the college game. With this generation of guys, you have to make some changes and be a little more careful in how you approach them. They are not used to constructive criticism and in-your-face coaching. Coach Boeheim has learned to adjust. It's a lot tougher to coach now. Coach has told us several times that he wishes he had guys like us."

Wendell Alexis, a member of Syracuse's 1,000-point club who played a few years after Bouie, Orr, and Shackleford, said that he heard from other players from his era who also thought Boeheim had softened up his practices a little. "Gene Waldron [who played from 1981 to 1984] told me, 'It's completely different from when we played.' When I played, Coach Boeheim was still a young coach and very demanding. We had a defensive drill where we would slide across the lane with bricks in our hands. A few years later when I went back and watched a practice, I asked Coach [Bernie] Fine, 'Where are the bricks?' Coach Fine said, 'We don't do that anymore.'"

Besides basketball, Bouie and Orr said Boeheim also taught his players a sense of community service. "Every year he would have us go to the Upstate Medical Center and spend some time with five-, six-, and seven-year-old kids who were terminally ill," remembered Bouie. "We would talk to them, play board games, and just play with them. I remember most of those kids having smiles on their faces. I remember going back to my room and crying," he admitted. Orr recalled a group of players getting together and going to the Auburn Correctional Facility to play basketball against the inmates. "It was a public relations type of thing that was legal back then. I remember feeling a little nervous playing basketball inside a prison."

Like Boeheim's teammates, his first group of players had their

Boeheim stories. Bouie told of Syracuse traveling to an away game in cars and having an accident that involved three SU vehicles. "Louis Orr, Eddie Moss, Chris Jerebko, and I were in the middle car, with Coach Boeheim driving. If you were in the back seat and talking to him [in the front], he would turn around to answer," he informed. "One time, the car in front braked, and we ran into it, and the car behind us ran into us." Orr also remembered the fender bender. Bouie also remembered Boeheim driving an orange Pontiac Bonneville. "As players, we were embarrassed and didn't want to be seen riding in it," he said. "We'd say that we had a reputation and that we couldn't be seen getting out of an orange car." Everyone knew Boeheim bled orange, but they probably thought that was taking it a little too far.

Alexis recalled the entire team going over to Boeheim's house with a cake to surprise him on his birthday. "He wasn't expecting us, and certainly his first wife Elaine wasn't expecting us, because she answered the door with facial cream on her face. I don't think she was too happy to see us. Coach Boeheim was downstairs watching a college basketball game on ESPN. I don't remember if we did that every year, but I know we did it a couple of times."

Boeheim's contemporaries say he likes fine food, but regarding his personality, Shackleford called him a "Coke and hamburger" type of guy. "He's low-key. He loves the game of basketball, but he doesn't like the limelight. He's a great guy. Anybody who doesn't like him is probably a guy who never played [in games]," stated Shackleford.

"Coach has always been very loyal to his players and to people who have been a part of his program," said Orr. "If you need him for anything, he's not too hard to reach. He's a real humble, down-to-earth guy."

The dramatic success early in his career should have established Boeheim as one of college basketball's rising coaching stars. However, for quite some time, Boeheim remained one of the sport's best-kept secrets, with some sportscasters and writers still struggling with his name. Not getting the respect that his record suggested that he should get, Boeheim had to console himself knowing that he had the respect of his peers and that most of the time he came out on top where it counted—on the basketball court.

5

THE CARRIER DOME, THE BIG EAST, AND THE 1980s

1980–81

In 1980, Syracuse began playing in the spacious Carrier Dome, the largest domed stadium in the Northeast and the largest on-campus basketball facility in the country. Boeheim, in one of the relatively few times that he proved to be shortsighted, railed against leaving the friendly confines of Manley Field House, a comfy setting where the Orange had compiled a 190–30 record that included winning streaks of 36 and 57 games. In its last 10 years at Manley, Syracuse was nearly unbeatable at home, winning 123 of 129 games. Visiting teams dreaded coming to the dust-filled arena where 9,500 fans packed the place for every game. The joint really started to jump when the Orange went through warmups to "Le Freak," an upbeat disco song by the band Chic. A rowdy student section called "The Zoo" was strategically situated close to the opponent's bench, where the "Manley Maniacs" stomped on the wooden bleachers a few feet from the basket and provided an atmosphere as raucous as anyplace in the country. Louis Orr recalled that sometimes students threw toilet paper on the floor before games. When opposing teams were introduced, after each person's name was called, the Zoo would scream, "Who's he?", "So what!", "Who cares!", "Big deal!", and finally "Big shit!" Bouie said that within The Zoo was another group called "The Kennel Club." He said the students in that group would research each player on the opponent's starting team and find out their girlfriend's name, mother's name, or anything else they could learn and then relentlessly ride the players, especially the first player that would look into the crowd after being called out. "The Kennel Club would then bark at and roast that player the rest of the game. They would ride that player like a pony," stated Bouie, who noted that the leader of the Kennel Club was SU player Marty Byrnes's roommate. His Kennel Club leadership skills must have paid off as he became and still is a CEO of a bank.

Asked about Manley, Danforth, who enjoyed such great success there, laughed and said, "It was like a circus in there. It was dusty and dirty. Visiting teams didn't like to play there, and a lot of teams wouldn't come in and play us. It was a great home court advantage." Syracuse only lost one game at Manley Field House in the four years that Shackleford played, which turned out to be his home finale against Georgetown, with the Orangemen going 49–1 from 1976 through 1979. "It was the best place to play. The fans were great; the atmosphere was unbelievable," he said. "You talk about a sixth man; well, Manley was a seventh man for us. The fans would start heckling the opposing players as soon as they got on the floor. Some began heckling them outside before they even came in the building."

Referring to it as a dirt bowl, Pitino said Manley Field House was very loud. "The Zoo was very aggressive. It provided one of the strongest homecourt advantages in the country." Lou Carnesecca, St. John's Hall of Fame coach, told writer Bud Poliquin, "I mean it was tough winning [in Manley]…Holy mackerel, I'm a little bit deaf now, but I wish I was deaf back then. Those fans were right on top of you, and they let you have it from all angles. They had a way of expressing themselves, let me tell you."

Roosevelt Bouie, who starred in Manley and suffered his only home loss in his last home game against the Hoyas, called it "an incredible place to play. When I played my first home game there, I knew I made the right decision to come here to play. The place was so loud with people stomping on the bleachers, clapping their hands, and screaming, it felt like you were going deaf. The atmosphere made the hair on the back of your neck stand up."

Back in the day, Manley Field House was every bit as intimidating for opponents as Cameron Indoor Stadium is for foes venturing to Duke. "It is a very fair comparison to Cameron Indoor Stadium," stated Krzyzewski, who experienced what it was like in Manley when he played for West Point and who has enjoyed the luxury of coaching in the Blue Devils' compact home court. "It was like a zoo. It was in a field house, so when you walked off the court, there was dirt. It was a rowdy, crazy place. We [Army] had one hellacious game there. It rivals Cameron. It was right there."

Boeheim thought whoever made the decision to leave Manley lacked both vision and brains. He felt that even if his team drew 12 or 13,000 people in the newly constructed football facility, the fans would be seated too far from the court and would hardly be heard in the cavernous building, negating the homecourt advantage that the team enjoyed in Manley. He couldn't have been more wrong. Who would have ever thought that Syracuse would begin an 11-year stretch from 1984 through 1995, during which it would lead the nation in attendance and the Carrier Dome would, for a period of time, become the Mecca of college basketball? Or be called the "Loud House" and would attract eighty-plus crowds in excess of 30,000 people? Carnesecca said it didn't get any easier playing the Orange in the Dome. "It was like playing in an airport hangar. No wonder I hardly ever won up there," he quipped.

Soon thereafter, Boeheim, realizing the influence that the Dome had on recruiting, stated, "[The impact] is much bigger than people would have thought in the beginning. Everybody says they've got a good place to play, but if you ask a kid in high school to name five places, I would guess the Carrier Dome might be the only place that every kid names." Dick Vitale put it this way: "You'd have to live in a cave not to know about the Carrier Dome."

Boeheim quickly acknowledged the importance of the new facility and the formation of the new conference. "Two things that made a big difference are the formation of the Big East Conference and the Carrier Dome," he stated. "Before the Big East, we were probably in the top thirty or forty teams in the country. No one really knew that much about us. The Big East brought recognition to all of the Eastern teams. The conference has a very respected commissioner in Dave Gavitt, who knows the game and the people in the game, and it has an excellent television package that gives the teams a lot of exposure. The Carrier Dome has certainly helped us with recognition and has helped us get exposure. It's a great place to play basketball. No one else has a place like it."

Wendell Alexis, who played when the Dome was relatively new and rocking, stated, "As an 18-, 19-, 20-year-old kid, it was the best place to play. Absolutely! That was during the formative years of the Big East. It was good for the university, the town, and for college basketball."

With John Wooden having won his last championship in 1975, ending UCLA's run of dominance, the college basketball scene was changing. It wouldn't be too long before Syracuse would move toward the forefront of that change.

In 1980–81, Syracuse triumphed in six of its first eight games but then dropped 10 of its next 18 to finish the regular season with a 15–11 mark. The Orange, however, won the Big East tournament when Leo Rautins scored on a tip-in with three seconds remaining in the third overtime period to secure an 83–80 win over Villanova, which had joined the league that year. Bypassed by the NCAA,

Syracuse went to the NIT where it defeated Marquette, Holy Cross, Michigan, and Purdue, only to suffer an 86–84 setback loss in overtime to Tulsa. Danny Schayes, Tony "Red" Bruin, and Rautins all fouled out in regulation, making Syracuse shorthanded during the extra session. Syracuse salvaged a 22–12 record when, considering the mid-year slump, it could have been worse.

The season concluded Danny Schayes's career at SU. A local product out of nearby Jamesville-DeWitt High School and the son of Syracuse Nats and NBA great Dolph Schayes, Danny had the misfortune of being at Syracuse during the same time period as Roosevelt Bouie. Much to the dismay of his famous father, Schayes had to sit and wait his turn, serving as Bouie's backup for three years. Going against Bouie in practice, however, significantly improved Schayes's game and, over time, Schayes progressed from a substitute to an honorable mention All-American and a first-round selection in the NBA draft. Despite being a starter for only one season, Schayes went on to enjoy an 18-plus year career in the NBA. His 1,138 games played in the NBA is the most of any ex-Orangemen and 79 more than Dolph, who was selected among the Top 50 NBA Players of all time. Although a journeyman as a professional, Schayes endured and had a respectable NBA career, scoring 8,780 points and pulling down 5,671 rebounds.

1981–82

Boeheim's poorest team, as it turned out, was the 1981–82 edition that settled for a 16–13 record, 7–7 in the conference, and a spot in the NIT, where it did reach the finals before falling to Bradley, 95–81. Unaccustomed to residing among the ranks of the also-rans and spoiled by Syracuse's previous successes, the natives were beginning to get restless. Boeheim never had a losing season, but his fifth year would be the low watershed moment in what would go on to be a marvelous career.

1982–83

In 1982, bang, just like that, Syracuse bounced back by winning its first 11 games. The Cuse climbed to No. 9 in the nation before stumbling at North Carolina and Georgetown, the latter despite Rautins recording the first triple-double (12 points, 13 rebounds, and 10 assists) in Big East history, something he would do again the same season against Boston College. Included in the win streak were victories over Ohio State and an upset of a Top 10 Phi Slama Jama Houston team on its way to the NCAA finals that reestablished credibility for the Orangemen. It was the Orange's best start since the 14–0 getaway in 1979–80 when the Cuse finished sixth in the nation.

The back-to-back setbacks to the Tar Heels and Hoyas knocked SU down to the lower echelons of the Top 20, but Boeheim, being a realist and knowing how hard it was to get to the Top 10, let alone stay there, stated, "Although it would be nice to be No. 1 or 2, I think we have the respect of most knowledgeable basketball people. It has taken us some time, but we have gotten to the point where people think we have a good basketball program."

But then the wheels came off, and SU flopped in six games down the stretch. On March 1, however, Boeheim recorded his first win over a Top 5 team, sticking No. 4 Villanova, 79–70. SU then got pasted at Connecticut and Georgetown to close the regular season. Turnaround was fair play as the Orange came right back three days later and upset the Hoyas, 79–72, in the Big East tournament. Syracuse was purged from the conference tournament by Boston College and from the NCAA tournament by Ohio State. SU had beaten the Buckeyes earlier in the season, 91–85, but, as SU did with Georgetown, OSU turned the tables on the Orange in postseason play, 79–74. The Orange hobbled to a 21–10 finish, 9–7 in the league, which that year had added Pittsburgh. Not a bad year, but subpar by Syracuse's rising standards, and a disappointment considering the way the season had begun.

As their reputation steadily rose, Boeheim began to get better players. "In the beginning, we got a lot of guys who were on the borderline who became good players for us," he explained. "People like Marty Byrnes, Marty Headd, and Hal Cohen come readily to mind, and there were a lot of others like that. We were strictly an Eastern program then. With the Big East and the Carrier Dome, we have been able to recruit the national blue-chippers. Before the Big East conference, we used to lose a lot of those kids to other parts of the country. We couldn't recruit the best players in New York City or on Long Island. Now we are right in there with those guys. We're starting to attract more blue-chippers now, but the key is to get blue-chippers who are not rated as such."

That last statement epitomized much of Boeheim's recruiting strategy through the years. Acknowledged as having a keen eye for talent, Boeheim was always beating the bushes for "projects," players with the potential to be good if their raw ability could be developed and refined. Capitalizing on that philosophy, Boeheim became recognized as a coach who many times did his best work with under-recruited players who were bypassed by other coaches. He had developed a successful system where year after year he was able to do more with less. A transformation was about to occur, however.

Pearl Washington

The perception of Syracuse basketball was soon going to be forever changed, and the bar was raised exponentially when the No. 1 recruit in the nation, Pearl Washington, declared that he was coming to Syracuse. Washington was such a special player that he had eyes across the country glued to their television sets whenever Syracuse played. In the Carrier Dome, students would raise signs with 10.0, 9.7, and 9.5 on them, judging Pearl's basketball acrobatics as if they were gymnastics maneuvers. Never did you see a sign below 9.0. Washington ushered in what was to be a whole new era of Syracuse basketball.

A 6-foot-2, 190-pound playmaker extraordinaire, Pearl was a real court gem, a man of many moves, some of them seemingly extraterrestrial. Although he lacked size and speed and was not a particularly good jumper, he was unusually strong for his size and had remarkable ball-handling skills, an uncanny court sense, elusiveness, and the ability to make amazing plays at the most opportune time. Pearl possessed a wicked crossover dribble, his signature move, and had a slashing, inner-city, take-it-to-the-hoop style that thrilled the fans. His ability to penetrate, draw defenders, and then pitch the ball to his teammates for easy layups and high-percentage jump shots was unparalleled. Pearl was the catalyst that made the team go, the extra gear that catapulted the Cuse into overdrive, the player that put the bop in the bop-a-tee-bop. But that is putting the carriage before the horse.

"The Pearl Watch" began a long time before Washington got to Syracuse, before he was eight years old when Dwayne Alonzo Washington picked up his nickname "Pearl" because he was making moves on the playgrounds of the Brownsville section of Brooklyn, that reminded people of Earl Monroe. It continued when Washington drew national attention while displaying his talents at New York City's Boys and Girls High School where, as a junior, he once scored 82 points in a game. As a senior, he averaged a stat-stuffing 35 points, 10 rebounds, eight assists, and four steals per contest. A prolific scorer, he tallied a school record 1,755 points for the Kangaroos. Kenny "The Jet" Smith, another Big Apple high school star during the Washington era who went on to play 10 years in the NBA, told TNT's *Inside the NBA*: "[Pearl] was without question the rabbit everybody chased and tried to be like. He brought attention to New York City (high school basketball) ... He was the guy everybody talked about. He was the guy everybody knew ... He was a celebrity from the time he was 17 years old ... cab drivers and people on the street would stop and call out his name ... [Before Jay-Z] he was what Jay-Z was for Brooklyn ... He was the first college basketball player in rap songs ... He was an unbelievable icon."

Washington's legend escalated even more when, playing against the best high school competition in the nation, he was named Most Valuable Player of the Wheelchair Classic and the Dapper Dan Roundball Classic, and co-MVP of the McDonald's East-West All-American Game. Super-scout Howard Garfinkel called Washington "the best one-on-one-player since Calvin Murphy." Recruited by more than 300 colleges from coast-to-coast, Washington announced to Al McGuire and a CBS national television audience that he had selected Syracuse because he wanted to showcase his enormous talents in the colossal 33,000-seat Carrier Dome. "I wanted to play on the biggest stage," he said. That he did, as the Orange drew thirteen home crowds in excess of 30,000 people when he played, many of whom came especially to see a player who would become arguably the most popular player in SU hoops history. The Pearl and the Dome, one might say, was a match made in hoops heaven.

After SU lost the preceding year's tri-captains (Leo Rautins, Erich Santifer, Tony "Red" Bruin), the Pearl arrived and gave the Orange more juice and another dimension. It didn't take long for him to make the Carrier Dome his personal playground. In what could be some kind of record, it took all of three seconds for Washington to score his first collegiate field goal. He set what at the time was the school scoring record for a freshman debut, with 16 points in that 88–49 SU romp over outmanned Colgate, a mark that has since been surpassed by John Wallace, who had 17 points against Cornell, Carmelo Anthony, who hung 27 points on Memphis, and Jonny Flynn, who blistered Siena for 28 points. That Colgate game was just a prequel of things to come.

During this time, Syracuse basketball was nearing its zenith in excitement, and contests in the Carrier Dome were more than just a basketball game. Many times, they were happenings. There was a big blue curtain on one side of the court with all the championship banners displayed. Behind the curtain were tables and chairs where people who didn't have seats could eat, socialize, and watch the game televised on a large screen. In games when SU was behind and catching up, ESPN color commentator Bill Raftery, feeding off the frenzy of the crowd, loved to say while accentuating it in his unique way, "And here comes the 'Cuse!'" Factor in the Dome Ranger running around riling up the fans and the aficionados screaming "Let's Go Orange … Let's Go Orange" in unison that sent chills down the spines of some, and the result was Cuse chaos.

Later in the 1983–84 season while playing Boston College, Pearl, in just his 15th game in a college uniform, showed his flair for the dramatic when, with the score tied, he took an outlet pass from Sean Kerins, dribbled a few times, and let fly a last-second, game-winning, 46-foot running one-hand push shot that grounded the No. 16-ranked Eagles, 75–73. Made in front of a sold-out crowd in the Dome and a USA cable network audience, it was a "shot seen around the country," with Washington, without breaking stride, running right into the tunnel as if it was something that he did routinely every day. It couldn't have been choreographed any better. It was one of many "Syracuse moments" that would come in the future and help define a storied Syracuse basketball program. In doing so, it set Syracuse apart from all but a handful of programs throughout the nation. During the mid-1980s at the Carrier Dome, when the Cuse needed to make a play or a run, someone would ask, "What time is it?" and the appropriate response was, "It's Pearl Time!"

The accolades came from everyone, and they were flattering. The late NBC and CBS analyst Al McGuire, who had his own way of talking by referring to flashy plays as "French pastry," close games as "white knucklers," and calling big, dominating centers aircraft carriers, stated, "Pearl is the best little PT boat in the country. He's the only freshman who has ever brought maturity to a college team in the history of the game. He's the next Oscar Robertson." Way before LeBron James was even born, "The Big O" was the standard by which backcourt players were compared. For a freshman to even be mentioned in the same sentence with Robertson was as big a compliment as one could get.

Dick Vitale called Pearl "an absolute blue-chipper, a thoroughbred in every sense of the word, a penetrator deluxe. With the ball, he's electricity. Pearl is the guard of the future." Following Syracuse's 78–74 overtime victory over St. John's, coach Lou Carnesecca said, "Pearl is one of the great ones because everytime he has it in his mind to score, he does." And after watching Washington score 28 and 27 points against his team, Villanova coach Rollie Massimino stated, "He's a great, great, great player. That's all I can say." At the time Boeheim, who had the chance to watch his jewel every day, simply said, "I don't know if there's a better guard anywhere."

Dribbling with his head bouncing and bobbing, Washington saw the whole court. "He gives you a lot of herky-jerky head and body motion, changes speeds, and creates openings in the opposition's defense, giving his teammates a lot of what Al McGuire calls 'chippie baskets,'" explained Vitale. "He has excellent ball control. The ball is like an extension of his arm. It's like a yo-yo. He's a much better shooter than people think. And he's so unselfish, maybe too much so at times because he passes up good shots. He made all of his team-mates better players."

Arguably the best open-court, fast-break, one-on-one player in the nation during the time he played, Washington fit right into Syracuse's running offense, and his shake-and-bake moves and exciting style were made for the huge crowds that flocked to the Carrier Dome. When Syracuse played on the road, he sold out arenas that generally did not sell out. More than that, because of the majesty and wizardry of the Pearl, Syracuse basketball games became must-see television across the country. In some ways, Washington turned an entire generation on to college basketball.

Another indicator of what Pearl meant to SU was that the Orange was unranked when Washington's freshman season began but jumped into the Top 20 following his dramatic shot against Boston College on January 21, 1984, and they remained in the rankings throughout his career. Averaging 14.4 points and 6.2 assists a game while controlling the offense, Washington, the highest-scoring freshman in SU history up to that time, led Syracuse to a 23–9 record and into the NCAA East Regional semifinals, where the Orangemen's season came to an abrupt end against Virginia, 63–55. Living up to his advance billing, Washington earned Big East Freshman of the Week honors five times, along with *Sports Illustrated* National Player of the Week, All-Big East, Big East Rookie of the Year, USA Network Big East Freshman of the Year, and *Basketball Times* Freshman of the Year. Simply put, to many, Washington was becoming the face of the Big East as the conference was heading into its peak years. Jumping ahead here, after Washington passed away in 2016, former Big East commissioner Mike Tranghese tweeted, "Pearl brought more excitement to the Big East and Madison Square Garden than any other single player." National broadcaster Michael Wilbon stated that "in writing the history of the Big East, [Pearl] is in the first paragraph, he's in the first line."

Eight years removed from the 1975 Final Four and the solid foundation that Danforth established, several things came together at Syracuse. The Carrier Dome was a building the Carrier Corporation, for the most part, funded, but it was the house that Pearl filled. Like flies to food, fans flocked to see Pearl, Boeheim, and the Orangemen. Washington, although not the best player, was the most important recruit in school history because snagging the most celebrated high school star in the country escalated Syracuse to a whole new level.

Washington was instrumental in turning Syracuse from a cold spot in Central New York to a basketball hotbed. It may have been snowing and freezing outside, but inside the Carrier Dome, things really heated up when the Pearl was doing his thing, as only he could do it. "When he took the court, it was like a rock concert in there [with Pearl the rock star]," stated Dick Vitale. "Pearl and the Cuse. Oh man, he had it rocking in there. There haven't been many with that kind of charisma." After the Pearl committed to Syracuse, the pipeline to the Salt City began as other future SU stars like Derrick Coleman, Rony Seikaly, Sherman Douglas, and Billy Owens followed. Thirty-thousand-plus crowds were a regular occurrence as Syracuse annually led the nation in basketball attendance for more than a decade. ESPN regularly televised Syracuse games across the country, helping the Orange to later persuade California stars such as Stevie Thompson,

Mike Hopkins, Tony Bland, and Jason Hart to leave the sunshine, seashore, sand, and surf for the snow, slush, and sleet.

"I remember in 1983 and 1984 being a kid in Southern California 3,000 miles away and watching the Pearl," stated Hopkins, who went on to become a longtime assistant coach at his alma mater. "I would rush home to watch the Big Monday game [on ESPN]. They were on at four o'clock in California. I met Pearl when I was in the ninth grade, and from that moment on, all I could think about was the Pearl and someday playing at Syracuse in the Dome. I bought a T-shirt on Marshall Street that had a caricature of Pearl spinning a globe with 'On the Seventh Day, God Created the Pearl' written on it ... Pearl started it all."

The Pearl, the brand-spanking new Carrier Dome, the formation of the Big East Conference, and the national exposure provided weekly by ESPN all propelled Syracuse from a regional to national power and put Syracuse on the national basketball map. Throughout the 1980s and early 1990s, Georgetown, St. John's, and Syracuse combined for five regular season championships, six Big East Championships, and a national championship, which was won by the Hoyas in 1984. The rivalry with Georgetown, which also was collecting stars, was revving up.

Coached by 6-foot-10 John Thompson Jr., the first prominent black head coach in college basketball, Georgetown had 7-foot Patrick Ewing at center. With Big John scowling on the sideline with a white towel draped over his shoulder to wipe off his sweat, equally imposing Ewing on the floor, and a supporting cast of hard-nosed, in-your-face players such as Gene Smith, Michael Graham, Michael Jackson, Horace Broadnax, and Reggie Williams that had size, speed, and played a suffocating trap defense, Georgetown was probably the most intimidating team in college basketball history. This was the era of "Hoya Paranoia." Like the Miami Hurricanes of that time in football, Georgetown struck fear into the hearts of many opponents. Battles between the Big East powers during the glory years of Big East basketball, especially when Georgetown was playing, were physical and rough, with key players sometimes fouling out of games. In one contest in the early 1990s in the Carrier Dome, when he complained a little too much and a little too loudly, Big John was ejected from a game.

1983–84

In 1983–84, it was Pearl Washington for the Cuse and Patrick Ewing for Georgetown. The Hoyas won both regular-season games against the Orangemen. In the finals of the Big East Tournament, Syracuse missed a chance to win the game at the buzzer, sending the contest into overtime. The heavily favored Hoyas scored the first seven points in the extra period of play en route to an 82–71 win. Washington and Ewing each scored 27 points. However, controversy surrounded the game. With 3:52 left in regulation and Syracuse ahead by three points, the Hoyas' Michael Graham shoved SU's Andre Hawkins to the floor and while doing so swung at Hawkins. The punch barely missed Hawkins's head. Initially, Graham appeared to be ejected from the game, having been charged with a flagrant foul and a personal foul, which would have awarded the Orange four free throws plus possession of the ball. However, after Thompson convincingly talked to the official, the call was changed, and Syracuse was awarded only two free throws instead of four. Momentum shifted the Hoyas' way, and Georgetown was able to tie the score and force overtime.

Unhappy with the officiating and the outcome, in the postgame press conference, Boeheim angrily stated, "Today the best team didn't win!" Then, in one of his best Bobby Knight impersonations, Boeheim stormed out of the pressroom, throwing a chair as he exited. Usually calm and collected in press conferences, Boeheim during his career would have a few more "Knight-like" episodes. To be clear, though, whenever Boeheim went off, it was never nearly as bad as when Bobby Knight, known for his infamous temper, went ballistic. The point being, when Boeheim got upset, he wasn't afraid to unload on some journalist or singe a few ears.

"If you ask a Syracuse fan about this game, he will refer to 'Graham throwing a punch.' If you ask a Georgetown fan, he will tell you to look at the *Daily News* photo of Patrick being punched in the groin by Pearl Washington," Georgetown senior sports communications director Bill Shapland told *The Washington Post*.

"It's certainly one of the best rivalries in college basketball because it comes out of an era when the Big East blossomed," Fran Fraschilla, former head coach at St. John's and current ESPN analyst, told *The Juice*'s Wesley Cheng relative to the Syracuse–Georgetown series. "I'm not sure the Big East would be as popular as it is today without John Thompson closing down Manley Field House and all of the great games the two schools have had with each other. When I think of this rivalry, I think of Patrick Ewing, Derrick Coleman, John Wallace, Alonzo Mourning, Billy Owens, Gerry McNamara—the names go on and on. But it's such a great rivalry because it basically helped form what may be the best college basketball league of all time. For much of the last 30 years, the competition has been magical.

"The last game at Manley Field House was the one that got it started for people like me," continued Fraschilla. "That to me was the most memorable because … the statement 'Manley Field House is officially closed!' resonates on both sides of the rivalry to this day." Sometimes little things kept the pot boiling. When Syracuse played at Georgetown in February 2011, Georgetown stopped selling tickets to the general public in an attempt to prevent Syracuse fans from buying them. With Washington, DC, being Syracuse's third-largest alumni base and the Cuse having always enjoyed good support when playing the Hoyas on the road, Georgetown purposely limited the number of Orange supporters in attendance. The move, and other little things, just added fuel to the fire. With all the drama that surrounded the contests, the Syracuse–Georgetown series caught the fancy of even the casual basketball fan.

Following the bitter loss to Georgetown during the 1983–84 season, Syracuse made what had become its customary trip to "The Big Dance," where it would defeat Virginia Commonwealth and lose to

Virginia. By this time, March had become a spot on the calendar that would become associated with Orange basketball for decades.

1984–85

In 1984, Syracuse started out 8–0 and ascended to No. 5 in the polls but then went 9–7 in the conference, losing to St. John's in overtime and splitting two regular-season games with Georgetown. On January 28, in the first matchup of the season with G-Town, Washington splashed a 15-footer with eight seconds left that enabled the No. 11-ranked Orange to edge the top-rated Hoyas, 65–63. It was Boeheim's first victory over a No. 1-ranked opponent. "Came down to the last shot," Boeheim told *The Washington Post*. "We called a play in the huddle. We were going to go to somebody else. And Pearl looked at me and said, 'I can make this shot.' [I said] 'All right, let's clear this side and let him go.' And he made the jump shot. He's a confident player. You want your best player to have the ball in that situation." The clutch shot was one of many defining moments in Washington's spectacular career. In that game in the Carrier Dome, with more than 32,000 people on hand and in front of a nationally televised audience, an orange thrown from the stands smashed against the backboard while Ewing was taking a free throw. After that, the Orangemen beat Boston College, again lost to hated Georgetown in the last game of the regular season, and then a third time in the Big East Tournament.

The 1985 Big East Tournament semifinal game between the Orange and the Hoyas was another walk on the wild side as Ewing again roughed up Hawkins and tempers flared. Ewing elbowed Washington in the stomach, and Washington, who confessed to not liking Georgetown or Ewing, reciprocated with a hard elbow to Ewing's ribs that enraged the Georgetown giant. Ewing then threw a haymaker at Pearl that would make a heavyweight boxer proud. The punch barely missed.

"That punch missed by a centimeter," stated Wendell Alexis, who was in the game. "Dwayne just was lucky he ducked out of the way, or he'd have no head," stated teammate Howard Triche. "The games with St. John's were physical, but every game with Georgetown was like a war. It was a very heated rivalry." Georgetown won that battle, 74–65. After the intense competition and tension in Madison Square Garden, in the first NCAA tournament with sixty-four teams, the Cuse won its first game, defeating DePaul, 70–65. SU was then tripped up by Georgia Tech in the East Regional in Atlanta, the home of the engineers, to finish 22–9 overall.

1985–86

In 1985, the Orange, picked by the pollsters as No. 4 in the preseason, roared back from the previous year, winning the first of back-to-back Big East Championships. One of the highlights of the season was Rafael Addison scoring 26 points as ninth-ranked Syracuse won a dogfight over the 13th-rated Georgetown Hoyas, 64–63. Syracuse entered the game with a 21–3 record, the only losses coming at Georgetown earlier in the season, 73–70, at Louisville in the next game, 83–73, and to Notre Dame, 85–81. In the rubber match with the Hoyas, it was another tough and physical contest in the semifinals of the Big East tournament, with Georgetown prevailing, 75–73, in overtime. The Orange made it to the championship game of the Big East Tournament, only to suffer a 70–69 loss to St. John's when Washington, who so often came through in critical situations, drove the length of the court only to uncharacteristically have his shot blocked by Walter Berry.

Syracuse returned to the Carrier Dome, which that year hosted the first round of the NCAA tournament, and blew out Brown, 101–52. SU clicked on all cylinders. The Cuse was comfortably in control throughout, making crisp passes and crowd-pleasing dunks. However, it was an about-face against 17th-ranked Navy. Buoyed by 35 points, 11 rebounds, and 7 blocked shots from All-American David Robinson, the Midshipmen sunk the No. 9 Orange. The disappointing 97–85 beatdown put a damper on what could have been a much better year. What made that loss sting even more was that the Orange had whipped the Middies by 22 points earlier in the season. Syracuse compiled an outstanding 26–6 record, including 14–2 in conference play. Syracuse fans, however, had developed increasingly high expectations. They did not easily accept or forget losses to Navy, much less losses on their home court. The sooner-than-expected season exits were starting to mount, with Boeheim building a reputation among some that he was a good in-season coach but a poor postseason coach.

Pearl Washington, who had made the college hoop world his oyster while earning All-American recognition in 1984, 1985, and 1986, opted to leave for the NBA after his junior year. The man with the mesmerizing moves and a galvanizing presence on the court concluded his career with 1,490 points. He set school and Big East single-game (18) and career (199) assist records. In 2004, he was named to the Big East Conference's 25th Anniversary first team. Besides his ability, what Syracuse lost was Washington's attraction. Wherever Pearl played, people came to the games in record numbers. Across the nation, people regularly tuned in to see his magic. From Syracuse to Sacramento and from Maine to Miami, Pearl Washington had become a household name and the Cuse a big-time brand.

Washington could put a ball in a hoop with ease but, like everyone, he sometimes experienced difficulty trying to put things into openings, as Mel Rubenstein shared in a humorous letter to the editor of Syracuse.com: "Pearl Washington and I had a good laugh together," Rubenstein related. "It was on a sunny day in May in 1986. I saw him wheeling a new bicycle he just bought ... I watched as he approached his car in the parking lot. It was a small four-door sedan with a sunroof. I became curious as to how he would get the bike in the car. He first tried to get it in the trunk, and then began to squeeze it in one of the doors when it got stuck. Then, pulling it free, he looked up at the open sunroof, lifted the bike, and got the first tire in when it got stuck again. At that, I walked over and said, 'Pearl, I know you have made a lot of great shots, but you can't make this one.' As I helped him get the bike out of the sunroof, we looked at each other and laughed. I said, 'Pearl, I have a van right over there, so why don't we put the bike in it, and I will follow you to your place and unload it there.' He gave one of those big Pearl smiles and thumbs up. Once we unloaded the bike at his apartment, we had another good laugh together. As I began to leave, he said, 'I did make a lot of good shots, didn't I?'"

The loss to Navy hurt and stuck in the craw of SU followers for years. Shortly after that, in March 1986, Boeheim was contacted about a job at Ohio State. He agreed to listen to an overture from Ohio State athletic director Rick Bay about becoming the Buckeyes' coach. Bay came to Syracuse and talked to Boeheim at his home. "Ten minutes into the conversation, I knew that I wasn't going to go," Boeheim told Adrian Wojnarowski of ESPN.com. Boeheim indicated that there were only a couple of jobs that he thought he might like but since they would require him to leave Syracuse, he wasn't interested. Boeheim loves Syracuse, as made clear in that frequently told story when he and his first wife Elaine were vacationing in Bermuda with Rick Pitino and Rick's wife, Joanne. Pitino said they were sitting on the beach getting some sun when the topic of where they would like to live, if given a choice, came up. Rick recalled that he thought he said Miami, Joanne said Hawaii, and Elaine said Paris or someplace like that. Boeheim, dead serious, said Syracuse. "When he said that, we all picked up our chairs and moved away," said Pitino, exaggerating how taken back they were by Boeheim's response. "We couldn't believe it because the winters in Syracuse are treacherous. They are extremely harsh." Boeheim, a Syracuse lifer by choice, acknowledged that it was a true story. He said he was serious and that he still feels the same way. Explaining his reasoning, he said, "For eight months of the year, Syracuse has the best weather in the country, and the other four months, we're playing basketball." He told *Sports Illustrated* the same thing. In 2014, Boeheim modified his feelings slightly but more strongly when, as a guest on a Syracuse radio station, he stated, "Ten months of the year [Syracuse] is the best place on Earth. Two months of the year, we're going somewhere where we can golf."

Back to basketball. The pain that lingered after being torpedoed by the Midshipmen was eased a little when Syracuse successfully recruited Derrick Coleman, another highly regarded prospect. A 6-foot-9 power forward from Detroit, Coleman was a great all-around player who could rebound and block shots. Despite his size, he was a very good ball handler who possessed a fine shooting touch from the perimeter.

Syracuse started the post-Pearl era at No. 15 in the preseason AP poll. Sherman Douglas, an unheralded recruit from Washington, DC, had replaced Pearl at the controls, and the Orange didn't miss a beat. Douglas did not possess Pearl's peculiar pizzazz, but he brought his own style and flash and, in some ways, proved to be a better point guard than Washington. From Spingarn High School, the same school that years earlier spawned Dave Bing, Douglas became the master of the "alley-oop," where he tossed the ball toward the basket and Coleman jumped up, caught the ball above the rim, and slammed it through the basket, bringing the Carrier crazies to their feet. In the following years, Rony Seikaly and Stevie Thompson were also frequent beneficiaries of Douglas's precision alley-oop passes.

1986–87

In 1986, with Douglas and Coleman leading the way, Syracuse stormed back to have one of its best years in its tradition-rich history. The Cuse won 31 games, another Big East championship, and advanced to the NCAA national championship game, only to have its heart ripped out at the very end. The season unfolded in set-em-up, shoot-em-down fashion, as the Orange disposed of its first fifteen opponents until it ended up on the short end of a 91–88 score at Michigan. The Orange came out on top in all Big East games, except for losing twice to Pittsburgh and twice to Georgetown.

In two close games against the Hoyas, a heavily favored Syracuse team, with a lineup of star players, came up short in both meetings against a Georgetown team that didn't have its customary big-name players. Perry McDonald, a solid but unsung performer, proved to be the thorn in the Orange's side. On January 31, McDonald posted low and made a buzzer-beating turnaround jump shot in overtime. Playing out of position, the 6-foot-4 Perry outplayed SU's 6-foot-10 Rony Seikaly, scoring 21 points and grabbing seven rebounds, while limiting Seikaly to four field goals and 13 points as the Hoyas upset the Orange at the Capital Centre, 83–81. Two weeks later Perry scored a career-high 26 points to lead Georgetown to a 72–71 win in Syracuse.

In the conference tournament, Syracuse defeated Villanova and got revenge against the Pittsburgh Panthers when Douglas scored 35 points and dished out 11 assists. SU bowed to the Hoyas a third time, despite a 20-point, 8-assist effort from Douglas.

In the NCAA tournament, SU got by Georgia Southern, Western Kentucky, Florida, and North Carolina. A big factor in the 87–81 win over the Gators and the 79–74 victory over the No. 2 Tar Heels that enabled the Orange to advance to the Final Four was that Seikaly, in much ballyhooed matchups against star centers, outplayed Dwayne Schintzius and then J. R. Reid. Seikaly hung 33 points and nine rebounds on the Gators' 7-foot Schintzius and 26 points and 11 boards on the Tar Heels' 6-foot-11 Reid. Also significant in the win over Carolina was Derrick Coleman, the other member of SU's "Twin Towers," grabbing 10 rebounds in the first half while Reid had zero. The advantage on the boards enabled SU to take a 41–30 lead at intermission. Coleman finished with 14 rebounds and three blocked shots as Syracuse defeated a North Carolina team of which Dean Smith had said, "This is a great team, and we don't use the word 'great' very often."

The Orange then beat Providence, which was coached by Pitino, Boeheim's protégé, 77–63, to make it to the national championship game for the first time in school history. The opponent was Indiana, coached by legendary Bobby Knight. In a city that loves its Orange, the headline the next day in the *Syracuse Herald-American* roared "EUPHORIA EXPLODES IN STREETS OF SYRACUSE!"

6

1987 NATIONAL CHAMPIONSHIP GAME

March 30, 1987, was the night the dream died in front of a Super Dome crowd of 64,959 and millions more watching on television. In a game that lived up to its hype, a 16-foot jump shot by Keith Smart with five seconds to go gave the Hoosiers a come-from-behind 74–73 victory. With Syracuse ahead 52–44 and twelve and a half minutes remaining, Indiana closed on the Cuse. With 38 seconds left and the score 73–70, Howard Triche missed the back end of a one-and-one free throw situation. Smart scurried down the court and made a field goal to cut the lead to 73–72. With less than a minute to go, Derrick Coleman, a 6-foot-9 freshman forward and a 69 percent free throw shooter who had eight points, 19 rebounds, and three blocked shots up to that point, missed the front end of a one-and-one. SU put everyone back on defense. IU rebounded the ball and raced down the court, with published reports stating that the intention was for Steve Alford, the Hoosiers' best shooter, to take the potential game-winning shot. Alford, however, was covered, so he threw the ball inside to Daryl Thomas, who started to drive but was guarded by Coleman. Thomas fired off a pass to Smart on the wing. Smart buried the shot over the outstretched arm of Howard Triche that squashed the Orange. SU had about five seconds left but wasn't able to get a timeout called until there was just one second showing on the clock. The long inbounds pass was intercepted, giving Knight his third national championship and denying Boeheim his first.

As for his game-winning shot, Smart told one writer, "I just threw it up. I didn't know where it went." Well, to the delight of the delirious Hoosier Nation and to the dismay of disheartened Syracuse fans, it went in the basket.

Alford clarified the last play. "No, it's not true that I was supposed to take the last shot," he stated. "No play was set up. We were a motion team and whoever got a good look would take the shot." Asked what he remembered about that game, Alford stated, "Just winning. Being the last team standing."

Questioned on his end-of-game management when he didn't call a timeout sooner to give the team more time to set up a better play, Boeheim told the media that it wouldn't have made any difference. He said that Syracuse would have run the same play because they were out of timeouts.

Indiana led at the half, 34–33. The game had nineteen lead changes. Syracuse effectively intermingled the 2–3 zone, man-to-man, and the box-and-one along with some traps in a defense that puzzled the Hoosiers and limited their scoring. Douglas, the sophomore point guard nicknamed "The General" for his overall floor leadership, had a game-high 20 points and seven assists. While shaking hands, Knight, in a show of respect for Boeheim, told Boeheim not to worry, that his day to win a national championship would come. Following the game, Boeheim stated, "It was a great game … It doesn't feel good. I've never had a loss that feels good, but this one hurts a little worse." What added to Boeheim's pain was that he thought the Orange had outplayed the Hoosiers but still failed to bring home the bacon. The front-page headline the next day in the *Syracuse Post-Standard* screamed "HEARTBREAK." That summed up the feelings of Orange Nation.

Unlike 1975, by 1987 Syracuse basketball had become a known commodity in the college basketball world. The team was young and inexperienced, but it had size and big-time players. SU had become accustomed to competing with the best teams in the country. The loss was difficult for Boeheim to digest, especially the way it happened. Syracuse seemed in control of the game but squandered an eight-point lead down the stretch.

Boeheim was so disheartened that he couldn't bring himself to watch a tape of the game. "I never really watched the whole game," he admitted. "I've watched highlights, different parts of the game by accident on tape at different times." In 2012, *The Sporting News* listed the 1987 IU–SU game, with Smart's oft-replayed jumper the highlight, the seventh best game since the NCAA tournament was expanded. Just as Syracuse beating Kansas to win the 2003 national championship is a game Orange Nation will always remember, the stinging loss to Indiana is a game Orange Nation will never forget.

Noteworthy is that following the 1987 championship game "One Shining Moment" was introduced. A song written by David Barrett that is played while the winning team is shown cutting down the nets while a composite of highlights and special moments from the NCAA tournament is shown, it has become a popular tradition and much-anticipated special closing to the CBS and TBS broadcasts of the tournament.

As his first decade on the job was coming to an end, Boeheim summarized his philosophy, which had been modified through the years but really hadn't changed an awful lot. "We like to run, and a lot of kids today like to play that up-tempo style of play. We're strictly a fast-break team. We'd fast break every time if we're able to take it. Of course, you need to be able to slow down at times.

"Offensively we run some motion, but we really try to go to specific guys and run certain things to get them the ball when it counts most," he explained of a system that is referred to as freelance by people who do not understand it. More accurately, it is an offense that allows players the freedom to use their individual skills to create plays within a structured system. Success requires proper spacing and players knowing when, where, and how to cut to get open. "Our offense and defense have evolved over a long period of time. Some of it is the same. Some of it is a little bit different," Boeheim said.

The defense, of course, was Syracuse's vaunted 2–3 zone, of which Boeheim is the guru. Basically, it was designed to limit offensive schemes and make opposing teams take shots that the Orange wanted them to take, not shots that the opponents wanted to take. The zone also created offensive rebounding and fast-break opportunities. With the guards out front, the Orange like to run following a rebound. "We play a 2–3 zone, but we trap out of it," Boeheim pointed out. "We adjust with it. We try to move our zone and be active in it. We pride ourselves on coming out and stopping three-point shooting teams, even though we are playing zone.

"Basically, we like to pressure for forty minutes, or as much as we can and get into a full-court, fast-tempo game. At Syracuse, we are offensive-minded and have been a high-scoring team. But we emphasize defense too and work on it. In the conference, we are always pretty high on field goal percentage defense, which is a better indicator of your defense than points given up, especially in our style of play where we run, score a lot, and play a lot of high-scoring games."

Boeheim said he looked for players who could fit into his system. "We look for what we are in need of. We look for players who can fit into our program and who can play a fast-break style of basketball. We want players who can play within the team concept. Basically, we're looking for good athletes who can run.

"We've been successful with kids who were not highly rated. We don't necessarily look for a finished product, but guys that we think we can develop. We look for good people who can play together, be good teammates, and are willing to work hard to improve and graduate," he continued. Boeheim's offensive and defensive philosophies obviously worked as the Orange were a model of consistency up to that point and continued to be throughout his career. That was a period when Syracuse didn't rebuild, it reloaded.

1987–88

In 1987, for the first time in its history, Syracuse started the season ranked No. 1 in the country. The Orange then promptly lost a heartbreaker in overtime to North Carolina, 96–93, in the Hall of Fame Tip-Off Classic in Springfield, Massachusetts. Following a couple of easy wins in the Great Alaska Shootout over Alaska–Anchorage and Alabama–Birmingham, SU got dismantled in the finals by Arizona, 80–69. Against much easier competition in its own Carrier Classic, the Orangemen trampled South Florida, Texas Christian University, and Cornell. Syracuse barreled through seven more opponents to make it 11 straight before Villanova put a stop to the run, 80–78. Syracuse suffered through five more losses during the regular season, all down-to-the-wire squeakers. The Cuse came up short against Connecticut, 51–50, Georgetown, 69–68, Georgetown again, 71–69, Kentucky, 62–58, and Pittsburgh, 85–84.

Syracuse finished strong to win the Big East tournament pretty handily. The Cuse cruised past North Carolina A&T in NCAA play, but they were surprisingly given a much earlier than expected exit by upstart Rhode Island, another loss that didn't sit well with the SU faithful. Syracuse recorded a 26–9 mark, but again, people were dejected because the team didn't make a much deeper run given the talent that it possessed. More precisely, a season that began with so much hope ended with a thud. Boeheim-bashers, as they tended to do when the Orange was an early out, resurfaced and complained.

1988–89

Prior to the season, Syracuse garnered one of its biggest pickups in school history. Billy Owens, a 6-foot-8, 230-pound small forward, came out of Carlisle High School in Pennsylvania generally rated the number one or two recruit in the nation, either ahead of or behind Alonzo Mourning. Owens was a *Sports Illustrated* cover boy before he ever suited up for the Orange. Howard Garfinkel, the founder of the Five-Star camp, compared Owens to Magic Johnson. Garfinkel called Owens the best all-around player of the 1980s and the player of the decade. After leading Carlisle to a 118–11 record and four straight state championships, Owens was pursued by colleges throughout the country. As a senior in high school, he scored 53 points in the state title game. Rated a little bit below the Pearl catch, securing Owens was a huge get for Syracuse. Giving the Orange a leg up on the competition was that Owens's older brother Michael was already at Syracuse and was a running back on the football team.

Sherman Douglas

The Orange went through the first thirteen opponents in 1988–89 like a hot knife through butter, except for nail-biting overtime wins over Missouri and Louisiana Tech. Missouri had a good team that year, and a tough game was expected, but the tussle with "La Who" was much too close for comfort. But a win is a win is a win. During the early-season Big Apple NIT in New York that featured a rematch between SU and IU, the two teams that had played for the national championship twenty months earlier, a memorable play occurred. Sherman Douglas caught an outlet pass near midcourt and, with his back to the Syracuse basket, hiked the ball between his legs to a streaking Stevie Thompson who took the pass in stride and stuffed it in the hoop, to the delight of the orange-clad SU fans that made up most of the crowd in Madison Square Garden. You would have had to be there to see it, or watch a video of it to believe it. It was a Harlem

Globetrotters-type play but in a real game against live competition. Another uniquely "Syracuse moment." After beating Bobby Knight and Indiana, 102–78, Syracuse edged Missouri, 86–84, in overtime to win the Big Apple NIT.

On January 28, Douglas set a school and NCAA record with 22 assists against Providence. As a senior, he led the nation in assists with 326. He was designated a first-team All-American. A three-year starter, Douglas finished his college career as the all-time NCAA leader in assists with 960, as well as Syracuse's all-time top scorer with 2,060 points and all-time leader in steals with 235. Not too shabby for a player who was an afterthought and second choice, not once but twice. Douglas took advantage of openings created by two academic casualties to put his name in the school and NCAA record books. Douglas was elevated to a starting position after Greg "Boo" Harvey and, a year later, Earl Duncan both failed to academically qualify to get into Syracuse. Harvey, a hot-shot point guard from New York City, and Duncan, a blue-chip guard from Los Angeles, were expected to start if they could get in school. They couldn't, and SU got a pleasant surprise. Douglas's NCAA assists record has since been broken, five Orange players have surpassed him on the school career-scoring list, and Jason Hart and Gerry McNamara have jumped him in steals. However, when the Pearl and the General played, it was showtime at Syracuse.

On February 26, in a made-for-television intersectional game, the Cuse whipped Kentucky, 89–73. Whenever he took down a program of Kentucky's stature, it was another feather in Boeheim's cap. As Boeheim progressed through his career, to accommodate all the feathers would require several caps. When Boeheim started out, Syracuse was trying to catch up with the big dogs. It wasn't too long into the Boeheim tenure before Syracuse became a big dog. Then beating Boeheim would become a feather in other coaches' caps.

The regular season ended with another Syracuse–Georgetown classic, won by the Orange, 82–76, in overtime in Sherman Douglas's Dome finale. The victory by SU enabled the rivals to break even in their season series. They would clash again in the conference tournament, with the Hoyas winning, 88–79. After breezing past Bucknell and Colorado State in the first two rounds of March Madness, Syracuse outscored Missouri, 83–80, but got outscored by an Illinois team that featured eight future NBA players, 89–86. Some thought the Coleman–Douglas–Owens-led 1988–89 team had the most talent in school history. With the horses the Orange had, many considered it a colossal letdown when the team couldn't advance past the Sweet 16.

1989–90

The 1988–89 season started in typical Syracuse fashion, with the Orange bolting to 10 wins highlighted by a 78–76 victory over Duke in the ACC–Big East Challenge. SU ripped through its Big East schedule to win the conference regular season championship, with its only losses inflicted by Villanova, UConn, Providence, and Villanova again. Standing out was the last game of the regular season against Georgetown with the Big East title at stake. With the Hoyas ahead by two points, Owens was foolishly fouled at midcourt with one second remaining in regulation. He made two free throws to send the game into overtime, a contest that the Cuse would win, 89–87, in another frantic finish. The difference was a layup by Stevie Thompson with 25 seconds remaining, but the outcome was not decided until Alonzo Mourning missed a 12-foot shot from the left baseline with three seconds to go, giving Syracuse its first sweep of two regular-season games against the Hoyas and the top seed in the conference tournament. The Orange's dynamic duo led the charge: Coleman with 27 points, 13 rebounds, six assists, and three steals, and Owens with 23 points, six rebounds, four assists, and three blocked shots.

The game will be remembered because Georgetown coach John Thompson got thrown out of the contest after getting three technical fouls from three different officials in a ten-second span toward the end of the first half. With 2:14 left before intermission and the Hoyas ahead, 36–33, Thompson was T'd up for complaining about a reach-in foul by Dwayne Bryant against Coleman, who was playing in his final home game before an NCAA on-campus record crowd of 33,015 delirious fans. Angered about the technical, Thompson got hit with another technical, resulting in automatic rejection and then, still in a rage, got nailed with a third technical. Leaving the court, Big John threw his trademark white towel and thrust both hands in the air, egging the Syracuse crowd on. A person the Orange Nation loved to hate, SU fans responded by mocking and serenading the Hoya boss as he made his way to the locker room. After the dust had cleared, Coleman made seven free throws and, with Syracuse retaining possession of the ball, Owens made a three-pointer to make it an almost unheard of 10-point possession. Down by three, Syracuse was suddenly up by seven.

Years later, Thompson told the *Washington Post* that the game still bothered him. "That one loss haunts me today," he stated. "They threw me out of the game … Had we won [that game], I would have come right out of the locker room and come out on the floor … Had we won that game, guarantee you, [my] Manley Field House statement wouldn't have been nothing compared to what I would have said to them!" Reflecting on it prior to the Big East's biggest rivalry ending in 2013, Boeheim told the *Post*, "That was the most memorable game, I think, in the series."

In the Big East tournament, Syracuse defeated Pittsburgh and Villanova, but not Connecticut. In the NCAAs, the Orange routed Coppin State and slipped past Virginia, 63–61, but got sent packing by Minnesota, 82–75. The loss marked the last college game for Stevie Thompson, the 6-foot-4 jumping jack who came to SU from the mean streets of Los Angeles and Crenshaw High School and ended up trailing only teammates Coleman and Douglas among Syracuse career scorers.

Rony Seikaly, Derrick Coleman, and Billy Owens

The careers of three of Syracuse's best big players intertwined during this time period. Rony Seikaly became a part of the basketball program in 1984. The 6-foot-10, 235-pound Seikaly grew up in Athens,

Greece, where he played other sports in high school. His basketball skills were limited, and he lacked an understanding of the game. Considered a project, he required a redshirt year to develop. Over the course of his career, Seikaly steadily improved to become one of the school's outstanding scorers and rebounders. Seikaly started in 133 of the 136 games he played. As a freshman, he led the Orange in rebounding and blocked 59 shots, more than anybody up to that point except Roosevelt Bouie. He was named to the Big East's All-Freshman team. As a sophomore, he blocked 97 shots, sixth best in the nation. He averaged 16.3 points per game as a senior and finished with 1,716 points, which was then fourth best all-time. Seikaly concluded his career as Syracuse's leading rebounder with 1,094, with an average of eight boards per game his final season. His 319 blocks made him the school's second-best shot rejecter, behind Bouie. A force on the inside, Seikaly and Derrick Coleman played together for two years, including on the team that reached the 1987 championship game. The pair provided the Orange with an intimidating front line. Selected with the ninth pick in the first round of the draft by the Miami Heat, Seikaly played 11 years in the NBA, where he averaged 14.7 points and 9.5 rebounds a game. He holds the Heat's single-game rebound record with 34 and the single-game block record with eight. He also is the team leader in double-double games.

Coleman, a 6-foot-9 power forward, came to Syracuse in 1986 from Northern High School in Detroit and played four years through the 1989–90 season, two with Seikaly and two with Billy Owens, who came in 1988 and played three years through the 1990–91 campaign. Influenced but not pushed by Dave Bing, Boeheim's former teammate and his connection in Detroit, Coleman left the Motor City to play collegiately in the Salt City. Just like Bing saying he went to Syracuse because it helped produce a quality person like Ernie Davis, Coleman said he went to SU because the school helped produce a quality person like Dave Bing. Bing impressed Coleman, not because of his basketball success, but because of his business achievements as CEO of Bing Steel.

Coleman played 143 games for the Orange, starting 141 of them.

He scored what was then a school-record 2,143 points. He averaged 15 points per game throughout his career and 17.9 points per game as a senior. He pulled down an at-the-time NCAA record 1,537 rebounds, an average of 10.8 per contest. He was named Big East Rookie of the Year and Big East Player of the Year en route to earning first-team All-American honors as a senior. In his last game, before a Carrier Dome crowd that for the first time numbered more than 33,000, the Coleman–Owens Orange defeated the Alonzo Mourning–Dikembe Mutombo Georgetown Hoyas, 89–87, in an overtime thriller. Pearl Washington stated that he would have stayed for his senior year had he known Coleman was coming on board. Coleman had a 15-year career in the NBA where he averaged 16.5 points and 9.3 rebounds per game.

Owens, a very versatile player, started all 103 games that he played. Like Coleman, he became an instant starter and played with Coleman for two years before becoming the top offensive player after "DC" departed. Owens totaled 1,840 points, an average of 17.9 per game over the course of his three-year career. In his last year, he averaged 23.2 points per game. Owens grabbed 910 rebounds, an average of 8.8 a contest. Following his junior year when he was Big East Player of the Year and led SU to a 26–4 record and a No. 6 ranking in the final poll, Owens opted for the NBA. He was the third overall pick in the draft by the Sacramento Kings. Owens had an 11-year run in the NBA where he averaged 11.7 points and 6.7 rebounds a contest. By skipping his senior year, he left Syracuse fans wondering what it would have been like had he returned to school for his last season. Boeheim stated that Pearl Washington and Owens were the best players he ever recruited, with Owens the most complete player. Boeheim also put Owens, who remains the third highest scorer in Pennsylvania high school history, in the same class as future SU superstar Carmelo Anthony. "Billy was one of the greatest players that we've ever had," Boeheim told Mike Waters in his book *Legends of Syracuse Basketball.* "He did all the things that Carmelo did. Carmelo was just a little bit better shooter, but Billy did everything else. He was just a great college basketball player."

Propelled by its prolongation of stars, Syracuse rocketed to national prominence. Boeheim, bolstered by the horses he had corralled, went 217–83 during the 1980s. Included during the decade were eight appearances in the NCAA tournament and a trip to the Final Four. The teams were characterized by a fast-break offense and a combination of the 2–3 zone with a lot of full-court pressure defense. With all the All-Americans, the winning, and the high profile that the program had achieved, it was a happy time and a great decade for Syracuse and Boeheim. However, just when the program was up to that point at its peak, the bottom almost fell out.

1990–91

Probation

In early March of 1990, *Raw Recruits*, a book by Alexander Wolff and Armen Keteyian, cited abuses in college basketball. One of the schools mentioned was Syracuse, which allegedly had connections with Robert Johnson, an influential street agent in New York City who supposedly had directed prized players to SU. Furthermore, it revealed Syracuse players were receiving extra benefits beyond those allowed by the NCAA. The book instigated an investigation into the Syracuse basketball program.

In late December of 1990, the Syracuse athletic program, especially its acclaimed basketball program, was rocked when the *Syracuse Post-Standard* published a two-part series, titled "Out of Bounds," that revealed NCAA violations in the recruiting of basketball players. With Syracuse approaching elite status as a basketball program, ESPN prioritized the reported allegations, repeatedly showing footage of the basketball team leaving the bus and entering an arena at an away game the evening of the day that the story broke, sensationalizing the news with dramatic background music.

A thirteen-month investigation that stretched into a twenty-two-month ordeal tarred the basketball program and held it in limbo, severely limiting its ability to bring in the type of talent that Syracuse had become accustomed to. Although no major violations were found, it was discovered that Boeheim had used Johnson to help steer players to Syracuse. There were also improprieties involving Bill Rapp Jr., a local car dealer, and Fred Grimaldi, owner of a popular local Italian restaurant. Rapp and Grimaldi were friends of Boeheim. The investigation found that other people and businesses were providing perks to players. The extended national coverage and the possibility of NCAA sanctions created a dark cloud that hovered over and haunted the program for years, hindering recruiting.

"We've lost some recruits because of this," stated Boeheim, who had to work on damage control while simultaneously moving the program forward. "We've talked to three or four kids who have eliminated us." Understating how stressful the situation was for him, Boeheim told William C. Rhoden of the *New York Times*, "The only thing I can say is these are difficult times, and obviously, there's nothing easy about what we're going through ... I've got to help this team get through this and be as successful as it can be."

Despite the tension that permeated the program and the longtime hindrance to recruiting, Syracuse started the 1990s as usual, feasting on the home cooking it enjoyed by playing most of its games in the Dome as it ran roughshod through the first 13 games of its schedule. The Orange had a notable victory over Indiana in the Maui Classic by three points, but otherwise enjoyed smooth sailing, except for a 92–86 overtime win against No. 9 St. John's. It was Boeheim's 356th win and enabled him to pass Lew Andreas to become the all-time winningest coach in Syracuse basketball history. Downplaying the personal achievement, Boeheim responded to a question about the milestone by stating, "That's nothing. It's not that I don't appreciate it, but I tell my players that we don't have individual awards. Individual awards do not matter in the game of basketball."

During the postgame press conference, Boeheim, worn out from the barn burner and the stress that he was laboring under, responded to those among the media and fan base who complained about

Syracuse's soft non-conference schedule by stating: "You guys all want us to play these [kind of games] in December. Play thirty of these and we'd have no teams, players, or coaches left. And the referees are gone because they can't take these games either. We can't play these kinds of games all year long. If we did, I'd be out of coaching 10 years early. [If you want them] you get into coaching, and you schedule them."

In its next outing, after winning the regular season conference championship and working its way to No. 3 in the nation, SU was taken down a peg or two by Villanova in the Big East tournament, 70–68. Following that disappointment, the day before Syracuse was to play Richmond in the first round of the NCAA tournament, Boeheim was required to attend an NCAA inquiry where he was grilled regarding rules violations. Distracted and upset, the timing couldn't have been worse for the coach and his team. The next day, the sixth-ranked Orange tanked badly. The Spiders stunned Syracuse, 73–69. It was the first time in tournament history that a No. 15 seed toppled a No. 2 seed. The Spiders didn't just bite the Orange, they bit them repeatedly and left serious wounds, some of which have never healed. It would be Boeheim's most embarrassing loss and one that critics would never let him forget, making him wear it like a scarlet letter throughout his career. Years later, Boeheim told Syracuse beat writer Mike Waters that the Orange lost to Richmond because the turmoil created by the NCAA situation took its toll on the team.

Led by Billy Owens, the bell cow and first player coached by Boeheim to average 20 points per game for a season, the Orange amassed a 26–6 record and a conference-best 12–4 mark. No matter. Syracuse was unable to advance past the first round. *Typical Syracuse, a classic example of underachievement,* some said.

7

EARLY YEARS OF THE BIG EAST

Early 1990s: Syracuse Survives the Down Years

With the NCAA investigation finally completed, on October 1, 1992, the NCAA Committee on Infractions slapped Syracuse with sanctions for violations in the men's and women's basketball, men's lacrosse, wrestling, and football programs that included two years of probation, a one-year ban from postseason play, and the reduction of one basketball scholarship for 1993–1994 and 1994–95. Some basketball analysts around the country called for Boeheim's firing. Years later, on November 1, 2011, Boeheim, ironically while his program was again under NCAA investigation beginning with the 2002 season, rehashed the 1992 probation with sports reporter Graham Bensinger. "The violations were in little things here and there, but they added up. No coaches were involved. There was nothing egregious," he said, pointing out that Syracuse was one of the last teams to be taken out of the NCAA tournament and that most coaches thought the punishment was excessive.

Although the sanctions were not severe, the lengthy delay from the time that the story broke until the NCAA released its decision significantly slowed the recruiting momentum the Cuse had gained in recent years. High school stars such as Donyell Marshall and Jalen Rose, both big on the Orange, decided to go elsewhere. It enabled other schools, especially Connecticut, which got Marshall, a McDonald's All-American who some thought was ticketed for SU, to gain ground on the Orange. Early in the recruiting process, Marshall was planning to sign a letter of intent with SU, but he changed his mind and went to UConn where he became the Huskies' first All-American and helped lay the foundation for the powerhouse that Jim Calhoun was putting in place at Storrs. Rose switched his allegiance to Michigan where he became a key cog in the Wolverines' famed "Fab Five" class that lost to Duke in the NCAA finals. Had they and some others who shied away instead committed to the Cuse, the Syracuse train would have kept on rolling down the track, keeping the program a destination of choice.

John Wallace, a high school McDonald's and Parade All-American in 1992 from nearby Rochester, was the only blue-chip player who still chose to go to Syracuse. The result was that Syracuse struggled for a few years. The drop-off in talent forced Boeheim to rely more and more on the 2–3 zone to camouflage the talent differential and reduce the chances of key players getting into foul trouble. A credit to the stability and tradition of the program, as well as his ability to coach-up the kids he had, Boeheim still won 20 or more games a year during these down years. The Orange just didn't play up to Syracuse standards, where 20-plus-win seasons and trips to the NCAA Tournament had become a given. Along with Lawrence Moten, a relatively unknown player from Washington, DC, who Syracuse had gotten a year earlier, Wallace stabilized a program that was teetering on the brink of falling off the national radar.

Because of his willingness to come to SU despite NCAA problems, Wallace, who finished third in both scoring and rebounding en route to earning second-team AP All-America honors in 1996, is seen by some as perhaps the second most important recruit in school history.

Under the circumstances, corralling him was considered a coup. "I think John's place in Syracuse basketball history is unappreciated," Boeheim told Scott Pitoniak of the *Rochester Democrat and Chronicle*. "We were facing some tough times, and he easily could have turned his back on us and committed someplace else, but he stuck with us. During the 1996 tournament, he literally carried us on his shoulders to the title game."

Lightly regarded after attending prep school in New Hampshire, the 6-foot-5, 185-pound Moten burst onto the Syracuse and Big East scene, shattering the conference freshmen records for scoring and scoring average previously held by Connecticut's Earl Kelley and St. John's three-time All-American and Wooden Player of the Year Chris Mullin. In the third game of his freshman season, Moten became a starter and never surrendered his place on the first team. A stellar and smooth performer who elicited the phrase "Poetry in Moten," he led the team in scoring all three years he played and averaged 19.3 points per game, fourth-best in school history behind Bing (24.7), Bill Smith (20.7), and Hal Cohen (19.7). Moten finished his career as not only Syracuse's all-time leading scorer with 2,334 points but the leading scorer in Big East history.

Moten, Wallace, and guard Adrian "Red" Autry kept the Syracuse ship afloat. Shorthanded, it just couldn't cruise like it had become accustomed to. The significant roles that Moten and then Wallace played during the probationary period helped Syracuse keep winning. Oh, not as much as in the recent glory years, but enough to sustain a respectable level of success. Therefore, their contributions to the program cannot be overstated.

1991–92 and 1992–93

1991 and 1992 were subpar years by Syracuse standards, with SU posting 22–10 and 20–9 marks. Like they did almost every year, the Orange opened each of those seasons with fairly lengthy winning streaks, and in each of those years, SU went 10–8 in conference play. In 1991–92, there was even an un-SU-like four-game losing streak. If Syracuse was sick, Boston College was what the doctor ordered as the Orange snapped the skid with a 76–71 win. Syracuse still won the Big East tournament in 1992. The Orange slithered past Villanova, 55–52, had little problem beating Seton Hall, 70–66, and came out on the high end of a 56–54 white-knuckler over Georgetown when Dave Johnson sank a game-winning jump shot over the outreached arms of Alonzo Mourning.

Boeheim solved Pete Carril's slowdown offense as Syracuse defeated Princeton, 51–43, in the first round of the NCAAs in Worcester, Massachusetts. That would be the end of the trail, however, as John Calipari's Massachusetts Minutemen, playing in their own backyard, put away the Orange in overtime, 77–71. Despite another good group of players, the Orange was again quickly kicked to the curb, bringing the Boeheim bashers out of the woodwork. Those who subscribe solely to the school of thought that it's the end result—how the team plays in the NCAA tournament—that counts, relentlessly raked Boeheim over the coals. The number of myopic fans was growing.

The following season was worse. The sanctions ensured that. With nowhere to go following the Big East tournament, Seton Hall exasperated the situation by annihilating the Orange in the finals of the conference tournament, 103–70. It was the biggest point differential in conference tournament history until SU blasted Boston College, 96–55, in 1999. Boeheim buried his head in his hands as Seton Hall sunk baskets by the bushelful. All the ghosts that had haunted Syracuse at various times throughout the season—offensive ineptness, defensive breakdowns, lack of intensity, and poor free-throw shooting—came back to spook them again. Boeheim's good friend P. J. Carlesimo coached the Hall, whose teams Boeheim regularly beat like a drum. Boeheim kidded Carlesimo after the game, "This is one game, you know. You can't count this two or three times." More bad news was that, despite winning 20 games, including 10 in the Big East Conference, probation stopped Syracuse's string of 10 straight NCAA appearances, a run that began in 1983 and tied Al McGuire's Marquette team for the fourth longest in NCAA history. Every year during the time period the Orange was ranked among the top 21 teams in the preseason and finished among the top 21 teams in the country. In its best glory run in the polls, Syracuse finished in the Top 10 six straight times from 1985–86 to 1990–91.

1993–94

Syracuse opened the 1993–94 season with a resounding 98–65 intersectional win over Tennessee, perhaps again indicating that The Big Orange was a more fitting moniker for the basketball team from Central New York than the one from Knoxville. Another nice non-conference win was the 93–85 victory over Kentucky, the bluest of the blue bloods. The Orange also split two games with Connecticut and Georgetown to finish second in the Big East. Syracuse lost its first game in the conference tournament to Seton Hall, 81–80, in overtime. The score was much closer than the debacle to the Pirates in the tournament finals the year before. Boeheim reiterated to Carlesimo that the slaughter the previous season only counted as one win. By the same token, the setback by the slightest of margins still counted as a loss, which was enough to turn the lights out on Syracuse's season.

After a one-year absence, SU was back in the NCAA tournament in 1994. The Orange beat Hawaii and Wisconsin–Green Bay before fading in overtime in a 98–88 Sweet 16 loss to Missouri that closed out a 23–7 campaign. For Syracuse, Adrian Autry, who would be named a Syracuse assistant coach in April 2011, set a school record in his final game by scoring 31 points in the second half against the Tigers. A captain as a senior and a four-year starter at point guard, Autry finished his SU career fifth all-time in assists and sixth in steals before embarking on an 11-year professional career overseas.

Jim meets Juli

For Boeheim personally, a high point in his life came on May 7, 1994, when Rick Pitino introduced him to Juli Greene, a beautiful University of Kentucky graduate, at the Kentucky Derby. "Pitino tells this story," said Boeheim's friend Rich Duffy. "Jim saw two beautiful girls across the room and asked Pitino who they were. Pitino told Jim they were twins and asked Jim which one he wanted to meet, and Jim said, 'Either one.'" Pitino is great for a good quote, and that sounds cute but probably was not the way it happened because one of the twins was engaged at the time. A couple of years later when asked about that, Pitino said he couldn't remember exactly how the introduction took place.

Boeheim and Greene became immersed in a backgammon game that continued well past when others at the social gathering had left for dinner. They enjoyed each other's company so much that Boeheim delayed leaving Kentucky for two days so that they could spend more time together. Despite Juli being about twenty years younger than Boeheim, the relationship flourished.

Let's backtrack for perspective. Boeheim, at the age of 32 married his first wife, Elaine, in June 1976, two months after he accepted the Syracuse job and about four months before he started his head-coaching career. Boeheim was 41 years old in 1985 when the couple adopted a daughter, Elizabeth. It didn't help the marriage that Boeheim brought his work home with him. He took losses hard, and he never really enjoyed winning as much as he should have. The pressures of the job escalated problems at home, taking a toll on the eighteen-year roller-coaster relationship. Jim and Elaine had separated twice, once in the mid-1980s and again in the 1990s, before finally divorcing in 1993. Following the divorce, Boeheim concentrated on basketball, which he pretty much did anyway. A year later, he met Juli. The following year, Juli relocated to Syracuse to be with Jim. On October 10, 1997, Jim and Juli got married at Hendricks Chapel on the Syracuse campus, with his daughter Elizabeth serving as the maid of honor.

Comically, Pitino, who had his honeymoon interrupted years ago by Boeheim, as it turned out, almost two decades later, introduced Boeheim to the woman who would become his second wife. Meeting Juli, for sure, took away much of the sting from the overtime loss to

Missouri in the Sweet 16 a month and a half earlier. "Go for Gin" won the Derby, but the big winner was Boeheim, who got the girl who many say changed his life.

Roosevelt Bouie related that when he met Juli's mother at the wedding, she asked him what Bouie thought of Boeheim and Juli getting married. "I said, 'Ma'am, I can tell you one thing for sure. I've known Coach Boeheim for a long time, and I've seen him smile more today than I ever remember him smiling.'"

Contradicting what Duffy said about Boeheim being a wallflower when it came to dancing, Bouie said that Boeheim was definitely putting down some steps that day. "He was 'breaking it down' and 'busting some moves,'" Bouie related. "He's really come a long way. So marrying Juli was definitely a good move for him." Duffy agreed that Juli has been a turning point in Jimmy's life. "Juli has been a tremendous asset of his, but all she did was bring out what was already there. He's not a nerd now," he said. "Juli is smart, obviously beautiful, and fun. Juli has changed his whole demeanor, his physical appearance, and, obviously, the way he dresses. Before that, he didn't really care how he dressed. It was not important to him," continued Duffy.

Boeheim has remained good friends with Elaine and has a very close relationship with his daughter Elizabeth. This is illustrated by Duffy's comment, "Every time my wife Karen and I have been with Jimmy, unfailingly he would call his daughter almost every night. Now that may be a slight exaggeration, but that always impressed my wife Karen."

After he remarried, Boeheim bought a house for Elaine right across the street. He said in his Hall of Fame acceptance speech that Juli is even better friends with Elaine. He also said that Elizabeth coming into his life at that time changed his life, probably alluding that his daughter gave him more perspective of where the importance of basketball fit in his priorities. He then thanked Juli, stating, "I really believe I owe it to my family, my wife who has been there for me and enabled me to just coach basketball. Everybody who's in this business understands that you don't get [in the Hall of Fame] unless your wife is there for you every day. I'm just blessed to have a wife like Juli Greene Boeheim."

Jim and Juli have since had three children: James Arthur Boeheim III, who was born in 1998 when Boeheim was 54 years old, and twins Jack and Jamie, born in 1999 when Boeheim was 55. With Boeheim having children in his mid-50s, Connecticut coach Jim Calhoun quipped, "Jim is going to be the oldest parent going to PTA meetings."

Boeheim still had basketball in his blood and on his brain, but everyone around him could see that he had mellowed, and much of that can be attributed to Juli and his kids. His priorities changed. He became a devoted husband and continued as a dedicated father. George Hicker, Boeheim's former teammate, observed a kinder, gentler Boeheim. "He's not the same as he was. I think we all grow up," Hicker said. "When he first started coaching, Jim was much more excitable. I think the relationships he has with Juli and the kids have pacified him a lot. He still wants to win every game, of course, but now there are other things more important to him than sports. I think he's realized that."

Boeheim acknowledged that Juli understands him and knows how to deal with him. "She's the only one who will absolutely stand up to me on every issue," he told writer Seth Davis. "She knows how to push the right buttons. She's the only one." One of the reasons the Jim–Juli relationship works so well is because Juli lets Jim do his thing, which is coaching basketball, and Jim lets Juli run the house and everything else. Boeheim, during an in-depth interview with Graham Bensinger, said that relative to their home, Juli is in charge of everything, inside and out. Whatever Juli says or wants, Jim said he agrees with. Boeheim said that when Juli wants something, he replies, "Good idea." When she suggests something, he responds, "I agree." When she asks what he thinks, Jim says, "Whatever you think." When Juli asks him if he has any ideas, Jim said he replies, "I have no ideas. I never have an idea. It's best never to have any ideas."

Boeheim also became much more involved in the community and giving back. Through the Jim and Juli Boeheim Foundation and beyond his Coaches vs. Cancer work, he became involved in a dozen or more charitable causes. And whenever his friends needed or called on him, he was there. Duffy told the story of a business venture that he became involved in where he needed immediate financial help. "In the fall of 2003, right after Jimmy had his surgery, I bought a Nestlé's chocolate factory in Fulton. It was an exceptionally good deal but a very fast-paced deal. I needed to come up with some money quickly, so I called Jimmy to find out the lay of the land locally," related Duffy. "Anyway, I'm on two phones trying to put together the money, and then I get a call-waiting, and it's Juli and she says, 'Count us in.' That they would send a check. They didn't even know the details of the deal, but they were willing to help. He and Juli were right there. That's the kind of friends they are. Jimmy's not a taker, he's a giver," stated Duffy.

1994–95

The following year Syracuse finished 20–10 overall and 12–6 in the Big East, but the thing about the 1994–95 season was that it should have extended further than it did. In the NCAA tournament, after defeating Providence and Southern Illinois, the No. 7-seeded Orange had No. 2 seed Arkansas beat, but Lawrence Moten, who had just recently become the school's all-time leading scorer, suffered a mental gaffe that enabled the defending national champion Razorbacks to come off the ropes and escape with the victory. After trailing by 12 points in the second half, Syracuse fought back to go in front. With 4.3 seconds left in the game and SU ahead, 82–81, Lucious Jackson stole Arkansas' inbounds pass but got tied up, with the possession arrow indicating Syracuse ball. In what might have been the game's last possession, SU had the ball in its hands, and the Razorbacks were down and almost out. A victory over an Arkansas team that had returned all of its starters from winning it all the previous year was all but in the scorebook.

Syracuse had the Razorbacks on their backs but couldn't seal the deal. During the held ball, Moten came unglued and instinctively called a timeout, but the Orange were out of them. The blunder resulted in a technical foul. Scotty Thurman made one of two free throws, sending the contest into overtime.

In the overtime session, with Syracuse down, 95–94, and 36.3 seconds to go, the Orange had the ball out of bounds. The Cuse called a timeout to set up a possible game-winning play. However, John Wallace threw a long inbounds pass that Arkansas' Corey Beck intercepted. Arkansas held on for a 96–94 victory in a game that would frustrate Syracuse fans for years to come. After the game Moten, the senior co-captain, stated, "I just had a mental lapse." Moten scored 27 points in the game, but all most people remember is the game-costing timeout. A great college career had ended on a sad note.

And so had the 1994–95 season. Always a target for criticism from a segment of the Syracuse fan base that had become jaded by the string of successful seasons, Boeheim caught increased flak. Despite doing a masterful job with mostly unheralded players in continuing to produce 20-plus win teams that finished third and second in the Big East in 1993 and 1994, rightly or wrongly, Boeheim's stock as a coach dropped.

1995–96

Notre Dame, West Virginia, and Rutgers joined the Big East in 1995, and the conference split into the Big East 6 and the Big East 7 for the next three years. The two divisions created interest for conference seedings but caused confusion for fans. Before the season, star forward John Wallace declared for the NBA draft. The Orange Nation was relieved, however, when Wallace reneged and decided to return to school for his senior season. And what a season it was. Syracuse remained unscathed through the first 11 games. A high point was a December 23 pummeling of No. 3 Arizona, 79–70, in Tucson in a game that wasn't as close as the final score indicated. Wallace had many great games while playing for the Orange, but noteworthy was his 26-point, nine-rebound performance as SU handed the undefeated Wildcats their first loss in the McKale Center in three years to a team outside the Pac 10.

As the team continued to win, "The Cuse is in Da House" became the mantra for the season. Back-to-back losses to Massachusetts and Miami brought the Orange back to earth. Although Syracuse was schooled by the No. 1-ranked Minutemen, 65–47, in the Rainbow Classic, the setback wasn't as bad as it sounded because John Calipari had built a juggernaut at UMass. SU responded by going 11–5 the rest of the regular season. They then beat Notre Dame and Boston College in the Big East tournament but bombed against UConn. Receiving a No. 4 seed in the West Regional, SU crushed Montana and defeated Drexel in Albuquerque, moving on to the Elite Eight to face Georgia in Denver in what would be one of the most dramatic games of the tournament.

Trailing by nine points with about three minutes to go, Syracuse staged a rally to jump ahead of the Bulldogs, setting up a wild finish. Up by one with seven seconds left, SU seemed to be in control of the contest until Georgia's Pertha Robinson hit a three-point shot that gave the Bulldogs a two-point lead. Following a timeout, Wallace, the team's best passer, fired a long inbounds pass cross-court to Jason Cipolla in the corner. Cipolla launched a 12-footer that sailed through the net to tie the game as time expired. The extra session was a seesaw affair. With Georgia clinging to an 81–80 lead with about 10 seconds to go, Wallace buried the game-winning three-pointer that gave Syracuse an 83–81 victory. The Bulldogs thought they had the game won on two occasions with the clock winding down. Then Syracuse pulled the bone out of the Bulldogs' mouth. A 6-foot-8 forward, Wallace ended up with 30 points and 15 rebounds.

Following the contest, CBS's Al McGuire got comments from an elated Boeheim, center Otis Hill, and Wallace. Toward the end of the interview, the Orange players spontaneously started dancing while singing, "The Cuse is in Da House! Oh my God! The Cuse is in Da House! Oh my God!" Overtaken by the hysteria, McGuire, on national television, joined in the dancing, hilariously making up his own moves before almost falling down. It made for a memorable conclusion to a thrilling game and became a highlight that would be replayed throughout the duration of the tournament. For several years, the clip was played to show the excitement of the NCAA tournament. Suddenly students and fans started wearing "The Cuse is in Da House" T-shirts. It became another in numerous "Syracuse moments" that defined the highly recognized basketball program.

In another down-to-the-wire job, Syracuse got past the second-seeded Kansas Jayhawks, 60–57, to punch its ticket to East Rutherford, New Jersey, for the program's third Final Four appearance. At the Meadowlands, SU defeated Mississippi State, 77–69, to earn its way into the title game.

8

1996 NATIONAL CHAMPIONSHIP GAME

Syracuse had started the season unranked. Now standing between the Orange and the national championship was Rick Pitino and his Kentucky Wildcats. Leading up to the game, Pitino told George Vecsey of the *New York Times*, "If we happen to lose, God forbid, one small part of me would be happy. If I had to lose to one coach, I would pick Jim Boeheim. He gave me my break twenty years ago." Up to that point, Boeheim had beaten Pitino six out of the seven times they had coached against each other, including in the national semifinals in 1987 when Pitino was at Providence.

The Sagarin Ratings, which had only been used since the mid-1970s, would later rank 1995–96 Kentucky as the best national championship team. UK finished with a 34–2 record, its only two losses coming to Final Four teams Massachusetts, early in the season when the Minutemen were ranked No. 2, and Mississippi State. The Wildcats had an unofficial record of nine players that went on to the NBA. The team was tabbed "The Untouchables."

Boeheim's tenacious trademark 2–3 zone defense held Kentucky to 38 percent shooting. By skillfully rotating seven players who knew their roles and played unselfishly, tired, injured, and troubled by fouls, Boeheim got the absolute most out of his tissue-thin team. Out-everythinged, Boeheim kept the Cuse in the contest, with SU down three with about two minutes to go. The Orange finally faded when Wallace fouled out with just over a minute remaining and Syracuse was within five points of the Wildcats. A team consisting of veterans and loaded with future pros, UK prevailed, 76–67. This group of Cats was simply too much for the Cuse. It was a game in which Boeheim outcoached Pitino, but he just didn't have the manpower to win.

"The zone was what kept the game close," stated Pitino. "Syracuse beat a very good Kansas team, and nobody expected them to," he said. "And we had to get by UMass, which had beaten us earlier in the season, so that was a very intense game."

Syracuse's third trip to the Final Four was a little different from its first two. Boeheim liked his team's chemistry but realized that it ran into a buzz saw in Kentucky, a team he called "the best team in the country, by far." The Cuse hung in there against tip-top competition, and in doing so, the team earned the respect of the national media and basketball fans around the country. All losses are tough to take, but this one was more digestible than the heartbreaker against Indiana in 1987.

With 2,119 points, Wallace departed Syracuse as the school's third all-time scorer, behind Lawrence Moten and Derrick Coleman, and third-leading rebounder with 1,065, trailing only Coleman and Rony Seikaly. Wallace's 845 points during the 1995–96 season remains the school's single-season record. Also on that team was Lazarus Sims, whom Boeheim had said, along with former player and longtime assistant coach Mike Hopkins, was one of his greatest overachievers.

It was a remarkable year for Boeheim as he took an unheralded Syracuse team that was ranked No. 41 in the Associated Press pre-season poll to the NCAA finals and almost upset a Kentucky team that was favored by 14 points. Arguably the most overachieving of any of his teams, what Boeheim got out of this group was a testament to his coaching ability. Like the stock market, Boeheim's image as a coach spiked.

When the 1996 team returned to the Dome for its twentieth anniversary in 2016, Boeheim told Chris Carlson of the *Syracuse Post-Standard*, "That team maximized what they could do. They got everything done you would ask to be done. It was a really unexpected Final Four, but we had a great point guard, a great scorer, and really good complimentary players. We had all the parts that we needed. It just fit," he said. "Lazarus [Sims] was the best point guard we've ever had for getting the ball to people. He was a great passer. He understood the game. He made sure the right guys got the ball ... He's probably the smartest point guard we ever had ... John [Wallace] was the most confident player that we've ever had. He believed we could beat anybody."

The critics and boobirds let up somewhat after Boeheim guided the Orange to 29 wins and into national championship contention in 1996, but his detractors were still there. Despite taking two teams into the NCAA finals, one of the ongoing knocks on Boeheim at the time was that he hadn't won a national championship, and therefore, he couldn't be considered a great coach. If Keith Smart's shot had clanged off the rim in the 1987 national championship game, would Boeheim suddenly have been a great coach? Back in 1996, Boeheim didn't think so, stating, "If one shot makes a difference between whether you're a good coach or a bad coach, that's really ridiculous. No, in some people's minds it wouldn't have made a difference at all. There are a lot of very good coaches who have never won a national championship. There are very few people alive who have won a national championship," he said. Boeheim also stated that he never thought that Buffalo Bills coach Marv Levy would have been a better coach if he had won one of those Super Bowls, where he and the Bills went 0-for-4. Case in point: Rick Pitino was being praised as one of the best coaches in the business long before he finally got the brass ring in 1996 and in doing so made Boeheim the bridesmaid again. Even if the Kentucky-Syracuse score were reversed, Pitino would still have maintained his sterling coaching reputation.

9

BOEHEIM BATTLES HIS IMAGE

Even though he was coming off a great season, the battle about Boeheim raged on. It took a while for Boeheim to begin to get his due. For the first ten years of his career, Boeheim was one of the best-kept secrets in basketball, with some sportscasters still mispronouncing and some writers misspelling his name. Without the attention and recognition, Boeheim methodically climbed uphill in a quest for respect, throughout his career taking two steps forward and one backward, receiving a little backhanded praise here and there and then turning his back and getting hit in the head with a rotten egg. It tended to happen after Syracuse would get off to another one of its customary good starts, only to suffer an equally customary late-season swoon. The fans, sometimes egged on by the media or vice versa, seemingly turned the thermostat up to express their dissatisfaction that another potentially good run in the NCAA tournament went out the window. Considering his consistent, career-long track record, Boeheim took more abuse from the media and from his own fan base than most. It seemed the more he achieved and the more accolades he received, the more his critics found fault with him. The more respect he gained professionally and nationally, the more the vocal minority, local and elsewhere, tried to belittle him and knock him down. A large part of the problem was that Boeheim had created a monster and that monster needed to be constantly fed. At times, the passionate but unforgiving fan base growled for red meat. By winning so early and so often, Boeheim set the bar so high that it created an insatiable appetite for Syracuse fans. In some ways, Jim Boeheim became a victim of his own success. Whenever the malcontents took potshots, and they did throughout his career, those in the Boeheim camp circled the wagons.

Disregarding Syracuse's virtual take-it-to-the-bank annual invitations to the NCAA tournament because he hadn't won a national championship, Boeheim's critics focused on his whining rather than his winning and his personality, which had been described as grumpy, cranky, crabby, sarcastic, bad-tempered, and, if you were kind, less than charming.

Some extended that by stating that Boeheim didn't win the big games. But what was a big game? During the 1996 NCAA tournament, were the Syracuse-Georgia, Syracuse-Kansas, and Syracuse-Mississippi State contests big games? They had to be, because if the Orange didn't overtake the Bulldogs in overtime, send the No. 2-seeded Jayhawks packing in a thriller and dispose of MSU in a Final Four matchup, Syracuse would not have met Kentucky center stage in the Meadowlands for all the marbles. Same thing in 1987. Had SU not taken care of business against Florida, North Carolina, and Providence, someone else would have played Indiana, and far fewer people would have ever remembered Keith Smart. Moreover, that's without mentioning all the hair-raising affairs where Boeheim came out on top against Georgetown and Connecticut and the other Big East powers when regular-season and tournament championships were at stake, as well as the big wins against the powers of the day, both at home and on the road. Before Boeheim won the national championship in 2003, an out-of-town writer during an NCAA tournament asked him about not being able to win the "big games," causing Boeheim to shoot back, "Some questions don't deserve an answer, and that's one of them."

"Jim Boeheim gets bashed and bashed, and that blows my mind," Dick Vitale said. "He's never been appreciated, but all he does is win and win. What he got out of [the 1995–96] Syracuse team was unbelievable. They overachieved all season and went to the Final Four. He can flat out coach."

No matter. Boeheim's faultfinders still insisted that he wasn't on par with some of his more acclaimed colleagues, forever pointing to long-past NCAA upset losses to the likes of Richmond and Navy and a blown game here and there. "We did lose those games," Boeheim conceded. "Everybody who has coached a long time has lost games like that. It happens to everybody over the course of ten to twenty years. You're going to get upset by somebody."

Periodically big-name coaches and big-time programs suffer humiliating and/or eliminating losses to lightweight opponents. During this season, Arkansas, then a power under Nolan "40-Minutes of Hell" Richardson, lost to Division II American University-Puerto Rico, and Indiana with Knight lost to Cleveland State. It happened every year. Bypassing all the years in between and quickly skipping to 2011, during the NCAA tournament No. 1-seed Kansas, coached by Bill Self, was never in the game against 11th-seeded Virginia Commonwealth, which was one of the four additional teams when the tournament expanded to sixty-eight. Thirteenth-seed Morehead State gave Rick Pitino's No. 4-seeded Louisville Cardinals the heave-ho in the first round. In 2012, No. 15 Lehigh disposed of No. 2 Duke. In 2013, unheard-of Florida Gulf Coast University, a fifteen-seed, sent the No. 2-seeded Georgetown Hoyas home. The No. 3 Dukies got decked again in 2014, this time by No. 14 Mercer. Then in 2018, the University of Maryland-Baltimore County Retrievers—yes, the Retrievers—became the first-ever No. 16 seed to dethrone a No. 1 when it embarrassed Virginia 74–54 a day after No. 13-seeded Buffalo blew out No. 4-seeded Arizona. Most of those coaches were forgiven, and their embarrassing losses were forgotten. Not so with Boeheim, who wore his stink bombs on his forehead whenever writers and television commentators reinforced the image they created and would perpetuate by digging up, dusting off, and dredging out the few dated blemishes on what was otherwise, even at that point, an extremely successful coaching career. The haters always reverted back to the same old tired complaints or created new ones to keep Boeheim from getting his due.

Boeheim heard the grumblings and digs, from near and far, but dismissed most of them stating, "If people respect our program … then I hope they have some measure of respect for me." He listened to a briefing of his perceived faults from a writer and took everything in stride but bristled when he was targeted for subpar bench coaching and being a poor strategist. Apparently hitting a nerve, he shot back: "That's nonsense. Any coach who has been in it a long time has had to make some decisions. Some work and some are wrong. It's funny. When I played, I was considered a very smart player," he said, recalling his days as Bing's backcourt mate at SU and in the professional minor leagues. "Every coach that I played for, and many that I played against, told me that. Maybe they told me that because I was non-athletic and I had to outthink other people. I must have gotten a lot stupider once I started coaching."

At that point in his career, Boeheim admitted that the continuous criticism sometimes got to him. "I'm sensitive to it. I read everything negative written about me and everything hurts, but it doesn't bother me as much as it used to," he said. "You hear something for a year or two, but some of this has gone on for fifteen or twenty years." Pitino said, "That's the one weakness Jim has. He's got 'rabbit ears.' He listens to his critics and tries to defend himself and his record, and they don't need defending."

On February 14, 2011, six years after Pitino said that, Boeheim demonstrated specifically what Pitino was talking about, and ironically, Boeheim did it using Pitino as the subject. Pitino, then coaching Louisville, had just beaten Boeheim for the seventh straight time.

When Syracuse beat writers pointed that out, Boeheim, who admitted that what he considered unfair criticism still bothered him, took issue with the media and lambasted them in a postgame press conference. He asked them why they didn't print that several years earlier he had beaten Pitino six straight times, including three times the year that Pitino took his Providence Friars to the Final Four. Boeheim also questioned the media on why they didn't write about his winning streaks against other good coaches, such as Bob Huggins and John Beilein. He also pointed out that he had won 80 percent of the time against some coaches who were in the Hall of Fame. "When people write and say things about me, it's personal to me. Always will be."

Pitino added, "We all have our critics. I have my critics. Bobby Knight had his critics. All coaches have their critics. Jim's record speaks for itself. Jim's record should silence his critics." However, it was Dick Vitale who, perhaps more than anybody else, exacerbated Boeheim's situation by calling Boeheim a crybaby and focusing on his so-called whining rather than his winning, his temperament rather than his triumphs. The image stuck. A few critics tagged the coach "Boewhine" and "Whineheim."

As for his bench behavior that apparently bothered some people, Boeheim acknowledged that he sometimes came across as a complainer. "I make no excuses for that," he said. "I do give that appearance. That's just part of my image, I guess. It's hard to change that. I'm active on the sideline. Sometimes somebody might not like your expressions or movements on the sideline, and if they don't like that, sometimes that can translate into he's a bad coach." In 1987, Boeheim told Mike Downey of the *Los Angeles Times*, "I'm a coach, and when I'm coaching on the floor, that's my act. That's my stage. A lot of that is emotional acting or whatever, and once the game's over, I'm fairly low-key. I'm not like that at all," he explained. "A lot of people don't like me, and then they meet me and say, 'Hey, you're not as bad as we thought.' Well, that's not really me out there. That's part of the job, part of what we do."

Almost all coaches complain to officials one way or another, sometimes as a strategy in hopes of getting the next close call. At the time Boeheim got tagged as a complainer, Purdue's Gene Keady scowled menacingly, John Thompson berated and intimidated with his sheer size, and Knight cursed and threw chairs, yet none of them had their coaching skills demeaned because of their tirades, technicals, or ejections, or were labeled like Boeheim was. Perhaps what grated on some people was the seemingly wimpy manner in which the balding, bespectacled, and blandly dressed Boeheim showed his discontent. Looking more like a philosophy professor, playwright, or preacher than a basketball coach, he shrugged his shoulders, gave a twisted half-smile, and extended his hands palms up as if pleading. OK, some called it whining. Harmless really, compared to the belligerent antics of some of his more forceful and demonstrative colleagues, but apparently irritating to some. Like in 1996 when Boeheim told of a West Coast writer who, throwing logic out the window and basing perceptions on personality rather than performance, stated, "I don't care what Boeheim does. I don't like him. And because I don't like him, he can't coach."

Vitale branded Boeheim a whiner, in fact perennially naming him captain of his "All-Crybaby team." It's a label, no matter how many wins he accumulates or what he achieves, Boeheim will never completely shake. It became permanently ingrained in people's minds. If you played that word-association game, it was probably the first thing that some people thought of when hearing Boeheim's name. Beyond that, because he never tried to appease the media, Boeheim didn't get the benefit of good press. "That was Jim's biggest problem early on," said Pitino. "He considered them his adversaries. But he's gotten a lot better. Right now, they see a man at peace with himself."

Mike Krzyzewski put it this way: "Jim is nonchalant about it. He doesn't make a big deal of himself. He's only on the microphone for a very short period of time. He doesn't make speeches. He makes statements." Perhaps former LSU coach Dale Brown, who like Boeheim never received due credit despite compiling 438 wins and putting Bayou Bengals basketball in the peoples' conscience, understood

Boeheim's plight better than most. "Some people don't like the way he looks, the way he talks, or the way he dresses," Brown said. "It's all image perpetuated by a few media people. What they have done with Jim Boeheim, like a litany of other guys, is a travesty. In this business, it's called the bottom line, and Jim Boeheim is a winner on the bottom line. Jim Boeheim is a great coach."

Boeheim admitted that up to that point in his career he hadn't really catered to the media and that hadn't helped his image. Oftentimes he came off as cantankerous, a curmudgeon, and downright ornery. He rarely smiled. He often projected a negative image and as much warmth as a bucket of ice. Even on his better days, he could find the dark cloud behind any silver lining. The belief was Boeheim treated the local media with disdain because the *Syracuse Post-Standard* investigated SU's basketball program in 1990. At a time when the Orange Express was camping out among the top five teams in the country, the *Post-Standard* broke the story about rules violations that resulted in knocking Syracuse off its high horse. The feeling was that Boeheim never forgave them for that. Therefore, when he was questioned about something he didn't like and responded sharply or sarcastically, they concluded that the long-standing grudge set him off. Whether that was true or not, Boeheim said during the 1996 postseason tournament that he tried to be more accommodating. "The perception is that I'm not very friendly or outgoing with the press," he said. "I guess I've always been feisty with the media because I never really felt that I had to play that PR game. But it works better when you do. I'm trying to be more outgoing, to be more personable in interviews. I made that effort during the [1996 NCAA] tournament, and I think it was well-received. You're never too old to try to change some things."

In fairness, though, to some journalists—and not necessarily Syracuse beat writers—Boeheim was more reachable, approachable, and accommodating than many other coaches. He returned telephone calls when many did not. He answered questions without giving the caller the feeling that he was in a hurry to hang up. He was everything that some felt that he was not. It was apparent though that Boeheim displayed a more relaxed, pleasing personality to the national media, though he did unload on ESPN's Andy Katz in 2013 after Boeheim thought Katz misled him in a previous conversation. Still, he maintained his surliness toward the Syracuse beat writers, as evidenced by his jumping all over them in 2006 when they called Gerry McNamara overrated and in 2011 when they brought up his losing streak to Pitino.

Vitale also contributed to Boeheim's negative image by annually criticizing Syracuse's preconference schedule and also referring to Boeheim as *Home Alone* star Macaulay Culkin because the Orange didn't leave the friendly confines of the Carrier Dome until after New Year's. Later, when the Orange regularly played big-name opponents in early season games in Madison Square Garden, Vitale came down on Boeheim for not leaving New York State. Vitale also solidified the perception that Syracuse played a soft non-conference schedule, when, in fact, there were years that the Orange played what was regarded as among the toughest schedules in the country.

Vitale had been chiding Boeheim for a long time. In a somewhat serious but beneficial event, Boeheim relished the opportunity to put Vitale in his place. In July 1991, the two agreed to play a one-on-one basketball game in Rochester with $1,000 going to Camp Good Days and Special Times in the name of the winner. Prior to the game, Boeheim, a good player in college, stated that he was not going to take it easy on Vitale. As rehashed by Syracuse.com's Johnathan Croyle, the two competed in 96-degree heat in front of 2,500 people. Boeheim dominated Vitale, winning 15–3. Not satisfied with the win, Boeheim then challenged Vitale to a best-of-ten free-throw shooting contest. Vitale, who prided himself on his ability to make foul shots—something he often did before games to excite the crowd—made eight free throws before Boeheim rallied to tie the score and then go on to win in a five-shot tiebreaker. Rubbing it in, Boeheim stated, "The only problem with this is, whom did you beat? Nobody!" Referring to Syracuse's annual soft preseason schedules, the quick-witted Vitale shot back, "You should be used to that, Jimmie."

When Boeheim took an underdog Syracuse team to the national

championship game during the 1995–96 season, Vitale still refused to elevate the Syracuse coach to the upper echelon of coaching, where only those Vitale considered the cream of the crop resides. In his book *Holding Court*, Vitale wrote: "In my mind, the great coaches have passed the test of time. Think about it. Guys like Dean Smith, John Chaney, John Thompson, Gene Keady, Bob Knight, Mike Krzyzewski, Rick Pitino, Denny Crum, and Nolan Richardson all fall into the same category. They've been there for ten years or more and gotten the job done year after year. Their teams are consistently in the Top 25." Several paragraphs later, Vitale adds that "one coach who hasn't got the credit he deserves is Jimmy Boeheim," although just by saying that, Vitale also slighted Boeheim. Along with the aforementioned, Vitale even unabashedly touted retired Princeton coach Pete Carril as a future Naismith Hall of Famer. However, he always stopped short of suggesting that the next probable member of the 550-Win Club belonged with the aforementioned coaches.

Asked then why he never mentioned Boeheim among the coaching elite, Vitale responded, "Some people have labeled him as a recruiter, but that's absurd. Some thought his personnel had been a little better than what he had ended up with in the postseason. And he still hasn't cut down the nets." Reminded then that Chaney at the Division I level and Keady also hadn't come close to cutting down the nets, Vitale conceded that some people feel Boeheim belonged in that select company but that certain members of the media didn't. "Jim doesn't jump out at you," he said, even though Boeheim had an impressive coaching resume. "A lot of that has to do with the world we live in today with television and press conferences. Jim isn't glib, and he doesn't have the one-liners. But I think [the 1996 tournament run] really, really helped him with the public. He finally got some recognition."

When pressed to separate personality from performance, Vitale said that "Jim Boeheim wins consistently, and he does it in a real special way. He allows his players to play their kind of game, and he's helped develop them to become pro stars by letting them play that way. Jim knows how to get the most out of people. He knows how to utilize their talents. People take for granted what he's done over the years. He's done an outstanding job. He knows how to win. He's never really given the credit he deserves."

Put on the spot with the suggestion that he himself was on the top of the list among those who had not given Boeheim the type of credit that Vitale was referring to, on September 6, 1996, for the very first time and for the record, he told this writer: "Look for Dickie V [in the future] to include Jim Boeheim among the great coaches. He's got to be accepted with that group. But Jim Boeheim doesn't have to worry about Dick Vitale," the non-stop analyst stated, before offering another first: "Jim has Hall of Fame numbers. It's going to be awfully difficult to keep him out of the Hall of Fame."

That conversation with Vitale took place in 1996. Regardless of what he said in that discussion, Vitale for several years publicly still did not include Boeheim unconditionally among the elite coaches whenever the topic was brought up. He really didn't start giving Boeheim his just due until Boeheim won the 2003 national championship and a couple of years later got elected into the basketball Hall of Fame. That said, to be fair, since that time, Vitale has been one of Boeheim's biggest supporters, particularly defending him when Boeheim got hit for the second time with NCAA sanctions in 2013 and inviting and honoring Boeheim with an award at his Dick Vitale Gala in 2015.

Steve Fisher, formerly the coach at Michigan and later San Diego State, now retired, stated, "For years, [Boeheim] was every critic's favorite mark because he'd never won a national championship." The perception about Boeheim's coaching ability began to change in the mid-to-late 1990s, but long-held, often-repeated beliefs die hard. When the dissonance surrounding Boeheim's image and coaching ability was mentioned to some elite coaches, they hurried to his defense. "I think Jim is starting to get some recognition now, but it's long overdue," said Krzyzewski, acknowledged as one of college basketball's finest coaches early on, despite a surname that also defies the rules of spelling and pronunciation. "At a school like Syracuse, with its rich basketball tradition, some people take sustained success for granted. I think that definitely happened in Jim's case. Jim has been one of the top coaches for a long time. He should have been recognized as such a long time ago. Frankly, I'm amazed that it hasn't happened. Jim is a close friend of mine and a great guy," continued Coach K shortly after Syracuse's 1996 national championship game appearance. "I admire him for what he has accomplished. I'm glad he's now starting to get some recognition."

Like many others, Rick Pitino thought that Boeheim got overlooked and disrespected because of his style. "If he were in the corporate world with its bottom line, Jim Boeheim would be a knight in shining armor because all he does is win," he said in 1996. "But in the basketball world, sometimes it's charisma and style. However, Jim has changed a great deal through the years. Right now Jim has more style and charisma than he's ever had. I know Jim in a way that a lot of other people may not know him. I know him as a charming person with a great personality. He's extremely funny and fun to be around. He can be the life of the party. I think Jim is able to poke fun at himself. He takes himself seriously, but then again, he doesn't take himself seriously. He has an ego, but it's because of high self-esteem and not in any condescending way. I like him so much as a person." What Boeheim has accomplished, as Pitino put it, "should silence his critics."

Pitino, who was 3–6 coaching against Boeheim at that point, took exception to those who picked on Boeheim's coaching ability. "Jim's a great bench coach. He's an excellent strategist on the bench," he stated. "He's one of the best coaches in the game. It's one of his strengths. From a technical standpoint, he's as sound as anybody. I think he's calm, very analytical, and he's poised to win. Jim is highly intelligent. He's a very bright basketball coach and an extremely bright person," continued Pitino, who was at the time already widely acknowledged as one of the best coaches in the game on any level after guiding Providence to the Final Four, turning around the New York Knicks, and winning the national championship at Kentucky. "Anybody who thinks he's not a good bench coach knows very little about basketball.

Jim is also a very good evaluator of talent and a great recruiter. He is one of the few coaches who can take a lower rated player and make him better than what the player was rated. Jim gives his players the freedom to create on offense. All of his guys really enjoy playing for him. Jim can also deal with problems better than a lot of other people.

"Now you may not like his style, such as his 2–3 zone, but that has nothing to do with his ability as a bench coach. I have great respect for Jim, and all the people in the business that I know think he can coach. He has many more admirers than critics, at least from people who know basketball. The people who say that Jim Boeheim can't coach are in the vast minority." Krzyzewski, several years before he appointed Boeheim his assistant on the Olympic team, agreed wholeheartedly, stating: "Jim has a real good basketball mind. His insights are intriguing. Because of that, he's opened my eyes to a number of different things. As a basketball coach, he can measure up to anybody."

The then-all-time leader in victories, retired and since deceased Dean Smith of North Carolina, simply said, "Jim has done a tremendous job. He doesn't get the credit that he deserves." Smith should have somewhat understood Boeheim's situation at the time because Smith had consistently won big throughout his career, and even he didn't get the monkey off his back until winning the first of his two national titles in 1982, after coming up short in six previous Final Fours. Roy Williams, with Kansas at the time, also couldn't believe the static that Boeheim received. "I definitely haven't heard of another coach who gets as little respect as Jimmy does," he told reporters after Syracuse beat his Jayhawks, 60–57, in the 1996 Midwest Regional final. "Syracuse outplayed us and outcoached us." Years later when he was at North Carolina, Williams was even more emphatic. He stated, "Jimmy's one of the best coaches in the game—ever."

In 2017, during his postgame comments after his team lost a thrilling 78–75 contest to the Orange, Krzyzewski stated, "You don't know what a treasure you have with [Boeheim]. . . . He's brilliant, competitive, loyal, and he doesn't need his ego scratched. He's humble."

One would think that an evaluation provided by Krzyzewski would carry considerably more weight than an opinion from some guy coming out of a grocery store with a six-pack or an accountant venting his frustration about Boeheim to his barber. One might surmise that an analysis by Pitino would have more validity than an emotional reaction from someone sitting on a sofa ranting, raving, and anonymously firing off complaints and criticisms on Internet chat lines and who, like the wild swings in the stock market, keeps changing his tone depending upon the flow of the game from half to half and game to game. Or that praise from Roy Williams and Dean Smith would be valued much more than criticism from someone who merely has a basketball goal in his driveway. Boeheim's peers stated he was an outstanding coach. So what if Joe Schmo, the bartender over at Pete's Pub, and the CYO coach from Who-Knows-Where didn't think so. Richie Duffy, Boeheim's old teammate, simply said that if he's around people who say Boeheim can't coach, "I'll get angry and walk out of the room."

Until he finally started getting some respect following the 1995–96 season and significantly more so after winning the 2003 national championship, Boeheim had to, by and large, console himself knowing that he had the respect of his peers and that most of the time he came out on top of where in his profession it counted the most—on the basketball court. According to some of the game's best coaches, Boeheim had finally made the leap from good to great. It wasn't until after he won the national championship and amassed over 900 wins that, at least among his admirers, he went from excellence to eminence.

However, it was still not to be with some in the media and others in the court of public opinion who clung to their beliefs that Boeheim was overrated. This assessment of Boeheim's dilemma may not be too far off. "I'm on Syracuse.com every day and read the posted comments, and I think most people give Boeheim the accolades he deserves. The people who criticize him are people who will criticize the President, the Pope, the Queen of England, etc.," emailed Rich Barone, a Syracuse fan. "To some, it's just human nature. The other groups of people who criticize him are the ones that Boeheim pisses off just by his actions, including in his pre- and postgame interviews where he comes off as being arrogant, snippy, cranky, and stubborn. He is not a people person, and that rubs people the wrong way, so they look for any little thing to throw him under the bus, if you know what I mean. I think that's the reason he doesn't get respect from the media and some fans. It's because he kind of gets under their skin. They know he's a good coach, but his personality gets in the way. He does, and more often than not, come across as a jerk. That's just Jim Boeheim.

"Then there are people, like me, who think they know more about basketball than him, which in my case, I do (lol). So there you have it, a complete breakdown of why Jim Boeheim, right or wrong, is not always respected. In other words, it's not really his coaching, it's because of his personality."

Boeheim understood and accepted the nature of his profession and the criticisms that came with it, stating, "I don't want credit. I never have. I want the players to get the credit. I'll take the blame. That's what I'm paid for. Our fans? All I care about is that they watch us, come to the games, and support us. They can have any opinion they want as long as they support us."

Some other members of the media did reluctantly come around, like a *Boston Globe* scribe who penned, "After years of being scorned as a roll-out-the-ball, laissez-faire coach who relied on extraordinary talent, Boeheim is now being recognized as a guy who has gotten more out of his talent than he should have." In a facetious response to Boeheim's critics, one television analyst stated, "For a guy who can't coach, Jim Boeheim sure wins a lot of games. Imagine how good Syracuse would be if Boeheim could coach."

1996–97

Many times Boeheim was at his best when his talent level was down and expectations were lowered. That was the case in 1996 when he was confronted with major problems from the get-go. Before the season began, Syracuse lost 6-foot-9 blue-chipper Winfred Walton because of academic issues, lost leading scorer Todd Burgan for the first seven games due to injury, and then the team lost its first four Big East games. Most people thought the Orangemen were dead in the water. Boeheim, however, resurrected the fast-sinking Syracuse ship and guided it to what had been considered an improbable 19-win season and almost into another NCAA tournament. In some ways, even though the Orange failed to make it for only the fourth time in his career up to that point, didn't win 20 games for only the second time, and in fact got bounced from the NIT in the first round, Boeheim, in prodding that team to come back like it did, may have done an even better coaching job than he did the year before when the Orange gave Pitino and Kentucky a run for its money.

A highlight of an otherwise subpar season was the Georgetown game when, after centers Otis Hill and Etan Thomas fouled out, Boeheim was forced to insert Donavan McNabb into the contest. An SU football star but a seldom-used substitute on the basketball team who rarely scored, McNabb responded with a much-needed 10-point performance on four of five shooting from the field in only 19 minutes of action, including two crucial free throws with seconds left to trigger a 77–74 Orange win. McNabb also stuffed a dunk attempt by 6-foot-9, 280-pound Georgetown center Jahidi White that got the fans out of their seats the way they did when as a quarterback he juked his way for a long gain or completed a long pass. Four games later, on February 22, Boeheim snagged win number 500, a 92–62 rout over Rutgers. Then the Syracuse season ended just the way it started, with an injured Burgan playing only seven minutes in an NIT loss to Florida State. The unavailability of his star at the beginning and the end of the season may have deprived Boeheim of chalking up what would have been yet another 20-win campaign.

1997–98

The following year it was back to business as usual as the Orange went 26–9. Syracuse pretty much breezed through the early portion of its schedule, only hitting a speed bump against Michigan in the Puerto Rico Holiday Classic. In league play, the 1997–98 Orangemen compiled a 12–6 record and captured the Big East championship. SU had tough games in the conference tournament, barely beating Villanova, 69–66, and St. John's, 69–67, in overtime, before bogging down against Connecticut, 69–64. In the NCAA South Regionals, Syracuse struggled against Iona but prevailed, 63–61, and proceeded to knock off New Mexico, 56–46. The Duke Blue Devils stopped the Cuse in their tracks, 80–67.

1998–99

In 1998–99 the Big East returned to a one-division format. Syracuse again waltzed through its pre-holiday schedule, but then, for the first time in the twenty-two-year history of the Carrier Classic, the host team lost in the first round. Unranked Ohio University shocked the No. 12-rated Orange, 61–55. SU rebounded, in Boeheim's 1,000th game at Syracuse as a player, assistant, and head coach, to defeat Santa Clara. The Orange had an up-and-down conference season, finishing 10–8. Included in those ups was No. 16 SU leveling No. 1-ranked Connecticut at the Hartford Civic Center, 59–42, by holding the Huskies to their lowest scoring total since Jim Calhoun arrived in Storrs in 1982. It was also the Orange's first game against a No. 1-ranked team since it lost to UMass in the Rainbow Classic in December 1995. One of the downs was Syracuse's first visit to storied Pauley Pavilion, where the Orange was flattened, 93–69, by a UCLA team that in name only resembled legendary coach John Wooden's dynasty-era clubs. Several of the losses that season were due to a lack of rebounding and poor free-throw shooting, things that had bitten Syracuse in the behind in the past and would also cost it in the future.

SU won its first two games in the conference tournament, but for the second straight year, they were beaten in the finals by UConn, this time 70–58. The Oklahoma State Cowboys ousted SU from the NCAA tournament. The Orange finished with a so-so 21–12 mark. Doug Gottlieb, a future ESPN and Fox Sports college basketball analyst who many SU fans dislike because they feel he doesn't like Syracuse, was the OSU point guard. He contributed 11 assists to the Cowboys' winning effort.

A pleasant surprise was 6-foot-6, 192-pound freshman forward Preston Shumpert, another diamond in the rough uncovered by Boeheim. A late signee overlooked by many, the Fort Walton Beach, Florida, product made his college debut by scoring 15 points in 15 minutes in a 93–40 demolition of Colgate. Although he tailed off toward the end of the year, the deadeye shooter deluxe would go on to make his mark at Syracuse, finishing as the school's all-time leader in three-point field goals made with 249 and three-pointers made in a single game with eight, a feat he accomplished twice. Boeheim, who handed out compliments about as frequently as he played man-to-man defense—especially to freshmen—favorably compared Shumpert's style of play, instincts, and shotmaking ability to Lawrence Moten, Boeheim's star who completed his career four years earlier as the Big East's all-time scoring leader. "He has a feel for the game and instincts like Lawrence had. He knows where to be, he has a knack of being where the ball is, knowing where the rebounds are," articulated Boeheim, who described his two players just the way Boeheim's teammates described Boeheim when he played. He made that analysis in 1999, and Shumpert made his coach sound like a prophet of sorts when he went on to be named a two-time Associated Press honorable mention All-American, just like Moten, although Moten tacked on a third-team AP All-American designation as a senior.

Following the season, Boeheim had a brief flirtation with the NBA. In April, *The Washington Post* reported that Boeheim had met with the Washington Wizards. The newspaper stated that it was not an interview, just an informal meeting to see if Boeheim had any interest in becoming the Wizards' head coach. Boeheim ended that discussion just as he did the talk with Rick Bay from Ohio State years before. He liked where he was, so he stayed. To Boeheim, if Syracuse was not heaven on earth, it was just on the outskirts.

1999–2000

In 1999 Syracuse returned all five starters, though Tony Bland beat out Allen Griffin to take over at point guard in the starting lineup. Going into the season, followers of the team didn't know if that was a good thing or a bad thing because some thought that during the previous year the team didn't play with passion, pride, or intestinal fortitude. Therefore the jury was still out on whether 1999–2000, with a veteran group that had played together, was going to translate to a big year or just be more of the same. The team surprised everyone by winning its first 19 games, the best start in Boeheim's career up to that point.

Characterized by solid defensive play but plagued by an inconsistent offense, the Cuse won its first nine conference games before losing two straight, to Seton Hall and then three days later to then non-conference opponent Louisville. Noteworthy was that UCLA came to the Carrier Dome and this time the Cuse bested the Bruins, 71–67. Syracuse went on to win the Big East regular-season championship with a 13–3 record, but the team proceeded to lose to Georgetown, 76–72, in the first round of the conference tournament. Receiving a No. 4 seed in the NCAA tournament, the Cuse handled small-time Samford, 79–65, and eked past big-time Kentucky, 52–50, before blowing a 14-point lead and falling to Michigan State, 75–58. The collapse, in part, may have been due to Preston Shumpert, the team's best outside shooter, going scoreless after having his vision impaired by an eye injury that later required stitches.

Despite the temporary dip from the heyday of the late 1980s, during the 1990s Syracuse still won a Big East championship, two Big East regular-season championships, went to eight NCAA tournaments, and came within five minutes of winning the national championship. In typical Boeheim fashion, the Cuse—led by Moten, Wallace, Adrian Autry, Jason Hart, Todd Burgan, and Shumpert, among others—experienced a ten-year resurgence to prominence as it went 232–91. Not bad since most schools would take a decade like that in a heartbeat.

However, the knock on Syracuse during that time, and on Boeheim in particular, was that the Orange, despite being a big winner during the season, played poorly in the NCAA tournament. To some people, it was no longer good enough to win 20 or more games a year and get into the NCAA tournament if SU didn't advance to the Sweet 16, Elite Eight, or get into the Final Four. The bar had been raised. Orange Nation wanted and expected more and bellyached when it didn't happen. By winning all those years, many Syracuse fans became spoiled. Some of the older fans had forgotten the pre-Fred Lewis years when the Orangemen were among the nation's biggest losers and the pre-Boeheim years when SU was happy just to get into the NIT. The younger fans didn't know about all that and didn't care. Some Orange followers were tired of Syracuse having opportunities and expectations, and they complained when, in their minds, the Cuse did not seize on or fulfill them.

Coaching basketball can be a cruel profession, but Boeheim proved to be resilient. Down a number of times over the years, Boeheim and his program time and again recovered, even if it was not always to the level or satisfaction of the die-hard but hard-to-please Syracuse Nation.

10

A NEW CENTURY

2000–01

In 2000 the University recognized the school's first one hundred years of basketball and named its All-Century Team, honoring the greatest players of the twentieth century.

After a tune-up win over St. Francis, the 2000–01 season was kickstarted by an early season championship in the Great Alaska Shootout that included victories over then non-conference opponent DePaul, Ohio State, and Missouri. After beating Colgate, the Cuse cakewalked through the Carrier Classic against significantly inferior competition to what it had faced in Anchorage and went on to tally a 10–6 record in Big East play. SU won its first two games in the conference tournament prior to getting edged out by Pittsburgh in overtime in the finals, 55–54. Syracuse then defeated Hawaii in the first round of the NCAAs but was brought down by Kansas, 87–58, to end the season.

2001–02

Syracuse pried the lid off their next season by winning the Carrier Dome portion of the preseason NIT and then continued on to New York to capture the NIT championship with nice wins over Michigan State and Wake Forest. In December, Boeheim was diagnosed with prostate cancer and traveled to St. Louis to undergo surgery. When his team lost twice in his absence—to North Carolina State and in the Peach Bowl Classic to Georgia Tech—Boeheim cut his recovery time short, returned to his team, and put out the fire. Asked by reporters in his postgame press conference why he came back so soon, Boeheim quipped, "It was either come back early and coach, or die from watching them play." Years later he explained more seriously, "We didn't play very well, and I got back out there. It was about fifteen days. I probably came back a little too soon."

While returning to courtside that quickly may not have been what the doctor recommended health-wise, coaching-wise it was needed because Syracuse rattled off seven consecutive victories before getting tripped up at Pittsburgh and Tennessee. Included during this span were two wins over Seton Hall, coached by Boeheim protégé Louis Orr.

"Coach is a competitor. He doesn't like to lose. That doesn't change, no matter who he is playing," stated Orr, who would win only twice in seven tries against his mentor during his five-year stint with the Pirates. "I don't enjoy playing against Coach. I preferred not to."

With a 20–11 record and a quick exit in the Big East tournament, the Orange was relegated to the NIT. Padding its record with victories over St. Bonaventure, Butler, and Richmond, Syracuse flamed out in New York, losing to South Carolina and Temple to conclude a 23–13 campaign.

2002–03

Carmelo Anthony

Then came Carmelo. A *Parade*, McDonald's, and *USA Today* first-team All-American, Carmelo Anthony became the first true blue-chip player that Boeheim landed since Billy Owens. Not as highly rated as Owens, Anthony was still a real big-time recruit. When marquee New York State prep players such as Elton Brand and Christian Laettner spurned Syracuse for Duke, some said that Boeheim had lost his mojo. However, just when some thought his career was on a down-tick, Boeheim brought in Anthony, and his arrival triggered another flurry of high school hotshots who followed suit, just as a decade or so earlier Pearl Washington's signing had made Syracuse an attraction for five-star talent.

Anthony was raised in a crime-infested area of West Baltimore known as "The Pharmacy" because of the drug dealing that went on. He played two years at Towson Catholic High School in Maryland. To escape the Baltimore ghetto and improve his grades and his game, Anthony transferred to Oak Hill Academy, a prep basketball power-house in Virginia known for its discipline and academic structure. Playing against significantly stiffer competition, Anthony got better. Consequently, college recruiters took an increased interest in Anthony, but Boeheim had gotten to him first. Like Pearl and so many others, Anthony wanted to play in the Carrier Dome. "It doesn't get much bigger than Syracuse when it comes to college hoops," stated Anthony. He committed to Syracuse before his senior year of high school.

Like some of Syracuse's prized recruits from a decade earlier, Anthony didn't disappoint. The Melo Watch began as soon as he put on a Syracuse uniform. Having the ability to dominate and take over a game at any time, Carmelo became an instant star at Syracuse. Like Elvis, Madonna, Cher, and LeBron, when people mentioned Carmelo, everyone knew who they were talking about. In his only season, Anthony, sporting his customary cornrows and headband, spearheaded the Orangemen to the 2003 national championship.

Anthony began his college career with a big game in The Big Apple. He scored 27 points, including 21 in the first half, and grabbed 11 rebounds against Memphis in the Coaches vs. Cancer Classic in Madison Square Garden. It wasn't enough, though, because the national championship season started out with a 73–60 loss to John Calipari's Tigers. It was all downhill from there for the Cuse until they ran into what was beginning to seem like an annual roadblock. Pittsburgh saddled Syracuse with its second loss, 73–66. After a couple of victories pushed its record to 13–2, the Orange experienced rough sledding at The RAC as Rutgers stunned Syracuse, 68–65. In regular season conference play, SU stumbled once more, this time at Connecticut, 75–61.

Syracuse mayor Matt Driscoll declared February 24, 2002, "Jim Boeheim Day" in the city. Later that evening before the Orange took on Georgetown, the basketball floor in the Carrier Dome was named "Jim Boeheim Court." Unfortunately, the Hoyas rained on Boeheim's parade by beating SU, 75–69. Fortunately, John Thompson II wasn't coaching at the time, or he might have remarked, "'Jim Boeheim Court' is officially christened!"

In what would be his final game in the Carrier Dome, Anthony poured in 30 points and snagged 14 rebounds as Syracuse ran over Rutgers, 83–74, in front of 33,070 fans who knew they were watching the one-and-done freshman phenom in an SU uniform for the last time. Throughout the one season that he wore orange, there were many Melo moments. Syracuse fans have their own special memories of the way Anthony brought joy to their town. Living there less than a year, they hardly got to know him, but they adored him.

The Orange beat Georgetown in the Big East tournament but not Connecticut. Syracuse began its run through the NCAA tournament with victories over Manhattan, Oklahoma State, Auburn, and Oklahoma to reach the fourth Final Four in school history.

In the semifinals, Anthony scored 33 points, an NCAA tournament Final Four freshman record, as Syracuse took care of third-ranked Texas, 95–84. He also grabbed 14 rebounds. In the win over the Longhorns, Hakim Warrick hammered home a dunk over Royal Ivey that ESPN.com ranked fourth in the Top 10 college dunks of all time, even though he was also assessed an offensive foul.

The Orange started the season unranked and remained that way until mid-January when they sneaked in at No. 25. They never got higher than No. 13, but nonetheless played their way to New Orleans.

National Championship Game

Playing for the national championship for the third time in the Boeheim era, in the 2002–03 season, Syracuse was not to be denied. Anthony and fellow freshman Gerry McNamara led the team effort, but it was Hakim Warrick's game-saving block of Michael Lee's potential game-tying three-point attempt that put the nail in Kansas' coffin and enabled the Orange to survive, 81–78. At the onset Kansas overplayed Anthony, leaving McNamara open. Like a kid in a candy store with eyes as big as saucers, G-Mac, who would go on to be one of the best clutch shooters in Syracuse history, stroked an NCAA-record-tying six three-pointers in the first half as the Orange bolted to an 18-point lead over the favored Jayhawks. The Cuse maintained a 53–42 advantage at intermission.

Kansas scored 11 of the first 15 points of the second half to whittle it down to 57–53 at the 15:37 mark. Syracuse responded with a run of its own to stretch the margin back to double-digits, 76–64, with a little over five minutes remaining. The Jayhawks fought back to make it a game again, slicing the lead to 76–70 with 3:20 left, and then to 80–77 on a Michael Lee layup with one minute showing on the clock. With 39 seconds to go, the Orange was clinging to a precarious 80–78 lead when Kueth Duany made a foul shot to push it to 81–78. It was still a one-possession game. With 14 seconds left, Warrick missed two free throws, painfully reminding Syracuse fans of Derrick Coleman's critical misfire on a one-and-one situation that opened the door for Keith Smart to make his game-winning shot that stunned SU in 1987.

With the final seconds ticking away and Kansas trailing by three, Kirk Hinrich, who was off the mark on a three-point attempt moments earlier, spotted Lee wide open in the left corner and rifled a pass to him. Lee caught the ball and went up for his shot. Seemingly out of nowhere came Warrick who, at 6-foot-8 and with long arms, jumped up and swatted the ball out of bounds with less than a second showing on the clock to preserve the win for the Orange before nearly 55,000 people and a worldwide television audience.

"Michael Lee was wide open, but [Warrick] closed so quickly because [he's] so athletic that he blocked the shot," stated disappointed Kansas coach Roy Williams. Years later Boeheim called Warrick's block "the single biggest play in Syracuse basketball history."

Ironically, sixteen years earlier in the same building and eerily from just about the same spot on the Superdome floor, Keith Smart shot down Syracuse when he got off his jumper over the outreached arms of Howard Triche. Had Lee made that trifecta, he would have joined Smart as someone SU fans would always remember with infamy. In missing it, he became a trivia question because, compared to Keith Smart, hardly anyone recalls who took that last shot. All that mattered was that Warrick blocked it.

"We just hung on," understated a relieved but happy Boeheim, who flashed a big smile that was throughout most of his career absent. "I was getting some flashbacks about some missed free throws," he said, in reference to Coleman's short-arming a foul shot in 1987. "Maybe this building owed us one." Straight outta Syracuse, the Orange on that night was the new blue (Duke, Kentucky, North Carolina, Kansas, UConn, and UCLA).

In the crowd that night were Coleman, Rony Seikaly, Pearl Washington, and Triche, among other former Orange stars. Finally, after sixteen years, they all felt vindicated. "I'm just glad we won it for Derrick Coleman, Rony Seikaly, Sherman Douglas, all those guys," said Boeheim.

As the story goes, after the high-flying Warrick rejected Lee's potential game-winner, Washington turned around in his seat and kiddingly told Triche, "If you'd done that to Keith Smart, we'd have won this thing a long time ago."

For Orange fans everywhere, time stood still. The spotlight was on Syracuse. For a few seconds, everything was right with the world. This was not just another "Syracuse moment" but the biggest SU basketball moment of all. Boeheim wished he could bottle the feeling and give a little bit of it in daily doses to his future players to motivate them to work hard to experience it for themselves.

Anthony, who had 20 points, 10 rebounds, and seven assists against Kansas, was selected the Most Outstanding Player of the Final Four, the third freshman in NCAA history to win the award. McNamara, another first-year star who scored 18 points and made 60 percent of his three-point shots against the Jayhawks, joined Melo on the Final Four first team. Billy Edelin, another freshman, had 12 points, and Kueth Duany, the steady unsung senior, contributed 11 points and four rebounds. Melo was the best player on the national championship team, but he had a good supporting cast that included sophomore Josh Pace, who chipped in with eight points, eight rebounds, three steals, and two assists.

Boeheim credited the good team chemistry of the national championship team, aka "The Comeback Kids," for winning 15 games when it trailed in the second half. Carmelo was the team's centerpiece and the go-to, take-over-the-game player. Despite being a rookie, McNamara was steady, unshakable, and a three-point threat. Duany was a senior captain and a player whom the players respected. Reserves such as Edelin and Pace stepped up to pick up the slack when the starters were a little bit off their game. "Obviously, Carmelo was a great player, but it was a good combination of upperclassmen and young guys," explained Boeheim, who pointed out that the team had three or four scoring options and peaked at the right time. Boeheim noted that Edelin and Pace were instrumental in victories over Manhattan, Oklahoma State, Auburn, and Oklahoma in the NCAA East Regionals. "They got us to the Final Four," he stated. "Anytime you have your sixth and seventh men playing that well, it's a huge plus. I thought we played our best offensive basketball of the season when we got to New Orleans," he continued. "We played our best game against Texas, which I felt maybe overall was the best team we had played."

Boeheim thought the team played to its potential in the first half against Kansas. "We couldn't play any better than that," he said, "but then we had to hang on" to win.

So in addition to being national champions and Big East West Division co-champions, Syracuse—after mowing down Oklahoma State, Oklahoma, Texas, and Kansas—could also be called the "unofficial champions of the Big 12."

Boeheim acknowledged that in winning the national championship he was finally able to put the disappointment of the 1987 loss to Indiana to bed. "It took sixteen years to get that '87 game out of my mind," he admitted to Graham Bensinger. "That was the first time that I was able to get it out of my mind."

After spending a little time on Bourbon Street enjoying the moment, Boeheim had enough of the partying. "Juli told me that Jimmy couldn't wait to get back to the hotel," related Richie Duffy, Boeheim's former teammate. "He said to her, 'Let's get this celebration over with.'" For those who say that Carmelo Anthony won that national championship for Boeheim, that simply is not entirely true. The Orange couldn't have won it without McNamara or any of the other key players who contributed at crucial times during the season, in the NCAA tournament, and in the championship game. Like all team sports, it was a team effort. And they couldn't have won it without Boeheim. He made all the decisions.

Following the championship, Boeheim and his team were honored on all levels. Soon after returning to campus the championship celebration attracted more than 25,000 fans that flocked to the Carrier Dome to show their appreciation for their hoops heroes, a gathering that was larger than any crowd at any basketball game at any other on-campus arena that season. On April 12, the city of Syracuse had a Parade of Champions. On April 15, Boeheim and his victors were invited to the governor's mansion in Albany. April 17 trumped that with the Syracuse contingent being guests at the White House in Washington, DC, where President George W. Bush recognized the Orange entourage as a part of Champions Day. In addition to Anthony, McNamara, Warrick, Duany, Edelin, and Pace, other members of the national championship team were Craig Forth, the starting center, his backup Jeremy McNeil, Matt Gorman, Tyrone Albright, Josh Brooks, Ronneil Herron, Gary Hall, Xzavier Gaines, and Andrew Kouwe. The associate head coach was Bernie Fine, and the assistant coaches were Mike Hopkins and Troy Weaver.

Syracuse became the first team since Rollie Massimino's Villanova Wildcats in 1985 to start the season unranked in the Associated Press poll and go on to win the national championship. The Orange was also the first No. 3 seed to win it all since Michigan in 1989. Roy Williams's record in NCAA tournament play dropped to 34–14, making him at the time the winningest coach to never win a national championship, a distinction previously held by Boeheim, who had been 37–21 before the victory and more than happy to pass that frowned-upon title to Williams.

Just as Boeheim had stated years ago that he didn't believe he was a poorer coach because Keith Smart had made that basket in 1987 to prevent him from winning the national championship, Boeheim stated that he didn't think he was a better coach because Hakim Warrick had blocked that shot to give him his first NCAA title.

This Final Four, clearly, was much different from the others. In 1975, Syracuse was the unknown quantity, the upstart, the low-profile program that somehow managed to play over its head for a couple of weeks and snuck into the tournament. The Orange was like the cast of a high school senior play that, unexpectedly and from out of nowhere, somehow got invited to perform its show on Broadway. They were just elated to be in the tournament and simply happy to drink up the experience. There were no expectations. The feeling was that they had already won just by being among the last four teams playing.

By 1987, Syracuse was a "name" program and the school was a regular participant in the NCAA tournament. The team was very talented, but it was a young and inexperienced group. The team definitely had potential, but most people thought SU was a year or two away. Regardless, the Cuse outplayed Indiana, and as the game wore on, the Orange really believed they could beat the Hoosiers. When they didn't, it was devastating.

In 1996, Syracuse had a star in John Wallace and good team chemistry. By this time Syracuse was recognized as among the top programs in the nation. Unfortunately, the Cuse faced a Kentucky team that was by far the best team in the country that season. The Orange hung with the Cats until almost the very end. The Cuse wanted to shock the world, as they boldly stated, but couldn't quite pull it off.

This 2003 team, although playing two freshmen and two sophomore starters, had a superstar in Carmelo Anthony and, again, good team chemistry. Syracuse successfully completed an exhausting sprint through the NCAA Tournament. The big difference, though, was the end result. For Syracuse, three was not a charm, but four was. The Orange was able to cut down the nets on its fourth trip to the Final Four. "Winning is always big. Don't let anybody tell you winning isn't big," Boeheim stated. "It's big."

Counting when he was an assistant in 1975, Boeheim coached Syracuse to Final Fours in four different decades, which was no small feat. Although he had taken SU to numerous NCAA tournaments and periodically reached the Final Four and even the national championship game, prior to 2003 Boeheim was the Susan Lucci of coaching, like the soap opera star, always leaving without the top trophy. No more, not this time!

With all due respect to the Syracuse lacrosse dynasty and its record eleven national championships in the modern era, in terms of significance, the basketball victory over Kansas placed the SU sports program on a pedestal that it had not experienced since the 1959 football team won the national championship by defeating Texas. In terms of national exposure, there was no comparison, however. In 1959, there were only three television networks, which were in black-and-white, and there was very little hype. The Cotton Bowl had to share the television audience with the other bowl games playing that day. With the 2003 NCAA basketball tournament, there was seemingly never-ending media coverage, and the excitement and hoopla continued to build up over the course of about three weeks to and through the Final Four. In the finals, Syracuse had pretty much the world's sports stage all to itself. For a one-day winner-take-all event, arguably only the Super Bowl was bigger.

The following year Boeheim, reflecting on Anthony with affection and appreciation for carrying him and his team to the national title, emphatically stated, "Carmelo Anthony was by far the best player in college basketball. It wasn't even close."

Syracuse fans, as they did when Billy Owens departed prior to his senior season, were again left wondering how good the Orange could have been had Anthony, defying economic logic, stayed another one, two, or three years. Boeheim knew what he had, having said on several occasions that a player like Carmelo only comes along once in a coach's lifetime.

Anthony led Syracuse in scoring (22.1 points per game) and rebounding (10 rebounds per game). Despite the fact that he was a freshman, his 778 points is the third highest single-season total in school history. He earned a Big East Rookie of the Week record ten times, joined former Orange star Pearl Washington as the only freshmen to make the Big East first team, captured National Freshman of the Year honors, and was an Associated Press second-team All-American. With a smile appropriate for a toothpaste commercial, matched only by Syracuse football great Donavan McNabb and later star guard Jonny Flynn, Melo had the same effect on his teammates that Bing did years before. When he got the ball, he was frequently double-teamed, and that left other players open to whom he passed the ball for easy baskets. Having helped Syracuse win the national championship, and with his basketball stock soaring and feeling there was little left to accomplish at the collegiate level, Anthony, with Boeheim's blessing, opted for the NBA draft. He was the third pick.

Playing for the Denver Nuggets, Anthony made the NBA All-Rookie Team and finished runner-up to LeBron James for Rookie of the Year. After playing professionally for a couple of years, Anthony donated $3 million to his alma mater to help fund the $19 million, 54,000-square foot Carmelo K. Anthony Basketball Center, a state-of-the-art practice facility for men's and women's basketball that had its ribbon-cutting ceremony September 24, 2009, and its official dedication on October 3. Boeheim's oversized and memorabilia-filled office is on the second floor of the building and overlooks two full-size basketball courts. Next to the courts are a well-stocked weight room and a training room that has a whirlpool and various therapeutic pools. There is also a spacious locker room, team meeting room, film room, academic center, and players' lounge. Another attraction is a Hall of Fame that honors Syracuse's basketball legends. The NCAA championship trophy is prominently on display, as are five large banners that recognize SU's four Final Four teams. Numerous trophies and pictures of former Orange greats remind visitors of the program's past successes.

Anthony's donation is the largest single donation made to the SU athletic department and thought to be one of the largest individual donations made by any current professional athlete to his alma mater. The facility enabled Syracuse to continue to attract and entice blue-chip recruits. Boeheim not only greatly appreciated Melo's many contributions on the court but his philanthropy as well.

In 2011, Melo, the best pure scoring small forward in the league, agreed to be traded to the New York Knicks. With Madison Square Garden now his stage, Melo immediately captured New York City's fancy. Shortly after being obtained by the Knicks, two huge billboards featuring Anthony went up in the Times Square area of Manhattan: a Jordan Brand billboard on the Southwestern corner of 34th Street and 7th Avenue, one block from the Garden, and then a giant 128-foot billboard on the corner of 33rd and 9th, just a couple of blocks from the famed arena in the middle of one of the busiest neighborhoods in the world. Then on June 26, 2012, a life-size wax likeness of Anthony was unveiled at the Madame Tussauds New York Museum. Wearing his white No. 7 home New York uniform, Melo is poised to shoot a free throw. Melo joined other wax celebrities in the museum's SportZone alongside other New York City sports heroes such as the Yankees' Derek Jeter, the Mets' David Wright, and the Giants' Eli Manning, while also near President and Mrs. Barack Obama, movie stars George Clooney and Whoopi Goldberg, and basketball icon Michael Jordan.

In 2013, Anthony, with his contract up, had the option to leave the Knicks. The Melo Watch was again in full vogue. The nation was captivated as several cities invited Anthony to visit and consider playing for their hometown teams. Los Angeles, Chicago, Houston, and Miami all gave Anthony the star treatment and showered him with affection in the hopes of enticing him to play for their team. In the end, Anthony opted to stay in New York where he finished as the league scoring champion. Also in 2013, Syracuse retired Melo's No. 15 jersey. In June 2016, ESPN listed Anthony as the 29th most famous current athlete in the world. He was among nine US athletes named, and just the fourth basketball player, behind LeBron James, Kevin Durant, and Kobe Bryant.

In 2018, Anthony was in his 16th season in the NBA where he averaged per game 24.8 points, 6.6 rebounds, and 3.1 assists en route to making ten All-Star teams, an all-time SU high. During his career, he became the second-youngest player in NBA history to score 30 points in a game, trailing only Kobe Bryant, and the second youngest to score 40 points in a game, behind only LeBron James, who beat him by three days. Anthony was the third youngest NBA player to score 2,000 points, again following Bryant and James, and he was the second youngest to tally 5,000 points, after James. On January 24, 2014, Melo shattered the New York Knicks' franchise and current Madison Square Garden scoring record with a 62-point performance against Charlotte. Prior to the 2017–18 season, Anthony was traded to the Oklahoma City Thunder. Anthony finished the season with 25,417 career points, which is 19th in NBA history. He is one of only six players to score 24,000 points, grab 6,000 rebounds, have 2,500 assists, 1,000 steals, and make 1,000 three-point field goals. During the summer Anthony was traded to the Atlanta Hawks. The Hawks then made Anthony a free agent and he chose to sign with the Houston Rockets.

On March 10, 2017, Marnie Eisenstadt at Syracuse.com reported that Ryan Homes was building a new housing development in Clay, just north of Syracuse, with the street names honoring players from the national championship team. The first streets named in "Orange Commons" were Melo Circle, McNamara Drive, Duany Avenue, and Pace Lane. Chris Baker, a public policy reporter for Syracuse.com and an SU grad, facetiously responded, "I'm assuming they were going to add a Warrick Way, but it got blocked at the last second." In jest, commenter Orangeinindy wrote, "Warrick Way is only a block away." Tucsondave, yet another reader, quipped, "In a show of good sportsmanship, Route 31 [which runs past the development] will be renamed Keith Smart Freeway."

2003–04

In 2003–04, the defending national champions started out with a belly flop, losing to Charlotte. It was a rarity for Syracuse to lose its first game of the season, but the Cuse also did just that the year before when it made its title run. SU then rebounded to win 13 consecutive contests, including nifty non-conference victories over Michigan State and Missouri before suffering back-to-back setbacks to Seton Hall and nemesis Pittsburgh. Syracuse went 8–3 in league play the rest of the way to finish 11–5, splitting games with Connecticut and getting a payback win over Pittsburgh. A highlight came on February 29 at Georgetown when McNamara bagged a three-pointer at the buzzer to beat the Hoyas.

In the first round of the Big East tournament, Boston College defeated the Orange, 57–54. Syracuse came back to beat BYU and Maryland in the NCAA Phoenix Regional, but Alabama pulled the curtain on Syracuse's season, 80–71.

In between seasons, Syracuse officially changed its nickname from the Orangemen to the Orange, a move that didn't resonate well with a lot of fans. Years earlier, giving way to political correctness, Syracuse discarded its mascot, the "Saltine Warrior," and created "Otto," a cute Orange caricature, which also didn't play well with the SU following.

2004–05

Led by returning stars Warrick and McNamara, Syracuse started the 2004–05 season ranked No. 4 in the AP and ESPN/*USA Today* coaches' polls. Ignited by the "Hack and Mac Attack," the Cuse opened by winning the Coaches vs. Cancer Classic, steamrolling Northern Colorado and Princeton in the Carrier Dome, and Mississippi State and Memphis in Madison Square Garden. A couple of weeks later, the Orange was back in New York for a marquee match-up against No. 5 Oklahoma State in the Jimmy V Classic. The Cowboys ended Syracuse's seven-game winning streak, 74–60. SU won 13 more games before Pittsburgh stuck it to the Orange again, 76–69. For the second consecutive year, Syracuse went 11–5 in the Big East. They then beat Rutgers, UConn, and West Virginia to win the Big East tournament but suffered a first-round loss to Vermont, 60–57. With a 27–7 record, the embarrassing loss to the Catamounts was a sad ending to what otherwise could have been a very good year.

2005–06

The Big East underwent another sea change in 2005–06. In a football-first move, Miami, Virginia Tech, and Boston College bolted for the Atlantic Coast Conference, with the Big East countering by adding Louisville, Cincinnati, Marquette, DePaul, and South Florida. With all of the newcomers, sans South Florida, having reached the Final Four since the formation of the conference in 1979, the additions enhanced the basketball reputation of the league, making it arguably the strongest hoops group in the country.

The Orange tapped off the 2005–06 campaign by hosting the first stage of the 2K Sports College Hoops Classic. After taking care of a couple of soft touches, Bethune-Cookman and Cornell, it was on to New York for stage two, where Syracuse stomped Texas Tech, 81–46, but fell to Florida, 75–70, and Bucknell, 75–69. Losing to the Gators was acceptable, but falling to the Bisons was not. Then with a 3–2 mark, Syracuse raced to 12 wins in a row before running into a brick wall. The 20th-ranked Orange was crushed by No. 3 Connecticut, No. 8 Villanova, No. 12 Pittsburgh, and Seton Hall. The Cuse recovered to beat Rutgers in overtime, 86–84, but quickly took it on the chin again, losing for a second time to UConn. Dropping four of its last seven conference games, Syracuse limped to the conclusion of its regular schedule, burdened with a losing record (7–9) in league play for only the second time in Boeheim's career.

The 2005–06 season will always be remembered for Gerry McNamara's great performance in the Big East tournament, as well as for Boeheim's tirade against some conference assistant coaches who downplayed the value of his star guard and the Syracuse papers for reporting it. In the first round game, Cincinnati's James White made a jump shot that gave the Bearcats a 73–71 lead with only a few ticks of the clock remaining that ripped the heart out of the Orange, only to have McNamara perform a transplant when he drove the length of the court and hit a running, one-hand three-point shot with less than a second to play to give the Orange a riveting 74–73 win. Boeheim started his postgame press conference on the McNamara topic calmly enough. He warmed up saying, "Gerry has been very consistent for us all year and throughout his whole career. I have to laugh a little bit when our own local paper and our student newspaper called Gerry McNamara overrated. And they actually listened to a couple of assistant coaches in our league, who I guarantee you will never become head coaches if they think Gerry McNamara is overrated." Then, with his voice rising and becoming as steamed as a cooked lobster and his eyeballs starting to bulge, Boeheim got pissed off and stated: "Without Gerry McNamara, we wouldn't have won ten f--king games this year! OK, not ten! These other guys just aren't ready. They needed him. Without him, not ten!

"Without Gerry McNamara, we wouldn't even be here to have a chance to play this game. Everybody's been talking to me and writing about Gerry McNamara being overrated. That's the most bullshit thing I've seen in thirty years! And especially when it comes from our own people and our own paper. He's been double-teamed all year. The head coaches in our league voted him first-team All-Conference, but the head coaches don't know shit I guess." Regaining his composure, Boeheim turned his head, smiled, and said to a pressroom attendant, "Now, am I going to get fined for that?"

Gerry McNamara

Not as good as Bing, Pearl, Melo, and some other SU superstars, McNamara was in his own way a very special player at Syracuse who deserved all the accolades that he got for what he did for the program. One of the most beloved players in school history, "G-Mac," as he was affectionately called, started every one of the 135 games he played for the Orange over the course of his four-year career. While Anthony did just about everything in his one glory year, and for that he will be forever revered in SU annals, McNamara also contributed so much, so consistently, for so long, and in such clutch situations that he too will forever be endeared in the hearts of SU fans.

McNamara had the statistics for sure—finishing fourth in school history in points (2,099), second in steals (258), third in assists (648), first in three-point shots made (400, which is sixth-best in the NCAA) and attempts (1,131), and first in free-throw percentage (91 percent). He also played in 63 Big East conference games, establishing the mark for three-point shots made (183) and career free-throw percentage (91.7 percent).

And then there are the honors and awards. In his first year, McNamara made the Big East All-Rookie team and closed out his collegiate career by winning the Chip Hilton Player of the Year Award, given by the Naismith Memorial Basketball Hall of Fame to a senior Division I player who demonstrates character, leadership, and talent. An AP honorable mention All-American, McNamara was considered for the Bob Cousy Award, which is given to the nation's top point guard.

However, G-Mac also had numerous spectacular moments for which he will be fondly remembered. In addition to his role in the national championship win over Kansas, in February of his freshman year, he nailed a three-point shot that beat No. 17 Notre Dame, 82–80, a basket he later called his biggest of the season. In March of the same year, he scored 22 points, including 10 in overtime, to help defeat Georgetown, 93–84. In the NCAA tournament, he made a school-record nine three-pointers, which was part of a career-high 43-point performance in a first-round victory over BYU. As a sophomore, he poured in 36 points against Davidson, the second-most points tallied by a Syracuse player in the Carrier Dome. As a senior, he took over the Big East tournament and, by his performance and mental toughness, willed the underdog Orange to four wins in four days to capture the title, up to that point an unprecedented feat.

The entire tournament was a G-Mac highlight reel, beginning with McNamara's last-second three-ball that beat the Bearcats and provided Boeheim with up-to-the-minute ammunition to blast anyone he thought was dumb enough to say that McNamara was overrated. The following night, G-Mac drilled a three-pointer in the closing seconds of regulation to knot the score against No. 1-ranked Connecticut that sent the contest into overtime. McNamara contributed 17 points and 13 assists, one shy of the Big East tournament record, in the Cuse's upset of the Huskies, the last time that Boeheim beat the top-ranked team in the nation. In the semifinals against Georgetown, G-Mac made five three-pointers in the second half, including one in the last minute of the game to whittle the Hoyas' lead to a single point, 57–56. As a sequel, with the game winding down, he got off a bounce pass to Eric Devendorf for the basket with 9.3 seconds left that put SU in front and then created a turnover to put the game on ice. G-Mac's 14-point, six-assist effort helped Syracuse defeat Pittsburgh, 65–61, and win what for all intents and purposes had become the "Gerry McNamara Invitational." For his heroics, McNamara was voted tournament MVP. When he accepted the David Gavitt Award, he wore a T-shirt with "Overrated" written on it. The entire tournament was a series of "Syracuse moments."

What Gerry McNamara had, beyond the statistics and accolades, was charisma. His status as a cult figure began when he was in middle school back in Scranton, a town with a population of about 75,000 in Northeastern Pennsylvania. The son of postal workers, McNamara grew up on West Market Street and fit in nicely in a city heavily populated with people of Irish descent. His deadeye shooting, willingness to pull the trigger on a long shot with the outcome of a contest on the line, and the all-out way he played the game made him a fan favorite at a young age. While still in high school, he was the talk of the town—in the local pubs, marketplaces, and anywhere two or more sports-minded people gathered. His penchant for making game-winning shots made him a hometown hero. His growing fame attracted followers like bees are attracted to honey. After graduating from Bishop Hannan High School, busloads of people from Scranton made the two-hour, 130-mile trip to Syracuse to see Gerry play, and G-Mac usually came through, making the return ride home a joyous one. While he remained the favorite son of Scranton, he also became the adopted son of Syracuse.

On Senior Day on March 5, 2006, in his final home game, McNamara was primarily responsible for attracting the first-ever advance sellout for a basketball game in the Carrier Dome. Included in the capacity crowd of 33,633 were a reported 3,000 Scrantonians who came to Syracuse in a string of cars and in six buses. G-Mac scored 29 points in his Dome finale, but it wasn't enough as the Orange lost to Villanova in front of what was at the time an NCAA record on-campus crowd for a regular season basketball game. Except for the final score, it was a farewell for the ages and would have been a great ending to a storybook career for someone who probably is the only player in the history of college basketball to have such a loyal, traveling fan base.

In his final college game, a 66–58 first round loss to Texas A&M in the NCAA tournament, he suited up but barely played. Being fiercely competitive didn't mean G-Mac was made of iron. Suffering from a severely strained groin injury, McNamara only played twenty-three minutes and only scored two points in the only game of his college career where he was held without a field goal. When he was on a roll, Gerry McNamara was money. Unfortunately, in his last college game, G-Mac was more or less relegated to the role of spectator as he helplessly watched his teammates get eliminated from postseason play.

Whereas Carmelo Anthony was wondrous, he was in town for less than a year. G-Mac was around for four years, and his legend grew each season. Because of what he uniquely brought to Syracuse, McNamara left a lasting legacy. For many people, because of his hard-hat, lunch-bucket mentality and his uncanny ability to light it up when it counted the most, G-Mac remains their favorite player. McNamara, after a few years in the lower levels of professional basketball, returned to his alma mater as a graduate assistant coach. In 2011, McNamara was promoted to full-time assistant. Many people feel he is being groomed to one day become the coach at Syracuse.

2006–07

If 1987 is remembered for the Keith Smart shot, 1996 for SU's second run to the NCAA Finals, 2003 for the national championship, 2006 as the year G-Mac dominated the Big East tournament, then the 2006–07 season is remembered by Syracuse fans as the year that the Orange got snubbed by the NCAA Tournament Committee. Despite a 24–11 record—10–6 in the Big East—and having finished strong by winning five of its last six games and seven of its last 10, including a 14-point victory over No. 9 Georgetown that snapped the Hoyas' 11-game winning streak, the Orange was left hanging by the NCAA tournament selection committee. The committee was chaired by Princeton athletic director Gary Walters, who, rest assured, is not on Jim Boeheim's Christmas card list.

In 2006–07, for only the sixth time in Boeheim's 31-year reign at SU, the Orange did not make the NCAA tournament. Losses in the eighth game to Wichita State in Buffalo and in the twelfth game to Drexel at home came back to bite the Orange. While both the Shockers and Dragons were ranked teams when they played Syracuse, SU was expected to beat both, but they didn't beat either. To make matters worse, Syracuse had a three-game losing streak in January, lost its last regular season game and then got bopped from the Big East tournament in the second round by Notre Dame. Regardless, Boeheim empathetically pointed out that his team had tied for fifth place in a strong BCS conference and finished strong by winning eight of its last 11 games, something he said other teams, such as Stanford, which only had an 18–12 record and lost four of its last five games and seven of its last 11, failed to do. He noted that Villanova, with a 9–7 Big East record, got in. "If you finish fifth in the Big East and don't make the tournament, something's wrong," he protested. "We had four league road wins and beat the best team in our conference by 14 points late in the year."

Boeheim was not a happy camper and let everyone know it, in no uncertain terms. He was everywhere, voicing his opinion to anyone who would listen and give him airtime. "This is the biggest shock of all time," he declared loudly and clearly as he expressed his dissatisfaction on the post-selection show, on ESPN, Fox Sports, ESPN News, and on numerous national and local radio shows. "I can't believe it. If we were on the bubble, I would see it, but we weren't on the bubble. If Gary Walters thinks we're not one of the thirty-four best at-large teams, then he's crazy," stated Boeheim, who wondered out loud if Walters and his group knew that the ball was round.

Not quite as boisterous as Bobby Knight would have reacted if he felt his team was slighted, Boeheim nonetheless was certainly no wallflower on this issue. Always one to speak his mind, for better or worse, the man should be credited for sticking up for his team. Immediately "We Got Screwed" T-shirts became a popular item in upstate New York.

Left out of the Big Dance, Syracuse landed in the NIT. By then, it was no longer the NIT of the mid-1960s. It was mocked by some as the "Not Invited Tournament," the "National Insignificant Tournament," and the "Little Dance." Regardless, rather than sulk like the 1996–97 SU NIT team that bombed badly at home against Florida State, Syracuse, seeking some balm to sooth its Selection Sunday sore spot, embraced the opportunity to play on. Its first opponent was South Alabama. The Orange faithful, just as angry and distraught as their coach, in a demonstration of support for their team and in reaction to the NCAA's decision, showed up 16,832 strong and loud in the Carrier Dome to watch the Cuse slay the Jaguars. And that was while the students were on break. In the second game against San Diego State, more came, and they were even louder, as an NIT-record crowd of 26,572 cheered the Orange to an 80–64 victory over the Aztecs. The Syracuse fans made their point. Boeheim thanked the fans for their vocal show of support, saying it was better than in some games during the season.

The third game was at Clemson, with the Tigers winning, 74–70. Lost in all the hoopla was the fact that Boeheim had coached in his 1,000th game, a 70–53 win over South Florida on January 25. In doing so, he joined Bobby Knight, Lute Olson, Jim Calhoun, and Mike Krzyzewski as the only coaches to accomplish that feat. The accomplishment represents more than simply longevity. To last that long in a profession characterized by what-have-you-done-for-me-lately attitudes, a coach has got to be successful year in and year out.

2007–08

The following year it was back to the NIT, not once but twice. Invited to the NIT Season Tip-Off, Syracuse, as expected, beat Siena and Saint Joseph's at home. The team then traveled to New York for the continuation of the tourney where they were beaten by Ohio State but defeated Washington. With a 21–14 mark and only winning half of its conference games plus getting hammered by Villanova in the first game of the conference tournament, Syracuse participated in its second straight NIT, the first time it had done so since the 1981–82 season. However, this time the Orange didn't have much of a leg to stand on, and there was no beef from Boeheim. Syracuse swallowed its poison and responded with wins over Robert Morris and Maryland before UMass showed Syracuse the exit door.

2008–09

Having had its fill of the NIT, Syracuse was back in the NCAA Tournament in 2009. With 28 wins and an 11–7 record in the league, there was no anxiety or bubble-wait on Selection Sunday. Whereas bad losses to Drexel and Wichita State hurt them the year before, impressive quality wins over Florida, Kansas, Virginia, and Memphis left no doubt of SU being NCAA tournament-worthy this time around. It was just a matter of where SU would be seated, who they would play in the first game, and where they would play the first round. After losing in the finals of the Big East tournament to Louisville, Syracuse was sent to the South Region where it won its first two NCAA games against Stephen F. Austin State and Arizona State before Oklahoma pulled the plug on the season.

Six-Overtime Win Over Connecticut

The 2008–09 season was highlighted by the Orange's six-overtime win over Connecticut in the quarterfinals of the Big East tournament in the second-longest game in NCAA history. Syracuse started out by beating Seton Hall in the first round, 89–74. Waiting for SU was the well-rested Connecticut Huskies, who had benefited from having received a bye. The Syracuse-Connecticut game was hard fought throughout and concluded regulation play at midnight with the teams tied, 71–71. The drama began when Eric Devendorf hauled in a long pass from Paul Harris and nailed a long three-pointer as time expired. The improbable ending appeared to give the underdog Orange, ranked No. 18 in the AP poll, an upset over the No. 3 Huskies. Instant replay, however, showed that the ball was touching Devo's fingertips just as the game clock struck zero, negating what would have been a highlight shot and a memorable ending all on its own. You can't find a closer call than that. What transpired after that, though, was what would be an epic game for the ages as the two teams played on, and on, and on, and on, and on, and on. Never ahead in any of the overtime sessions, the undermanned but gritty and gutsy Orange stayed with, wore down, and outlasted the Huskies. The marathon in Madison Square Garden had a tip-off on March 21 at 9:36 p.m. and didn't end until 1:30 a.m. on March 22, three hours and forty-six minutes later, when the depleted and exhausted Orange, out of gas and playing on fumes, not only survived but won, 127–117.

Syracuse fans were glued to their televisions throughout the lengthy war of wills, including alumnus and nationally-known sportscaster Bob Costas who was with his wife in Hawaii celebrating their wedding anniversary. Being six hours behind, it was mid-afternoon in Honolulu. Costas and his wife had planned to watch the game at the motel and had timed their reservations at a seaside restaurant so they could eat a nice meal and watch the beautiful sunset. When the game went into overtime, Costas called the restaurant and requested that the reservations be pushed back a little. When the game kept getting extended, Costas kept calling the restaurant to push back their reservations further.

"By the third overtime, I told my wife, 'We'll still see the sunset, just during dessert,'" he related. But the game continued. When the game finally ended, Costas told his wife, "Hey, this is my alma mater, and a six-overtime game occurs once in a lifetime. The sun sets every day. We'll just celebrate tomorrow and pretend that it's our anniversary."

For SU fans that watched it on television back home and had to get up early to go to work the next day, it was sleepless in Syracuse.

Syracuse lacked the depth to begin with. Going into the fourth quarter, with Arinze Onuaku, Rick Jackson, and Kristof Ongenaet having fouled out, the Orange seemed in big trouble. Then in the fifth overtime, Devendorf fouled out. Severely undermanned and undersized, the Cuse dug deeper and captured the hearts of the nation who stayed up until the wee hours of the morning to watch the conclusion of the historic event. It was a game that saw four players on each team foul out and Syracuse finish the contest with a walk-on player. Justin Thomas, who had only seen 23 minutes of action the entire season, was forced to play seven minutes in the pressure-cooker situation. Jonny Flynn, who played 67 of the 70 minutes in an iron-man performance, scored a game-high 34 points, including 16 of 16 free throws. He also dished out 11 assists and had six steals and three rebounds. Paul Harris had 29 points and 22 rebounds. Devendorf put up 22 points. Speaking at the postgame press conference, Flynn stated, "I can't even feel my legs right now."

In sold-out Madison Square Garden, the most famous sports arena in the country, and in front of a full house of 19,375, it would be called The Most Memorable Game of the 2008–09 college basketball season by *The Sporting News* and the No. 1 Greatest Moment of the Decade by ESPN. The all-sports network showed the game on the day it ended as part of its sports classics series, making the game an instant classic. For those who stayed up to watch the finish, it was worth every minute of lost sleep. That didn't include the President of the United States, however, as Barack Obama said he needed to go to bed. He said that he did watch the highlights the next day on *SportsCenter*.

Immediately after the game, an unidentified writer for AllKYHoops. com penned: "Yes, I realize that this is Bluegrass Basketball State basketball, but occasionally, something happens that just deserves respect. Tonight was one of those occasions. I just watched perhaps the greatest college basketball game of all time. Syracuse defeated Connecticut 127–117 in six overtimes. That's right, six overtimes! All I can say is WOW!" Quite a statement, especially from someone who lives where basketball is king.

The late Jim O'Connell, a Hall of Fame writer for the Associated Press, told Pete Thamel of the *New York Times* that the game was the best that he had ever seen in the 574 games that he had covered at Madison Square Garden. "I've got no words," stated Boeheim after the marathon win in the city that never sleeps. "I've never been any prouder of a team that I coached. It was just two teams going at it. An unbelievable effort by both teams. History [was made] tonight." Connecticut coach Jim Calhoun couldn't appreciate the significance of the game at the moment. "I'm sure in the summertime I'll look back at what a historic battle it was," he said. "Right now, it's just a loss." Big East commissioner Mike Tranghese, who had witnessed all thirty conference tournaments, simply stated, "This is the best ever." It was the second-longest college basketball game in NCAA history, just short of the seven-overtime affair that saw Cincinnati beat Bradley, 75–73, on December 21, 1981. Shortly after the Cuse win, T-shirts were produced that on the front stated "Syracuse Marathon Men" and on the back had "244 points, 226 minutes, 6 overtimes, 2 days, 1 for the ages." It became the highest-selling T-shirt in Syracuse history. Another "Syracuse moment!" In this case, a "Syracuse 3 3/4 Hours!" For sports fans who could stay awake, the spotlight was squarely on Syracuse. For sure, everybody got his moneys worth.

Just ten hours later, Syracuse had to suit up again to play West Virginia. Despite very little sleep, tired legs, and weary bodies, in another magnificent show of courage and stamina, the Orange, in another overtime game, gallantly outfought the Mountaineers, 74–69. The Cuse had played two regulation games plus seven overtime periods over the course of two days. With no rest for the weary, Syracuse faced a Louisville team that applied relentless pressure in the finals. After leading at the half by eight but with nothing left in the tank, Syracuse subdued to Rick Pitino and the Cardinals, 76–66. Nonetheless, it was a gutsy effort by the boys from Syracuse. With their feel-good performance, they had won over the hearts of television viewers across the country that were pulling for SU to spring another upset.

After that game, Boeheim seemingly put pressure on himself and his team by stating, "Five years from now there is going to be two things that people remember from this Syracuse team and only two things. The UConn–Syracuse game, and what we do in the [upcoming] NCAA Tournament." For Syracuse, the good news was, after a two-year drought, the Orange would be dancing again.

Years ago while at Virginia Commonwealth University, Oklahoma coach Jeff Capel purchased Boeheim's video *Complete Guide to the 2–3 Zone*. No doubt it helped him dissect SU's fabled defense because Oklahoma ousted the Orange from the NCAA Tournament. The 84–71 loss to the Sooners was a disappointing ending, but it didn't take away the exhilaration that Syracuse fans received from the team's six-overtime victory over Connecticut, which, along with the other aforementioned "Syracuse moments," became a part of Syracuse basketball folklore. The overtime win over West Virginia that followed that same day just added to the legend. The season-ending loss to Oklahoma also left Boeheim stalled at 799 wins and having to wait seven long months for the next milestone victory.

2009–10

On November 3, 2009, Syracuse elected a new mayor, but as Brent Axe of Syracuse.com wrote, "The biggest story in the Salt City came from an exhibition basketball game." Le Moyne College, a Division II Jesuit school of 2,300 students, shocked preseason No. 25-ranked Syracuse, 82–79, when Christopher Johnson splashed a three-point shot with 8.3 seconds to go that deflated the Orange. Even though the mega-upset came in an exhibition game, one that SU won by an average of 42 points the previous two seasons, Le Moyne's win became the lead story on ESPN's *SportsCenter* where it continued to loop seemingly forever to the delight of Dolphins fans and chagrin of

SU followers. The unlikely victory set off an unparalleled publicity blitz that paid dividends to the small private school well beyond the $15,000 it received to take what usually is a whooping from the basketball power that sits a few miles crosstown. The benefits included an immediate boost in interest, national recognition, and applications. It was a dream win for the Dolphins and a nightmare for the Orange.

Le Moyne coach Steve Evans told Donna Ditota of the *Syracuse Post-Standard,* "They've got McDonald's All-Americans, and we've got guys who buy Happy Meals at McDonald's." David did slay Goliath on that evening, and Le Moyne got its fifteen minutes of fame, but the Dolphins were brought back to earth in a hurry when shortly thereafter they lost to Pace University. With the clock winding down, the Pace student section chanted, "We want Syracuse, We want Syracuse." Le Moyne, a respectable Division II program, went on to finish 18–10 that season and 14–8 in the Northeast-10, a league that includes Bentley, Merrimack, Stonehill, and similar schools. Given a wake-up call, Syracuse got off to a 24–1 start en route to a 30–5 overall record and 15–3 in the Big East. So much for exhibition games.

Much more significant about that loss, however, was that Syracuse played man-to-man defense the entire game, except on the last play when it switched to zone in a futile attempt to win. The Dolphins repeatedly dissected the man defense with drives and cuts as they matched the Cuse basket-for-basket. Maybe Boeheim was trying to prove a point to the fans that relentlessly voiced their displeasure for his exclusive use of the zone. Whether that's true or not, Boeheim did state in his book, *Bleeding Orange,* that after that game, "I decided that we were a zone team and that I was a zone coach. Period. It was probably the best decision I ever made."

Jumping ahead to the five-year anniversary of the win, Le Moyne had a promotion where "Miracle Men" T-shirts that included the score were given away free in exchange of an old school shirt. Evans said, "I'll forever be known as the coach who won that game that doesn't count."

Syracuse started the season at the bottom of the rankings and clawed its way to No. 1. With its trademark 2–3 zone defense again being the difference and with a mantra of "Shut it Down," Syracuse won the Big East championship and finished 30–5 and ranked No. 4 in the final Associated Press poll.

Rewinding a bit, on November 9 in the first game of the year, Boeheim got his 800th win, a 75–43 victory over Albany, to become the eighth coach to reach that plateau and the fourth-fastest to do so. After the game, standing at the center of the court named after him, Boeheim showed his appreciation by saying, "I'd like to thank all the fans that make this the best place in the country to play basketball." The Le Moyne loss was forgotten, at least for the moment. Everything was again going well in Jimmieland.

Although the win total put Boeheim on a stratospheric level where only seven other coaches resided, detractors cutely said that he had compiled many of those victories by feasting on the "ABCs" of New York State— Albany, Buffalo, and Colgate. When Syracuse scheduled such teams and, depending on the year, others such as Siena, Binghamton, Morgan State, Iona, and Northern Iowa, it's safe to say that preseason pickers could pencil in, or more accurately darken with a bold magic marker, a "W" in the Syracuse win column, though upsets can and do happen and not just in the NCAA tournament where they are magnified.

Nothing new or different about that strategy. Almost all big boy basketball schools scheduled so-called pre-conference "cupcakes." And they did it every year. The 2010–11 Kansas schedule included the likes of Washburn, Emporia State, Longwood, Valparaiso, Northern Texas, Texas-Corpus Christi, and Ohio University, none of which are household basketball names by any stretch of the imagination. Indiana's 2010–11 slate was sprinkled with Florida Gulf Coast, Wright State, Mississippi Valley State, Evansville, North Carolina Central, Northwestern State, Savannah State, Southern Illinois–Edwardsville, South Carolina State, and Northern Iowa, none of which should strike fear in the eyes of the Hoosiers. North Carolina loaded up with Lipscomb, Hofstra, UNC–Asheville, the College of Charleston,

Evansville, Long Beach State, William & Mary, and St. Francis (PA), none of which regularly resides in the Top 25. Duke padded its record with Princeton, Miami (OH), Colgate, Bradley, St. Louis, Elon, UNC–Greensboro, and UA–Birmingham, none of which are regulars in the NCAA tournament. The Kentucky Wildcats gobbled up East Tennessee State, Portland, Boston University, Mississippi Valley State, Winthrop, and Coppin State. Ohio State warmed up with North Carolina A&T, Indiana University of Pennsylvania, Western Carolina, Florida Gulf Coast, and UT-Martin. Arizona piled up wins against Idaho State, Northern Colorado, Bethune-Cookman, Santa Clara, Cal State, Fullerton, and Robert Morris. The year before, for example, 'Zona feasted on Seattle Pacific, Humboldt State, Valparaiso, Duquesne, Ball State, Northern Arizona, Oakland, and Bryant. And skipping around, in 2015, Louisville entertained Samford, Northern Florida, Hartford, St. Francis, Grand Canyon, Eastern Michigan, Kennesaw State, Utah Valley, and University of Missouri-Kansas City. Not a world-beater in that bunch. That kind of scheduling happened every year, and certainly not just at Syracuse.

Boeheim-haters also brought up that Syracuse never left the state before the New Year began, conveniently failing to acknowledge that Duke, Kansas, and many other top programs also pretty much played all of their pre-conference games instate, at home, or relatively close to their campuses. Boeheim stocking his schedule with home games was nothing out of the ordinary, according to Roy Danforth, his predecessor at Syracuse. "Adolph Rupp started that," he stated, referring to the "Baron of the Bluegrass" who ruled the roost when he was at Kentucky. "Rupp never played a lot of [non-conference] road games."

Some national cynics, disregarding neutral-site games, even extended their complaint about Syracuse's preseason schedule to the tri-state area. They referred to games not only in New York City but in New Jersey or surrounding states such as Pennsylvania and Connecticut as "home" games for the Orange, even though New York City, Atlantic City, and venues close to the Main Line are anywhere from 200 to 275 miles from the Carrier Dome. And when Syracuse plays in New York City, UConn is a lot closer to Madison Square Garden than Syracuse.

Asked by Brent Axe on his local radio show during the 2010-11 season if the away game issue bothered him, Boeheim laughed and said, "I don't even think about that anymore. Every team does that. Most teams don't play true road games. Most teams at this stage of the year only play a couple of true road games. They play neutral court games. It's nonsense.

"Georgetown won three of the toughest road games in the country this year. They won at Missouri, at Old Dominion where it's almost impossible to win, and they won at Memphis, and they've [already] lost four games in our league. The fact that you've won tough non-conference games does not mean that you're going to win in the Big East, as we've seen. They don't relate. If you're a good team and you've won 18 games in a row at home and then you play on the road, you'll win. If you're not a good team, you'll lose. It's as simple as that."

In the May 21, 2014, *Syracuse Post-Standard*, beat writer Donna Ditota interviewed Renee Baumgartner and Kip Wellman, two people who worked on the basketball schedule. They explained the factors and variables that go into developing SU's schedule. Being a power program, Syracuse, like other schools on its level, is in the envious position of picking and choosing its non-conference opponents because most other schools, especially mid-majors, relish the chance to play the Orange in the Carrier Dome. For the non-league portion of the schedule, Baumgartner and Wellman researched databases for teams needing games and analyzed the RPIs of those teams, looking for the proper balance and strength of competition that would enhance Syracuse's chances of being successful and making it into the NCAA Tournament, which is the goal of almost all teams. The Syracuse philosophy was to typically schedule five or six "buy-out" games from the fifty or so requests it annually received from lower-echelon programs seeking big-time opponents. Sometimes it depended upon if Syracuse wanted a buy-out game against a team ranked 100 to 200 in the RPI versus a home-and-home series with another top program. Rivalry games were considered. Syracuse also wanted one game a year in New York City. Non-conference games, of course, had to be mutually agreed upon and had to fit into each team's schedule. After everything was taken into consideration, Boeheim looked at and approved the schedule. It is pretty much the modus operandi of schools of Syracuse's tier.

In late June of 2011, ESPN's Joe Lunardi analyzed the strength of schedule of teams throughout the country during the preceding four years and not only determined that Syracuse did not play a weak non-conference schedule but, contrary to the beliefs of Boeheim's critics, played the seventh most difficult non-conference schedule in the nation. In recent years, Syracuse continued to play tough opponents, with its 2017–18 non-conference schedule ranked the 14th toughest in the nation and its overall schedule the 18th most difficult. Furthermore, against the top programs in the nation over the years compiled through 2018, Boeheim held his own. His won-lost record: Michigan State (6–1), Indiana (5–1), Florida (4–1), Kansas (3–2), Arizona (2–1), North Carolina State (7–4), Michigan (4–4), Duke (4–5), Kentucky (3–5), North Carolina (3–10), Gonzaga (2–0), Purdue (3–0), and UCLA (1–1). Likewise when facing his most frequent opponents: UConn (42–34), Georgetown (39–37), Villanova (37–33), Notre Dame (26–14), Pittsburgh (44–28), and Louisville (9–14).

In head-to-head competition against the best coaches, Boeheim again held his own. In August 2013, ESPN's Jeff Goodman polled 250 Division I coaches and asked them to rank the Top 25 coaches based on their ability to strategize. Chris Carlson of Syracuse.com pointed out that Boeheim enjoyed a winning record (73–36) against fifteen of the eighteen coaches he had competed against who made the list and is now 5–1 against Tom Izzo, who was ranked No. 1. According to Syracuse beat writer Mike Waters, in a 2014 survey, Boeheim managed a 31–21 record against the top coaches ranked ahead of him. In another comparison of top coaches, meaning those with 500 wins or more or who had won 70 percent of their games over the last ten years, Boeheim was 176–139. More specifically, Boeheim finished

28–27 against Jim Calhoun and 21–25 against John Thompson II, his two biggest Big East rivals, and 11–15 against Rick Pitino. Against the top two coaches in the Atlantic Coast Conference, Boeheim was 4–5 against Mike Krzyzewski and 4–6 against Roy Williams. Some other notable conquests include: Bobby Knight (4–1), Tom Crean (4–0), Gene Keady (3–0), Billy Donovan (3–1), Denny Crum (3–2), Mark Few (2–0), John Beilein (9–2), Mike Brey (16–6), Jim Larrañaga (4–3), Norm Stewart (2–1), Lute Olson (2–1), Norm Sloan (1–0), Bill Self (1–0), John Calipari (1–3), and Lou Henson (1–2), and with losing ledgers only against Krzyzewski, Williams, Pitino, Smith, Calipari, Henson, and former Big East archrival John Thompson, although Boeheim won the last four meetings before Thompson retired. The record shows that Boeheim had a winning record against the heavyweights. Moreover, unlike some coaches considered on the top tier, such as Krzyzewski, Knight, Smith, and Calhoun, Boeheim never experienced a losing season. The closest Boeheim ever came was 16–13, while even legendary Adolph Rupp, "The Baron of the Blue Grass," went 13–13 one year at Kentucky.

Shifting gears a bit, those who harp on the Richmond and Navy losses in the NCAA tournament should remember that Boeheim pulled off plenty of upsets of his own. He won a truckload of white-knuckle games through the years—in the Big East conference, the Big East tournament, in the ACC, against Top 10 and Top 20 teams, and in NCAA play. Those who dislike Boeheim dismiss all that, preferring to chalk his long string of 20-win seasons up to soft scheduling.

Returning to the 2009-10 season, respected ESPN commentator Jay Bilas wrote in his blog, "There are no geniuses in college basketball, but Jim Boeheim is close. The Orange coach believes in the matchup zone down to his socks, and playing it, he makes his opponents adjust to him ... The Orange defense also invites you to take challenged three-point shots. Year-after-year Syracuse leads the Big East in three-point percentage defense. That means lower percentages, less reliable offensive rebounding, and fewer free-throw opportunities ... Syracuse's defense will win a lot of games." He was right.

After Boeheim notched No. 800, he added 12 more consecutive wins, including victories over California and North Carolina in the 2K Sports Classic and over Florida in the Big East Challenge. They were resume-building wins that came in handy when NCAA tournament selections and seedings were determined. Jamie Dixon and his Pittsburgh Panthers put a halt to the win streak with an 82–72 victory at the Dome. The Orange mowed down eleven more Big East opponents before Pitino, who, like Dixon, had Boeheim's number, grounded the Cuse on its own home court, 66–60. Four more conference wins followed. Syracuse steadily worked its way up the charts and was ranked No. 1 in the nation during the first week of March before Pitino did in Boeheim again, this time at Louisville, 78–68, in the last game the Cardinals played at Freedom Hall. It also was the last time a Boeheim team was ranked No. 1 until December 12, 2012.

Syracuse came back by winning the Big East championship. That set up another matchup with Georgetown. For the thirteenth time, the most ever between two schools in the Big East tournament since its inception in 1980, the Orange squared off against the Hoyas. Going into the contest, Georgetown center Greg Monroe stated, "[The rivalry] is very special. Georgetown and Syracuse is one of the Big East's [best] rivalries. Everybody is going to be amped up." The Hoyas prevailed, upsetting the No. 3-ranked Orange, 84–71.

In the NCAA tournament, Syracuse drew Vermont, a team that pinned a humiliating overtime loss on the Orange in the 2005 tournament. Not this time, as SU handily beat the Catamounts, as they should have, 79–56. Syracuse moved on to play Gonzaga, a relatively low-profile school at the time that in recent years had beaten some of the big boys and, by doing so, had become a fan favorite across the country. The Orange got past the Zags and faced Butler, another under-the-radar team that turned out to be the Cinderella story that year. The Bulldogs upset a favored Syracuse team that played without injured Arinze Onuaku, the school's all-time leader in field goal percentage, 63–59. Butler went on to play Duke tough in the national championship game, before losing to the Blue Devils. With Onuaku,

Boeheim was confident the Cuse could bring home the bacon. "You only get so many shots at the title, and the way that team was playing I really would have liked our chances [to win it all]," he lamented. It was Boeheim's fourth 30-win season and his NCAA-best 32nd 20-win season.

Boeheim added to his extensive collection of awards as more members of the media jumped on the Boeheim bandwagon. The Associated Press, *The Sporting News*, the United States Basketball Association, the National Association of Basketball Coaches, and the Naismith Foundation all named him their national coach of the year. On October 15, prior to an NBA exhibition game between the Detroit Pistons and the Minnesota Timberwolves in the Carrier Dome, Boeheim was presented with *The Sporting News* Coach of the Year Award. More than twenty of his former players were in attendance, along with his former teammate Dave Bing, then the mayor of Detroit, who tossed up the ceremonial jump ball.

Boeheim was also recognized for his many accomplishments by the 111th Congress, 2nd Session, and House Resolution 1318. Those accolades were on top of his 2004 Clair Bee Coach of the Year Award and the John Wooden Legends Coaching Award, given in 2006. He had already been named NCAA District II Coach of the Year ten times by the National Association of Basketball Coaches and Big East Coach of the Year four times. Although he had accumulated a boatload of state and local awards over the years, Boeheim was finally making up for lost time in the national recognition department.

(Left) Boeheim's 1962 Lyons Central High School senior yearbook photo.
Courtesy of Lyons Central School District.

(Right) Boeheim as a player at Syracuse.
Photo courtesy of Finger Lakes Times.

1962 Lyons High School team photo.
Photo courtesy of Lyons Central School District.

Boeheim warming up before an SU game during the 1965–66 season.
Photo courtesy of Don Cronson.

Dave Bing, Boeheim's teammate and roommate at Syracuse.
Photo courtesy of Don Cronson.

Frank Nicoletti, Dave Bing, Jim Boeheim, and Sam Penceal,
March 5, 1964.
Daily Orange photo.

SU players and friends, 1965. From the left, Dave Bing, Claude Young,
Boeheim, Bruce Heath, George Fair, and Larry Rubin.
Photo courtesy of Don Cronson.

Boeheim in 1981 relaxing with his former SU teammates. From the left, Dave Bing, George Hicker, and Richie Duffy.
Photo courtesy of Don Cronson.

Boeheim speaking early in his coaching career.
Photo courtesy of the Finger Lakes Times.

Boeheim enjoying a moment in 1981.
Photo courtesy of Don Cronson.

Roosevelt Bouie, a star in Boeheim's first recruiting class in 1976. *AP photo.*

Roosevelt Bouie and Louie Orr, the stars of Boeheim's first recruiting class, when their jerseys were retired on February 21, 2015. *AP photo.*

(Right) Pearl Washington
dribbling in front of
Wendell Alexis. *AP photo.*

(Below) Pearl Washington
and Boeheim. *AP photo.*

Rony Seikaly and Derrick Coleman. *AP Photo.*

Derrick Coleman, a
beast on the boards, with
Howard Triche and
Sherman Douglas, mem-
bers of Syracuse's 1986–
87 NCAA runner-up
team. *AP Photo.*

(Left) Derrick Coleman dunking with Sherman Douglas looking on. *AP Photo.*

(Below) Boeheim addressing Rony Seikaly and others during a timeout. *AP Photo.*

Billy Owens against Villanova with Derrick Coleman looking on. *AP Photo.*

Lawrence "Poetry in" Moten. *AP Photo.*

John Wallace. *AP Photo.*

Carmelo Anthony celebrating
with an NCAA championship
towel. *AP Photo.*

Boeheim's hometown of Lyons, New York.
Photo courtesy of Mike Cutillo.

Boeheim holding the
2003 national champion-
ship trophy. *AP Photo.*

Boeheim and Duke coach Mike Krzyzewski coaching the USA Olympic basketball team. *AP Photo.*

Jim and Juli Boeheim on the evening of Boeheim's induction into the Naismith Memorial Basketball Hall of Fame.
Photo courtesy of Don Cronson.

Connecticut basketball coach Jim Calhoun, Boston-based sportswriter Bob Ryan, and Boeheim on the night of Calhoun's and Boeheim's inductions into the Naismith Memorial Basketball Hall of Fame.
Photo courtesy of Don Cronson.

Boeheim speaking when he was honored in his hometown of Lyons, New York, after Syracuse won the 2003 national championship. *Photo courtesy of the Finger Lakes Times.*

Eric Devendorf and Gerry McNamara.
AP Photo.

Gerry McNamara shooting a jump shot.
AP Photo.

Jim Boeheim. *AP Photo.*

11

A NEW DECADE

2010–11

Unlike the previous year, the Orange started the season ranked No. 10. Despite losing three key players—Wesley Johnson, Andy Rautins, and Arinze Onuaku—the team believed it could be good and took the motto "Unfinished Business" to proclaim to the world that they had something to prove. However, Syracuse slogged out of the gate. Although they won early, SU won ugly. Following an 86–67 win over Canisius, an unhappy Boeheim, always a straight shooter, stated: "Right now we're the most overrated team that I've ever had ... We are not a good basketball team."

Considering that Boeheim had been in the head coaching business since 1976, that statement encompassed thirty-five teams. Syracuse did win its first two games by an average of 20.5 points, but in its fourth game, they barely beat William & Mary, 63–60. After defeating Cornell, 78–58, on November 30, Boeheim, always the perfectionist, told the media: "You can't look at this game and who we're beating ... It's how you play, not who ... you're playing ... You can't play bad basketball and win games against good teams. We're playing bad basketball, and we've been playing bad basketball from the first game until now."

One school of thought was that Boeheim, at times a sly fox and motivational mastermind, was trying to light a fire under his team by declaring that they were overrated. If he indeed thought the team needed a spark, he lit the fuse because after beginning the season on wobbly legs, the Orange gained traction and shot out to an 18–0 start for the second time in Boeheim's career. Then they got derailed at Pittsburgh, which continued to be a thorn in Syracuse's side. But beating No. 8 Michigan State in Madison Square Garden was a huge hurdle and confidence builder.

With a group of versatile athletes, Boeheim had a deep bench that enabled him to play a nine-man rotation instead of his customary seven. He put together one of his best transition teams and, as good as the 2009–10 team was defensively, the 2010–11 team early in the season appeared to be even better. Although Boeheim was displeased early in the season, clearly the Cuse was pretty good, and as the season progressed, they were certainly better than expected. Thirty-five years into his career, Boeheim again seemed to be doing some of his best work. On January 12, Syracuse beat St. John's, 76–59, in Madison Square Garden to record the 1,800th victory in school history. SU was fifth on the NCAA's win list behind only Kentucky (2,035), Kansas (2,020), North Carolina (2,015), and Duke (1,927). Boeheim was part of 849 of those victories, and he ranked second among active coaches in wins and fifth all-time.

Following Syracuse's destruction of a pretty good St. John's team, Red Storm coach Steve Lavin, speaking on the difficulty of playing against Boeheim's zone defense, stated: "It's a cumulative effect over the course of a game as a result of Coach Boeheim having a great sense and feel for the zone to teach it and make changes in personnel. They recruit well for his system and style ... He can plug players into roles. Because of the size and length [of his players] there just aren't many openings and, even when there is an opening, it closes so quickly because they move in concert so well. This year is no different than other years because he tweaks it so well game-to-game, even timeout-to-timeout. He's the master of the zone, and tonight it was really effective. [Now] you know why Mike Krzyzewski used him as an assistant in international competition for our national team."

The litmus test came on January 17 when undefeated Syracuse, which had reached No. 3 in the national polls, traveled to Pittsburgh to play the No. 5-ranked Panthers, the Big East preseason favorite. It was a game everyone had circled on the calendar. But if the man from Mars happened to be reading what the trolls on the Syracuse Internet chat lines were writing, there was no way he could have figured out that the Orange was 18–0 and rated among the best teams in the nation. Considering the criticism and less than complimentary comments being directed at Syracuse, the guy from outer space would have been hard-pressed to think Syracuse had a winning record and was guided by a Hall of Fame coach.

Syracuse was 3–11 against Pitt going back to the 2001–02 season, with Pittsburgh having won the last seven times. The Panthers were also very tough at home, sporting a 144–11 record in the Petersen Events Center where they had won 50 of their last 51 games, including going 9–0 against visiting Top 5 teams. One of those losses was inflicted by Syracuse, 49–46, in overtime in 2004. SU entered the contest having won 48 of its last 53 games and was trying to match the school's best getaway since the 1999–2000 team started 19–0. ESPN televised the showdown between the top two teams in the Big East and two of the top five teams in the country as part of what the network billed as the best Big Monday ever. The afternoon game on the all-sports station had No. 6 Villanova at No. 7 Connecticut. The SU–Pitt game played in the prime-time slot, with No. 3 Kansas meeting Baylor in the nightcap.

As was the case most years but perhaps more so in 2011, the Big East conference was a meat grinder that ate its own. The Huskies upset the Wildcats, which helped Syracuse, but the Orange suffered its first loss of the season before a record crowd in The Pete. Before the late arrivers had a chance to find their seats, the Panthers had bolted to a 19–0 lead. Seemingly left for dead, Syracuse valiantly fought back to score 17 unanswered points to get back in the game. After knotting up the contest at 41–41, the Cuse caved in. The 74–66 loss left the country with only three undefeated teams.

Whereas Pitt went inside to carve up the zone, back home six days later in front of another 33,000-plus crowd in the Carrier Dome, Nova went over the top. The Wildcats shot lights out in the first half, making 8 of 13 three-point attempts, some from downtown, to build a double-digit lead and hand SU its second consecutive loss. "It was just the opposite [of what Pittsburgh did]," stated SU guard Brandon Triche. Villanova coach Jay Wright acknowledged that his team made some difficult long-range bombs. "You can get threes off against their zone, but you can't get good threes," he said. "[Some] weren't great shots, but we made them." Wright was on an uptick, and some SU fans openly wished he could be their coach, not just because he was winning but also because he appealed to the public with his pleasing personality, tailored GQ suits, Gucci shoes, and George Clooney-like good looks.

After falling to two top six teams, Syracuse dropped to No. 9 in the polls. Things then went from bad to worse as a Seton Hall team with a 9–12 record, 3–6 in the Big East, came into the Dome and dominated the Orange, 90–68. The Pirates pinned the worst loss on Syracuse since the DePaul debacle in 2006 when the Blue Demons totally embarrassed SU, 108–61. It was also the third-worst home loss suffered during the Boeheim era. The worst perimeter shooting team in the league, Seton Hall blistered the zone by making 11 of 17 three-point shots. Soon thereafter, Pittsburgh promptly lost at home to Notre Dame, which Syracuse had beaten soundly, and a few days later, Villanova went down against Providence, proving that navigating the Big East conference gauntlet was akin to traveling through shark-infested waters on a rubber raft. When a top team was beaten and there was blood in the water, even the smaller sharks like Seton Hall started circling. However, as John Pitarresi of the *Utica*

Observer-Dispatch pointed out, in 2009, SU lost seven of 10 games in January and February and then won seven in a row to claim the Big East championship and reach the third round of the NCAA tournament. So there was still time to right the ship.

Critics panning for complaints struck gold as, for just the third time in the Boeheim era, Syracuse lost its fourth straight game. It was something the program hadn't experienced since the 2005–06 season. As for the Big East race, Syracuse had shot itself in both feet, it seemed. Going through its customary mid-season swoon, it appeared a season that started out in first class was quickly being downgraded to coach. People thought the sky was falling. Boeheim got battered.

In disarray and with an away game at No. 6 Connecticut where it had not won in seven years, Syracuse went from the frying pan into the fire. Boeheim with 847 wins and Calhoun with 840 set a record for the most combined wins (1,687) among opposing NCAA Division I coaches. Through the years the Boeheim–Calhoun head-to-head matchup had been pretty even, with Calhoun holding a slight 26–25 edge against SU and a 26–22 advantage while he was at Connecticut. Calhoun had won seven of the last nine regular-season meetings, but in the Big East tournament, Boeheim had come out on top the previous three times, including the six-overtime game. But all that could be thrown out the window once the game started. When it did, it was the same ole, same ole, with Syracuse quickly falling behind, 23–14. Having not won a game in sixteen days, the Orange's psyche was fragile and its confidence low. Things pointed toward a first-time-ever five-game losing streak for Boeheim. The 'Cuse could have quit, but it didn't. SU left Storrs with a 66–58 win that put a stop to the NIT talk and got the Orange back in the NCAA conversation. It was Boeheim's fourth straight win over Connecticut and evened his personal record with Calhoun at 26–26.

In his postgame press conference, Calhoun called Boeheim the best coach in the country. In his opening remarks, in response to Jeff Jacobs of the *Hartford Courant* having written that Rick Pitino was the best "game coach" in the country after Louisville beat UConn in overtime, an irritated Calhoun said: "I guess I was outcoached for the second game in a row. The last game I think somebody wrote I coached against the best coach in the country. I happen to think Jim is a better coach than anybody.

"I couldn't wait to get that in there because ... some people ... don't understand anything," stated Calhoun, who can be as sarcastic and surly as Boeheim or anybody else. To which Jacobs printed the next day: "Fair enough, but I do understand how my tape recorder works. You've got a hall-of-fame coach, Syracuse. We've got a hall-of-fame coach. Advantage Syracuse, says our hall-of-fame coach." Maybe it was "coach-speak," maybe it wasn't. Regardless, Calhoun publicly acknowledged that he had the utmost respect for Boeheim.

After Syracuse won big at South Florida, for the first time since 2002, the No. 13 Orange lost at home to No. 11 Georgetown, 64–56. A loss at Louisville followed. SU beat West Virginia to prevent the school's first four-game home losing streak in forty-nine years, going back to the year before SU moved into the then new Manley Field House. It was Boeheim's 850th win. But in the postgame press conference, the thin-skinned Boeheim pulled a Jim Calhoun, angrily criticizing local media who noted that in the previous game's write-up he had lost seven straight games to Pitino. "When people write and say things about me, it's personal to me. Always will be," he stated. The blow-up went national and didn't help Boeheim's image. It also reinforced what Pitino had said, that Boeheim had "rabbit ears." The next day Boeheim stood by his opinion, telling Danny Parkins on *The Score 1260* radio show, "I'm just reacting to things that have been said or written about me. That's the only time I have to express my opinion about what I feel."

Syracuse then struggled with lowly Rutgers at home but managed to win in overtime. Next was payback in Philadelphia, where No. 17 SU upset No. 14 Villanova, taming a Wildcats team that couldn't miss from outside a month earlier in the Dome by limiting Nova to 32 percent shooting from the field and only 5 of 26 from three-point range. It was on to Washington, DC, where—despite Senior

Day, Alonzo Mourning being inducted into the school's Hall of Fame, former president Bill Clinton being in the house, and a Georgetown ploy to prevent Syracuse fans from attending the game by stopping the public sale of tickets—the Orange got road revenge with a 58–51 win over the No. 11-ranked Hoyas. It was Syracuse's fourth consecutive win and its seventh over a ranked team, which surpassed Texas for the most in the season to that point.

Next, the Orange demolished DePaul, eating DePaul's breakfast, lunch, and dinner and then gobbling the Blue Demons themselves in a 107–59 rout. The 48-point differential was the largest in Big East history. The point total was the highest since Syracuse put 108 on Connecticut during the 1993–94 season. It was the Carrier Dome finale for senior workhorse Rick Jackson, who joined Derrick Coleman, Billy Owens, and Carmelo Anthony as the only Boeheim-coached players to average double-doubles for a season. Jackson led the league in rebounding and blocked shots and was runner-up in field goal percentage. Having played 139 games, he trailed only Stevie Thompson (144) and Coleman (143).

Syracuse finished the regular season 25–6 and entered Big East Tournament play on a five-game winning streak. Expectations for a run in the conference and NCAA tournament ratcheted up significantly. Well rested, the Orange put away St. John's, 79–73, in the quarterfinals of the Big East tournament. It was the long-awaited coming-out party for 7-foot McDonald's All-American Fab Melo, the preseason pick for Rookie of the Year in the Big East. Relegated to the bench for most of the year, Melo came through with a career-high 12 points, grabbed four rebounds, got an assist and a steal, and stood his ground underneath the basket. It was a very good all-around game for the young man from Brazil, whom many had quickly dubbed a bust. As Fran Fraschilla, who was broadcasting the game for ESPN, stated, "Melo was so far in the doghouse that you couldn't even smell him."

In their first tournament meeting since Syracuse won the epic six-overtime game in 2009, this Syracuse-Connecticut semifinal contest only took one extra period to decide. The Huskies outlasted the

Orange, 76–71. Simply, it was too much Kemba Walker as UConn's 6-foot, cat-quick All-American guard chewed up the Orange for 33 points, 12 rebounds, five assists, and six steals. The Connecticut win snapped a four-game Huskie losing streak to Syracuse and enabled Calhoun to take a 6–5 advantage over Boeheim in their head-to-head matchups in the Big East tournament.

Possessing a 26–6 record, the Orange was rewarded with a No. 3 seed. SU began March Madness with Midnight Madness. Its first-round game against Indiana State started at 10:20 Friday night. Syracuse didn't dispatch the Sycamores until 12:40 Saturday morning. Big East brethren Marquette, seeded 11th, bounced the Orange, 66–62. So the season that started with the mantra "Unfinished Business" was finished.

Immediately, Syracuse's fickle fans reappeared. The fans who a few weeks earlier—before Villanova, Pittsburgh, and Louisville suffered early NCAA exits—preferred to have Jay Wright, Jamie Dixon, or Rick Pitino coach the Orange, now voiced their opinions on how SU would be better off with Marquette's Buzz Williams, Butler's Brad Stevens, or even Virginia Commonwealth's Shaka Smart—the latest flavor of the month. As one person said, "As soon as Syracuse loses, no matter the circumstances, the nuts will fall from the trees." And they did, with Boeheim getting zinged left and right. Membership in his fan club was again on the decline.

For the second straight year, Syracuse had lost three starting players. In 2009, the Orange overcame the loss of All-American point guard Jonny Flynn, Eric Devendorf, and Paul Harris to go 30–5, win the Big East championship, and advance to the NCAA West Regional. In 2010, with first-team All-American Wesley Johnson, Andy Rautins, and Arinze Onuaku gone, Syracuse shot out of the blocks with 18 wins and finished 27–8. Despite replacing three-fifths of his starting team in two consecutive years, Boeheim and the Cuse surprised everyone by becoming one of the best teams in the country, finishing fourth in 2010 and 12th in 2011.

And reinforcements were on the way. Boeheim had landed two

McDonald's All-Americans—Michael Carter-Williams, a 6-foot-5, 175-pound combo guard from Hamilton, Rhode Island, and Rakeem Christmas, a 6-foot-8, 180-pound center out of Bryn Athyn, Pennsylvania. Also coming on board was Trevor Cooney, a 6-foot-3, 180-pound shooting guard considered one of the best three-point threats in the country and whom Syracuse fans were hoping would be the next coming of Gerry McNamara. In signing Christmas and friends, it seemed like Santa Claus was coming to Syracuse early.

Despite Boeheim's consistent success and a seemingly very bright future, a relatively small but vocal portion of the SU fan base still wanted its coach fired. They complained whenever he lost a game. They complained even when he won, sometimes by double-digits, because they didn't like how he won. They complained when he started off numerous seasons with extended winning streaks, in some years reaching as many as 17 and 19 games. They complained when the Orange was one of two or three remaining undefeated teams in the nation as the season moved into mid-January. They complained about Boeheim only playing seven players most years. They complained when he played some players too much and other players not enough. They complained about his total reliance on the 2–3 zone defense. They complained when he slowed things down to preserve a lead with too much time remaining. They complained about the non-conference schedule, especially his penchant for not scheduling any true road games. They complained about his coaching decisions and bench behavior. They complained about his demeanor with the local press. They complained about almost everything and anything. They complained and complained and complained, and, almost always, Boeheim just continued to win and win and win.

On September 16, 2011, Dave Gavitt, the first commissioner of the Big East Conference, died of congestive heart failure. Ironically, two days later he probably turned over in his grave when Syracuse, a charter member and arguably the anchor team in the league that he guided during its early years when it became a dominant force in basketball, bolted the Big East to join the Atlantic Coast Conference.

After initially reiterating the party line that the move was in the best interests of the school, Boeheim acknowledged the move was difficult for him. "I spent thirty years in the Big East, so this has been hard for me," he told Andy Katz of ESPN.com. "Dave Gavitt made us all. Without him, there would be no Hall of Fame for me, no national championship for Jim Boeheim."

Syracuse leaving triggered the demise of the league. ESPN.com's Dana O'Neal was quick to lambast Syracuse for bailing. In her column, she stated, "From Derrick Coleman to Billy Owens to Carmelo Anthony to Hakim Warrick to Gerry McNamara, only a handful of schools can match the college star-power wattage of the Orange. And in the Mount Rushmore of coaches who have personified the league, the chin-in-his-hand image of Jim Boeheim stands alongside John Thompson, Lou Carnesecca, and Jim Calhoun. Now, on the same weekend Gavitt died, Syracuse has helped bury the league he so adored. Because this is the end of the Big East. Let's not kid ourselves here."

At a September 2011 speaking engagement in Birmingham, Alabama, Boeheim was asked about retirement. "After thirty or forty years, they finally figured out that I'm not going anywhere," he responded. "Most of the critics are dead now, so they leave me alone."

However, after a 2011 Big East tournament game, Boeheim alluded to retirement stating, "You won't see me here four years from now." But as the 2011 season approached, Boeheim was singing a different tune. He sounded like he might coach forever. "I love coaching. I feel as strongly about it as I ever have. I've talked to coaches who said after they retired that they retired too early. I don't want to make that mistake. I think I'd rather stay a little too long than [getting] out a little too early. Then I'll have no regrets."

12

A SEASON OF ON-THE-COURT HIGHS AND OFF-THE-COURT LOWS

2011–12

Practice began with "Midnight Madness" that included a legends game with the rosters filled with some of SU's biggest stars from the past. The event drew almost 30,000 people, three times what many schools attract for a regular-season game. "This is the most incredible Midnight Madness ever. In history," John Wallace told Mike Waters of the *Syracuse Post-Standard*. "It's an epic event."

In 2011–12, the Orange was loaded. Catching lightning in a bottle with homegrown product DaJuan Coleman playing at nearby Jamesville-DeWitt—a hop, skip, and a jump from the Syracuse campus—Boeheim added the fourth-best center and overall 14th-best high school player to the talented frontcourt that he already had. However, it wasn't a given, and it wasn't easy. To reel in the 6-foot-10,

280-pound man-child, Boeheim had to beat out Kentucky and recruiting guru John Calipari, who had persuaded Coleman to attend UK's Midnight Madness where he was exposed to Big Blue mania.

"Plucking a five-star recruit from the backyard of one of college basketball's elite programs wasn't going to be easy," wrote Ben Roberts of the *Lexington (KY) Herald-Leader*, "but Calipari targeted Coleman early in the recruitment process and stayed on him until the end." Adding Coleman to a team already stocked with big-time talent at almost every position set the Cuse up to make a run for the national championship in the near future. Boeheim was on the verge of bringing in more prep school stars than he did at any one time over the course of his long career. Expectations shot through the roof. As good as the Orange had been, it appeared that they were going to be even better. The glory days were back at Syracuse. With Kris Joseph tabbed as a preseason All-American, Syracuse started 2011–12 No. 5 in the nation.

Bernie Fine Scandal Rocks Syracuse

Just as Syracuse was piggybacking blue-chip recruits to become an elite program in the late 1980s when the NCAA investigation short-circuited the program, the Orange's resurgence suffered another crushing blow that threatened to knock SU off track again. On November 17, 2011, two days before the Colgate game, the program was shaken when a former SU ball boy accused longtime assistant coach Bernie Fine of molesting him beginning in 1984 when he was 12 or 13 years old and continuing to do so until he was 27. This was just one week after Penn State was rocked by a similar sexual abuse case in its football program where an assistant coach was accused of molesting as many as ten young teenagers. The Penn State case resulted in the firing of the University president, a couple of high-level administrators, and legendary football coach Joe Paterno.

Penn State was severely criticized for failing to report the allegations to the police and for failing to act promptly in addressing the issues for fear of tarnishing the up-to-then pristine image of the University's highly acclaimed football program. Aware of the lambasting Penn State had taken for its slow and indecisive reaction, Syracuse Chancellor Nancy Cantor placed Fine on administrative leave a couple of hours after the story broke nationally on ESPN.

Bobby Davis, a former ball boy for six years in the 1980s, went to ESPN with his story. He said the abuse took place at Fine's home, at the university's basketball facilities, and when he went to away games as a guest of Fine, and that it continued for nine years. Davis, 36, first reported the allegations to the *Syracuse Post-Standard* and to the Syracuse police department in 2002, to ESPN in 2003, and to the university in 2005, but investigations into the matter by all the aforementioned failed to find a single person who would corroborate Davis's story. None of the people who Davis said would also state they were abused by Fine did so. Therefore, the case was not pursued further at any level.

In 2011, eleven years later, Mike Lang, then 45 years old and also a former SU ball boy and a stepbrother to Davis, told ESPN that Fine began molesting him when he was in the fifth or sixth grade. Because Davis now had someone who supported his story, the investigation of Fine was reopened. Playing through the distractions, Syracuse dispatched Colgate for its third win of the season and then went to New York City where it beat Virginia Tech and Stanford to win the Preseason NIT. With Connecticut and then North Carolina losing, Syracuse rose to No. 3 in the coaches poll and No. 4 in the Associated Press poll. Things were looking very rosy for the Cuse on the basketball court, if not so good in the court of public opinion and the court of law.

Bernie Fine was fired on November 27. Fine began as Boeheim's assistant in 1976 and, after 36 years, his coaching career was over but not the case that his alleged sexual behavior instigated. Not by a long shot. With new information coming forth in bits and pieces, the case continued to drag on. The Associated Press would vote the Bernie Fine allegations of child molestation ninth on its Top 10 list of the biggest sports stories of 2011. With Boeheim getting heat from various sources, on November 29, Cantor gave Boeheim a vote of confidence stating, "Coach Boeheim is our coach. He's getting the team ready tonight."

Meanwhile, Syracuse was in the midst of a basketball season, and a highly successful one at that. Having advanced to No. 3 and 4 in the national polls, the Orange hosted Eastern Michigan, coached by former Boeheim assistant Rob Murphy. When Boeheim entered the arena where the basketball court bears his name, he was greeted by a standing ovation by the 16,000-plus people in attendance. The Orange grounded the Eagles, 84–48, but that wasn't the story that night.

Following the game, Boeheim walked into a jam-packed press conference that included media representatives from *USA Today*, the *New York Times*, ESPN, and numerous other national outlets. The press conference focused on the Fine case, not the game. After reading a brief statement, Boeheim said that's all he had to say about the case but then continued to address the situation for another twenty minutes where he backed off from fully supporting Fine to now wanting to wait for the investigation to be completed. Boeheim's postgame comments received a mixed reaction from national and local media and the general public. Three days later, not the least bit distracted, the Orange disposed of No. 10 Florida, 82–78. In his postgame comments, Boeheim finally offered a sincere apology, which is what his critics wanted him to do much earlier. "It was insensitive what I said earlier … I'm sorry." Although it received little publicity, years before the Fine scandal, Boeheim and Juli donated $20,000 from their Boeheim Foundation plus some personal funds to the McMahon/Ryan Child Advocacy Center.

Syracuse #1

As the season progressed, the defensive-minded and ten-deep Orange beat George Washington to begin the season 10–0 for the third consecutive year. Earlier in the day, No. 2 Ohio State lost at Kansas and

No. 1 Kentucky went down on a buzzer-beating three-point shot at Indiana. The two upsets opened the door for SU to ascend to the top of the AP and ESPN/*USA Today* Coaches Polls. It was the fourth time Syracuse has been ranked No. 1 and its first top ranking since March 1, 2010. Before that, the Orangemen were ranked No. 1 in the 1987–88 preseason poll but promptly lost its opening game against No. 3 North Carolina. In 1989–90, the Cuse again started the season No. 1 and held onto the ranking for six weeks until they went down against Villanova on January 6.

Ironically, the week Syracuse reached the top of the polls was when the Bernie Fine sex scandal became an even bigger soap opera due to Davis and Lang having hired high-powered, high-profile attorney Gloria Allred and suing Boeheim and Syracuse University for the disparaging comments Boeheim at first had directed toward them. Working overtime, the rumor mill had more legs than a centipede. Whereas some questioned the merits of the suit, it nonetheless grabbed headlines across the country and took away some of the shine from the basketball team's accomplishment. Through it all Boeheim bore the brunt of the scandal. Like the Teflon Dome in some ways served as a cocoon to shelter the team from the turmoil while on the court, Boeheim took the arrows and buffered his players from the controversy surrounding the season by keeping their attention focused on winning the Big East championship.

As the dueling national stories of Syracuse's success on the court and its problems off of it played on, the Orange, with more distractions and a newer and bigger target on its back, traveled to North Carolina State to make its first defense of its No. 1 ranking. Venturing to its first Atlantic Coast Conference venue since being selected to join the league in 2013, Boeheim faced off against Mark Gottfried, NC State's first-year coach who added interest to the game because he reacted to Boeheim's preseason statement that he preferred that the conference tournament be played in New York City rather than Greensboro by stating: "Jim Boeheim popping off up there that he thinks it needs to be in New York. He needs to get in the league first before he starts making demands on the league."

Boeheim responded by schooling Gottfried. With arguably the most depth and the best defense that it ever had, the Cuse destroyed the Wolfpack, 88–72. Syracuse's bench outscored NC State's bench, 46–4, and its 2–3 zone created 19 turnovers as SU shot out to an 11–0 start and garnered a road win against an ACC foe that would help its NCAA resume in March.

Continuing to go with the flow, SU started the season by winning 15 straight. And the band played on. The Cuse Nation had very little to gripe about as SU kept rolling over opponents. However, a relatively small but vocal bunch of critics continued to bemoan Boeheim's "easy" schedule and lack of road games. Countering that Mike DeCourcy of *Sporting News* in a January 3 column pointed out that Boeheim's scheduling pattern was no different from other elite coaches. "The non-conference schedules compiled by the coaches at Syracuse, Connecticut, Duke, Kentucky, Louisville, and North Carolina … are all very similar," wrote DeCourcy. "Every one of those guys—Jim Boeheim, Jim Calhoun, Mike Krzyzewski, John Calipari, Rick Pitino and Roy Williams … Their teams have played a combined 78 non-conference basketball games to date. Only six of those were on the road—an average of one per man."

DeCourcy stated that the top veteran coaches knew the formula to make the NCAA tournament. The way they schedule "has not hurt them at all … Their teams have won 91.7 percent of their games overall, 93.5 percent of their non-conference games, and 100 percent of the home games they arranged for themselves. None is ranked lower than No. 11 in the most recent Associated Press poll … That these teams mostly choose to play non-league games at home doesn't hurt them in the least in the court of public opinion. Neither will it damage them when it comes to NCAA Tournament seeding. By March, they'll have played on the road plenty because their conference schedules demand it. They'll have played plenty of elite opponents because their conferences include such teams. Whether their non-league schedules register as challenging with the NCAA Tournament selection committee will have only a marginal bearing, if any, on where they are seeded in the field."

That same day, ESPN Top Line stated, "There are some awfully good teams in college basketball this season, but Syracuse (15–0) has emerged as No. 1 in the polls and the clear No. 1 overall seed for NCAA tournament projection purposes. More importantly, the Orange boasts the nation's best slate of quality wins and have, obviously, not hurt themselves with any bad losses. The first half of the Big East schedule is relatively friendly, so Syracuse could still be perfect at the end of January. All of that combines to give the Orange the best shot of securing a No. 1 seed come March, as reflected in their No. 1 odds of doing so at 65 percent. But that doesn't mean they won't be passed for No. 1 overall."

Continuing to create turnovers, forcing opponents into taking poor shots, utilizing a transition offense that was among the best in the nation and having several players capable of being the "go-to" guy on any given night, Syracuse won at Providence and then held off Marquette to extend its record to 17–0, making the Orange—along with Baylor and mid-major Murray State—one of three remaining undefeated teams in the country. Whereas Villanova was usually a tough game for Syracuse, especially in Philly, it was not so this time as the Cuse cruised past a young Wildcats team. With its 19th season-opening win, a 78–55 pounding of Providence that provided Boeheim with his 875th win, the Orange matched the school record set in the 1999–2000 season. Syracuse tied its school record when it was ranked No. 1 in the Associated Press and ESPN/*USA Today* Coaches polls for the sixth straight week. The 1989–90 team started out No. 1 and stayed on top of the totem pole until it suffered a setback at Villanova on January 6.

That evening, on ESPN's first *Big Monday* of the season, the 2011–12 Orange snapped a five-game losing streak against Pittsburgh and established a new school record with it 20th straight season-opening victory. The win provided a little redemption since the Panthers, a pain in the butt for years, ended Syracuse's 18-game winning streak the year before. At 7–0 in the league, the Orange continued to separate itself from the rest of the Big East conference. The 71–63 win extended Boeheim's own mark by notching his 34th 20-win season. In the postgame press conference, Boeheim, all business as usual, brushed off any personal achievements. "No significance. None whatsoever. The only thing I think about is this season."

Then there were two. Later that evening Baylor lost badly at Kansas, leaving Syracuse and mid-major Murray State as the only unbeaten teams in the country. The Cuse was on a crusade, beating opponents by an average of nearly 16 points a game. Mid-season discussions had Boeheim's name in the mix for National Coach of the Year. Not bad for a guy who some still said couldn't coach or recruit and played too much zone.

Before leaving for a two-game road trip to Notre Dame and Cincinnati, Syracuse learned that it would be playing without Fab Melo, its 7-foot starting center, who did not make the trip due to academic problems. With SU minus its big man in the middle, the Fighting Irish burst the Orange bubble, winning, 67–58, while holding Syracuse to its lowest point total of the season. The Cuse went into the Joyce Center with a target on its back, and Notre Dame scored a bull's-eye. Following the stunning upset, fans stormed the court at Purcell Pavilion. Syracuse dropped to No. 3 in the AP poll and No. 4 in the coaches poll, ending a school-record six-week reign as the nation's highest ranked team. Toward the end of January, Syracuse remained in the driver's seat in its quest for a Big East regular-season championship.

Some thought the Orange might have trouble at Cincinnati, but Syracuse surprised a lot of people by beating the Bearcats, 60–53. Christmas came a month late for Syracuse as freshman center Rakeem Christmas, playing in the absence of Melo, had a breakout game with nine rebounds and three blocks. Although SU was winning, Boeheim got questioned by the media about why his team in the early going of two straight games got torched from long range. Boeheim responded, "My wife asked me the other night, 'Can't you play man-to-man?' So

I even get it at home. It's funny, when you're playing zone and three or four guys make threes, everybody sits there and says, 'Can't you play man-to-man?' But when a man-to-man coach is coaching and they make three or four threes, they don't tell him to change defenses. The man-to-man coach says, 'We've got to play better defense.' Well, we had to play our zone better.

"There's a few advantages to playing zone," he explained. "We play zone because we think it's our best defense overall to win the game. But at the end of games, you'll see at least half the time in a close game, there's a foul called on a drive to the basket because that's what people will do. They'll try to get to the basket, and they'll foul because you're playing man-to-man. Very seldom is somebody going to go to the foul line and beat us. That almost never happens." With his 877th victory, Boeheim passed Adolph Rupp to take over fourth place on the all-time victory list. "I used to look at Adolph Rupp's record [of 876–190 in 41 years], and that was winning twenty games for forty years plus. I could never even imagine coaching for forty years," stated Boeheim, who was then within four years of the unimaginable.

Fab-less, Syracuse squeezed by West Virginia at home, 63–61, to improve to 22–1 overall and 9–1 in the Big East. The following Monday, Syracuse moved back up to No. 2 in both polls. The Orange had a week off before going to New York to play St. John's. Just when the Fine case seemed to be losing some of its steam, drama continued to keep it in the news as attorneys for Davis and Lange filed an affidavit against Syracuse University and Boeheim.

In Madison Square Garden, Syracuse, in front of a predominately orange-clad crowd, easily blitzed a young St. John's team, 95–70. Fab Melo returned to the lineup following his academic-related absence and was Fab-u-lous as he put in a career-high 14 points on 5 of 6 shooting from the floor and 4-for-4 from the free-throw line. He also grabbed three rebounds and reestablished his dominant defensive presence underneath the basket by blocking and contesting shots and taking charges, all in 21 minutes of play. Boeheim bagged win number 879, tying Dean Smith for third on the career all-time wins list as the Cuse improved to 23–1 and 10–1 in the Big East.

Syracuse was staring at the teeth of its schedule, with three games in six days against teams expected to make the NCAA tournament. First up was archrival Georgetown. In anticipation of what at the time might have been the Hoyas' last Big East game against the Orange in the Carrier Dome, a couple of days before the hyped-up game, students began camping out in front of the Carrier Dome to ensure seeing Syracuse, the Big East's best scoring team (78.1 points per game) go toe-to-toe with No. 12 Georgetown, the conference's best defensive team (58.6 points per game). Like many Orange-Hoya contests of years gone by, the game lived up to expectation as it took overtime for the Cuse to come out with a 64–61 victory to improve to 24–1, 11–1 in the league. Although the game went back and forth and then into overtime, Boeheim was unimpressed. Asked by a reporter where the game ranked in the storied SU-Georgetown series, Boeheim, in all seriousness, said, "Oh, about 28th or 30th." He then added, "Before you were born there were more than twenty better than this." In the signature rivalry of the Big East conference, the win extended Syracuse's advantage over Georgetown to 48–39. As for people who constantly complained about Boeheim's defense, Hall of Fame former coach and ESPN color commentator Bobby Knight stated, "Jim Boeheim's 2–3 zone is the best in basketball history."

Connecticut came to town hoping a big upset of the Orange would turnaround a disappointing season for them. SU squelched those hopes. An 85–67 victory propelled Syracuse to its 25th win in 26 games, the best start in school history. Two days later, SU squared off against No. 19-ranked Louisville, which had rolled Syracuse seven straight times. Not this time though, as Syracuse scored the last six points of the game to escape with a workmanlike 52–51 win. It was a "white-out" at the KFC Yum! Center, with "Slick Rick" looking dapper as ever in his white suit. With both teams playing the 2–3 zone, something that Boeheim taught Pitino years ago, SU's version prevailed as the Cuse improved to a school-best 26–1, including 13–1 in the conference.

Boeheim periodically implied that the 2012 edition of the Orange was something special. He sensed it might be the year Syracuse could win its second national championship. He didn't want a mistake here or there to cause the opportunity to slip away. More so than other years, it was like he was preparing the Orange for March.

As the season progressed, talk of Boeheim for National Coach of the Year picked up. Not just because the wins had piled up but also because Boeheim skillfully navigated the Bernie Fine scandal that had the potential to bring the program down and for the way the maestro masterfully mixed and matched all the stars on the team in a way that got them to forget their egos, buy into the team concept, and willingly come off the bench when called upon to give Syracuse the spark that it needed to continue to win games. Fitting all the pieces into the puzzle was no easy task, considering the me-first mindset that Dion Waiters brought with him to Syracuse, that Scoop Jardine was a fifth-year senior with diminished minutes, and others like C. J. Fair and Rakeem Christmas could have started elsewhere.

"I'm really impressed with how he handled everything, how he handled this team," Villanova coach Jay Wright said. "I don't know if people realize how difficult it is when you have a lot of good players and you're successful. Dealing with success sometimes is much harder than dealing with losing. And he's handled it as well as anybody I've ever seen. This is definitely one of his best jobs." It was not an ordinary season by any means, but Boeheim got extraordinary results. Therefore, his name remained in the discussion for the best coaching job of the year.

After successfully getting past three big hurdles, the Orange scored 26 unanswered points to beat Rutgers, 74–64, and clinch at least a share of the Big East regular-season championship. Boeheim, who had now guided Syracuse to 40 consecutive winning seasons—a school- and NCAA-best—summarized one of the reasons for the team's success. "I think that we've been very, very good in late-game situations.

I think we've had six games that were in real doubt late in the game, and we've won all of those," he stated. "It's difficult to do that. We felt [before the season] we had a chance to be a good team and winning those close games has been the difference."

Only two conference games remained on the regular season schedule: at Connecticut, and at home against Louisville. Against UConn, Syracuse zoomed out to a 17-point lead in the first half but then had to hang on for dear life to break a four-game losing streak in Gampel Pavilion. Melo made a put-back dunk following a C. J. Fair shot with 31 seconds remaining to give Syracuse a 71–69 win. Fair then blocked a UConn shot underneath the basket that would have tied the game. The hard-fought victory over a hungry Huskies team that was fighting to wiggle its way into the NCAA tournament improved SU to 29–1 and 16–1 in the conference. Sticking UConn earned the Orange its third outright Big East regular-season championship and its second in three years. Besides enabling Kris Joseph and Scoop Jardine to become the first Syracuse players to play on two teams that won undisputed Big East regular-season championships, it also gave Boeheim an all-time best 400 Big East victories and upped his career total to 885 wins.

Boeheim's colleagues remained impressed with the job he was doing. "Jim's the Mick Jagger of college coaching," quipped Villanova coach Jay Wright. "He gets better with age." The *Boston Globe*'s Bob Ryan became the latest member of the media to hail Syracuse as the team to beat come NCAA tournament time. Already assured of a No. 1 seed in the Big East tournament and a likely No. 1 seed in the NCAA tournament, Syracuse concluded the regular season with a 58–49 win over No. 19 Louisville. With its 10th straight victory, the Orange finished 19–0 at home, only the second time Syracuse went undefeated in the Dome since it opened in 1980. The other time was in the 2002–03 national championship season when the Cuse went 17–0. Even bigger accomplishments were that the 2011–12 team was the first to win 30 regular-season games and the second Big East team to win 17 conference games during the regular season. Boeheim also recorded his fifth 30-win campaign.

Ranked in the top five nationally all season and, in the last three months, no lower than No. 3 in the AP poll, the Orange was readying for the Big East tournament. Then on the Monday of conference tournament week, after it seemed that the Bernie Fine story was dying a slow death, another distraction flared up. Charles Robinson and Pat Forde posted on Yahoo Sports that, according to their three-month investigation, Syracuse basketball players going back ten years had tested positive for illegal recreational substances, some repeatedly, and were still allowed to play. The report, citing four anonymous sources and an unidentified former player, stated that Syracuse had violated its own internal drug policy. The alleged violations, which Robinson and Forde said surfaced during their investigation of the Bernie Fine scandal, went back to the 2001 season and included the 2003 season when the Orange won the national championship.

Boeheim responded to Yahoo Sports, "I would not comment on anything like that. Good luck with your story." With another scandal swirling around him, Boeheim managed to stay zoned in on the mission at hand. When Reid Forgrave of Fox Sports asked him about the drug-testing issue, Forgrave said that Boeheim bristled and stated, "Let me just tell you this, and we can put this to rest. I just coach this team. That's it. I don't care if there's an earthquake down the street, as long as it's not my house. I don't care. I'm worried about this team, getting this team to play well. That's all I'm focused on. Nothing else is even in my mind or thoughts when I'm coaching." Clear enough. Many coaches are single-minded, but none more so than Boeheim and Alabama football coach Nick Saban, who said that he didn't vote in the 2016 presidential election because he was so consumed with his job that he was unaware of the voting day.

Beginning in his early 60s, Boeheim periodically had been asked about his retirement plans. He always shrugged it off, saying at different times that it could be sometime soon or sometime in the distant future. When Pete Thamel of the *New York Times* asked if he thought his legacy would be tainted by the off-the-court problems, Boeheim shot back, "I don't care what you think or anyone else thinks. When

I leave, I'll leave, and I don't care if it's good reviews or bad reviews. I think legacy and tainted and all that is a bunch of bull ... That's all media nonsense." Again, clear enough.

It was sniping like that though that gave people the impression that Boeheim didn't like the media. But Boeheim told Graham Bensinger, "People think I don't like the media. That's not true. I like the media. There are very few people [in the media] that I don't like. Now I may not like something someone said, and I'll react to it. I like to react, then I move on." Boeheim then admitted, "Sometimes I come out a little too harsh."

In between the first-round games of the conference tournament, South Florida's Stan Heath, to the surprise of some, was named Big East Coach of the Year over Boeheim, who had guided the Orange to a 30–1 record, including 17–1 in the Big East. Heath got the nod primarily because he overachieved, taking a team picked to finish 14th in the Big East and leading it to a 12–6 mark and a tie for fourth place. Good coaching for sure, but Boeheim supporters argued that Boeheim, although Syracuse was picked along with Connecticut to win the conference championship, also overachieved by going 30–1 during the regular season and winning a conference record-tying 17 games with a team that did not have a scorer in the top 15 in the league. Lacking a star or "go-to player," Boeheim skillfully blended a basketball machine by managing the egos and personalities of ten players who could have started for many college teams, the minutes they played and their rotations, while keeping his team focused on winning basketball games and simultaneously dealing with two major scandals that grabbed national headlines.

St. John's coach Steve Lavin voted for Heath, stating, "Every year [Boeheim] could get coach of the year. It's almost not fair. It could be the annual Jim Boeheim national coach of the year award. He sets such a standard, as Coach [John] Wooden did at UCLA or Dean Smith and, more recently, [Mike] Krzyzewski. Jim Boeheim's in that discussion with the greats in college basketball. It's not taking anything away from him, but sometimes when you've had such a dominant run as Coach Boeheim has, it's almost taken for granted."

In the quarterfinals, Syracuse beat Connecticut for the third time that season and the sixth time in the last seven Big East tournament meetings. As had been the case in several regular-season games, the Orange dug deep to pull it out, 58–55, at sold-out Madison Square Garden in yet another memorable meeting between the two conference powers. Boeheim with 887 wins and Calhoun with 869 broke their own record for combined coaching victories for opposing coaches. The two schools faced off in the tournament for a conference-record 14th time, with the Orange holding an 8–6 edge.

Some people believed that Boeheim and Calhoun, despite sharing the bond of being cancer survivors, deep down disliked each other. However, in his postgame press conference, Calhoun stated, "I love Jim Boeheim like a brother and through everything else. I've told people this through the whole year, including other things that have gone on, he's done an incredible job coaching his team and being unselfish and giving to each other. They're just a terrific basketball team, capable, in my opinion, of winning a national championship."

In the semifinals Syracuse played fourth-seeded Cincinnati, which had upset No. 13 Georgetown, 72–70, in double overtime. Leading from start to finish, Cincinnati pulled off a 71–68 victory. Licking its wounds with its No. 1 seed in the NCAA tournament still intact, SU got its wish. It would play its first two games in relatively close-by Pittsburgh and Boston before moving to New Orleans for the Final Four. Then another off-the-court shocker happened in a season filled with such occurrences. Just before the team flew to Pittsburgh, it learned that Fab Melo, the 7-foot, 244-pound game-changing defensive presence that solidified the zone, was declared ineligible for the NCAA tournament. The seemingly snake-bit Orange, a popular pick to reach the Final Four, faced a situation eerily similar to 2010 when, also as a No. 1 seed, their chances for a deep run in the tournament took a big hit when it lost solid center Arinze Onuaku due to a quadriceps injury suffered in the Big East tournament. Syracuse had to find an answer to make up for such a critical loss as basketball analysts and people throughout the country scampered to redo their brackets. March Madness without Melo resulted in lowered expectations for the No. 2 ranked team in the country. Many who had predicted Syracuse would win the national championship backed off from that belief and, despite its gaudy 31–2 record, now said the Orange was the most vulnerable No. 1 seed. Not bothered by the multitude of issues that popped up periodically throughout the season, the players disregarded the latest obstacle as well, assuming an "us against the world" mentality.

The scrutiny surrounding the Syracuse basketball team had lingered for months, starting soon after the season began. A group that had somehow survived the November Bernie Fine molestation allegations, the firing of a long-time assistant coach, a defamation lawsuit against its head coach, stories stating that Fine's wife was sexually involved with some SU basketball players, Melo's three-game suspension in late January when Syracuse suffered its only regular-season loss, and the university being called to task for failing to monitor its drug policy when it allowed ineligible athletes to compete, absorbed still another body blow. Melo, a difference-making bedrock underneath the basket, was disqualified for the most important part of the season.

In a drama-filled season that had more twists and turns and bumps than a winding, pot-holed country road, Syracuse, in its first NCAA game, got a scare from No. 16 seed UNC–Asheville but managed to sneak past the pesky Bulldogs, 72–65. Syracuse lived to play another day. UNC–Asheville coach Eddie Biedenbach complained, "Syracuse is better than Asheville, [but] tonight Asheville was better than Syracuse." A little irked by Biedenbach's putdown, Boeheim shot back, "That's why they make scoreboards."

Syracuse fans complained about the subpar performance and wondered out loud why the Orange always seemed to underperform in the Big Dance. While they were bellyaching, a couple of No. 2s were brought down by a pair of No. 15s. Duke got leveled, 75–70, by Lehigh—a team that had lost during the season to Cornell and Holy

Cross—and Missouri bit the dust as Norfolk State slithered by the Tigers, 86–84.

Syracuse continued to stay in the news, as much for non-basketball problems as for its basketball prominence. US Secretary of Education Arne Duncan took a swipe at Boeheim for what he said were poor graduation rates. Duncan cited several "basketball powerhouses," including Syracuse, which he said had Academic Progress Rates (APR, sometimes called Academic Performance Rating) below 930. "If they don't improve, you just simply won't see them in the tournament." The APR, instituted in February 2005, is an NCAA metric calculated by allowing points for eligibility and retention—the best indicators of graduation—that gauges the semester-by-semester progress of student-athletes as they matriculate towards graduation. Referring to Boeheim, Duncan said, "One Hall of Fame basketball coach told *USA Today* [last year] that the proposal to require teams to be on track to graduate half their players was, and I quote, 'completely nuts.'"

Peeved at the personal attack that apparently hit a nerve, Boeheim, forced to deflect still another distraction, took issue with Duncan's calculations and used the last part of his Asheville postgame media session to straighten Duncan out. "I think people need to get better information ... We are qualified. We are over 930 ... If they would have called us, we could have told them that," he stated. The SU Athletics Communications office quickly issued a statement corroborating Boeheim's statements.

Waging battles on several fronts, Boeheim sometimes circumvented controversies like water rolling off his back and, at other times, like he just had a root canal. To hammer home his point about student-athletes leaving school early for the pros, Boeheim noted that Bill Gates, the multimillionaire founder of Microsoft, didn't do too bad after dropping out of Harvard. When the NCAA moderator tried to bring the session to a close, Boeheim stated, "I'm not finished yet," and continued his verbal sparring with Duncan: "We've also had five or six guys who left early, went to the NBA, played, and came back and graduated. We helped them graduate. We have two or three right now that are very close to graduating who are done with their NBA careers. So education is paramount to me. We want every guy to graduate, and we work very hard on that. So I think it's fair to say that I'm upset right now."

That issue addressed, it was back to the business of the NCAA tournament and the next opponent—Kansas State. No Melo. No problem. The Orange's esteemed zone was so effective in the 71–68 win that the commentators on two occasions said, "It looked like Syracuse had six guys out there on defense." The victory kept Syracuse's incredible season going and sent SU on to Boston for its third straight trip to the Sweet 16 and the school's 17th. Count Kansas State coach Frank Martin as another in a long line of Boeheim admirers. "I told Coach Boeheim before the game that when I grow old, I'll be able to tell my kids that I coached basketball against Jim Boeheim and Mike Krzyzewski ... It was an honor to line up against a Hall of Famer." Martin also said "[Boeheim's] a helluva coach ... As a fan of the game, Syracuse is one of the teams that I enjoy watching."

Against No. 4 seed Wisconsin, Syracuse relied on teamwork, a flexible and stifling defense, and accurate shooting to escape with a nail-biting, heart-throbbing 64–63 win in what CBS college basketball writer Matt Norlander afterward called the best game of the 2012 tournament. When Kris Joseph missed the front end of a one-and-one, Wisconsin rebounded the ball and had a chance to win the game, but the Orange's stop unit forced an off-balance shot that was short. SU improved its mark to a record-setting 34–2. The victory, Boeheim's 48th, moved him ahead of John Wooden for sole possession of fifth place in all-time NCAA tournament wins.

Syracuse now had to get by another Big 10 power: the Ohio State Buckeyes with their 280-pound All-American center Jared Sullinger. No small task there. Syracuse and OSU had previously met one time in the NCAA tournament, with the then No. 3 Buckeyes defeating then No. 6 SU, 79–74, in 1983. The Buckeyes, this time the No. 2 seed in the East, again punctured the Orange, 77–70. The Orange missed Melo in this game. Not just his rebounding and shot-blocking ability, but his massive presence in the middle, ability to alter shots, willingness to take charges, and just his big body pressing on Sullinger to make everything a little more difficult for the Buckeyes' big man. It was a tough end to a triumphant campaign. Ohio State coach Thad Matta heaped praise on the program and its coach. "From the time I've been around basketball, Syracuse has been a pillar," Matta said. Asked by a member of the media if Syracuse deserved to be compared to Kentucky, North Carolina, Duke, and Kansas in the pantheon of great college basketball programs, Matta replied, "I view Syracuse as one of the elite programs in college basketball. I mean, they just have stood the test of time, year after year after year."

Like in 1980 and 2010 when they were seeded No. 1, Syracuse failed to reach the Final Four. Despite a series of off-court scandals that lingered around the program like a bad cold, SU remained in the Top 5 throughout the season, making it a record-setting year for the Orange. The 34–3 campaign would go down as the second-best in school history, behind only the 2003 national championship season. Boeheim was a finalist for the Naismith Coach of the Year Award, an honor that he earned the year before. Following the season *Sporting News* writer Scott Smith ranked Boeheim sixth on his list of the best coaches of the NCAA tournament expanded bracket era, behind Mike Krzyzewski, Jim Calhoun, Roy Williams, Rick Pitino, and Tom Izzo, and ahead of John Calipari, Billy Donovan, Lute Olson, and Dean Smith. Pretty good company.

It's safe to say that although Boeheim enjoyed great success in 2011–12, he had little peace. The Teflon coach demonstrated his skill and resiliency in guiding the Orange through one of the most tumultuous seasons imaginable. If some others did not, Boeheim's colleagues very much appreciated and admired the job Boeheim did that season. They understood the storm clouds and, at times, seemingly hurricane winds that Boeheim endured while not just keeping his Syracuse ship afloat but successfully keeping it running efficiently and navigating it toward its destination. "I've always marveled at [Jim's] ability to shake things off," Connecticut's Jim Calhoun told ESPN.com's Dana

O'Neil. "I don't know what happens when his head hits the pillow, but publicly there aren't many guys who could have done a much better job."

St. Josephs' coach Phil Martelli told O'Neil, "I have been fascinated by this. I'd read a headline and think, 'That's the one. That's going to crack him.' Not one time has that happened. I couldn't do it. Some of these blows would bring you to your knees, but not him. Maybe 5 percent of coaches could handle what he's handled." After pausing for a moment, Martelli told O'Neil, "No, that [percentage] is too high."

For Boeheim, coaching was not fun. He said that it was serious work. To make his point he used the analogy that if a doctor was operating on him, he hoped that the doctor was not having fun. He expected the doctor to get his satisfaction from successfully completing the surgery. Therefore, the little fun that Boeheim got from coaching came from winning.

After the season ended, Waiters, the explosive sophomore who seemed destined to blossom into a potential All-American, and the much-improved Melo declared they were going to enter the NBA Draft. Including seniors Joseph and Jardine, Syracuse lost four key players. Most programs that took a hit like that would fall off the radar. Not the Orange. Boeheim and Syracuse simply reloaded. With high school All-American DaJuan Coleman and coveted recruit Jerami Grant already committed, Boeheim set his sights on the No. 1 recruit in the nation, 7-foot, five-star center Nerlens Noel, a proclaimed difference maker and program changer who had narrowed his choices down to SU, Kentucky, and Georgetown. On April 1, during a high school all-star game in New Orleans that featured the best prep players in the country, Coleman, Grant, and Noel were all on the East team and on the floor together and played the exact same number of minutes, something that had to please Boeheim because the trio worked well together. The Orange Nation thought that around the holidays "Christmas and Noel" would have a nice ring to it. It turned out to be a cruel April Fool's joke because following a long, drawn-out process that played out on social media over several months, Noel, on an ESPNU live broadcast signing show on April 11, turned his back to show the nation a UK shaved on the back of his head. The collective sigh that reverberated throughout Orangeland was the deflating of SU hopes that were banking on Noel for a 2012–13 preseason No. 1 ranking. The disappointment was short-lived, however, because SU fans and basketball buffs realized Syracuse had enough talent and experience returning to again compete for the conference and national championship—with or without Noel.

In April, Jim and Juli hosted their 13th annual Basket Ball, their foundation that had given away half a million dollars for charities that served children and battled cancer. Sportscaster and Syracuse alumnus Sean McDonough served as master of ceremonies for the event. Referencing Boeheim's recent string of comments on various issues from Bernie Fine to the NCAA's APR rating, McDonough roasted Boeheim. Noting that Boeheim was limping due to plantar fasciitis, McDonough quipped, "That's what happens when you stick your foot in your mouth all the time."

On May 11, Boeheim won another one, only this victory was not on a basketball court but in a court of law. State Supreme Court Justice Brian DeJoseph dismissed the slander case, an offshoot of the Bernie Fine situation that Davis and Lang and their celebrity lawyer Gloria Allred had filed against Boeheim back in November. The judge ruled that Boeheim's remarks weren't statements of facts but simply opinions that were protected from defamation suits. It didn't count as Boeheim's 35th victory of the season and 891st of his career, but it was another big win for the coach nonetheless.

13

BOEHEIM'S 50TH YEAR ON THE SU CAMPUS

2012–13

The 2012–13 season was Boeheim's 50th year on the Syracuse campus. It would be his first without Fine on the bench. It would also be SU's farewell tour through the Big East conference. Boeheim needed 10 wins to reach the 900 mark and 13 to pass Bobby Knight and trail only Krzyzewski in all-time victories.

The Cuse had been residing in the Top 10 and the immediate future looked very good. Due to the Carrmelo K. Anthony Center and with the future move to the Atlantic Coast Conference, in three of the previous four years, only Kentucky, North Carolina, Texas, North Carolina State, and the Orange had recruiting classes that were ranked in the Top 10 by ESPN. Syracuse basketball was in the midst of what could be its greatest era. Going into the season, Syracuse had the ingredients for another deep run in the NCAA tournament, even with the toll of losing two senior leaders to graduation and two players who opted early for the NBA. Kris Joseph, first-team Big East and a second-team NABC and USBWA All-American, and Scoop Jardine both received their degrees. Joseph was taken in the second round of the NBA draft by the Boston Celtics. Dion Waiters and Fab Melo were both first-round draft picks, Waiters the fourth overall selection by the Cleveland Cavaliers and Melo the 22nd pick of the Celtics. Even with their departures, Syracuse was picked No. 9 in the AP preseason poll. The forecast was for an interesting year right from the beginning.

The Orange opened the season against San Diego State in the Battle of the Midway. It was an unusual and historic setting with the game played on the flight deck of the decommissioned USS *Midway* aircraft carrier in San Diego Bay. Despite blustery winds capable of altering shots and bright sunlight sometimes shining directly in the players' faces, the Orange beat the No. 20 Aztecs in what would be a once-in-a-lifetime experience for the participants. The game was ESPN's highest-watched November game in nineteen years.

After easily running over some relatively early season competition, Syracuse, which had risen to No. 6 in the polls, in late November traveled to Fayetteville to take on Arkansas in Bud Walton Arena, where they would be greeted by a "white-out." Coming off the bench, James Southerland poured in a career-high 35 points that included a school-tying nine three-pointers to lead the Orange to a 91–82 victory that not only was SU's 47th straight non-conference win but snapped the Razorbacks' 25-game homecourt winning streak against non-conference opponents. It was the second quality road win of the season although detractors, who like to say that Boeheim never played a true road game until January, joked that Fayetteville is located on the eastern outskirts of Syracuse. In actuality, Syracuse, in its last four true away games, had beaten Memphis, Missouri, NC State, and Virginia, as well as Kansas in Kansas City, Florida in Tampa, and San Diego State on the ship in San Diego. However, the critics weren't going to let facts spoil a good joke.

After the Eastern Michigan game on December 5, Boeheim

explained the knock on his philosophy of usually only playing seven men: "Most teams play six or seven guys. We have nine. Sometimes seven or eight, but about 99 percent of college basketball teams play seven guys. Some teams really play five. The teams that usually play everybody, they lose, and I don't want to be that team. I want to play the guys that we need to win."

As had become customary at the Cuse, the Orange zipped through its first nine games unscathed. In the midst of a nation-best 29-game home winning streak and a school-record 50-consecutive non-conference wins, Syracuse ascended to No. 3 in the polls, only to have another off-the-court incident mar the early season success. Star point guard Michael Carter-Williams, who was leading the nation in assists and among the leaders in steals, was reportedly, and ironically, caught shoplifting after security at Lord & Taylor in the Destiny USA Mall discovered a bathrobe and gloves in his backpack. Another public relations problem, the matter was settled to the satisfaction of the store, the Syracuse police department, and Carter-Williams, with the point guard playing flawlessly through the embarrassment. Regardless, the talented sophomore set himself up as the target of jokes from hostile crowds, whether innocent or guilty of what he described as "a misunderstanding."

December 17 was truly a "Big Monday" as ESPN was on hand when SU defeated Detroit, 72–68, enabling the 68-year-old Boeheim to notch milestone win No. 900. The win didn't come easy, though. With the No. 3-ranked Orange leading by as many as 21 points early in the second half, the Carrier Dome public address announcer reminded the fans to stick around after the game to witness the ceremony to celebrate the accomplishment. But that premature mention may have awakened Detroit as the Titans came close to crashing the party when they trimmed the advantage to three points with 28 seconds to go in the game. However, Syracuse escaped with the historic victory in the Gotham Classic. With former SU teammate and roommate Dave Bing, ironically the mayor of Detroit, in the house, Boeheim reached rarified air where only Mike Krzyzewski and Bobby Knight resided. James Southerland, whose first game at Syracuse took place when Boeheim won his 800th game against Albany, led the Orange with 22 points. It was Syracuse's 30th straight homecourt win, the longest streak in the nation, the 52nd straight conquest over regular-season non-conference foes, and brought Boeheim's career ledger to 900–304. In his 37th year coaching, Boeheim had gotten better—his .862 winning percentage from 800 to 900 victories was higher than any of his other 100-win periods.

On the giant Carrier Dome video board, postgame tributes came from Krzyzewski, Boeheim's Olympic boss, Rick Pitino, his first hire, Bing, his college roommate, Bill Raftery, the ESPN analyst and former Seton Hall coach who contributed to the win total, and SU Newhouse School of Communication grads Mike Tirico and Sean McDonough. Several former players tweeted their congratulations. Deflecting the attention from himself, Boeheim credited his players, coaches, and the fans of the program over the years for his success, especially noting the influence Bing had on him and his career. Criticized by many for many years, Boeheim was now recognized by many as being among the best college basketball coaches of all time.

As he had over the course of his career, Boeheim brushed off the accomplishment as if it were a little dandruff on his collar, stating that the players didn't care about it and that the big 9-0-0 didn't matter, that the only thing of importance was winning the game. Regardless, it was a grand testament to the loyalty, longevity, consistency, and sustained success that Boeheim had enjoyed through the years.

Quite a feat for someone who said his first goal was just to make it through his first four-year contract. "[Syracuse] wanted to give me a three-year contract, but I thought I needed four years in case I got fired," he said on the *Mike and Mike in the Morning* radio show.

The March to 900 Wins

Still Some Critics Remained

Boeheim had outlasted most of his critics, but not all of them. Those who remained turned up the volume. They tried to undermine the monumental achievement by monotonously moaning about Syracuse's weak non-conference schedule while overlooking the early-season foes of Duke (Georgia State, Florida Gulf Coast, Delaware, Elon, and Santa Clara), North Carolina (Gardner-Webb, Florida Atlantic, Long Beach, East Tennessee, and McNeese State) and Kentucky (Lafayette, Morehead State, LIU, Samford, Portland, and Lipscomb). Even though Syracuse had ventured to San Diego and Arkansas and won, teams such as Notre Dame, Connecticut, Georgetown, and Pittsburgh had not yet played a road game. Even though Syracuse had played and beaten Ohio State, UMass, and Virginia in 2007; Florida, Kansas, Virginia, and Memphis in 2008, Florida in 2009; Michigan, Michigan State, and North Carolina State in 2010; Florida and NC State in 2011; San Diego State and Arkansas in 2012; and would go on and beat North Carolina and Duke in 2013, the worn-out complaint about Boeheim beating up on the sisters-of-the-poor kept resurfacing. Few cared that Kentucky's 2012–13 schedule included Lafayette, Morehead State, LIU, Samford, Portland, Lipscomb, Marshall, and Eastern Michigan, while North Carolina's slate had Gardner-Webb, Florida Atlantic, Long Beach State, East Tennessee, and McNeese State. And that Indiana played Stony Brook, Chattanooga, Evansville, Savannah State, Gardner-Webb, Stetson, Howard, North Carolina Central, and University of Maryland-Baltimore County, while Duke played Georgia State, Florida Gulf Coast, Delaware, Cornell, Elon, Santa Clara, and Davidson. Those who harped that Boeheim's won-lost record was inflated because of the teams he played, to be fair, must recognize that the ledgers of Krzyzewski, Knight, and a host of other big-time coaches would also be far less impressive minus the annual "chippie" wins they accumulated. For some reason, however, other coaches were rarely called out about it.

On the contrary, Syracuse's schedule had generally been rated nationally in the top twenty because the Orange played in the Big East, a conference that from top to bottom was always ranked among the best and most competitive in the country. From the 2007–08 season through 2010–11, Syracuse had played forty-four ranked teams, which was more than Duke (thirty-eight), Louisville (thirty-seven), Kentucky (thirty-five), and Kansas (thirty-four). Moreover, at the time Boeheim was 5–2 against the two coaches ahead of him, Knight and Krzyzewski. Furthermore, after Knight beat Boeheim for the 1987 national championship, Boeheim went on to beat Knight four straight times, the last being when Knight finished his career at Texas Tech.

After reaching 900 wins, Boeheim, like Knight and Krzyzewski, lost the next game. The Orange traveled to Madison Square Garden where—*splat!*—they fell flat in an 83–79 loss to Temple in the Chevrolet Gotham Classic that snapped Syracuse's 52-game regular-season winning streak against non-conference competition. SU dropped to 10–1 and No. 9 in the rankings.

After polishing off Alcorn State, Boeheim tied Knight when he recorded win No. 902 with a 96–62 romp over Central Connecticut. With the preseason concluded, No. 7-ranked Syracuse embarked on its 34th and final campaign in the Big East conference. The Orange started conference play 12–1, with a national-best 32-game home-court winning streak. The swan song season began with the Orange scoring the final 21 points of the first half to coast to a 78–53 victory over Rutgers. The usually dead serious Boeheim, knowing the game was no longer in doubt, cracked a smile and even laughed when conversing with officials. It was "Good Knight," as Boeheim zoomed past the Indiana coaching legend for win No. 903. *CBS Sports Eye on College Basketball* blogger Matt Norlander noted that Boeheim's 903 wins paradoxically matched Rutgers' 903-win total compiled since 1947 under twelve coaches.

Boeheim, as always, was modest in his assessment of his momentous accomplishment. "It's a great honor. I couldn't be prouder," he said immediately after the game, choosing to give credit to others. "We've had great coaches and great players [here] for a long time." Asked about the unusual feat of compiling all the victories at one school, he said, "It's a great honor to coach at Syracuse. I came here when I was 17 years old. I love the place. I've never felt any reason to leave, and I'm glad that I didn't." And so were a lot of Orange fans that appreciated what he had accomplished at their school and in their city.

Boeheim's climb up the win ladder retriggered the discussion of where the Syracuse icon ranked among the all-time coaching greats. Boeheim stated his feelings on the matter to John Feinstein: "There are four coaches who are on a different level from the rest of us," he said. "Coach [John] Wooden, [Bobby] Knight, Coach [Dean] Smith, and Mike [Krzyzewski]. Forget any numbers. The rest of us aren't there. They're Mount Rushmore."

Boeheim was at peace with himself and his achievements, explaining to Feinstein that, "Everyone wants to be liked and respected. Some people care more [about that] than others. I was always someone who cared a lot—more than I should have—but I did care. It bothered me when people said I wasn't a good coach ... I still worry about it sometimes, but not nearly as much as in the past. I've reached the point where I know I'm a pretty good coach. For a long time, I hoped that when I stop coaching people wouldn't say I was a bad coach. I think now that won't be the case. How good they think I was, well, that's up to other people."

No longer distracted by the countdown to 900 and Knight, Boeheim and Syracuse gave their undivided attention to the Big East race. After running up a 16–1 record, 4–0 in the conference, and minus sharp-shooter and second-leading scorer James Southerland, who was declared academically ineligible prior to the win over Villanova, the No. 6-ranked Orange traveled to No. 1-ranked Louisville.

The Cuse vs. the Ville. Boeheim vs. Pitino. Mentor vs. former assistant. The last time the two teams met with a No. 1 ranking at stake was in 2010 in the last game played in Freedom Hall. Louisville upended the top-ranked Orange, 78–68. This meeting was in the KFC Yum! Center in front of a raucous, record-setting crowd. The 22,814 in attendance, plus all the Orange fans who watched the game on television, chewed their nails to nubs as they watched Syracuse ground the Cardinals, 70–68, in what was an NCAA tournament-type test and atmosphere. It was a gritty, hard-fought, and exciting game that lived up to its billing and would go down as one of the most memorable games in SU history. Michael Carter-Williams, the acclaimed freshman point guard, was turnover prone and struggled mightily in the first half but settled down in the second half and starred down the stretch, including during the last minute of the game. He stole the ball, streaked down the court, and hammered home an emphatic two-handed dunk that proved to be the margin of victory. He quickly grabbed a rebound, was fouled, and added a free throw. He then ripped the ball from the hands of Louisville's 6-foot-11, 245-pound Gorgui Dieng and flung it away as time expired, putting an end to the Cardinals' 11-game winning streak. ESPN.com stated that Carter-Williams "turned in what may be the clutch performance of college basketball this season to date."

Brandon Triche, with 18 of his 23 points coming in the first half, carried Syracuse in the early going. Filling in for Southerland, freshman Jerami Grant provided a shot in the arm with 10 points and five rebounds in 35 minutes. Carter-Williams put the nails in the Cardinals' coffin with his late-game heroics as Boeheim won his third straight over Pitino to pull even at 10–10 in head-to-head matchups. The ending was eerily reminiscent of the previous year in the Yum! Center when Dion Waiters stripped the ball in the final seconds to enable Syracuse to beat Louisville, 52–51. It was the Orange's fourth win in 11 contests against a No. 1 team in the AP Top 25 poll, with all of the victories coming against Big East teams. Like snow in Syracuse in January, SU was 17–1 overall and 5–0 and in first place in the conference.

As he had done most of the time throughout his extraordinary career, Boeheim pushed the right buttons that enabled Syracuse to win. Even the decreasing number of detractors who continued to gripe about the same old complaints had to admit that. Internet commenter OJkillz perhaps stated what more and more people were learning: "When Jim Boeheim talks, E. F. Hutton listens."

With business taken care of in Kentucky, the Orange faced another stiff test two days later against Cincinnati, which that same day playing at home required overtime to beat Marquette, another conference contender. For the second consecutive game, Carter-Williams shrugged off a sluggish first half to spark the newly elevated No. 3 Orange to a 57–55 win over the No. 21-ranked Bearcats. After scoring 11 of Syracuse's last 13 points against Louisville, the supremely confident and extremely competitive Carter-Williams scored five of SU's final seven points to enable the Cuse to overtake Cincy.

Like clockwork Orange, Syracuse had won an all-time Big East-best 28 of its last 29 conference games heading into the Villanova game. Not impressed, the Wildcats upset the nation's No. 3 team, 75–71, at the Wells Fargo Center, dropping SU to 6–1 in the league and 18–2 overall, with both losses coming against Philadelphia teams. Syracuse then lost at Pittsburgh in the Petersen Events Center, a house of horrors for the Orange as it had lost 7 of its last 9 games in the building. Syracuse returned home, regained its composure, and easily defeated Notre Dame. Then, aided by the return of three-point laser-shooter James Southerland who had missed the previous six games, No. 9 Syracuse defeated St. John's, 77–58. The win enabled Boeheim to extend his string of 20-win seasons to an all time best 35 over the course of a 37-year career. The Orange extended its nation-leading homecourt winning streak to 37 games.

SU then bowed to Connecticut, 66–58, in the last Big East meeting between the two conference powers. The bigger story, however, came from Boeheim's postgame press conference when he refused to answer a lead question from ESPN's Andy Katz. Boeheim stated, "I'll answer anyone's question but yours because you're an idiot and a really disloyal person and a few other things that I could add, but I'm not gonna go there."

The next day Boeheim explained his putdown of Katz was because in November 2011, when Syracuse was in New York for the NIT Season Tip-off tournament during the Bernie Fine investigation, Boeheim agreed to be interviewed by Katz, with the stipulation that the questions would only be about the tournament and any questions about the Fine case would be off-limits. Boeheim related that as soon as the interview started, Katz immediately and repeatedly asked him questions about the Fine case, with Boeheim then telling Katz that he would never talk to him again, which he didn't until he shot down Katz when he asked him that question at the postgame presser. Beyond that, the Orange dropped to 20–4.

After victories over Seton Hall and Providence, next up for Syracuse was the much anticipated game against longtime, hated rival Georgetown in what would be the Hoyas' last Big East regular-season visit to the Carrier Dome. Even with additional seating installed, the game was declared a sellout early in the week. Beginning on Monday, six days before the Saturday afternoon showdown, dozens of students braved the cold weather. Bundled up like Eskimos, they camped out overnight in front of the Dome in tents and makeshift shelters. In an expression of appreciation, on Friday morning Boeheim and assistant coaches Mike Hopkins and Adrian Autry distributed coffee and pastries and visited with the students.

Going into the game SU, GT, and Marquette were sitting on top of the Big East standings with 10–3 marks. With the Orange ranked No. 8 and the Hoyas No. 11, the last Big East meeting in Syracuse between the two powers promised to be another Syracuse-Georgetown classic. There was a lot of hoopla leading up to the historic contest, including the retiring of Carmelo Anthony's No. 15 jersey during a halftime ceremony. Numerous former players, including several from the 2003 national championship team, returned for the game. The atmosphere was charged, or as the *New York Times* put it: "The Dome glowed like the inside of a jack-o'-lantern. It sounded like the inside of a jet engine." Marshall Street was jumping the day of the game. It was a happening, with the potential of producing another "Syracuse Moment."

Before a Syracuse, Carrier Dome, and on-campus NCAA-record crowd of 35,012, Georgetown spoiled the party, 57–46, deflating the Orange faithful that had been so pumped up. It was Syracuse's lowest point total in Carrier Dome history. Poignantly, it was Otto—no, not the SU mascot—Porter who did in the Cuse. The Hoyas' sophomore poured in a career-high 33 points, the most by an opponent in the Dome in seven years, to figuratively puncture the big bubble that was stuffed with Cuse-a-holics. The 2–3 zone cuts both ways, with the Hoyas employing SU's trademark defense to hold the Orange to 34 percent shooting that included 4-for-20 from beyond the arch.

With Marquette also losing later that day, the Hoyas took sole possession of the top spot in the standings. Adding salt to the wounds, Georgetown, which had the propensity for such things, snapped Syracuse's 38-game home winning streak, the longest in the nation, and SU's string of 11 straight regular-season wins against ranked teams that tied Indiana for the longest such streak. Only the 57 consecutive wins in Manley Field House is longer, which was coincidentally also ended by Georgetown in 1980 when John Thompson II declared, "Manley Field House is officially closed!" With the game being the last regular-season Big East game, Thompson's son, JTIII, had the opportunity to make a similar statement that would have further infuriated the Orange Nation. In a show of class, he refused to do so. Syracuse's last homecourt loss was also to the Hoyas, 64–56, on February 9, 2011.

So the Syracuse-Georgetown rivalry, as good as any during its heyday in the 1980s and early 1990s when twelve contests went into overtime and twenty were decided by one or two points, came to an end. The teams would go on to meet in the future, but the games would not have the same meaning as the Big East clashes that helped make the conference what it was during its salad years. Boeheim managed a 37–35 record against Georgetown up to that point.

With the loss to Georgetown, Syracuse slipped to No. 12 in the polls, the first time Syracuse was out of the Top 10 in almost two years. Tied for second place in the conference behind the Hoyas, the Orange traveled to Milwaukee and was beaten by Marquette, 74–71. Louisville then handed Syracuse its third straight loss, two of which were to Top 10 teams and the other, Marquette, a Top 25 team on the road.

On Senior Night, SU stopped the skid by easily defeating bottom-feeder DePaul in what was the last Big East regular-season game at the Carrier Dome. But then a few days later in its final Big East regular-season game at Georgetown, the Hoyas humiliated Syracuse, 61–39. The Hoyas held the punchless Orange to its lowest point total ever in a Big East game, the lowest point total ever during the Boeheim era, and the lowest point total since SU beat Kent State, 36–35, on December 1, 1962, when Boeheim and Bing were on the school's freshman team. In one month, the Hoyas had crushed the Orange twice on national television, this last one witnessed by the biggest crowd to watch a college basketball game in the Washington, DC–Baltimore area. In the first meeting on February 9, Georgetown stymied Syracuse with a zone defense, but in this game, it was the Hoyas' man-to-man defense that suffocated the Orange. In both games, as it had been in several previous games, SU's offense was stuck in quicksand.

When the outcome of the game became evident, the Hoyas' student section, which prior to the contest held up a banner that stated, "Our Hatred is Eternal," taunted Syracuse fans by chanting "ACC! ACC!" Toward the end of the game, they serenaded them with "Na Na Na Na Na, Hey Hey Hey, Goodbye!" Hated Georgetown coach John Thompson II, with a big grin on his face, raised a Georgetown scarf over his head and ran his thumb across his neck, symbolizing the beatdown his son's team had put on SU.

Regarding the ending of the rivalry, John Thompson III, always more polite than his famous father, in his postgame press conference inserted a little dig by stating, "It's special because the Big East, as we have known it, is ending. Georgetown won the first [meeting with Syracuse], and now Georgetown has won the last [one]." That wasn't enough for his father, though, who from the back of the room interrupted his son by bellowing, "And kiss Syracuse goodbye," a biting remark similar to his famous "Manley Field House is officially closed!" statement made in 1980 that pissed off the Syracuse faithful and ignited the heated rivalry.

For sure, it was not the way Syracuse wanted to end the rivalry with

Georgetown or the regular season. Like Humpty Dumpty, Syracuse had a great fall. The Orange finished 23–8, 11–7 in league play, but wilted by losing four of its last five games. That dropped SU to a fifth seed in the conference tournament, quite a comedown for a team that ripped through the non-conference and early Big East portion of its schedule on its way to an 18–1 start, 6–0 in the conference, and rose as high as No. 3 in the nation. Boeheim bashers piled on. They blamed the in-some-cases close but still-the-same losses, as well as the meltdowns against the Hoyas, on the Hall of Fame coach as if he suddenly had gotten dumber during the course of the last month.

Slumping Syracuse staggered into its farewell tour of the Big East Tournament. Playing in the second round, SU was pitted against Seton Hall, a poor team that barely got past South Florida, another poor team. The reinvigorated Orange won as its offense resurfaced. The No. 17 Cuse then got a solid victory over No. 19 Pittsburgh. About two weeks after Georgetown thrashed Syracuse by 22 points, SU slipped past the No. 5 Hoyas in overtime, 58–55, to even its conference tournament record with GT at 7–7. The win wiped that smile off the face of John Thompson II, who spoke too soon when he said, "And kiss Syracuse goodbye." Boeheim said, although he liked Thompson, he didn't appreciate his comment. Rather than come back with a similar quip, Boeheim took the high road and kept quiet as the Orange waved goodbye to the Hoyas. The curtain closed, ending a bitter, sometimes brutal rivalry and an era, and Jim Boeheim had the last laugh.

Syracuse advanced to the finals for a Big East-best 15th time. Pitted against No. 4 Louisville, a team they split with during the season, SU opened up a 16-point lead with about 15 minutes to go, only to watch the Cardinals not only erase all of it but shoot out to an 18-point advantage, a 34-point swing, to win going away, 78–61. The Cuse collapsed, and the Ville wanted it more. Syracuse departed the Big East tied with Georgetown for the most tournament wins with 78.

For its strong play in the conference tournament, Syracuse (26–9) was rewarded with a fourth seed in the NCAA tournament but was shipped out west to San Jose where they were matched up with the Big Sky champion Montana Grizzlies, who were seeded 13th. On the eve of the game, however, CBSSports.com reported that the NCAA was investigating Syracuse for major and widespread rules violations within the program. Accustomed to controversy swirling around his program before and during tournament time, Boeheim shrugged off the allegations.

In Boeheim's 30th NCAA tournament, the Jekyll and Hyde Orange, after leading by 50 points, rocked the Grizzlies, 81–34. Standing in the way of SU advancing to the Sweet 16 was the California Golden Bears, who were playing forty-five miles from their Berkeley campus. The contest matched Boeheim with 917 wins against his friend Mike Montgomery, who had compiled 656 wins. The pair ranked second and ninth in victories among NCAA coaches. With little prepara-tion to get ready for a defense they rarely saw, Cal was completely befuddled by Syracuse's suffocating zone and lost, 66–60, in a game that was not as close as the score indicated. Boeheim recorded his 50th NCAA tournament win, and Syracuse advanced to the Sweet 16 for the fourth time in five years, the 12th time since the NCAA tournament expanded to sixty-four teams in 1985, and the 17th time in Boeheim's tenure.

Syracuse (28–9) faced No. 1 seed Indiana in Washington, DC, a meeting that immediately revived twenty-six-year-old memories of that killer baseline shot by Keith Smart over the outstretched arms of Howard Triche, Brandon's uncle. Reminded of that, Boeheim, in his Sweet 16 press conference, said, "I got over it in 2003. I used to think about it most of the time. It took me sixteen years to get over it. I hardly think of it anymore."

Syracuse and Indiana had played three times since that champion-ship game over a quarter of a century earlier, with the Orange winning all three easily. Syracuse's 2–3 defense smothered Indiana, completely confusing, frustrating, and harassing the Hoosiers in a 61–50 victory. One of the best offensive teams in the country, IU unraveled under the stifling pressure as Syracuse advanced to the Elite Eight for the ninth time. "Let's face it. We haven't seen a zone like that," stated Indiana coach Tom Crean, after watching his team get spanked. "They're very good. They're where they are for a reason." Boeheim said his teams were always good defensively, but this unit was his best ever, and statistically, it was.

A couple of days later, Marquette coach Buzz Williams, if he wasn't already, became a believer after the Orange bottled up his Golden Eagles, 55–39, in front of President Obama and a slew of former Syracuse stars who were in the arena. "It's the zone. It's the players," he stated. "To compare Syracuse's zone to someone else's zone I think is unfair to Coach Boeheim and disrespectful to their players because every game is a different game. They beat us from start to finish. We tried everything we knew [and couldn't stop them]." President Obama wanted to go into the locker room to congratulate the winners but was told by his security that he couldn't. "Can't I go see the Cuse?" he asked.

In addition to winning the East Regional trophy, the Orange cut down the nets on the Hoyas' home floor, making the conquest even sweeter. The victory sent Syracuse to its fifth Final Four in five decades (1975, 1987, 1996, 2003, and 2013), the last four of which were coached by Boeheim, making him the fourth coach to take teams to the Final Four in four decades. In the game, Carter-Williams set a school single-season steals record when he got his 104th takeaway. With its tenacious, swarming defense that had long arms and legs stretching out across the court like the tentacles of an octopus that closed passing routes and prevented people from penetrating, the Orange's one-of-a-kind zone won over new admirers after holding Montana, California, Indiana, and Marquette to a combined 29 percent shooting from the floor (61 of 211) and 15 percent (14-for-91) from three-point range. Syracuse became the first team in the shot clock era to hold three of its first four NCAA tournament opponents to 50 points or less, and its 183 points allowed was the fewest in the Elite Eight since the tournament expanded in 1985. In winning by an average of 20 points a game against teams that had compiled a combined 101–31 record, Syracuse combined an efficient offense with a dominating defense that forced more turnovers (76) than it allowed opponents to make field goals (61).

Coaches, analysts, and people who had criticized the zone or hadn't bought into its effectiveness were hailing Boeheim, who had just notched his sixth 30-win season, as if he were suddenly a genius. Consequently, more and more teams began incorporating the 2–3 zone into their defenses. If you can't beat them, join them, they apparently thought.

Boeheim's Fourth Final Four

Still dancing, the Cuse headed to Atlanta to take on Michigan, coached by former Le Moyne College coach John Beilein, who had lost all nine of his previous contests against Boeheim. Before 75,350 people in the Georgia Dome, the second-largest crowd to ever attend the Final Four, Syracuse squandered some chances toward the end of the game and came up short against the Wolverines. After trailing at the half, 36–25, its largest deficit of the season at intermission, SU scrapped its way back to pull within one, 57–56, with 40 seconds to go. Behind, 59–56, with 19.2 seconds remaining, Syracuse had the ball with a chance to tie the score. Following a timeout, the plan was to get the ball to sharpshooter James Southerland for a three-point attempt, but he was covered, and Trevor Cooney resorted to driving to the basket. The Wolverines stuffed his shot and ended the Orange's season. Hindered by a couple of questionable calls during the last two minutes of the game—a blocking call against Carter-Williams and a charging call against Triche—the Orange went south in the 61–56 loss.

Syracuse's stingy defense held Michigan to 61 points, but the Orange offense, its Achilles' heel in several losses, struggled again. "Our defense was good enough to win tonight, but our offense was not," stated Boeheim, who orchestrated an incredible turnaround that began with the conference tournament. Boeheim took a team with flaws—poor shooting and poor post play—and again a victim of distractions—Carter-Williams being charged with theft, Southerland forced to sit out some games for academic reasons, rumors swirling about an NCAA investigation, and Boeheim trading barbs with a couple of national writers—and overachieved by guiding them to the Final Four and within a few seconds of another national championship game. Opportunities knocked, but Syracuse didn't take advantage of them. Michigan seized the moment and prevented two Big East teams from playing for the national championship in the conference's swan-song season as they would go on to lose to Louisville.

The loss closed the college careers of Triche and Southerland. A nephew of former SU player Howard Triche and cousin of former Orange guard Jason Hart, Triche started all of his school-record 147 games at Syracuse. Triche also made 34 consecutive free throws, matching Mike Lee's long-standing record set in 1971–72, and tied Derrick Coleman for playing in the most SU tournament wins with 10, although Coleman was a team member for 11 victories, but a back injury caused him to sit out the 1989 first-round win over Bucknell. Triche finished his career as the winningest player in school history.

Going 121–26 (.823) during the previous four years, a tad below the 100–18 (.847) mark he posted in his first four seasons, Boeheim was hardly losing his edge. The longtime Orange coach had accumulated 920 wins, 57 behind Krzyzewski, the all-time leader. With 52 NCAA tournament wins, Boeheim was fourth on the all-time list. Yet there were a few complainers hanging around.

A few days after the season ended, sophomore point guard Michael Carter-Williams became the eighth SU player to declare for the NBA draft since 2008, with Syracuse behind only Kentucky (15) and Kansas (10) in the number of undergraduate players lost to the professional ranks during that time period. Carter-Williams finished fifth nationally in both assist average (7.3) and steal average (2.8) per game. He broke the school record for steals in a season (111), while his 292 assists were second all-time behind Sherman Douglas's 326 total. For the third straight year Syracuse lost three starters, and this time the departures included its backcourt. As it did before, the Orange simply replaced good players with more of the same. Boeheim and his assistants brought in another Top 10-ranked recruiting class. Just as Carter-Williams stepped right in for Scoop Jardine, Syracuse had already lined up highly regarded point guard Tyler Ennis to slide into Carter-Williams' position. Ennis was named to the Wayman Tisdale watch list for national freshman of the year.

Carter-Williams had a spectacular NBA debut with Philadelphia when he scored 22 points, handed out 12 assists, and grabbed seven rebounds. He set an all-time NBA record for a rookie playing in his first game with nine steals as the 76ers, picked to finish last, upset the LeBron James-led, two-time defending champion Miami Heat. Carter-Williams started fast. Within the first two minutes of his professional career, he stole the ball, slammed home a dunk, got an assist, and made a three-point shot as the Sixers bolted to a 23–2 lead. He also finished strong, snaring three rebounds, dishing off two assists, and making three of four foul shots in the last two minutes of play as Philly, behind 108–104, overtook the Heat for a 114–110 victory. With the game winding down and the 76ers up by two, Carter-Williams grabbed a rebound and calmly buried two free throws with 8.5 seconds left to ice the contest. Sinking four of six shots from beyond the three-point line, committing only one turnover, and coming within one steal and three rebounds of a rare quadruple-double, Carter-Williams not only stole the ball several times in his first NBA game, but he also upstaged James and stole the show. He even swiped the ball from "The King," topping the theft off with a dunk. Carter-Williams's nine steals tied a Philadelphia team record.

After following up with a 14-point, five-assist, three-rebound performance against Washington in his second game and a 26-point, 10-assist effort against Chicago that helped the 76ers burst out to a surprising 3–0 start, Carter-Williams was named NBA Eastern Conference Player of the Week, the first neophyte to garner that honor since Shaquille O'Neal in 1992–93. Carter-Williams concluded an outstanding first season by being named NBA Rookie of the Year.

Picked 11th by Philadelphia, Carter-Williams represented Syracuse's fourth lottery selection in five years, with Jonny Flynn going No. 6 to Minnesota in 2009, Wes Johnson No. 4 to the Timberwolves in 2010, and Dion Waiters No. 4 to Cleveland in 2012. Waiters was named to the NBA All-Rookie Team, joining an SU club that included Billy Owens, Derrick Coleman, Sherman Douglas, Dave Bing, and Carmelo Anthony.

14

SYRACUSE'S BIG EAST
RIVALRIES: GEORGETOWN AND
CONNECTICUT

In the early years of the Big East conference, Georgetown, St. John's, and Syracuse were the best teams. The retirement of Lou Carnesecca at St. John's following the 1992 season and the subsequent demise of the Redmen (later known as the Red Storm) left Georgetown and Syracuse as the two prominent powers in the Big East. John Thompson's Hoyas, with a string of great centers beginning with Patrick Ewing and followed by Alonzo Mourning, Dikembe Mutombo, and Othella Harrington, along with players like Eric "Sleepy" Floyd and Allen Iverson, was the more dominant team throughout most of the 1980s. Georgetown won four regular-season championships, six conference tournaments, and 19 of 27 games against the Orange, while Syracuse managed just three regular-season titles and two Big East tournament championships. At its zenith, the games between the Orange and Hoyas were all-out wars, as evidenced by the elbowing and punching that occurred during a couple of games and by the sheer physicality of the confrontations during the regular season. The Hoyas' relentless, swarming, in-your-face, five-headed monster pressure defense that double-teamed, harassed, pushed, disrupted, and did-everything-within-the-rules style turned every game into a 94-foot street fight. As expressed in *30 for 30: Requiem for the Big East*, the attitudes of the two coaches spurred on the contentiousness. "John and I were not friends," informed Boeheim. "We were face-to-face in a few games yelling at each other, and there was a lot of bitterness. I didn't like Georgetown. I didn't like any part of them. We were enemies." Thompson simply stated, "The feeling was mutual." When Syracuse and Georgetown clashed, the intensity and everything else was turned up a couple of notches. Before the games, it would have been apropos for the Carrier Dome crowd to be warned with an announcement, "The pilot has turned on the fasten your seatbelt sign as we will be experiencing significant turbulence. Thank you for flying Orange Air."

However, in 1990, when it went 8–8 in league play, Georgetown started to fade. The Hoyas then experienced a losing season in conference play in 1992–93. On the decline, Georgetown finally bottomed out in the 1997–98 season when the Hoyas barely finished above .500, with a 16–15 overall record and 6–12 in the Big East. In 1998–99, Georgetown started out 7–6 and 0–3 in the conference, causing Thompson to step down with his program in free fall. What was a heated rivalry between Syracuse and Georgetown started to lose a little of its luster. Regardless, the games between the two schools remained intense. Georgetown still considered Syracuse its top rival. The Hoyas' fan base annually declared the days leading up to the SU game "Syracuse Hate Week."

Following a few years of slippage, as if given a shot of adrenaline, Georgetown got good again. The Syracuse-Georgetown rivalry picked up steam. Beginning with the 2008–09 season, the Orange and Hoyas met nine more times as members of the Big East, six times when both teams were ranked in the Top 25, with Syracuse holding a 5–4 edge.

Connecticut became a conference contender soon after Jim

Calhoun was named coach in 1986. After going 9–19 in Calhoun's first year and then experiencing a couple of mediocre seasons, in 1990 UConn emerged as the Big East's biggest power. The Huskies, with Donyell Marshall, Ray Allen, Richard "Rip" Hamilton, Khalid El-Amin, Caron Butler, Emeka Okafor, and Ben Gordon hit their stride in the mid-'90s and continued to play at high level through 2006. In the 1990s, UConn captured nine regular-season championships and six conference tournament titles, while SU only mustered five regular-season championships and three tournament championships. In head-to-head games, Connecticut held the whip hand, going 24–18 against the Orange. However, like Georgetown, the Huskies tailed off a little bit and experienced a few subpar seasons, even missing the 2010 NCAA tournament.

By 2011 Syracuse, Georgetown, and Connecticut were again pretty competitive with each other during the regular season and all made the NCAA Tournament. UConn came back with a vengeance when do-everything guard Kemba Walker carried and willed the Huskies to an unprecedented five wins in five days in the Big East tournament and six wins in the NCAA Tournament. Led by the crusty and grizzled Calhoun and the amazing and magical Walker, Connecticut, despite going 9–9 and finishing ninth in the conference, surprised everyone by winning 11 games in twenty-seven days to go from a middle-of-the-pack team to the leader and win its third national championship under Calhoun. The following year, however, Connecticut, with a starting team stacked with NBA talent, fell flat on its face, finishing tied for ninth with an 8–10 conference record and being ousted in the first round of the NCAA tournament by Iowa State.

Meanwhile, Syracuse continued its sustained success, advancing to the Elite Eight in 2012 and the Final Four in 2013, while UConn was eliminated in the first round of play in 2012 and Georgetown followed suit in the second round. Villanova and Pittsburgh, also pretty good teams, returned to the lower echelons of the conference, with the Wildcats missing out on postseason play completely and the Panthers relegated to the NIT.

During the Georgetown and Connecticut glory days, Syracuse was always in the mix and pretty competitive with the Hoyas and Huskies, but in many years, they lagged a step behind. SU clashed with its two biggest rivals nine times in the Big East tournament but won only once. Georgetown was the Orange's biggest rival from the 1980s through 1990, and in the minds of many people, they remain its most hated foe. However, because of UConn's rise and Georgetown's demise, for some, the Huskies replaced the Hoyas as Syracuse's biggest rival. The opponent that is the most disliked would depend upon which Syracuse fan you asked. The older fans probably still consider Georgetown the bigger rival because they remember the salad days of the series, while perhaps the younger fans begrudge Connecticut more because those battles are what they grew up on.

Syracuse, the Big East's Most Consistent Team

Whereas Georgetown experienced several down years and Connecticut was a losing program before Calhoun turned it around and toward the end of Calhoun's career again suffered a brief but drastic downtick, Syracuse was the most consistent top-level program and arguably the Big East's biggest winner since the formation of the conference. The Orange may have dipped a little some years and were not as dominant even in its best seasons, but for the most part, Syracuse had been the best program year in and year out. As the dean of Big East coaches, Boeheim's teams won a conference-record ten Big East championships, a first place in the now defunct Big East 7 Division, five tournament titles, and played in the conference championship game a league-record fifteen times. With a Big East-best 416 overall conference wins through the 2012–13 season when Syracuse left the league, Boeheim finished well ahead of Calhoun and Thompson, who were a distant second and third. Excluding latecomers to the league Louisville and Marquette, Syracuse also had the fewest losing seasons in Big East play with two: the first in 1980–81 when the Orange finished 6–8, and the second in 2005–06 when the Cuse came in at 7–9. Georgetown had suffered through seven losing seasons and Connecticut experienced five losing seasons. St. John's, one of the original powers, endured 13 losing seasons. Powers that emerged later, Villanova, which shocked the world by beating Georgetown to win the 1985 national championship, and Pittsburgh, had six and 11 losing seasons respectively. During the thirty-four years that Syracuse, Georgetown, and UConn were members of the Big East, Syracuse had the best overall regular-season record (366–186), followed by Georgetown (338–213) and UConn (325–226). During that time, the Orange also compiled the best road record a league-leading twelve times.

Therefore, a strong argument can be made that Syracuse, although not the most dominant, had been the Big East's best team overall since the conference was formed. Not experiencing the roller-coaster ride of other teams, Syracuse, solid and stable, in some ways had been the Big East's Rock of Gibraltar. It was the only program that had consistently been a national player year in and year out. Moreover, Syracuse also produced conference-bests with 101 All-Big East players and 35 first-team and 25 second-team selections. And the man responsible for that was Boeheim.

15

==

SYRACUSE JOINS THE ATLANTIC COAST CONFERENCE

2013–14

After thirty-four years as a charter member of the Big East, on July 1, 2013, Syracuse, along with Pittsburgh and Notre Dame, officially became a member of the Atlantic Coast Conference, instantly and arguably making the ACC the strongest college basketball conference ever assembled. Because of Syracuse's basketball reputation, the Cuse's entrance bolstered the conference's strength, like a rising tide that lifted all of the boats. For SU, it meant the big-name programs coming to the Carrier Dome in the future would be Duke and North Carolina, not Georgetown and Connecticut. Whereas the Hoyas and Huskies at times towered over the Big East, the path to the top of the ACC ran right through Tobacco Road. A whole new era had begun, one that the Orange was expected to benefit from on a lot of levels, especially financially.

As Boeheim's career was seemingly headed toward the finish line, it got fresh legs. Deciding to again join Krzyzewski for the 2016 Olympic Games gave people the impression that Boeheim would now continue coaching at Syracuse up until or through the Olympics. Winning more than 82 percent of his games over the last four years enabled Boeheim's recruiting to pick up steam. On September 9, 2013, recruiting guru Dave Telep ranked the top recruiting teams over the previous four years based solely on their NCAA tournament results, and Syracuse, with a 10–4 record, ranked fourth, behind Kentucky (bolstered by John Calipari's one-and-done philosophy), Duke, and Kansas. And with the Orange right in the mix for some of the nation's top high school talent in 2014, 2015, and 2016, projections were for the Cuse to remain among the elite teams with a serious chance to make a run at the national title during those years. The thinking was that Boeheim would want to stay aboard and enjoy the ride. After all, the fun is in the winning, and Boeheim appeared to position himself to win big over the next few years.

Syracuse entered the new conference with three major contributors in the backcourt gone. The Orange transitioned from a guard- to a forward-oriented team. Leading the way was C. J. Fair, the preseason ACC Player of the Year. Discounting Fair's numbers, with Baye Moussa Keita, Jerami Grant, Rakeem Christmas, and DaJuan Coleman also returning, the Orange opened ACC play with a big front line that combined to average 17.5 points, 15.3 rebounds, and 3.8 blocks per game in its last season in the Big East. Boeheim called the group of bigs one of the best defensive groups that he had ever coached.

Syracuse was ranked No. 7 in the *USA Today* and No. 8 in the Associated Press preseason polls, the fourth straight year that SU started the season in the Top 10. The Cuse also got respect from the ACC as they were selected second behind nationally No.1-ranked Duke and ahead of conference power North Carolina. Furthermore, Fair was picked as the league's top player. Putting any retirement talk to rest, seemingly for another three years until after he coached the Olympic team, Boeheim at the ACC Media Days seemed recharged by the challenge of banging heads with the likes of the Blue Devils and Tar Heels. A little glamor was added to the 2013–14 season when rapper King Vega came out with his upbeat Syracuse basketball and Jim Boeheim anthems and videos, sideshows not common at most other schools.

As Boeheim hoped and expected, Tyler Ennis, a poised, pass-first point guard, comfortably and capably fit into the Syracuse system and immediately took control of the team, sophomore Trevor Cooney finally began to make three-point shots the way SU coaches knew he could when they recruited him, Jerami Grant demonstrated even more of his immense potential, DaJuan Coleman offensively showed glimpses of his high school All-American ability, and C. J. Fair was C. J. Fair only better, all of which made the Cuse jell with only a minimum of growing pains. Juiced up, the Orange, in typical SU fashion, began the 2013–14 season by winning its first seven games, including its third Maui Classic championship where it defeated Minnesota, California, and No. 18 Baylor, all of which were undefeated entering the tournament. Like Billy Owens in 1990 and Jason Hart in 1998, Fair garnered MVP honors as the team returned to Central New York with another trophy earned in Hawaii.

Fully recovered from jet lag, SU improved to 8–0 with a 69–52 rout of Indiana in the Carrier Dome in the ACC/Big Ten Challenge, bettering the margin in the 61–50 victory over IU in the previous season's Sweet 16 game. It also made it five wins in a row over the Hoosiers since Indiana edged SU for the 1987 NCAA title. Meanwhile, the Orange also advanced to No. 4 in the AP poll, making it the fifth straight year that the Cuse had been ranked in the AP Top 5, the first time that had happened since 1986–87 through 1990–91. After defeating Binghamton in its next game, along with Michigan State and Kentucky losing, the Cuse rose to No. 2 in the nation, its highest ranking since finishing the 2011–12 campaign No. 2 in the land.

More good news came when Malachi Richardson, a 6-foot-5, 190-pound shooting guard/small forward with octopus arms, ranked the No. 12 overall player in the nation, verbally committed to Syracuse.

Recruiting over the course of the past decade had been the best that it had ever been on the Hill. Unlike programs that went after one-and-done players and then tried to build a team around them, during the Orange's latest rise to elite status Boeheim became increasingly more successful in consistently bringing in players who fit his system and the program's immediate and long-range needs, rather than previous to that when he sometimes settled for players who possessed particular skills such as shooting while being deficient at ball-handling or who could leap but not shoot.

Syracuse traveled downstate to face old Big East rival St. John's. In front of a packed house that sported plenty of orange, SU went up 15 in the first half. Syracuse then got punched as the Johnnies took the lead in the second half before the Orange punched back, only harder, to regain control over the final four minutes to come away with a hard-fought 68–63 victory that made it the fifth straight season that Syracuse had started 10–0. It took an incredible performance from freshman sensation Tyler Ennis, who looked poised and for the most part polished playing his first game in "The World's Most Famous Area." Boeheim gave his remarkable rookie the highest praise, stating, "As a freshman point guard, he's playing better than anybody I've ever had," meaning Ennis surpassed the first-year performances of former Syracuse stars Pearl Washington, Jason Hart, and Jonny Flynn. In Carter-Williams, Syracuse lost an NBA lottery pick but surprisingly enjoyed a step up at the point guard position. Regardless of what the weather was outside in Gotham, for Cuse fans, the sun was bright orange in The City.

The neutral site or away victories over creditable teams Minnesota, Baylor, and St. John's, which entered the games with a combined 28–3 record, provided no fodder for those who annually complained about Syracuse's non-conference schedule or the Cuse not leaving New York State before January. Following the Christmas break, in a battle of former Big East foes with identical 11–0 records, No. 2 Syracuse entertained No. 11 Villanova before a crowd of nearly 30,000 in the Carrier Dome and a CBS national television audience. The Orange absorbed an early barrage of Wildcat three-point bombs to quickly fall behind, 25–7, but, like a Sasquatch sighting, whatever spark Nova had was swiftly extinguished when SU answered with a 20–0 run to take the lead enroute to a 78–62 victory. The Wildcats, which at first lived by the three, later died by the three when the long-range shots that went in at the beginning were consistently off the mark later. In what had become a staple of the program, the Orange, after easily beating Eastern Michigan, 70–48, like the previous four years, cruised through the non-conference portion of its schedule unblemished.

Sporting a 13–0 mark and No. 2 ranking, Syracuse ventured into virgin territory as it began its first season of play in the Atlantic Coast Conference. A coach in the Big East since Jimmy Carter was president, Boeheim went from "Dean of the Big East coaches" to a rookie coach in the new league. SU, one of seven remaining unbeaten teams, hosted a Miami team that was the defending conference regular-season and tournament champion but, with most of its best players having departed, had slipped to mediocrity. Like the subfreezing temperature outside, inside the Dome, Syracuse's offense was cold. Against a deliberate, methodical Miami offense and a matchup zone defense that dictated the pace of the game, SU shot a frosty 36 percent from the field and an even icier 20 percent from beyond the arc. The Orange offense thawed out enough to put together an 8–0 run in the last six minutes of the contest to prevent a major upset as Syracuse prevailed over the 'Canes, 49–44, in its historic ACC debut. The first ACC road stop was at Virginia Tech where the Cuse beat the Hokies by 20. That set the table for North Carolina's highly anticipated visit to the Carrier Dome.

Carolina, a basketball thoroughbred and longtime ACC giant, was a wildly erratic team. Over the course of three weeks, they defeated defending national champion Louisville, preseason No. 1 Kentucky, and then No. 1 Michigan State, all while going down to Butler at home, UAB on the road, lowly Wake Forest in its conference opener, and then to Miami three days prior to its trip up north. All the losses were to unranked teams. Inconsistency and unpredictability aside,

Carolina was still Carolina, but the Tar Heels found Syracuse's 2–3 zone harder to solve than Rubik's Cube. Syracuse humbled them, 57–45, in front of 32,000-plus feverish fans and a national television audience, holding UNC to its lowest offensive output in the shot-clock era and the fewest points ever scored by a Roy Williams-coached team. It was also the fewest points North Carolina had scored since it managed only 44 points against Duke in 1979. In the game between two Hall of Fame coaches and tradition-rich programs that came into the contest with a combined 3,989 wins—2,100 by Carolina and 1,889 by Syracuse—Boeheim's juggernaut imposed its will on the Tar Heels to even the series between the two storied programs at 4–4. Recognized for its "Carolina blue" colors, North Carolina departed New York State with the Carolina blues.

The Carolina slamdown, followed by Duke suffering its fourth loss of the season a couple of hours later, at the moment hinted of a changing of the guard in the ACC. Two former top-tier Big East teams, Syracuse and Pittsburgh, surged to the head of the pack with 3–0 conference records—the Orange, nestled in at No. 2 in the nation, and the Panthers with a 15–1 overall record.

With SU putting together another in an assembly line of outstanding teams, ESPN's Seth Greenberg asked Boeheim how he had been able to consistently produce excellent teams over the years. Explaining his formula to a national television audience, Boeheim said, "We try to have one or two guys good enough maybe to play in the NBA but who need four years to mature and then throw in one or two talented players or a couple of juniors. If you can do that, you can be successful consistently." Greenberg then asked Boeheim how he had been able to keep players who didn't play much from transferring. Boeheim responded, "Everybody's different. [We tell them] if they stay they get to play right away next year, rather than sitting out a year if they go someplace else. A lot of guys just don't understand that, and that's why you have 500 transfers in college basketball. Smart players get it."

Asked why he had stayed at Syracuse for so long, Boeheim said, "I'm from here. I've always been comfortable here. I'm one of those guys who absolutely doesn't think the grass is greener on the other side of the fence. I think it's greener on my side. Syracuse University really has everything you need to be successful."

Although Boeheim had strongly hinted in years past that he was very close to retirement, he told Greenberg, "I honestly thought that I would have retired ten or fifteen years ago. Most coaches I've talked to said they retired too soon. That's a mistake you don't want to make. If I retired five years ago, I would have missed five 30-win seasons, and I wouldn't have been too happy. I'm going to coach until I finally come to that day, but I haven't thought in a long time that it was going to be soon."

One of four remaining unbeaten teams, the Cuse continued in cruise control, topping Boston College, 69–59. Straight ahead was Pittsburgh, a team that many times gave SU fits, including stopping SU's season-opening win streaks of 13 games in 2009–10 and 18 games in 2010–11. Old foes in a new conference, Syracuse and Pittsburgh battled in what was a typical Big East-type contest with the Panthers leading, 52–49, with 4:41 to go, causing the stomachs of SU fans everywhere to churn. The Orange avoided the upset when freshman Ennis, steady and poised beyond his years, scored on two driving layups and two foul shots in the final two minutes. Not done, he calmly sank the critical free throws with 4.8 seconds remaining to make the score 59–54 and enable Syracuse to start the season 18–0 for the fourth time in school history and the third time in the previous four years. In sole possession of first place in the conference with a 5–0 mark, Boeheim, at least for the time being, was the new sheriff in ACC country. With Wisconsin falling to Indiana, a team the Orange had beaten earlier in the season, SU, Arizona, and Wichita State were the only undefeated teams in the country.

However, just when Syracuse seemed to have it all together, for the third time in recent years, it lost a big man. DaJuan Coleman's season was short-circuited due to surgery, reminiscent of when Arinze Onuaku and Fab Melo went out, although Coleman's injury happened mid-season while Onuaku's injury and Melo's absence for academic reasons occurred during the NCAA tournament. Regardless, the Orange Express kept rolling along. After frittering away an 18-point advantage and watching Miami storm back to take a 47–46 lead late in the game, the Cuse calmed the 'Canes to leave South Florida with a 64–52 victory. Syracuse then avoided an upset bid by Wake Forest, doing just enough in Winston-Salem to get by the Demon Deacons to match the 20–0 program-best start recorded by the 2011–12 team.

Syracuse-Duke I

The first-ever visit by Duke to Syracuse would have made a good movie script. Like New Year's Eve, the countdown to the biggest college basketball game in the 2013–14 season to that point began early. The thought of the Dukies coming to town had caused a stir in Central New York going back four months to when the date of the game was announced. The drama began to build over the course of the 171-day wait for the clash between the longtime anchor of the ACC and the new kids on the block. In Boeheimburg, an area outside Gate E of the Carrier Dome, numerous Syracuse students in upwards of twenty-five tents camped out overnight in frigid temperatures for two weeks leading up to the contest.

Let's set the stage. On August 22, 2014, Paul Swaney on the website StadiumJourney.com published the results of a four-year study that involved visiting all 351 college basketball arenas. Based on several categories, the study rated the Carrier Dome the second-best college basketball venue in the country, behind only Rupp Arena. Among the things that separated the Dome from other places were the new video boards and the overall atmosphere, especially the noise factor at certain junctures of a game and the Syracuse tradition of fans standing and clapping until the Orange made its first basket, while "Welcome to the Jungle" by hard-rock group Guns N' Roses blared over the loudspeakers. "There's a reason why the Carrier Dome has been called the 'Loud House,'" he wrote.

The day had finally arrived for the most anticipated home game in SU history. A polarizing team, Duke is to college basketball what Notre Dame is to college football and the New York Yankees are to baseball. People either love the Blue Devils or hate them. With ESPN's *College GameDay* in town, like ants to a picnic, people began entering the Carrier Dome around 7:00 a.m. for the 6:30 p.m. tip-off. New York State Governor Andrew Cuomo even tweeted, "Let's Go [Orange]," apropos for a school that marketed itself as "New York's College Team," with NY stickers on the school's football helmets and banners of the Statue of Liberty inside the Dome, to SU adverts on top of New York City taxicabs and occasional Syracuse promotions in Times Square. It was Super Bowl week, but for the Orange Nation and many Blue Devil and college basketball fans, the talk was about Syracuse-Duke, not Seattle-Denver. The big sports event was going to take place in Syracuse, not New Jersey.

Going into the game, the series between two of college basketball's premier programs was locked at 4–4, with Boeheim scoring 15 points against Duke in the first meeting between the teams when the Blue Devils prevailed during the 1966 NCAA tournament. Coaching head-to-head, Krzyzewski and Boeheim were 1–1. The two legendary coaches had combined for 1,914 wins, the most ever between opposing coaches and 154 more victories than when Boeheim and Jim Calhoun were on opposite sides of the court in the quarterfinals of the 2012 Big East tournament.

After the game had been dissected a couple of dozen different ways for days, the hour had arrived for what Boeheim told Dick Vitale was the most hyped game in the history of the Carrier Dome. Before a record-breaking Carrier Dome and NCAA on-campus crowd of 35,446 people, in a game that featured the two winningest coaches in college basketball history—Krzyzewski with 974 wins and Boeheim with 940—the two best freshmen in the country—Ennis and Jabari Parker—and SU alum Vanessa Williams, the first African American Miss America in 1983 singing the national anthem, it had all the makings of another "Syracuse Moment" before the game even started. "When the Carrier Dome is rockin' and rollin' it's one of the great spectacles of all of college sports," stated television color commentator Fran Fraschilla. And on the evening of February 1, the 34-year-old gray concrete and steel structure with a 165-foot high, air-supported, Teflon-coated, fiberglass-inflatable roof that is the signature of the Syracuse skyline was packed. The people inside were animated like never before. Courtside seats went for $3,400, while those in the first ten rows were going for $1,500.

Moments before the game, just after Williams concluded the national anthem with a "Go Orange," ESPN courtside reporter Shannon Spake opened her comments by simply stating, "Wow!" During the telecast, Dick Vitale called Syracuse "the sports capital of the world tonight." The atmosphere in the building was electric, the noise deafening, and it stayed that way throughout the contest. Seemingly there was no way the game could possibly live up to its billing, but Syracuse squeaked out a thrilling 91–89 overtime win that exceeded the buildup to what arguably was the greatest and most exciting game in the history of the Carrier Dome, which opened in 1980, the year Krzyzewski started coaching at Duke.

Duke's Rasheed Sulaimon splashed a game-tying three-pointer to knot the score at 78–78 as time expired to send the game into overtime. With 1:21 left in the extra session, Andre Dawkins drained a three-ball to put the Blue Devils in front, 87–84, only to have SU score six straight points to bolt to a 90–87 advantage. Sulaimon converted two free throws to make it 90–89 with 0:09 to go. C. J. Fair closed out the scoring by making one of two free throws, but the hotly contested game from start to finish was not decided until the Blue Devils' Quinn Cook missed a potential game-tying shot with four seconds remaining in overtime, sending the already hysterical crowd into even more of a frenzy. In a high-scoring affair played at a Ping-Pong pace that saw the Blue Devils make an astonishing 15 three-point shots and Syracuse make a season-high 57 percent of its shots from the floor, the Cuse yet again found a way to win.

Duke went down. Syracuse had slain the devil, all dressed in blue. Being undefeated and the No. 2 team in the nation, after defeating the No. 17 team that had entered the game with four losses—albeit Duke—the crowd remained classy and did not storm the court. The Domers reacted as a power program should, like they had been there before. Soon after the game ended, ESPN put out a hilarious *Pulp Fiction*-inspired cartoon of Otto, the SU mascot, shoving an orange into the mouth of a Blue Devil, with the caption reading, "How's that orange taste?"

Fair and Grant both had career-high scoring days, with Fair firing in 28 points and Grant 24 in addition to grabbing 16 rebounds. Rakeem Christmas couldn't have picked a better time to play his best all-around game, with a line of 10 rebounds, seven points, six blocks, and two assists in support of being an intimidating force underneath the basket. Tyler Ennis, cool as a cucumber as always, contributed 14 points and nine assists, along with going 8-for-8 from the free throw line. Trevor Cooney was steady with 14 points.

It couldn't have been scripted any better. The game was as good as it gets, with Boeheim in his press conference stating, "We've had a lot of games in here that have been good, but there has never been a game as good as this one." Long-time assistant Mike Hopkins told Syracuse scribe Bud Poliquin, "This was the best regular-season game that I've ever been a part of." Former star guard Gerry McNamara told Syracuse beat writer Mike Waters, "This was one of the greatest regular-season college basketball games that I've not just been a part of but have watched. This was a special game." Dick Vitale tweeted, "This is one of the top five games that I've done in thirty-five years."

Other commentators, coaches, fans, and social networking contributors couldn't find enough superlatives to describe the game, the atmosphere, and what they had witnessed—whether in person or on television—with some calling it the greatest college basketball game they had ever seen, even surpassing the Orange's epic six-overtime win over Connecticut in the Big East tournament. It was an incredible game in an incredible atmosphere. It was a spectacle, a historic, drama-filled event throughout that had people biting their fingernails while sitting on the edge of their seats or sofas. It was theater at its absolute best, a night to remember. An instant classic, Syracuse-Duke was more than just a basketball game. It was an event that twenty years later 75,000 people will claim to have been in the house. With 4.1 million television viewers, it garnered a Nielsen rating of 2.9 that tied it for the fourth-highest watched regular-season college basketball game on ESPN since 2002. Simply put, the entire evening became quite the "Syracuse Moment."

With the huge win before a national television audience, the status of Syracuse basketball and Jim Boeheim as a coach continued to skyrocket. For those not yet fully on board, the Orange took another giant step toward being recognized as a truly major player on the college basketball landscape, and Boeheim, already the king of Syracuse to hard-shell Cuse fans, toward nationally being recognized as one of the all-time greats of college basketball.

Beyond that, Syracuse started the season 21–0 for the first time in school history, the record-breaking win made even sweeter because it came at the expense of Duke. The victory also propelled the Orange to No. 1 in the country because, shortly after the final buzzer in Central New York, across the country, top-ranked Arizona fell to California, 60–58. It was Syracuse's first No. 1 ranking since the 2011–12 season and left the Orange as one of only two undefeated teams in the nation, the other being Wichita State that along with SU was a Final Four participant the previous year. There was still a long way to go in the season, but coincidentally, the Cuse's unblemished record occurred during the 100th anniversary season of the school's only undefeated team that in 1913–14 went 12–0.

Unlike some rivalries that are based on hate, such as SU and Georgetown and in football with Ohio State and Michigan as well as Alabama and Auburn, the budding Syracuse-Duke rivalry, because of the relationship between Boeheim and Krzyzewski, was based on respect. People were already talking about the sequel, which was going to take place three weeks later when Syracuse would be traveling to Durham to play Duke in Cameron Indoor Stadium.

But first things first. In less than 48 hours, Notre Dame, the team that on January 21, 2012, snapped Syracuse's season-opening 20-game win streak, was coming to the Dome. However, that 68–57 victory the previous year was in South Bend and was the first game that Syracuse played without Big East Defensive Player of the Year Fab Melo. No such luck for the Irish this time, however, as Trevor Cooney, like fireworks on a dark night, lit up the Irish. As if he was shooting the ball through a Hula Hoop, the Orange sharpshooter lasered 11 of 15 shots from the field, including a school-record-tying 9 of 12 from three-point range for a career-best 33 points. With his mentor Gerry McNamara grinning from ear to ear while watching from the bench, Cooney, the only double-figure scorer, bailed out the Orange as it played through off nights by stars C. J. Fair and Jerami Grant in a 61–55 win that protected its newly minted No. 1 ranking. The crowd, although close to 26,000, seemed to have a hangover following the electrifying victory over Duke. After having played three games in six days, the Syracuse players sleepwalked to the win. The team, and maybe even its fans, was tired and needed and deserved the six-day rest period before hosting Clemson.

Another one bites the dust. Attracting everyone's best effort as the top team in the country, the Cuse, in a contest played at a snail's pace, patiently subdued Clemson, the nation's best defensive team, 57–44. The win extended Syracuse's season-opening streak to 23 games and matched the school mark for consecutive victories set over the course of two seasons by the 1916–17 and 1917–18 teams. Syracuse took its 10–0 conference record to Pittsburgh, always a tough place to play. In the 12-year history of the Petersen Events Center, in nine match-ups with top five teams, Pitt had never lost. Trailing throughout the game, the Cuse closed hard, outscoring Pittsburgh, 10–3, in the final two minutes. Before the second largest crowd in The Pete, freshman phenom Tyler Ennis quickly dribbled past midcourt and heaved a shot that sailed through the net as time expired to give the Orange a dramatic 58–56 win that snatched victory away from the Panthers and stunned the raucous crowd that was getting ready to celebrate. The fast finish took the jump out of the delirious jumping students in

Pitt's Oakland Zoo section who were anxiously waiting to storm the court in anticipation of their No. 25-ranked Panthers taking down the undefeated, top-ranked team in the nation. Not on this night, though, as Syracuse simply refused to lose. In the end, Pitt played physical, but Syracuse made plays. Pitt pushed the action, but Syracuse had answers. Superman, err Syracuse, had been punched in the nose by an adversary just as big, just as strong, and maybe just as talented, and the Panthers had drawn blood. A lesser team may have quit. Syracuse, showing the heart of a champion, did not. Boeheim in years past had difficulty overcoming Pitt's tenacious pit-bull defense. He now had beaten Jamie Dixon three straight times and in four of the last five games between the former Big East and current ACC rivals.

Reminiscent of Pearl Washington's 45-foot buzzer-beater thirty years before that beat Boston College, Ennis's 35-foot jump shot arguably surpassed it because it was in a hostile environment and enabled Syracuse to maintain its No. 1 ranking, remain undefeated, and win its school-record 24th straight game. Like Pearl's thrilling game-winner, Ennis's exciting curtain closer was seen on ESPN, with Cuse fans rejoicing throughout the world. The next day, Vice President of the United States Joe Biden called Ennis to congratulate him on the last-second dagger that slayed the Panthers. Ennis's heroics were replayed and discussed nationwide the following week. For all that and the excitement that it created and the interest that it generated nationally, the shot qualifies as another "Syracuse moment." Other college teams and programs have their share of highlights, for sure, but Syracuse just seemed to have the penchant for periodically doing things with a little more pizzazz.

The city of Syracuse was on board with this team as 31,572 fans showed up for the North Carolina State game. They were treated to yet another heart-stopper as the Orange, trailing, 55–54, with less than 15 seconds to go, found yet another way to win. This time, after the Wolfpack got caught in a couple of traps, it took a steal by Rakeem Christmas who passed to Ennis who fed Fair for a fast-break layup that ripped the victory away from the Wolfpack and extended the

Cuse's enchanted run to 25–0 overall and 12–0 in the ACC. After pulling a rabbit out of a hat against Pitt and the Houdini-like ending against NC State, Syracuse continued to be the talk of the basketball world. Fans in Cuse Kingdom were giddy.

Having already defeated High Point, Wake Forest, North Carolina, Duke, and now NC State, Syracuse swept Tobacco Road. Much more significant than that, Syracuse, in its first season in the ACC, recorded the third-best start in conference history, a mark bettered only by NC State (27–0) in 1973 and North Carolina (32–0) in 1957 in the years that both those teams won the national championship.

Syracuse, however, had been living dangerously, and it caught up with them. The Orange was ripening on the branch, and BC picked it. In a game played at turtle-like speed, Boston College, which entered the contest with a 6–19 record and in last place in the ACC with a 2–10 mark, exposed the Cuse. Losers of five straight, the Eagles planted a 62–59 overtime loss on SU. For a giant-killer to slay a giant, it usually needs some help. SU provided the help by shooting a season-low 32.2 percent from the field, including going 2-for-12 from long-range. When trailing or tied in the final two minutes, Syracuse had been 17–0. This time, unlike during the string of recent wins, the magic never materialized. It took the Eagles' best performance and Syracuse's worst performance for BC to win, and it happened.

Syracuse-Duke II

Syracuse had to regroup because its next foray would be to Durham for a rematch with Duke, which had inched its way up to No. 5 in the polls. An indicator of the magnitude of the contest was that in Syracuse the game was shown free at two theaters, the Landmark on South Salina Street and the Palace on James Street. The already bloated Syracuse following had grown, as evidenced by the Turning Stone Resort Casino hosting Syracuse basketball viewing parties for all remaining SU games. Like the theaters, Turning Stone provided food and festivities. Like sometimes in the past, SU hoops had again become more than just a basketball game.

After playing a game for the ages three weeks earlier, the Orange and Blue Devils were both coming off losses entering SU-Duke II. However, the contest still featured two top five teams who were competing for the ACC championship. In its first-ever appearance in the famed building where the "Cameron Crazies" cozy right up to courtside, the Orange invasion of Cameron Indoor Stadium highlighted the biggest weekend of the college basketball season. Even by its standards, the "Crazies," many with not just faces but bodies painted blue, were amped up and crazier than usual, as if on steroids.

Like the classic in the Carrier Dome that ended on a questionable call, this proved to be a dandy in Durham that also concluded with a controversial call. The game matched the intensity of the first game and, even without its wild finish, became another instant classic. Whereas the first was an offensive battle, this was a defensive struggle. The lead swung back and forth with Duke clinging to a 60–58 advantage with 10.4 seconds to go when C. J. Fair drove baseline and scored what appeared to be the tying basket while being fouled in the process, only to have the points erased with Fair called for charging into Rodney Hood. Instead of Fair going to the foul line with a chance to give the Orange a one-point lead, the Blue Devils were given possession of the ball with 10 ticks left.

The controversial call sent Boeheim into a rage. Hot under the collar, Boeheim went ballistic, trying but failing to tear off his sport coat as he stormed onto the court and unleashed an expletive-filled tirade at Tony Greene, the official who made the call. The picture of the open-mouthed and screaming Boeheim going bonkers was photoshopped and quickly became a hilarious meme that went viral across social media platforms. There was Boeheim running with the bulls, performing an acrobatic flying dunk, riding a baby weasel on top of a flying woodpecker, ski jumping, in WWE wrestling, hanging with the movie stars at the Oscars, with the *Baywatch* babes, with Leonardo

DiCaprio on the *Titanic,* with Maria von Trapp in *The Sound of Music,* with Tom Hanks in *Forrest Gump,* with a swimsuit model, with Michael Jackson, in *Breaking Bad,* and in *Ghostbusters,* among several other comical settings and scenarios, one funnier than the previous one. In its own unique way, it was another "Syracuse Moment."

The temper tantrum resulted in Boeheim drawing two technical fouls and being ejected from the game, the only time in his 38-year career that he was tossed from a contest, not counting an exhibition against Le Moyne College in 2005. Duke's designated free-throw shooter Quinn Cook converted three of four foul shots that sealed a 66–60 Blue Devils victory that toppled Syracuse from its No. 1 ranking. In another down-to-the-wire thriller that had fans of both teams on pins and needles from tip-off to the final buzzer, the Orange had a chance to pull out another squeaker in the style of Pitt and NC State had Boeheim not lost control. In his postgame press conference, the Orange coach was composed and even joked a little bit. "That's the new rule. It's been explained a hundred times," he said. "C. J. got in his motion. I saw the replay. [Hood] was moving. That's it. Simple as that. That was the worst call of the year. That was the game-decider right there. I just hated to see the game decided on that call." Asked if he regretted his actions, Boeheim said, "No regrets, not tomorrow, not next week either." For the record, four days later Boeheim acknowledged on ESPN Radio that he "definitely went too far" in his reaction to the referee's call.

Compared to his younger years, Boeheim, toward the latter half of his career, had mellowed and matured. The surprising meltdown surpassed his kicking a chair in anger while exiting a postgame press conference after the loss to Georgetown in the 1984 Big East tournament and his "Ten f---ing games" outburst in defense of Gerry McNamara during the 2006 Big East tournament. Boeheim bashers said the coach overreacted and cost his team a possible victory, but Boeheim supporters applauded their 69-year-old coach for still having the burning desire to win and for sticking up for and supporting his players. In doing so, Boeheim effectively diverted the criticism for the loss away from Fair. Beyond that, something good resulted from Boeheim's fiasco. The sport coat he wore later fetched $14,000 at a charity auction that went to the Jim and Juli Boeheim Foundation.

Just as he applauded the competitiveness and intensity of the first game and the atmosphere in the Carrier Dome, Mike Krzyzewski stated, "The game was spectacular. Absolutely spectacular." Of course, he liked the outcome better.

The two battle-royal games with the Blue Devils, acknowledged by many as the two best regular-season games played to that point in the season, kick-started a highly anticipated competition between the two basketball powers. Some thought Boeheim going berserk could quickly trigger a major rivalry in much the same way John Thompson declaring Manley Field House closed and later getting thrown out of a game at the Carrier Dome instigated the SU-Georgetown rivalry. People were already talking about a possible rubber game in the trilogy if Syracuse and Duke were to meet again in the ACC Tournament in Greensboro in a few weeks.

Two days later, Syracuse, suddenly on a two-game losing streak and having dropped to No. 4 in the country, played at Maryland. The Terrapins came to the Comcast Center bearing gifts, in the form of 18 turnovers, and the Orange readily accepted them. Playing on tired legs while the Terps had six days to rest, Syracuse led comfortably throughout the game but then had to withstand a late Maryland rally to eke out a 57–55 win when a potential game-winning three-point attempt by the Terps' Seth Allen, who had already made six three-pointers, banked harmlessly off the backboard as the horn sounded. Nothing came easy for the "Cardiac Cuse," a nickname that found its way onto T-shirts. Just another game where the Orange Nation had its fingers crossed and collective heart racing. Even though there were a few close calls at the end that went against Syracuse, Boeheim was on his best behavior. Like Boeheim against Duke, after the game, Maryland's Mark Turgeon complained about a call with seven seconds left and the Terps down by one that went against his team and cost them the victory. Such was life in the ACC.

Looming ahead was a big game at No. 12 Virginia, which had jumped Syracuse to take over first place in the ACC. Having lost two straight and with its offensive productivity at a 50-year low the Orange was in a rut, while the Cavaliers came into the contest riding a 12-game winning streak. John Paul Jones Arena was a sea of orange—Charlottesville Orange. Virginia was sitting on an ambush, and fourth-ranked Syracuse walked right into it. With the ACC regular-season championship on the line, the Cavaliers (25–5, 16–1), the best defensive team in the conference, shredded SU's zone and beat the Orange, 75–56, to win the regular-season championship for the first time since the Ralph Sampson days in 1981.

Georgia Tech came to the Carrier Dome with a 13–16 record, 4–12 in the league and having lost four straight games and eight of its last 10. The Engineers still prevailed, causing Syracuse to slip to No. 7 in the polls. After dodging several bullets on its way to a 25–0 start, the Orange, on the short end of four of its last five contests, was suddenly hit by a few. Back-to-back losses to two of the worst teams in the conference acerbated the Syracuse slide. In any event, the Orange changed from a 25–0 team with dreams to a 26–4 team with problems. As Cooney turned into more of an offensive liability than an asset, Syracuse started to lose its swagger. Although some Syracuse fans became depressed, others recalled that the previous year's Final Four team also lost four of its last five including a 61–39 drubbing by Georgetown, before regaining its mojo. While Syracuse's fair-weather fans were again berating Boeheim for losing to poor teams, Krzyzewski and No. 4 Duke promptly lost to lower-level Wake Forest. Instead of finishing the regular season with a head of steam, SU wobbled its way to the ACC tournament. With Ennis as the captain and point man, Fair as the horse and stabilizer, Grant as the gazelle and equalizer, Cooney as the glue and sniper, and Keita as the heart and soul, the Orange had the recipe for success. The problem was when one or more of the key ingredients were lacking, the Cuse was cooked.

In the regular-season finale at Florida State, one of the ingredients was back. Recovered from an aggravated back, Grant contributed a much-needed 18 points and eight rebounds that reinvigorated a sleeping offense and resulted in a 74–58 win over the Seminoles. The win pulled the Orange out of its mini funk. Fair found the mark with jump shots and three-pointers and Ennis, relying more on savvy than size, again drove and twisted past defenders for layups. Cooney, however, continued to be in a shooting coma, although he did dial up a couple of critical three-pointers when the game tightened up toward the end. It was a seamless effort where every component of a battle-worn starting five and limited roster contributed as a part of a fully-functioning machine, reminiscent of the 25–0 team that was exponentially better than the one that came to Tallahassee with a 1–4 record in its last five games. The victory reinstalled confidence in the Cuse and its fan base and earned SU a No. 2 seed and a double-bye in the ACC Tournament.

Syracuse, which had dropped to No. 11 nationally, brought a 27–4 overall and a 12–4 conference record into postseason play against NC State, a team with a chip on its shoulder after feeling that its regular-season game against the Orange was stolen from them on a referee's call. Having called out Syracuse, the Wolfpack wanted SU and the opportunity to administer a little payback. Except for Ennis, SU was off the mark offensively and missed six shots in the final 25 seconds that included a layup, dunk, and four three-point bricks that would have tied the game. Consequently, Syracuse went down, 66–63, to another unranked team. Many concluded the 25–0 start was an aberration of sorts. Now a figment of the team that spent six weeks on top of the national charts, Syracuse staggered into the NCAA tournament. Some people who were riding the Orange wave earlier in the season deserted Boeheim and his band of beaten down warriors.

Regardless of its tailspin that resulted in SU falling to No. 14, its lowest national ranking of the season, Syracuse's overall body of work earned the team a No. 3 seed in the NCAA tournament and the advantage of playing in nearby Buffalo. SU drew Western Michigan as its opening opponent. Even though Western Michigan coach Rob Murphy was once Boeheim's assistant and the copycat Broncos employed the Oranges' 2–3 zone, the sleeping Syracuse offense, especially Cooney, awakened as the Cuse tamed the Broncos, 77–53. The defense also regained its intimidation factor. With the go-and-stop units finally meshing again, Syracuse advanced to play Dayton.

Just when many thought the Orange had turned the corner, Syracuse laid another egg. Its offense again atrocious, SU, in a game that was painful to watch, came up short against the unranked and No. 11-seeded Flyers, 55–53. The Cuse was only going to go as far as Ennis would carry them and the freshman, who led the team in scoring with 19 points that came mostly on layups and free throws, took two questionable outside shots in the waning seconds of the game and missed both. The Orange finished 28–6 and failed to make the Sweet 16 for the first time in three years. Syracuse started the season on the fast track and, in the minds of some, ended up in a ditch. Boeheim faultfinders resurfaced in full force. To others, Syracuse, considering that it had lost three starters from the previous year, exceeded expectations. Fair was named a consensus second-team All-American and Ennis was selected to the Freshman All-American Team by the Basketball Writers of America and was an Associated Press honorable mention All-American.

2014–15

The timing of announcements is sometimes for effect. Before the 2014–15 season, an hour before basketball media day was about to begin, it was reported that the NCAA was investigating Syracuse for a number of violations. As if that wasn't enough drama for one day, the old slander suit against Boeheim by Bobby Davis and Michael Lang that spun off the Bernie Fine litigation was being reinstated.

On the court, Boeheim was challenged with the single biggest rebuilding job of his career. The nucleus of last year's team was gone. The epochs in college basketball had changed, and Syracuse faced a double-edged sword. The program was good enough to attract top talent, but the talent was also good enough to leave the program after a year or two to play professionally. From 2012 through 2016, Syracuse had ten players drafted by the NBA, a number surpassed only by Kentucky, Kansas, and Duke, indicative that SU was still among the top programs in developing and producing professional talent. In 2016, Malachi Richardson was picked 22nd by the Charlotte Hornets, making it nine straight first-round selections from Syracuse since 2008.

The flip side was that despite enjoying its longest run of success in program history, the Orange continuously had big holes to fill. Donté Greene, Tyler Ennis, Chris McCullough, and Richardson all left after their freshman year, and Jonny Flynn, Dion Waiters, Fab Melo, Michael Carter-Williams, and Jerami Grant all left following their sophomore year. It was a different era in college basketball. It was the fourth straight year that Boeheim had to break in a new point guard and the third consecutive year the point position was going to be manned by someone with little or hardly any experience. It was also the second straight season Syracuse had to replace its two leading scorers. With all the going and coming it was hard for the Orange to get traction. During Boeheim's first thirty-one years, only three players left early: Pearl Washington and Billy Owens after their junior years, and Carmelo Anthony following his freshman season. Boeheim was accustomed to replacing players, but 2014–15 was a little different because not only did the team not have any stars, of its two returning starters, Christmas was a foul-prone center and Cooney an inconsistent three-point shooter. Therefore, expectations for the team were lowered. Some predicted the Cuse was headed back to the NIT.

The Orange began the season by polishing off Kennesaw State. In the second game, on his 70th birthday, Boeheim got win No. 950 against Hampton. He had now amassed more wins than all of his SU coaching predecessors combined. Despite his lengthy and high-profile career, some people still had never heard of him. On November 4, as a guest on *CBS This Morning* with Gayle King, Charlie Rose, and Norah O'Donnell, King mispronounced Boeheim's name not once, but three times, calling him "Bayham" before being corrected by O'Donnell.

The 2013–14 team won its first 25 games, but the 2014–15 team, after a couple of easy victories, fell to California in its third contest. The Golden Bears made up for two losses to SU in the previous two seasons. After the cookie wins, Cal made the Orange feel like it had bitten into a rock. The setback snapped Syracuse's consecutive 96-week run in the Top 25. There was a decent win over Iowa in the consolation game of the 2K Classic in Madison Square Garden followed by blowout victories over Loyola (Maryland) and Holy Cross. Then a respectable 68–65 road loss at then-No. 17 Michigan turned out to be not as impressive after the Wolverines immediately got beat in Crisler Center by the New Jersey Institute of Technology and then Eastern Michigan. St. John's came to the Carrier Dome and, for the first time since 2007, stung Syracuse 69–57. The loss ended Syracuse's 55-game homecourt winning streak over non-conference foes, a streak that trailed only Duke's consecutive wins dominance at Cameron Indoor Stadium. The Orange had suffered three losses by December 6 for the first time in school history, although it should be noted that basketball season started much later in the earlier years of the program. Syracuse was still licking its wounds when Louisiana Tech came calling. SU continued to commit turnovers, shoot poorly, and blow leads, but the Cuse got away with all the mistakes and escaped with a two-point win after leading by 10 with four minutes to go. None of the buttons Boeheim pushed worked. He didn't try to hide his frustration during his brief postgame press conference when he complained about the fundamental errors his team repeatedly made.

In its next game, Syracuse had a chance to grab a big win, but frittered away a 15-point lead and wasted a gallant effort in suffering a heartbreaking 82–77 overtime loss at undefeated and No. 7-ranked Villanova. To make matters worse, SU blew a five-point lead with 17 seconds to go and never trailed until overtime. SU had an inbounds pass picked off that enabled the Wildcats to tie the contest with 4.9 seconds remaining. It was the first time since the 1981–82 season that the Orange had lost four non-conference regular-season games.

Syracuse came back to win seven straight games, albeit against

Colgate, Long Beach State, Cornell, and the ACC's lower-echelon teams to improve to 13–4 and a league-leading 4–0. Cooney heated up, Michael Gbinije began to come into his own, and rookie point guard Kaleb Joseph was starting to get it. Just when things looked like they were beginning to fall into place, freshman blue-chipper Chris McCullough suffered a season-ending injury in their 70–57 victory over Florida State. With DaJuan Coleman already ruled out for the year, the loss of McCullough made a thin frontcourt even thinner. Down to one quality big man, Boeheim complained to officials that opponents were fouling Rakeem, hanging on him like ornaments on a Christmas tree. After beating Boston College, the Orange was treading water at 14–5, 5–1 in the league, but it became evident that Syracuse was going to have a hard time hanging on. A week and a half later, the dog-tired Orange, with too many players forced to play 40 or close to 40 minutes a game, had to scramble from down nine points late in the game to somehow steal a 72–70 win over Virginia Tech when Gbinije dropped a little runner with 0:00:01 showing on the clock. It took everything Syracuse had to catch and pass the last-place Hokies. The Cuse won that game on heart. It was apparent at the onset of the season but became painfully clear at this point that, minus high school All-American DaJuan Coleman who had not played for two years because of a knee injury, the unexpected departures of Tyler Ennis and Jerami Grant to the NBA and then the season-ending loss of McCullough, this Syracuse contingent lacked a bench and, more specifically, depth at key positions. The Cuse was only a shell of what it could have been. A team that if it had all its components probably would have been ranked preseason in the Top 5 in the country, Syracuse was faced with the possibility that it could end up with a losing season, something unheard of in Orangeland since the 1960s. Adding to the burden, rumors and speculation over the NCAA investigation shadowed Syracuse for the remainder of the season.

The mystery whether Syracuse was going to make the NCAA tournament or not, or play in the NIT, was solved the next day, February 4, when the school self-imposed a postseason tournament ban as punishment for violations that occurred between 2007 and 2012 when players who should have been ineligible were allowed to play. It was determined that some players had received extra benefits and Syracuse had not adhered to its own school-instituted drug policy. The result was that the current players, including lone senior Rakeem Christmas who was in the midst of a great season, took the hit for the ill-advised actions of past players. Since the NCAA had the prerogative of imposing harsher penalties, the thinking was that Syracuse jumped the gun to hopefully soften any further action since SU's chances of making the NCAA tournament already appeared out of reach. Critics quickly concluded that SU wanted to pay the price that season when postseason play was iffy at best, rather than possibly pass along the penalties to the following season when the Orange was expected to be very good based on a highly rated recruiting class that was coming on board. Having been no less than a No.4 seed in the previous six years, this was a big comedown for a program that had NCAA tournament play in its DNA.

In the aftermath of the self-imposed tournament ban, many felt the Orange would simply go through the motions as it played out the last nine games on its schedule. Not so. Playing with the pride of the Orange, depleted and foul-plagued SU battled Pittsburgh tooth and nail on the road before fading in the final moments, 83–77. Reporters asked a few questions that prompted a couple of salty "Boeheimisms." Asked if he was surprised by his team's gallant effort, Boeheim said, like anyone who plays basketball at any level, regardless of the score, he "expected [his team] to play their asses off." When probed by a Pittsburgh scribe if his second NCAA violation would give a reason for others to think that he ran a dirty program, Boeheim bluntly retorted, "I don't give a shit what those people think." In short, Boeheim being Boeheim. Some people liked that. Some didn't.

Syracuse hosted Duke on Valentine's Day, but Mike Krzyzewski didn't show any love to his good friend Jim Boeheim. The fourth-ranked Blue Devils overcame an 11-point first-half deficit to power past the Orange, 80–72, in front of an NCAA record-tying crowd of 35,446 that equaled the attendance in the previous season's epic encounter with the Dukies in the Dome. Although the pregame buildup didn't nearly match that of the previous year when SU came into the game 25–0 and ranked No. 1 in the land, the unranked Orange, with a 16–8 record and an NCAA investigation looming over its head, still played hard. However, with less talent and tired legs, the Cuse couldn't keep up with the Blue Devils. Even with Duke transfer Michael Gbinije's career-high 27 points and a career-best 19 points and 12 rebounds from Tyler Roberson, Syracuse went down. The Blue Devils' freshman sensation Jahlil Okafor outplayed senior Rakeem Christmas in a battle between two of the best big men in the country. Krzyzewski's 1,004 wins and Boeheim's 964 wins for a combined total of 1,968 set a new NCAA record for most victories by opposing coaches in a game.

Showing there was still juice in the tank the Orange upset No. 12 Louisville, 69–59. In its fifth attempt that season, Syracuse finally managed a win over a ranked team. In another contest pitting Hall of Fame coaches who are good friends, Boeheim bested Rick Pitino as Christmas poured in 29 points to help SU improve to 19–9 and 8–5 in conference play. At that point that was still a good record for many schools, but not for a school with Syracuse's basketball history and for a team that in the preceding few years hovered around the 30-win mark.

Continuing to play inspired basketball Syracuse—despite its thin bench, being hobbled by injuries, plagued by fouls, and gasping for breath—came back from 11 points down in a ferocious contest against Pittsburgh, only to fall to the Panthers, 65–61. It was unfortunate that a questionable call against Christmas helped decide the outcome. Pulling to within one point at 62–61 with 54 seconds to go and with the ball and a chance to go ahead, Christmas, with 36 ticks of the clock remaining, was whistled for a debatable illegal screen. Although beaten up and bruised with Tyler Roberson playing with five stitches over a swollen and partially closed eye and cotton stuffed in his nostril, Cooney lacking mobility because of a bad back, Christmas taking a physical pounding due to being double-teamed whenever he touched the ball, and Syracuse playing simply for self-respect, the Orange put forth a gutsy effort in battling back. On a night when Roosevelt Bouie and Louis Orr of the late 1970s "Louie and Bouie Show" became the 11th and 12th SU players to have their jerseys retired, Christmas did fellow post player Bouie proud with a 20-point, 12-rebound performance. Averaging 14.2 points a game coming into the contest, Cooney, his shooting as cold as the temperature that accompanied the coldest February in Syracuse history, was held scoreless. In a show of support for their team, which was out of gas and playing on fumes, the 30,144 fans that made their way to the Dome despite the frigid weather applauded. It was the 80th crowd in Dome history in excess of 30,000.

When all but the most ardent Syracuse fans had given up on the season, the Orange, who had already upended Louisville, again rose to the occasion to upset another ranked team. Back from among the walking dead, B. J. Johnson's 19 points off the bench led resuscitated SU to a 65–60 victory over No. 9 Notre Dame in South Bend. But as good as Syracuse was against the Fighting Irish, it was as bad against No. 4 Duke in its next outing. In a game where the Syracuse basket seemed to have a lid on it, the Orange only managed to make 19 of 62 field-goal attempts and 3 of 20 three-point tries in a 73–54 blowout loss. A year after an irate Boeheim got tossed out of the game after going ballistic trying to take his sport coat off after arguing a call, the SU boss got to see the end of this game as he remained calm while watching his team fall behind by 20 points in the second half. Billed as the newest big rivalry in the ACC, the contest lost its shine when Syracuse dropped from the rankings early in the season, never to return, and then banned itself from the NCAA tournament. For the series to become a rivalry, both teams needed to be competitive. Syracuse wasn't in this game.

Syracuse closed the home portion of its schedule by entertaining a No. 2-ranked Virginia team that had prevailed in 27 of 28 games. Following the beating by Duke, the ACC's best offensive team, the Orange was confronted with the Cavaliers, the ACC's best defensive team. Limited to only two points during the first 14 minutes of the game, Virginia completely took over the contest and coasted to an easy 59–47 win to clinch its second consecutive ACC regular-season championship. The loss meant Boeheim would fail to win 20 games for only the third time in his 39-year coaching career. On a positive note, the 25,338 people in attendance assured Syracuse of winning the 2014–15 NCAA season attendance crown, its 14th including 11 straight from 1985 through 1995. That the crowds kept coming out to support, by Syracuse standards, a subpar team during one of the harshest winters in upstate New York history was a testimony to the long-running culture of success that Syracuse had established. Summing it up, Syracuse lost nine of its last 14 games, including its last three to finish 18–13, 9–9 in ACC play. At best it was sitting marginally on the NCAA tournament bubble, even if it didn't disqualify itself.

NCAA Sanctions

Having been banned from the NCAA tournament following the 1992–93 season, Syracuse was a repeat offender. The school should be credited for self-reporting its own failings, but it also deserved to be reprimanded to some degree for not learning its lesson to follow the rules, both institutional and NCAA. Armored with additional ammunition, Boeheim critics rejoiced and amped up their pleas for the aging and again controversial coach to retire since both run-ins with the NCAA came under his watch. Pointing out that Boeheim's two controversies with the NCAA were merely blips on an otherwise honorable four-decade career and all the humanitarian causes he had supported, Boeheim fans argued that coaches such as Roy Williams, Jim Calhoun, Pete Carroll, and John Calipari had scrapes with the NCAA and continued coaching, and therefore so should Boeheim.

Friday, March 7, 2015, started out like many winter days in Syracuse: cold and dreary. By mid-morning, the howling surrounding the second NCAA scandal shook the Syracuse basketball program and the school to the core, or so it seemed. In the biggest national sports story of the day, after a prolonged eight-year investigation into the SU basketball operation, the NCAA hit the Orange program with some of the harshest sanctions handed out in recent years. Citing more than a dozen violations over ten years, including lack of institutional control, academic misconduct, misplaced priorities, and failure to enforce the institution's drug policy, the NCAA suspended Boeheim for the first nine conference games during the following season, vacated 108 of his victories, reduced the number of scholarships allowed over four years by twelve, and forced the university to refund $1 million that it received from the Big East. All this on top of Syracuse's self-imposed 2014–15 postseason ban.

In a scathing ninety-four-page report, the NCAA stated that the university committed fourteen violations and for almost ten years, beginning in 2001, allowed players who were caught smoking marijuana to continue to play. Particularly problematic was in 2012, when the Orange was 20–0, ranked No. 2 in the country and positioned to compete for the national championship, then-athletic director Daryl Gross assembled a group of athletic and academic leaders, sans Boeheim, to somehow finagle a way to keep Fabricio Paulino de Melo (Fab Melo) eligible. With Melo about to be academically disqualified, the rationale was that the group manipulated a professor who in a course over a year earlier had given Melo a C-minus to now allow Melo to do additional work to raise the grade. The professor agreed to raise Melo's grade if Melo, who grew up in Brazil with English as his third language, wrote a satisfactory four- or five-page paper with references. With only hours to complete the task before Melo would become ineligible, speculation was that one or more members of the group essentially wrote the paper that enabled him to receive a B-minus in the course and therefore maintain his eligibility. The NCAA report, which also revealed violations within the football and women's basketball programs, in sum stated that Syracuse "placed the desire to achieve success on the basketball court over academic integrity, demonstrated clearly misplaced institutional priorities" and in doing so disregarded "the most fundamental core values of the NCAA."

The NCAA took Boeheim to task for not prudently overseeing his program. The national collegiate sports governing body's chief hearing officer Britton Banowsky stated, "The rules are pretty clear. The head coach has the duty to monitor activities in his program." Therefore, the captain went down with his ship. Boeheim became the first coach punished under the then relatively new NCAA ruling that assumed that the head coach was knowledgeable of and responsible for the misdoings of those involved in his program.

Boeheim had never micromanaged his coaches or his players, pretty much expecting and trusting them to follow the rules and do what they're supposed to do and do it well. He considered and treated his players like adults. Generally considered positive qualities in a leader, Boeheim adhered to his philosophy to a fault. Much like John Wooden during his heyday at UCLA, Boeheim didn't really want to know about the bad things that may have been going on, sometimes turning his back on problems while expecting his assistant coaches to handle and correct situations. As he explained in his book *Bleeding Orange*, which came out the preceding fall: "I have no desire to be a police officer … I'm a coach, not an inquisition judge." The problem was the NCAA expected head coaches to take full accountability for supervising the behavior of their players and coaches and punishing them when they did not follow the rules. In that regard, Boeheim failed.

The severity of the penalties made the sanctions the school received in 1992 look paltry. Syracuse Chancellor Kent Syverud immediately disputed some of the findings. Detailing SU's own internal investigation, he strongly supported Boeheim. The Syracuse investigation stated there was not a single documented instance where Boeheim was aware of any of the claims that were made against him. Syverud admitted Syracuse committed some violations, but not everything or to the extent that the NCAA concluded. He felt the sanctions were disproportionate for the offenses. The school later appealed.

Syracuse was cited for academic misconduct, but the misdeeds were not systemic throughout the athletic department. They involved one high-profile basketball player and three football players. Syracuse did violate its own drug-testing policy, which is something that most other institutions did not have. SU claimed that any rules broken did not result in a competitive advantage. Boeheim soon followed up with his own statement emphasizing his disappointment in the NCAA's penalties. Mike Krzyzewski, Jay Bilas, and Dick Vitale came to Boeheim's defense, all stating that the punishment was way over the top. At the local level, Onondaga County Executive Joanie Mahoney totally supported Boeheim and Syracuse University. "I wholeheartedly disagree with the sanctions and think the punishment far outweighs any crime," she stated. Citing what he and many others considered more serious improprieties at North Carolina, Penn State, and Miami, US Congressman John Katko thought in comparison the investigation into Syracuse was unfair and the sanctions extraordinary. He co-sponsored the National Collegiate Athletic Association Accountability Act, a bipartisan bill that pushed for a presidential commission on intercollegiate athletics that would force the NCAA to be more transparent and accountable. On January 20, 2016, Katko told the Syracuse Media Group editorial board, "The NCAA is a joke … [NCAA] corruption is profound … [across the board the sanctions given to other schools are] so uneven it's ridiculous."

The New York Times published a story with the second paragraph in part stating, "a ninety-four-page report by the NCAA exposing some of the most widespread and damning transgressions in college basketball in years" most assuredly caused many among the Syracuse University administration, faculty, students, and alumni to cringe. A public relations disaster, the institution's credibility and image were severely damaged. However, looking back at the Reggie Bush situation at USC, for instance, where it was determined that he received cash and gifts from aspiring marketers in 2004 and 2005, and later after an investigation where North Carolina went unpunished after an academic sham continued unabated for eighteen or more years, led some to believe that comparatively that newspaper's depiction of SU's improprieties was exorbitant. Athletes at SU were not living in luxurious homes, given new cars, or, in general, taking bogus classes and receiving passing grades.

Figuratively speaking, the embattled Boeheim absorbed some heavy body blows from the NCAA, along with a few right overhand punches and a couple of uppercuts. When national and local critics piled on, Boeheim almost went to his knees. Forever a competitor and fighter, Boeheim, like Muhammad Ali when he took a brutal beating in his ill-fated bout against Larry Holmes, refused to go down. Instead, a couple of days later, gearing up as if preparing to go to war against the NCAA, he told the hometown Hardwood Club, "There's a hell of a battle ahead of us … I came here in 1962, and I'm going nowhere." The 700 Boeheim backers in attendance applauded their feisty coach who made it clear he was not ready to sit on his porch in a rocking chair. When it seemed like the program was being torn apart, Boeheim struggled and somehow managed to keep the team together.

New York Times op-ed columnist Joe Nocera, in a piece published on March 13, 2015, opined that Boeheim appeared to have made two mistakes: hiring Stan Kissel to oversee the basketball team's academic progress, and in 2009, recruiting 7-foot Brazilian Fab Melo, who some said didn't belong on a college campus. Stating that Kissel and/or former basketball team mentor Debora Belanger almost assuredly wrote and submitted a paper that kept Melo eligible, making it a major transgression, Nocera also noted that Kissel and his secretary were fired long before the NCAA completed its investigation. Acknowledging that ten years prior three SU football players received credit for an internship, Nocera pointed out that was four cases of academic fraud in ten years while also noting that Syracuse University students were charged with 184 cases of academic dishonesty in 2013–14 alone. He also noted that some Syracuse athletes were paid for charity benefits without approval and three players were paid for disputed volunteer work.

"I have dwelled on this report because it illustrates that despite the blows it has taken recently—in court and elsewhere—the NCAA remains not only a powerful institution but one that is all too willing to abuse that power. To nail Syracuse's basketball program—for who knows what reason—it had to pad one serious 2012 offense with a handful of extraneous, at times silly, allegations that had occurred, here and there, over the course of a decade." Nocera ends with: "Syracuse, concluded the NCAA, violated the association's 'fundamental core values.' Not really. Very soon, the annual March Madness college basketball tournament will be upon us. The NCAA will reap somewhere on the order of $800 million. Now we're talking core values," he wrote.

Jay Bilas summed it up this way: "What a colossal overreaction and much ado about very little ... The penalties were disproportionate to the violations ... It makes the NCAA look inept because they are inept."

Therefore, relatively and comparatively speaking, to some, what occurred at Syracuse were in most instances isolated cases where a small number of athletes, and not necessarily the stars, were provided with a few extra benefits and extra academic help. Those were violations and should be punished, but most agreed not to the extent that they were. It also must be noted that numerous big-time basketball-playing universities throughout the country recruited Melo, and had Syracuse not accepted him, they would have welcomed him to their basketball programs with open arms.

Boston Globe correspondent Bob Ryan referenced a March 16 *Sports Illustrated* article written by S. L. Price that detailed North Carolina's scam involving bogus classes that kept athletes eligible. He called it "the eighteen-year farce" that extended back to 1993, meaning that UNC's academic misconduct happened under the watch of Dean Smith through Roy Williams. Ryan pointed out that the NCAA rulebook is "ludicrously large" because no one trusts anyone, in part making the NCAA "practically unmanageable." Therefore, Ryan believed that violations ran rampant among NCAA schools stating, "Whatever Jim Boeheim did, believe me, someone else [coaching in the 2014–15] NCAA Tournament [field] did something ten times worse." Apparently so since University of Maryland president Wallace Loh on April 10, 2017, stated, "The things that happened in North Carolina [are] abysmal. I would think that would lead to the implementation of the [NCAA] death penalty." Ryan concluded, "It is a waste of time to chastise these alleged rogue schools when the truth is that they are only trying to keep the customers satisfied." Ryan thought that, because the "schools are addicted to money," it was too late to get the system back on track since it would have required a change in values that was probably unrealistic with the current emphasis on winning.

For years the NCAA had been under attack as being more or less dysfunctional, arbitrary, and inconsistent on various fronts. Severely understaffed, they had difficulty effectively policing its member schools. After the almost two-decade academic farce that occurred at North Carolina went unpunished, Yahoo Sports columnist Pat Forde on October 16, 2017, stated, "Let history record this week that the NCAA completed its descent from flawed to failed. The governing body of college sports is useless when it comes to policing itself. The NCAA's impotence can no longer be debated." Mark Titus of *The Ringer* stated, "North Carolina facilitated the most widespread academic scandal in the history of college sports."

On October 23, 2017, Boeheim finally responded to his take on the North Carolina investigation, telling Syracuse basketball writer Chris Carlson, "I'm supposed to know about a ten-page paper and [North Carolina] doesn't know about eighteen years of As? ... Well, [the NCAA rules] are certainly applied differently." Therefore, if Syracuse offered a "cookie course" like North Carolina, Fab Melo could have taken it and received an A grade and stayed eligible.

On October 30, 2017, a poll conducted for the NCAA found that in part more than half of the respondents felt the NCAA was part of the problem. Syracuse.com's Mark Weiner reported that NCAA President Mark Emmert told the Knight Commission on Intercollegiate Athletics that, based on public perception, "only a small portion of

Americans believe [the conclusion in the North Carolina case] was the right decision ... The public doesn't have any significant confidence in any of us."

The late Jerry Tarkanian, who battled the NCAA for years, once stated, "Nine out of ten teams cheat, and the 10th team is in last place." That's probably overstating the situation, but Tarkanian, who accused the NCAA of hypocrisy and opacity, made his point. He twice sued the organization and won a $2.5 million verdict. Regarding the unfairness of the way he thought that the NCAA handled cases, he also once stated, "The NCAA was so mad at Kentucky [for all its perceived violations] that it gave Cleveland State two more years on probation." In his autobiography, he wrote that he liked transfers from major colleges "because they already have their cars paid for." Tarkanian was angry with the college sports governing body that many thought acted as judge, jury, and executioner in determining verdicts. Then University of Southern California athletic director Pat Haden, in reference to the sanctions given to USC in the Reggie Bush case, questioned the NCAA's own institutional controls, stating in 2013 that "it should be concerning to all schools that the NCAA didn't appear to follow its own rules."

Commentor Moondog23 posted on a Syracuse chat line, "The NCAA gave Syracuse University an eight-year colonoscopy. They really wanted to find Stage 4 cancer but could only come up with a couple of polyps. That's good news." Another, Billydrew, followed up with, "Except they treated them for cancer." That pretty much summed up the viewpoint of the pro-Boeheim, pro-SU crowd.

The basketball purists adamantly stated that Syracuse and Boeheim knowingly and continually disregarded and broke the rules. They vented that the violations badly hurt Syracuse's academic reputation, embarrassed those associated with the school, and tarnished SU's image. The school and coaches committed the crime, therefore they should graciously accept and suffer the penalties, the supporters of the NCAA's sanctions said. All that is true. The basketball purists wanted Syracuse to get its priorities straight. Stress academics, in effect de-emphasize athletics and put everything back into its proper perspective, they purported. It's the right thing to do. Simple as that. Except in reality very few major university sports programs operated that way. True, just because many if not most other schools cheat and are unethical in various ways does not mean that Syracuse should continue to swim in that cesspool. On the other hand, if Syracuse downplayed sports as some pontificated, SU would pretty much become a lower-tier Division I athletics program, like Colgate or St. Bonaventure. The Ivy League has things in perspective, but few Ivy League teams are competitive at the big-time level, and some draw crowds less than what you would see at some high school games. The only way that Syracuse could "put athletics in proper perspective" and still successfully compete at the championship level in Division I sports was if all the other big-time sports-playing universities did likewise. Of course, that's not going to happen.

March 18, 2015, twelve days after the NCAA released its report, became a big news day in Syracuse. Athletic Director Daryl Gross, claiming that he was not forced out, announced that he was stepping down from that post to accept a position within the university as vice president and special assistant to Chancellor Kent Syverud along with becoming an adjunct professor in the David B. Falk College of Sport and Human Dynamics. Syverud announced SU would appeal the sanctions involving loss of scholarships and wins, Boeheim announced he would retire in three years, and two executives of the Tri-Valley YMCA, where some of the rules violations were said to have occurred, denied any wrongdoing.

As expected, the response to Boeheim's retirement plan was mixed. His loyalists were happy that he could stay on board to help restore the school's successful basketball image while trying to climb back to No. 2 in the all-time wins category. His censors were angry that he wasn't fired immediately and upset that they would have to put up with his antics and shenanigans through the 2018 season.

The following day, despite being the first day of the NCAA tournament, much of the college basketball world stayed focused on Syracuse as ESPN covered forty minutes of a Boeheim press conference where he gave his take on the sanctions. Muzzled for quite a while, it was clear that he had looked forward to challenging the findings that he firmly believed were inaccurate and unfair. Feisty and defiant, Boeheim was at his best as he painstakingly dissected the NCAA's conclusions by either disputing or explaining each allegation. Talking slowly with measured words and changing his tone for effect, Boeheim, reading from a prepared statement, pointed out the arbitrary manner that the NCAA dished out its penalties, not just from school to school but even within a single institution.

"Although the infractions report does not find that I had personal involvement in any violations of NCAA rules, the Committee on Infractions has asserted that for the past ten years I did not promote an atmosphere of compliance within the basketball program, and I did not monitor the activities regarding compliance of those within," he read from his prepared statement. "This could not be further from the truth ... That is the farthest thing from the truth that Syracuse admitted student-athletes who couldn't do the work ... This is far from a program where student-athletes freely committed academic fraud," stated Boeheim in disputing the NCAA's claim that Syracuse placed basketball success above academic integrity. Boeheim admitted that he and Syracuse were not sinless and had made some mistakes that he was responsible for and that he and the school should be penalized for, but he stated that the sanctions were "unduly harsh." "I'll take the punishment," he said. Boeheim also made it clear that he felt he and his program were victimized and singled out. As commonly done at other schools, Boeheim acknowledged taking "at-risk" students. He stated they can be successful academically and graduate in four years, citing Rakeem Christmas as an example of someone who was once labeled at-risk but graduated in three years and as a senior was halfway through a master's degree program.

Following Boeheim's press conference, Dick Vitale again immediately came to Boeheim's support, stating, "I know Jim Boeheim, and Jim Boeheim is not a cheater. He's a man of integrity. I firmly believe that … he did not orchestrate all this, he did not plan [what happened] … in any way, shape, or form … Jim Boeheim is guilty of one thing—trust[ing people within the program to do the right thing when doing their jobs]." The next week when his team was playing an NCAA regional game in Syracuse, Louisville coach Rick Pitino told Syracuse beat writer Mike Waters, "I do know that [Boeheim] is a man of great integrity. I worked with him. There's not an ounce in him that would ever break the rules knowingly. I know him very well."

The contrarians believed none of this, holding fast to their opinions that Boeheim and Syracuse deserved what the NCAA gave them, and perhaps should have been penalized even more. However, the besieged coach's legacy received another boost when a group of former SU players covering 13 seasons banded together to form a team, respectfully called "Boeheim's Army," that played in The Basketball Tournament with a winner-take-all prize of $1 million that would go to the squad that won the 17-team summer single-elimination tournament championship.

The shake-up in the SU athletic hierarchy continued as Joe Giansante, SU's athletics chief communications officer, was placed on an administrative leave of absence. A few days later, the editorial board of the *Rochester Democrat and Chronicle* called for Boeheim to resign, making it another eventful week at the University. In early June, Syracuse named Mark Coyle, who had been at Boise State, as its new athletic director. On June 25, three days after tapping Coyle to take over athletic operations, Syracuse officially changed Mike Hopkins's title from "coach-in-waiting" to "coach-designate" and announced that Hopkins would succeed Boeheim as head coach in three years. That reaffirmed the plan put in place by Boeheim several years earlier under Daryl Gross's administration.

In the final game of the 2014–15 campaign, Syracuse got whipped by NC State, 71–57, putting a fitting end to a forgettable season. For only the second time in Boeheim's 39-year tenure, the other being 1993 that also followed NCAA sanctions, Syracuse did not participate in postseason play. The Orange finished 18–13 and 9–9 in the

ACC, good for some schools, but a bitter pill to swallow for a proud program accustomed to waiting for Selection Sunday to see who and where it would play in the national championship tournament. Rakeem Christmas closed out a stellar senior season by being named first-team All-ACC and a third-team Associated Press All-American.

In the previous season, SU's basketball future looked rosy when Syracuse was sitting at 25–0 and No. 1 in the nation, but the series of aforementioned occurrences and others caused the rose to lose its bloom. Jerami Grant and Tyler Ennis left for the NBA, Chris McCullough suffered a season-ending injury, and the program got hit with harsh sanctions that caused Boeheim's reputation that had climbed to near the top of the pack to plunge. Then McCullough decided to leave early for the NBA, and coveted recruit and McDonald's All-American Thomas Bryant from nearby Rochester chose IU over SU. In the course of a year, the Syracuse train that seemed to have been picking up steam started to stall. Even though Syracuse still had the No. 4 recruiting class coming in, projections of an anticipated dream season started to go down the drain. The doom-and-gloomers reacted as if the sky was falling. Some thought the overall level of talent that Syracuse had was down to the pre-Pearl Washington days, pointing out that since 1998 Boeheim had reeled in twenty Top 50 recruits but only two Top 10 recruits. Syracuse beat writer Chris Carlson, however, pointed out that the Orange had eight players drafted by the NBA in the previous five years, fourth behind Kentucky (19), Kansas (11), and Duke (9). SU also had produced eight first-round selections in the previous ten years. Whereas Syracuse could still attract big-time talent, the downside was that with eight SU players bolting for the NBA after either their freshmen or sophomore year it made it hard for the Orange to make headway.

The hardcore critics continued to make noise, strangely stating that the program was suddenly in demise, despite a 167–45 record over the previous six seasons that represented the best run in school history. They dismissed the fact that the Orange had been in the Final Four just two years before and had big-time ballers on the way. Inexplicably, the complainers maintained their willingness to damage what they claimed they loved—SU basketball.

Amid the Storm, There Was Sunshine

The critics were quieted a couple of weeks after Coyle was hired when five-star guard Tyus Battle gave a verbal commitment to SU that signaled Syracuse could still bring in elite recruits despite the sanctions. Battle's announcement came on the heels of 7-foot-2, 226-pound Paschal Chukwu stating he was transferring to Syracuse from Providence. The acquisitions provided the Cuse with a couple of battleships that showed Syracuse should maintain its momentum with Hopkins waiting in the wings.

In 2014–15, Syracuse averaged 23,854 fans for home games to maintain its college-attendance championship. It was the 14th time SU had led the nation in attendance. So, despite the gripers, there still were a lot of good things going on in Cusedom. Digging out from the aftermath of the sanctions took work. Consistent winning might not solve all problems, but it made it easier to shift the attention away from lawsuits. On August 6, 2015, Syracuse University and Jim Boeheim settled the slander suit filed by Bobby Davis and Mike Lang, finally putting to rest a part of the off-the-court drama that had engulfed the program. Terms of the settlement were not disclosed.

16

SYRACUSE'S UNLIKELY RUN TO ANOTHER FINAL FOUR

2015–16

Following that disappointing 18–13 season, Syracuse was a program in need of a reboot. SU opened 2015 unranked for only the fifth time in the previous fifteen years. Embarking on his 40th campaign, Boeheim reinvented his offense yet again. Whereas the year before Syracuse was offensively a center-dominated team with Rakeem Christmas, the Orange underwent almost a complete makeover as Boeheim, with guards galore at his disposal, assembled a backcourt-oriented team that could not only shoot three-pointers but also make them. In addition to Michael Gbinije, Trevor Cooney, Tyler Roberson, and Kaleb Joseph returning and DaJuan Coleman back after sitting out almost two years with a knee injury, a trio of sharpshooting freshmen—Malachi Richardson, Tyler Lydon, and Frank Howard—were coming on board to bring a spark to the SU offense. Just the thought of that brought a seldom-seen smile to Boeheim's face.

In a season that promised a lot of surprises, some came early. Roberson got off to a slow start, but Richardson immediately proved that he was as good as advertised and Lydon became acclimated to the college game earlier than expected. Coleman, though, showed signs of rust. The Orange won its first two games, the second being a come-from-behind 79–66 win over St. Bonaventure on Boeheim's birthday. Syracuse had its turkey early, before traveling to the Bahamas during Thanksgiving week for the Battle 4 Atlantis Tournament, eating up Elon, a team picked to finish dead last in the Colonial Conference.

The day before Thanksgiving, Syracuse had something to be thankful for, but not much. Just hours before SU was to play Charlotte, the NCAA announced it was giving Syracuse back one scholarship per year but still vacating 101 victories, seven less than originally declared. Consequently, Boeheim officially dropped from No. 2 on the all-time wins list to No. 6, his 969 wins reduced to 868, again putting him behind Adolph Rupp (876), Jim Calhoun (877), Dean Smith (879), Bob Knight (902), and Mike Krzyzewski (1,022 wins). At 71 years of age, his quest for 1,000 victories was seemingly over.

Before and during the Syracuse-Charlotte game, ESPN2 commentators Jay Bilas, Seth Greenberg, and Jay Williams, using the televised contest as a platform, ripped the NCAA. Greenberg stated, "Jim Boeheim coached those games. Syracuse won those games. I don't understand … taking the wins away makes no sense." The reaction by Boeheim's supporters was swift and clear. Social media lit up with many agreeing with the announcers' comments. Fans can credit Boeheim with as many wins as they want, but the university must follow NCAA rulings. The Orange took its anger out on Charlotte, beating the stuffing out of the 49ers.

With the "warm-up" games finished, the heavy lifting began. Pitted against No. 18 Connecticut, the Orange outlasted the Huskies, 79–76, in a game reminiscent of the classic Big East rivalry games between the two old foes. The contest showcased freshman phenom Tyler Lydon to the nation. Starring in all facets of the game, Lydon recorded his first double-double with 16 points and 12 rebounds to support 17-point efforts by Gbinije and Cooney. Syracuse moved on to the finals to play No. 25 Texas A&M, which had upset No. 10 Gonzaga earlier that day. Entering the tournament unranked and unrespected, the Orange's late-game surge overtook the Aggies, 74–67, to win the Battle 4 Atlantis championship. Doing so provided hope for a team that began the season with little hype. Boeheim, usually right-on with his player and team assessments, stated previously that the 2015–16 Orange could be a good perimeter-shooting team. The Cuse broke the tournament record for three-point shooting percentage (46.5) and tied the mark for most three-point shots made (34). Gbinije, the tourney MVP, set a new mark for the most three-pointers made (12) while Lydon, no longer a Syracuse secret, smashed the standard for three-point shooting percentage (70). Possessing two good fifth-year seniors (Gbinije and Cooney), two freshmen stars (Lydon and Richardson), two extremely versatile performers (Gbinije and Lydon), four legitimate three-point threats (Gbinije, Lydon, Cooney, and Richardson), a solid contributor and excellent rebounder (Roberson), and an improved 6-foot-9, 268-pound monster in the middle (Coleman), Syracuse showed the country that potentially it could be a force in March.

Winning the championship in a tournament that included three ranked teams springboarded Syracuse, a 6–0 team that previously had no votes in the polls, to a No. 14 ranking by the AP. However, what happened in the Bahamas stayed in the Bahamas. After riding high for a few days, the Orange was brought back to reality by Wisconsin, with the Badgers dealing SU an overtime loss. The next day Boeheim learned his appeal to reduce his nine-game suspension was denied. He would not be allowed any contact with his team, the coaches, or his program over the duration of the suspension that began immediately. Longtime assistant coach Mike Hopkins, on forty-eight hour notice, assumed the Syracuse basketball head coaching duties. A few days later, he cut his coaching teeth against Georgetown, SU's biggest adversary. No easy task.

When Hopkins walked into the Verizon Center, he was greeted by a sign, "WE HATE HOPKINS TOO." In a road game reminiscent of old,

Syracuse showed true grit in clawing its way back from a 20-point deficit to make it a two-possession game before being subdued by the Hoyas, 79–72. The Hoyas bit the Orange from the onset and continued to chew away to give Hopkins his first coaching defeat. Boeheim missed just his fourth game in forty years.

As suddenly as Syracuse soared in the rankings after the Atlantis championship, it immediately dropped out after its second straight loss. Stung, the Orange redeemed itself by beating Colgate, its nearby punching bag, for the 50th consecutive time, the longest active winning streak over an opponent in the nation. It was Hopkins's first win. In his postgame remarks, he implied he didn't want to fail in his responsibility, which was to improve the team during his boss's absence, "or it's not gonna be good … I'm trying to hold the fort down for one of the greatest coaches of all time," he stated, before humorously and metaphorically acknowledging Boeheim and the power program he built. "The father comes back and says, 'I gave you the keys to my Bentley and look what you did! You left the Doritos in the back, and you didn't wash it.'"

Against a St. John's team picked to finish last in the Big East, Syracuse slumbered its way through an 84–72 upset loss to a Red Storm team that then went on to lose 16 straight games. With Boeheim watching on television at home, it couldn't have been a pleasant afternoon. Five days later, St. John's got plastered by the University of Incarnate Word, 73–51. Quick now, what is UIW's nickname and where is it located? Times up—the Cardinals, in only their third year of Division I play, are located in San Antonio, Texas.

Rebounding and free throws matter. Syracuse found that out in a 72–61 loss at Pittsburgh in Hopkins's ACC debut, causing SU to lose a conference opener for the first time since 2007, also at The Pete. Leading, 59–58, the Orange folded like a tent when the Panthers closed the game on a 14–2 run, dropping SU to 10–4. Next game, a repeat performance. Tied, 44–44, with about five minutes to go at No. 13 Miami, the Cuse again completely caved in as the Hurricanes closed on a 20–7 run. Everything that could go wrong did go wrong.

Then for the last time Boeheim-less, Syracuse, a five-point favorite, lost at home to Clemson in overtime, 74–73. Surrendering a three-point lead with 18 seconds to go in regulation, the Orange croaked in OT when Cooney stole the inbound pass but airballed a three-point attempt with one second left—the kind of shot that Gerry McNamara used to can. The fight, especially at the end, was there. The desired result was not. Another gallant struggle with nothing to show for it. Looking more like an SU team from the pre-Dennis DuVal/Rudy Hackett days, this edition of the Orange (10–6) had lost three straight and appeared to have its hands full trying to make the NIT. Hopkins went 4–5 in his substitute stint, not the prelude that his backers wanted relative to his taking over the team one day. He returned the Bentley to Boeheim, not just dirty and with Doritos in the back, but with a couple of dents in it. Even Boeheim haters couldn't wait for Boeheim's return to the bench. In reality though, the 2015–16 Orange was more Buick than Bentley. SU had decent talent and versatile players, but too many were young, inconsistent, and often forced to play out of position. It was a team of potential but unreliable show horses, including Cooney, who was a workhorse.

Four days later, Boeheim, after being in his words "torture(d)" during his thirty-six-day suspension and chomping at the bit to get back to work, was back on the bench. No wading in. With the No. 6-ranked North Carolina Tar Heels in town, the well-rested and seasoned coach was reentering the fray in the deep end of the pool. Boeheim walked into the arena to a standing ovation. The loud and long reception that greeted Boeheim included North Carolina coach Roy Williams who joined in with the clapping. "He's been good not only for Syracuse University but for the entire world of college basketball," Williams stated after the game.

The Orange continued to fight hard, but the script was similar. Behind 66–64 with 3:30 remaining, the Tar Heels scored nine straight points to win, 84–73, the fourth time in the last five games that SU hung tough but failed to finish. In ACC play, freshman star

Lydon—unfortunately competing inside against bigger and stronger players—played like a freshman, and Gbinije's statistics dipped. In losing its first four ACC games, Syracuse tied its worst start in conference play and fell to 10–7 overall. In his postgame comments, Boeheim refused to discuss his NCAA punishment that reduced his win total by 101 games, except to sarcastically say, "I've coached 1,200 games. Although I've only coached 1,100, forgot that."

Gbinije thought the difference between Boeheim and Hopkins was the intensity. "Boeheim wants to win every game and every possession," he said. No different from Nick Saban, the iconic Alabama football coach, who wants to win every down and every game.

After a ho-hum win over Boston College, it was bombs away in Winston-Salem as Cooney shot Syracuse out of the blocks by scoring the team's first 11 points in three-plus minutes en route to an easy 83–55 victory over Wake Forest. Beyond that, it was a dunk-a-thon for Gbinije and a pickpocket parade for the defense that had 12 steals. For one game at least, they looked like the Orange of old.

Despite Duke having dropped to No. 20 and SU being unranked, the rivalry between the schools heated up when SU won a 64–62 barnburner for its first win in Durham, making Boeheim the winner in the latest matchup of the winningest active coaches in Division I, with a combined 1,906 victories. Reminding him of his escapade the last time he was in the building, students chanted at Boeheim, "Take off your sport coat," which he playfully started to do. Just as Boeheim was angry at the end of that 2014 game when C. J. Fair got called for a questionable offensive foul, Mike Krzyzewski was fuming at the end of this one when, in a hectic last possession, Malachi Richardson and the Blue Devils' Matt Jones had a no-call collision scrambling after a missed Duke shot. The script was flipped, with the only thing missing from escalating the drama even more being Krzyzewski trying to rip off his sport coat. Regardless, this was not going to escalate into a rivalry like Syracuse-Georgetown of old. Boeheim and Krzyzewski liked each other too much. "I love Syracuse, and obviously I love Jim and his family," Krzyzewski said. "Congratulations to him ... I love the guy, and I'll be forever grateful for him. It's hard for me to think of a rivalry with Jim or Syracuse."

Tyler Roberson, performing like a jumping jack ala Dennis Rodman, recorded another double-double with a visiting-player arena record 20 rebounds to go with 14 points. His 12 offensive boards tied Billy Owens's SU standard. Great defense and balanced offense were instrumental in the win. Clearly, with Boeheim back, the Orange was revived. After defeating the reigning national champions and with a 13–7 record, 3–4 in the ACC (9–2 and 3–1 under Boeheim, and 4–5, 0–3 under Hopkins), it was a confidence, momentum, and NCAA-credential builder as the Orange ventured on to tackle No. 13 Virginia.

A blizzard caused Syracuse to arrive in Charlottesville on the morning of the game. Down by 10, SU stormed back to pull within 55–51 with less than five minutes left before freezing up toward the end in a 73–65 loss that ended a modest three-game winning streak. Poor inside defense did in the Orange. Having beaten Boeheim three straight times, the Cavaliers' Tony Bennett joined Jamie Dixon and Rick Pitino as coaches who had regularly solved Syracuse's tricky zone.

Back in the Dome, it was "Dress like Boeheim" night, and the team played like Syracuse of yesteryear when decades ago Boeheim wore those tacky various shades of orange sport coats. The Cuse smoked 25th-ranked Notre Dame, 81–66. Tagged the "Irish Killer" by Notre Dame coach Mike Brey, Trevor Cooney, who feasted on Notre Dame like Popeye thrived on spinach, contributed a team-leading 22 points, including his 250th three-pointer. The trifecta moved Cooney past Preston Shumpert, leaving Cooney behind only Andy Rautins (282) and Gerry McNamara (400) on the school's all-time three-point list. Inconsistent all season, individually with the players taking turns on who played well and who did not, and collectively when the Orange beat four ranked teams but lost to a poor St. John's team, someone pushed the on-switch as four Syracuse players scored in double figures while the zone confounded the Irish.

In the next game, Syracuse honored its 1975 Final Four team and passed out "Prayers for Pearl" T-shirts to support the legend who was battling brain cancer. Washington was first diagnosed with a brain tumor in 1995. He underwent two operations to remove the tumor. The cancer went into remission but later reoccurred and, over the course of a few years, took its toll. By 2015, the situation was very dire, and it was thought that it might be only a matter of time. By 2016, it became clear that the end was near. Always kind, gentle, humble, and maintaining a great attitude and the personality that, as Boeheim said, "made him probably the most beloved player in Syracuse basketball history," the young man who brought screaming fans to their feet with standing ovations grew to become a middle-aged man who brought people to their knees with prayers and donations. SU scratched out a too-close-for-comfort 60–57 win over Georgia Tech in one of those take-the-win-and-run games.

The nine-game suspension ended up proving just how good a coach Jim Boeheim was. Regaining control over a team on the skids that many had put on the scrap pile, Boeheim guided the Cuse to its fifth straight win. The Orange, in a war of wills, topped Virginia Tech, 68–60, in overtime as part of what may have been a season-saving victory. After playing poorly and trailing the entire game and down by seven with 1:37 to go, Gbinije tied the game at the end of regulation by drilling an NBA-distance three-point shot. Syracuse took its first lead of the contest in the extra session and improved its record to 15–8 and 6–5 in the ACC. Boeheim, who usually has his tie on in his postgame press conferences, appeared without it, perhaps indicative of the catfight his team just came through. He noted that many fans were leaving early, thinking the Orange was going to lose. "They must have gave up," he said, "[but] we didn't give up." Demonstrating dramatic improvement since his return, the enigmatic Orange crept closer toward NCAA contention, leaving many to wonder what SU's record would have been had the Hall of Fame coach been at the helm for the entire season.

With another heavy dose of defense plus a heaping helping of offense, Syracuse ran away from Florida State, 85–72. On Valentine's

Day, the Orange beat Boston College, 75–61, to win its eighth game in its last nine tries to push its record to 18–8, 8–5 in conference. For those who had prematurely lost interest because of SU's early season doldrums, their love for the team returned, and keeping up with the Cuse again became an addiction. Syracuse traveled to Louisville but played like a no-show as the Cardinals, despite its own self-imposed postseason ban from the NCAA tournament, stifled the Orange, 72–58, leaving Boeheim 10–12 versus his former pupil Rick Pitino. When Syracuse hosted Pittsburgh, it was a rerun of the earlier matchup as SU was again outrebounded, outmuscled, and out-hustled. After tying the game, 45–45, with 7:15 left, Syracuse again fizzled out in a 66–52 loss that gave Jamie Dixon his fourth straight win over Boeheim and improved his success rate to 7–2 in the Carrier Dome. An SU team that was on a roll prior to Louisville had now been rolled twice.

Hope for an NCAA berth was renewed when on Senior Night Michael Gbinije exited the Dome in style by scoring a career-high 34 points to lead the Cuse to a 75–66 win over NC State. "Silent G" left the court to a standing ovation, joining Leo Rautins and Ryan Blackwell as only the third transfer in school history to score over 1,000 points.

With Syracuse being an NCAA bubble team and a 14-point underdog, the SU–North Carolina game lacked the pregame excitement of past meetings between the two heavyweights. Except for rallying to make it 69–68 with 2:23 to go, the Orange never seemed to be in the game in losing to the No. 8 Tar Heels, 75–70. It was the same scenario against Florida State. In a game that could have clinched a spot for Syracuse in the NCAA tournament, the Orange fell behind but fought back to make it a one-possession game in the final seconds, only to falter at the end. The loss meant that in the ACC tournament SU would face Pittsburgh, which had already beaten Syracuse twice and had proven to be a nightmare in recent years. In a case of history seemingly repeating itself, Syracuse shot out to a 10-point lead in the first half against Pitt, only to fall behind by 14 points in the second half before putting together a 14–2 run to tie the contest at 68–68 with 1:58 remaining. The Panthers responded by scoring the next four points before Gbinije sank a three-pointer to pull the Cuse back to within one, 72–71. A missed Pitt free throw gave Syracuse life, but the Orange squandered the opportunity. Cooney, with 2.2 ticks showing on the clock, raced down the court and bonked a three-point shot off the rim. Jaime Dixon beat Boeheim for the fifth straight time and 14th time in 20 matchups. A Syracuse team with a 19–13 record, including five losses in its last six games, was leaking oil at every turn and now had to sweat out Selection Sunday to see if it would play in the NCAA tournament or settle for the NIT.

Syracuse had been on the tournament bubble four times before and each time was bypassed. This time the chance to make the tournament was even dicier. CBS scheduled an extended two-hour selection show that frustrated a lot of people as it dragged on. A Twitter leak prematurely exposed the brackets an hour into the show. When the Syracuse coaches and players unofficially learned that they had made the tournament, based on five wins against top 50 teams including three on the road and eight wins against top 100 teams, there was a big, collective sigh of relief. However, the selection of Syracuse, which had the lowest RPI of any team selected in the history of the tournament, produced a firestorm of criticism from talking heads and print journalists around the country. Regardless, after teetering on the brink with one foot in the NIT and only its shadow in the NCAA discussion, SU was making its 38th trip to the NCAA tournament. Boeheim was going to the dance for the 32nd time in his 40-year reign, the accomplishment tying Krzyzewski for the most all time. Like flowers in spring, it was the Orange playing basketball in March. As they had done since 2003 when Carmelo Anthony led the Cuse to the national championship, Freedom of Espresso's four Syracuse-area stores came out with its tournament-themed drinks, one of which was amply named "Let's Go Orange."

Grateful and happy just to be selected, the Orange was pitted against Dayton, the opponent that slipped by SU, 55–53, in the second round of the NCAA tournament in Buffalo in 2014, the last time Syracuse danced. Meeting again in St. Louis, 10th-seeded Syracuse floored the seventh-seeded Flyers, 70–51. In doing so, SU avenged the loss in 2014, made a statement to the naysayers, gave the battle-hardened Boeheim his 50th NCAA tournament win, and extended his record-setting run of 20 on-court win campaigns to 37. Tyler Roberson, of whom Boeheim a month earlier said, "If I had anyone else, he wouldn't play a minute," became as Mike Hopkins had called him when he's on his game, "Plugged-in Robie," as he snared 18 rebounds to compliment his 10 points. The Orange's 2–3 zone lived up to its reputation, holding Dayton to a season-low 51 points. As Malachi Richardson, who scored 21 points stated, "Keep advancing, keep dancing."

Reminded that the media lambasted Syracuse for being selected, Boeheim snapped back with, "Anybody that said we didn't deserve to be in obviously doesn't know anything about basketball." Syracuse caught a break when No. 15-seed Middle Tennessee upset No. 2 seed Michigan State, setting up a second-round game against the Blue Raiders instead of the Spartans. Before it played MTSU, the Orange was aware that No. 11 Gonzaga blitzed No. 3 Utah, giving SU a very favorable matchup if Syracuse could get past the Blue Raiders. That they did. In the 100th NCAA tournament game in program history, it was the Cuse, with one of the country's top three-point shooting defenses, against Middle Tennessee, one of the nation's top three-point shooting teams. Giddy Potts, the country's best three-point shooter, was going to test the zone. No contest. Syracuse put Potts in its pocket. The Blue Raiders flamed out in the second half in a 75–50 loss, shooting a paltry 29 percent from the floor while going 8-for-24 from three-point range to join a long line of tournament teams that were overwhelmed by "The Zone." It was on to Chicago for Boeheim's 18th Sweet 16.

Facing a Gonzaga team that presented two matchup problems in 6-foot-11 Domantas Sabonis and 6-foot-10 zone buster Kyle Wiltjer, mastermind Boeheim made the adjustments that enabled Syracuse to eliminate the Zags, 63–60. Trailing by 13 at one point, the Orange charged back and took the lead, 61–60, when Gbinije made a layup with 24 seconds remaining in the game. With two seconds to go and with Wiltjer bottled up, Josh Perkins attempted a potential game-winning shot, but freshman Tyler Lydon leaped toward the foul line and rejected it to make the second biggest block in SU history. Lydon grabbed the ball, was fouled, and made two free throws to close out the scoring. The Lydon slamback sent the Cuse back to the Elite Eight for the third time in eight years and the seventh time since 1985 when the tournament was expanded to sixty-four teams. After the Zags bagged 5 of 6 three-point shots to start the game, the Orange defense limited Gonzaga to 3-for-21 from long distance the rest of the way. Perhaps it was karma, because Perkins had provided locker room fodder by stating that "Gonzaga couldn't be zoned." Holding Gonzaga to a season-low in points scored while forcing a season-high number of turnovers proved the Zags got zoned.

Syracuse's two fifth-year seniors, Michael Gbinije with 20 points and Trevor Cooney with 15, fittingly led the Orange to victory. Tyler Roberson stayed plugged in, with nine points and 12 rebounds. Vice President and SU Law School alum Joe Biden tweeted Cooney, whose grandfather had graduated from high school with Biden: "From one Delaware and Cuse man to another—all heart and pure Orange. Great game last night." Straight ahead was Virginia (29–7), the top seed in the Midwest Region and the only team in the ACC that SU had not beaten since entering the conference.

Syracuse was the only school with both its men's and women's basketball teams competing in the Sweet 16, making it only the ninth school to do so and making March 26, Easter Sunday, a big day in Central New York. A couple of hours after the women's team easily beat Tennessee, the Orange men, down 16 points to Virginia midway in the second half, came back from the dead. After losing nearly every battle for the first 30 minutes of the game to fall behind, 54–39, and after all but the truest of SU's die-hard fans had given up, Syracuse miraculously stormed back to win the war and send the Orange to the

Final Four for the sixth time in school history and the fifth time under Boeheim. It would be Syracuse's second trip in four years to college basketball's magic kingdom. The turning point came with about 10 minutes to go when Boeheim, out of desperation, called for a suffocating full-court press that speeded up the game against a fundamentally sound Virginia team that thrived on its preferred slower pace of play. As CBS analyst Charles Barkley put it, "Virginia wanted to play at 55 miles per hour, but the press pushed the tempo to 65 miles per hour, and the Cavaliers crashed." Considering the stage, the significance of the game and that it came against the KenPom No. 1-rated defensive team, the 68–62 win signified the greatest comeback in SU history. Boeheim called the comeback the greatest in his 40 years of coaching.

Much to the chagrin of the NCAA, which had thought sanctioning the program would derail the precision Syracuse basketball machine, and to the dismay of those who complained that Syracuse did not belong in the tournament and they did not deserve a No. 10 seeding, and to others who said that SU had won its first three games because it beat low-seeded teams, the Orange proved its worthiness by taking down the No. 1 seed. Syracuse became the first No. 10 seed and only the fourth double-digit seed to reach the coveted Final Four. The Cuse got loose because Malachi Richardson scored 21 of his 23 points in the second half to ignite SU's courageous, improbable, uphill climb to overtake the Cavaliers. The Cuse, on the back of its two seasoned seniors and fueled by big-time contributions from its outstanding freshmen, saved the last dance for Houston, where in the national semifinals it would again face ACC foe North Carolina. For the fourth straight time, Boeheim had beaten a No. 1 seed, improving his mark to a respectable 4–5 when facing top seeds.

The men's and women's teams winning made everything right in Cuse country. Hundreds of students and Cuse crazies congregated near campus as a spontaneous party erupted to celebrate the dual wins. Chants of "Let's Go Orange" reverberated throughout the area. Downstate and apropos for a school that promoted itself as New York's team, a photo showed an orange sky over the Big Apple. SU's school colors lit up the new World Trade Center. Governor Andrew Cuomo tweeted congrats to the men's and women's teams. The series of events made this more than just another "Syracuse Moment." With its fans, former players, and followers on social media jubilant, this was a "Syracuse Day."

During the week, the Syracuse spirit spread throughout the city, county, and beyond, with SU flags flying in Clinton Square as well as at the top of the State Tower Building, the tallest building in the city that also had "Go Cuse" prominently written in its windows. Orange and blue lights were aglow in the Niagara Mohawk building. SU displays of all kinds showed up on storefronts of businesses, eating and drinking establishments, and in schools. St. Joseph's Hospital dressed up its newborn babies in SU gear. Democratic presidential hopeful Hillary Clinton, sporting an orange blouse and necklace, stopped by the Varsity pub and signed two basketballs, one for the men's team and one for the women's team. Syracuse's success inspired several new songs about the Orange, including "Cuttin' Down the Nets," a revved-up tune by blues guitarist Duke Tumatoe, an original member of REO Speedwagon. Syracuse native Chris Mac came out with "We Ballin' on 'Em," a peppy hip-hop mix. Irv Lyons Jr. and Richie Melito put out "The Cuse is On the Loose." Another local musician, George Day, contributed, "I'm Still Standing." It was reminiscent of when "Cuse Yourself" by rapper Fame sprang up following the 2003 National Championship and Jake Ober (J.O.) came out with "Let's Go," which was accompanied by a video by Sam Bone Dean in 2010. A noon pep rally on Wednesday at Manley Field House provided the appropriate send-off for the teams. Meanwhile, Orange fever dominated the NCAA tournament on social media.

In a news conference in Houston before the Final Four, Boeheim was again asked about the violations committed by his program. He readily admitted that Syracuse broke the rules but stated that SU did not cheat. He said breaking rules is a lot different from cheating. "Cheating, to me, is intentionally doing something, like you wanted to get this recruit so you arranged a job for him, or you wanted to see him when you shouldn't ... to gain an advantage in recruiting. That's cheating." The Hall of Fame coach said he didn't think Syracuse gained any competitive advantage at any time during the entire ten-year investigation. "When they say we cheated, that's not true," he reiterated before admitting losing his wins bothered him. "Losing the [victories] is the most irritating thing to me because there's many situations and past cases [at other places] where similar things, exact same things happened, and games were not taken away. We presented all that stuff, but you know, nobody listened."

Many speculated that the NCAA came down hard on Boeheim because over the years Boeheim came across as crass, arrogant, and at times even combative, unlike former coaches such as John Wooden and Dean Smith, who were mild-mannered, charming, and grand-fatherly. Some hypothesized that certain members of the media were waiting for the chance to take down the cantankerous coach and, now given the opportunity, were giddily growling like a dog gnawing the last piece of meat off a bone.

Amidst all this there was a perception that some Syracuse fans were paranoid. They thought ESPN Radio's Doug Gottlieb, Yahoo's Pat Forde, *Newsday*'s Greg Logan, and ESPN, among others were against them. ESPN Radio's Mike Greenberg provided a reason for that perception by pointedly stating that an undeserving Syracuse team reaching the Final Four proved that the NCAA tournament was not designed to determine the best team. He alluded to what everyone had always known for years, that the NCAA tournament—and by extension the college football championship playoff and even the World Series with all the mediocre at-large qualifiers—was formatted to increase fan interest and revenue. Those events, of course, would only prove the best team at that particular tournament, playoff, or series. Greenberg's *Mike and Mike Show* colleague Mike Golic agreed, stating that if the tournament, and again by extension that if a play-off or a World Series were replayed, there was a reasonable chance that it could produce a different champion. No great revelation there. However, unlike other years when unexpected teams forged their way into the Final Four without being told they didn't belong there, Greenberg's dig was clearly directed at Syracuse.

Greenberg's comments were strange because upsets by bracket-busting Cinderella teams were precisely why people loved the NCAA tournament, ala the excitement of watching Jim Valvano's 1983 underdog NC State team take down Houston's "Phi Slamma Jamma" Cougars, who were led by Akeem "The Dream" Olajuwon and Clyde Drexler. Golic, however, thought much of that excitement was lost when the Orange crashed the party because Syracuse was not a true Cinderella team.

"[Syracuse] is a blue-blood, especially with its coach," he stated. Fine, but then how come nobody complained when a mediocre Connecticut team that finished ninth in the Big East got hot and rode Kemba Walker to the 2011 national title? Maybe it's because, as Carmelo Anthony emphatically screamed on the video he posted on social media, "They hate us. They don't want us to win." Apparently, Boeheim didn't hold a grudge against Greenberg because a few months later at an NBA Finals game between the Cleveland Cavaliers and the Golden State Warriors the two were smiling broadly when they posed together for a picture.

In reference to the recent NCAA problems at Syracuse and North Carolina, Forde began championship week by calling the SU-UNC game "awkward … for those who want to believe that NCAA crime doesn't pay … because you've got two scandal-scarred coaches who beat a messy system to reach the pinnacle of their sport again." Even though Syracuse had already been severely punished, that apparently wasn't enough for Forde, who wanted them punished again. Thus Carmelo Anthony's rant.

Syracuse was in the NCAA tournament. Unwanted, yes, because many felt they didn't belong. Unliked, yes, because of its skirmishes with the NCAA. Unappreciated, certainly, because people disregarded how they battled once they were selected. Disrespected, yes, because people chose to overlook the school's basketball tradition. But a Cinderella team? No, because, as Golic pointed out, the Cuse is a blue blood and a brand. A team with six appearances was no stranger to the Final Four. The Orange was a Cinderella team in 1975, for sure, but not this time. Syracuse was more like Donald Trump in the 2016 presidential election. People tried to configure all kinds of ways to keep him out, but Trump disregarded all the negativity, brushed away all the damaging perceptions, and bullied his way to the front of the Republican pack. He couldn't be stopped and, on its way to the Final Four, neither could the Cuse. Boeheim now ranked fifth among active coaches and ninth all-time among coaches reaching the Final Four.

By steering his flawed team through a myriad of distractions and over several obstacles and hurdles both on and off the court to reach the fabled Final Four, Boeheim again outdid himself. As he had in several other challenging campaigns, Boeheim may have again matched or bettered his "best coaching job ever." If not his best, Boeheim said that it was "his most satisfying year, with the possible exception of the year we won it all." For those who kept clamoring that Boeheim was over the hill, he recorded three Final Fours in his first thirty-six years and two Final Fours in the last four years, reached the Elite Eight four times in his first thirty-five years and three times in the last five years, and made the Sweet 16 thirteen times in his first thirty-two years and five times in the last eight years.

Motivated by Pearl, who was honored when mayor Bill de Blasio proclaimed April 9 "Pearl Washington Day in New York City" but who then was fighting for his life, big underdog Syracuse was fighting for the national championship against No. 1-seed North Carolina, a team with a 32–6 record and loaded with the most talent of any of the Final Four teams, which also included Villanova and Oklahoma. The Orange made a go of it early but fell behind and trailed by 11 at the half. Behind 17 in the second half, Boeheim's gritty band of warriors charged back to pull within seven, 57–50, with just under 10 minutes left. The Tar Heels, who had shot 0-for-12 from the three-point line up to that juncture, canned back-to-back threes to pull away for an 83–66 victory. Like in 1996 when the Orange lost to a better Kentucky team, in 2016, the Cuse lost to a better North

Carolina team. Demonstrating the same effort and intestinal fortitude as it did against the Wildcats, the Orange's all-out effort against the Tar Heels earned respect and admiration from those who watched the game. The loss ended another historic season for the proud and accomplished program. Playing with a lot of heart and a never-say-die attitude, Syracuse's incredible and exciting run throughout the tournament to the national semifinals delighted its fans and alumni, including Vice President Biden, who went to the locker room to tell the players and coaches how proud he was of his alma mater's tournament performance.

A couple of weeks later while on a campaign stop in Syracuse, Ohio Governor and presidential candidate John Kasich, who watched the SU-Virginia and SU-UNC games on television, told the Syracuse. com editorial board, "I could not believe how effective Syracuse was against Virginia ... They put that press on, and it was like Virginia collapsed like a house of cards." About the loss to the Tar Heels, he said, "Hey, you get to the Final Four, that's pretty significant." Continuing to politick, he inserted about Boeheim, "He's a great coach. There's no question about it ... [Syracuse] is a great program."

So after a 0–4 start in the conference in what began as a down year where some thought maybe the program was on a downtick, the Orange's second appearance in the Final Four in the previous four years was a feat topped only by Kentucky. Moreover, SU's three trips to the Elite Eight in the last five years were matched only by Kentucky, Louisville, and Florida. Syracuse was at least in the discussion when speaking of basketball royalty. They finished No. 10 in the final *USA Today* Coaches Poll.

Cooney was arguably the Orange's best player during the NCAA tournament. He scored a game-high 22 points against North Carolina. A streaky but inconsistent shooter, Cooney finished his checkered career with 1,437 points, placing him 29th on the school scoring list. He made 281 three-pointers, behind only Gerry McNamara's 400 and Andy Rautins's 282. His 207 steals rank ninth all-time at SU. A three-year starter, Cooney stands alone as the only Syracuse player to play in two Final Fours. Like Cooney, fellow senior Michael Gbinije was by turns scorned and praised by SU fans. "Silent G" scored in double-figures in all 37 games his senior season, one short of John Wallace's school-record 38 games.

As noted on Syracuse.com, DaJuan Coleman (Jamesville-DeWitt High School) became the fifth Syracuse native to play in the Final Four for the Orange, joining Chris Sease (Nottingham) who played in 1975, Howard Triche (Corcoran) in 1987, Lazarus Sims (Henninger) in 1996, and Brandon Triche (Jamesville-DeWitt) in 2013. Amazingly each started every game during their Final Four seasons. Boeheim finished the season with 989 on-court victories, behind only Krzyzewski's 1,043 wins. Since Boeheim had an annual salary of $2.144 million compared to K's $7-million-plus salary, Syracuse had a great deal. In November 2014, *Forbes* magazine, using a detailed formula, stated that Boeheim's calculated $2,131,424 salary was the second-best bargain in college basketball for a school, bettered only by the salary of Mark Few at Gonzaga.

The Passing of Pearl

Syracuse Nation was radiating with joy but shortly thereafter it was deeply saddened. On April 20, 2016, after a gallant fight for his life, Pearl Washington, at the age of 52, died from brain cancer. Like Ernie Davis, Syracuse's Heisman Trophy winner and another cancer casualty, Washington died with dignity. An emotional Boeheim called Washington "a unique player ... a unique person ... the most exciting player to ever play in the Big East ... He was one of a kind ... People wanted to watch him play ... I hadn't seen anything like him before and haven't seen anything like him since." Tributes came from all segments of the SU fan base as well as from celebrities across the country that tweeted their condolences and recollections.

NBA great Earvin "Magic" Johnson tweeted, "[Pearl] was the best ball handler I've seen in my lifetime." National sports reporter Steven A. Smith stated, "[Pearl put on] the greatest college basketball show that I've ever seen." Renowned movie director Spike Lee said, "[Pearl] was one of Brooklyn's finest." Teammate Rafael Addison put it this way: "Traveling with him was like traveling with a rock star." Dick Vitale called Washington "one of my all-time favorites." Patrick Ewing, a fierce competitor on hated-rival Georgetown who years earlier exchanged elbows to the gut with Washington, wrote: "Pearl was one of the great phenoms of my era. To me, he's one of the great college athletes of all time." From college basketball analyst Jay Bilas: "Dwayne 'Pearl' Washington, one of college basketball's all-time greats. An extraordinarily sad day."

Seth Greenberg, another national basketball analyst, posted: "[His] games were not games but events. He changed the Big East. Pearl was playing chess when everyone else was playing checkers." Vice President of the United States Joe Biden said, "God bless the Pearl. Dwayne Washington's No. 31 hangs from the rafters of my alma mater and in our hearts." New York Governor Andrew Cuomo tweeted, "My heart goes out to the family, friends, and the many adoring fans of Brooklyn native and Syracuse basketball legend Pearl Washington." Madison Square Garden, the world's most famous arena, memorialized Washington by quickly placing a picture of Pearl on one of its marquees with the words, "Thanks for the memories and magical moments at The Garden." And on and on, and all deserving for a man who was so embraced by everyone partly because, as Chris Cordes in a letter to the editor of the *Syracuse Post-Standard* so aptly put it, "Pearl was never too small for the biggest shot and [more importantly because of his mythical status] was never too big for the smallest fan."

Making that point, Mike Maestri, in a letter to Syracuse columnist Bud Poliquin, told how Washington took the time to make his daughter feel special. In a youth sports game, Maestri's daughter made a half-court shot just prior to the halftime buzzer. A short time later, Maestri and his daughter had a chance to meet Washington, and Maestri mentioned his daughter's shot. He said, "Pearl got down on a knee, looked at my daughter eye-to-eye, and said, 'I bet your shot was better than mine.'"

Washington's unassuming nature was exemplified by a story tweeted by Adam Himmelsbach, who as a high school student worked for the Syracuse Parks Department where he was supervised by Washington. "One day Pearl shows up and after looking around says that the bathrooms could be cleaner," wrote Himmelsbach. "I and the other workers say 'OK.' He then disappears for a bit, and I go in the field house, and he's in there scrubbing the place. He said that he just wanted it to look good. Then he finished, smiled, and left. The little kids there had no clue he was a hoops legend, and Pearl didn't bother to tell them or anyone else. [In his mind] he was just a parks department employee, and that was just fine with him."

Former Syracuse star Derrick Coleman told Kevin Armstrong of the *New York Daily News*, "I guess he's in heaven now. Pearl probably crossed-over Jesus to get inside the gates," in reference to Washington's famed crossover dribble that paralyzed defenders as he zipped past them for easy layups. Pearl Washington was Syracuse royalty. Pearl's light will shine forever in the folklore of Syracuse basketball and in the hearts of Orange Nation.

At his final viewing and public remembrance ceremony, an emotional Boeheim stated, "Pearl Washington came to Syracuse, he made our basketball program, he made our conference, and he made me." With his voice cracking, he ended by saying, "Pearl was the most humble player … and person … that I have ever known. And that is why we remember him the way we do. Because there are a lot of great players, but there's only one Pearl Washington."

Like Ernie Davis, Pearl exemplified the best in people. Famous as he was, he was humble, kind, selfless, and cordial with everyone he met. He made friends as easy as he made baskets. A competitor extraordinaire on the court, off the court he was shy, more regular guy than superstar, more Dwayne than Pearl. So iconic, yet so down-to-earth, Pearl touched the lives of a lot of people by the dignified way he lived his life. Whereas his head was always bobbing every which way when he dribbled and fired off no-look passes during intense basketball situations, Washington was courageous and kept his head held high, never complaining, as he suffered through the final agonizing days of his life. He gave back to the Syracuse community more than SU gave to him. Many wanted, and deservedly so, a statue erected for Pearl to accompany those of SU's former football greats. Although he would never have wanted the personal acclaim, Pearl created another, in fact one of the biggest "Syracuse Moments," because his passing resulted in an outpouring of national attention for his beloved alma mater.

Pearl Washington is buried in Maple Grove Cemetery in Queens. Skipping ahead, in April 2018, two years after his passing, Washington's fiance Debra Busacco told Don Cronson, a friend of Boeheim, that Washington's grave still did not have a headstone because the family couldn't afford one. Cronson said he would contact his Syracuse friends and they would pitch in to pay for the headstone. Cronson's first call was to Boeheim who, without knowing the cost, immediately said, "Send me the bill and I will take care of the whole thing."

2016–17

Syracuse hired John Wildhack, an ESPN executive, as its new athletic director. A longtime friend of Boeheim, immediate speculation was that Wildhack might allow Boeheim to coach beyond his announced retirement date. That notion gained credibility when Boeheim told James Szuba, a writer for the *Troy Nunes is an Absolute Magician* blog, "Retirement? You'd have a better shot at winning the Kentucky Derby with the Trojan horse before you see me retire!" He also said, "I'd like to get one more player like [Carmelo Anthony] at Syracuse before I retire … I've got a few more years left to pull it off." It was comments like that that kept Syracuse fans guessing how long he would coach.

Malachi Richardson, riding a great game performance against Virginia in the NCAA Tournament, entered the 2016 NBA Draft and was selected with the 22nd pick by the Sacramento Kings. Richardson was the third straight Syracuse one-and-done player to leave the program, following McCullough and Ennis, and the fifth overall with Carmelo Anthony departing after his freshman year in 2003 and

Donté Greene doing the same in 2008. When Michael Gbinije was picked by the Detroit Pistons in the second round, it was the fifth time that two SU players were drafted in the previous seven years. Beginning in 2010, 2011 aside, it also was the ninth time in ten years that Syracuse produced a first-round draft choice. Yet many Orange followers continued to complain that Boeheim couldn't recruit.

Boeheim emphatically put the kibosh to that theory by restocking his 2016 recruiting class with the summer additions of point guard John Gillon, a fifth-year transfer from Colorado State, coveted 6-foot-10 freshman forward Taurean Thompson, the No. 75 recruit in the nation according to ESPN, and 6-foot-7 wing Andrew White III, a graduate transfer from Nebraska where he averaged 16.6 points a game and 5.6 rebounds a game while making 41 percent of his three-point shots and 56 percent of his two-point attempts. White was a Top 50 recruit in 2012 when he originally signed with Kansas and, in 2016, was considered the best graduate transfer available.

With White stepping right in for Richardson, Gillon as a true point guard, Lydon back after establishing an SU record with 20 blocked shots in five tournament games, Roberson and Coleman returning, the addition of 7-foot-2 Providence transfer Paschal Chukwu plus highly touted freshmen Tyus Battle and Matthew Moyer, the Orange suddenly went from a young, inexperienced team to a veteran team with maturity and leadership. When White became Orange, the Cuse quickly rose from a Top 20 team to a legitimate Final Four and 2016–17 national-title contender. "It was an opportunity to compete on one of the biggest stages in all of college basketball," White told Syracuse beat writer Mike Waters. "It was too good of an opportunity to pass up."

After losing three starters and 70 percent of his scoring, Boeheim yet again outdid himself by putting together a group that, at least on paper, had size, speed, quickness, experience, depth, and the potential to score a lot of points. Balanced, two deep at every position, and now with two seniors and two grad transfers, Boeheim assembled one of his most complete teams in years. His challenge was to develop chemistry, figure out how to parcel out the minutes among the high-end talent he had collected, teach the new players how to play zone defense, and temper the exuberant expectations around Central New York that quickly took a Final Four-or-bust attitude.

The NCAA intended for the severe sanctions to set Syracuse back. However, in year two following the sanctions, Boeheim stated, "We have everything that we need [to be successful]." Usually a sandbagger, Boeheim went out on a limb when he told ESPN's Andy Katz in the preseason, "This is one of the best teams that we've had in a long time." In doing so, Boeheim got the already excited Orange fans even more excited about the upcoming season.

As in the past, it seemed that whenever the Orange program picked up momentum something surfaced to slow down the pace. This time it was another hit from the NCAA. Just as Syracuse was gearing up for an anticipated great season, on October 17, 2016, the NCAA formally announced that several key wins and seasons were among the 101 losses Syracuse would be forced to vacate. Included were the dramatic Gerry McNamara-dominated 2006 Big East tournament championship run and the program's all-time best 34–3 won-lost record amassed during the 2011–12 season. Fifteen wins from the 2004–05 season were also erased, lowering the record from 27–7 to 12–7. All 23 wins from the 2005–06 campaign were vacated, making the official record 0–12. The 2006–07 season record dropped from 24–11 to 2–11 after 22 wins were taken away. Seven wins were removed from the 2010–11 season, adjusting the mark from 27–8 to 20–8. Syracuse was left with a 0–3 record in 2011–12 after all 34 wins were stripped. Also affected were Boeheim's personal accomplishments that included his national-best string of 18 straight 20-win seasons and the school's nation-leading 45-season winning streak. Officially, Boeheim began the 2016–17 season with 884 wins instead of the 989 victories he amassed on the court.

Disagreeing with the severity of the sanctions, Boeheim told Doug Gottlieb, "Most of the [violations] were about tutoring. Most but not all … We've accepted the punishment. I've accepted the punishment.

I'm responsible. I've said that many, many times … I've said it enough."
Regarding the vacating of 101 of his victories, Boeheim brushed that
off by saying, "They're just numbers."

As he prepared for the 2016–17 season, Boeheim was aware that
the clock was ticking; the sand was slowly slipping through the hour-
glass, and the Jim Boeheim Era was inevitably going to end in the
next couple of years. In an attempt to finish his career with another
national championship before the end of the 2017–18 season, the
stated time of his retirement, Boeheim got involved in intense head-
to-head recruiting battles with Kentucky, Duke, and Kansas for some
of the best players in the country. He went all-out to land five-star
point guard Quade Green, anticipating that collaring Green would
get other five-stars to follow, but the plan backfired when Green, long
considered a strong Syracuse lean, at the last minute chose Kentucky.

Following a No. 10 final ranking in the AP poll the previous year
and starting out No. 19 in the preseason poll, Syracuse's enthusiastic
and hopeful fanbase put as much stock in the low ranking as Trump
supporters did in the 2016 presidential election. During a spruced-up
Orange Madness, ESPN analyst Seth Greenberg, defying the NCAA,
egged on the crowd by proclaiming that Boeheim was closing in on
winning his 1,000th game. Needing 16 wins, the countdown to the
unofficial 1,000 began with an 83–55 pounding of Colgate. After
burying South Carolina State, 101–59, Syracuse started the season
4–0 but in its next outing quickly discovered that big brother South
Carolina was a bit stronger, as the Gamecocks' defense smothered SU,
64–50. The Orange followed that up with a 17-point loss at No. 17
Wisconsin that, although early in the season, put all that Final Four
and national championship talk on hold.

In the first few games, Syracuse cherry-picked against weak opponents and got overwhelmed by Power Five opponents when its zone
turned to Swiss cheese, the offense disappeared, and the team became
discombobulated. Boeheim tinkered with various lineups. In some
games, the highly anticipated transfers and freshmen looked good,
and the Orange had quality depth as touted, while in other games

there were indications that Boeheim was going to be left with a six- or seven-man rotation again.

Then the unimaginable happened. Against former Big East rival UConn, playing in Madison Square Garden, where the two power programs played the epic six-overtime game in 2009, the two schools combined to play an awful game where neither team could put the ball in the basket. The worst Connecticut team since before Calhoun came to the rescue in 1986 slipped past Syracuse, 52–50, in a game that was painful to the eyes. Both teams played hard, but they both played terribly. Boeheim had told ESPN's Andy Katz, "This is one of the best teams I've had in a long time," but the Huskies, with four early seasons losses including to Wagner and Northeastern, made it clear that the preseason projections of SU as a possible Final Four team were folly. At that point, the Orange had all it could handle just to make the NIT. In a game consisting of offensive ineptitude on both sides, it seemed the only person who could make a shot was the fan who nailed a half-court heave during intermission to win $5,000. All the pieces were there. They just didn't fit together. The Jim Boeheim fan club was silent. At a school where, when the football team starts to tank, the groupies cry out "When does basketball season start?" the cry out was "When does lax [lacrosse] start?"

On Pearl Washington Day, when the late SU star had his No. 31 inscribed on Jim Boeheim Court during a halftime ceremony and with the Orange wearing early 1980s retro uniforms in his honor, Georgetown, like they had repeatedly done in the past, spoiled still another Syracuse ceremony by beating the Cuse, 78–71. Just as the Hoyas ended Syracuse's 57-game home winning streak by sticking SU, 52–50, in the "Manley Field House is Officially Closed" game in 1980, Georgetown ruined "Jim Boeheim Day" on February 2, 2002, by dumping the Orange, 75–69. The Hoyas also snapped Syracuse's 38-game homecourt winning streak by downing SU, 57–46, on February 23, 2013, in its last Big East regular-season game in the Carrier Dome on a day when Carmelo Anthony's jersey was retired. Now came this slap in the face. Beyond losing to a mediocre Hoyas team (7–4), Syracuse (6–4) put itself in a precarious position for post-season play. Given that Syracuse falling to UConn and Georgetown were now considered bad losses, when the Huskies and Hoyas enjoyed hoops respect not that long ago, showed how much the college basketball landscape had changed.

Whereas Syracuse did almost everything wrong in its four losses, it did virtually everything right in routing Eastern Michigan, 105–57. As beat writer Mike Waters pointed out, it was the first time in forty years that eight SU players scored in double figures in the same game. Still, it was a "so-what" win. Then a second-rate St. John's team embarrassed Syracuse, 93–60, their worst loss in Carrier Dome history and in the Boeheim era. Near the end, the usually rabid Orange crowd had had enough, booing as people left in droves with about five minutes remaining. For many who had thought in December that the season was toast, the feeling went from disappointment to disgust. Pitiful in all aspects of the game, Boeheim simply stated, "This game is all on me. I didn't get them ready … on defense or on offense." Boeheim had suffered through five non-conference losses for the first time ever. Four days before Christmas, Santa Claus delivered not a lump but a bushel of coal. Boeheim's preseason assessment of his team took a 180-degree turn when he said that unless Syracuse made some drastic improvements, the Orange would lose many more games.

The Orange crushed Cornell, 80–56, but a disgruntled Internet writer stated, "Jimmie eats another cupcake," expressing the sentiment of many of the unimpressed who debated about whether underachieving Syracuse was even going to have a winning season or whether Boeheim would pick up the needed seven more wins that season to tally 1,000 on-court victories. On New Year's Day, a hapless Boston College team that earlier had lost at home to Nicholls State and Hampton, ended a 20-game ACC losing streak by humiliating Syracuse, 96–81. The high point for the Orange was that BC didn't crack the 100-point mark. What went right for SU? Nothing. What went wrong? Everything. In a season of historic program lows in the Jim Boeheim era, Syracuse hit rock bottom. A year removed from the

Final Four, the Orange was floundering around East of Eden. Internet troll skcusexa posted that new T-shirts were out that said, "We Stink" on the front and "Retire" on the back.

Like an aged warhorse left behind at the stable, Boeheim became frustrated as more and more teams figured out how to solve his zone, with the low-flying Eagles the latest by making a record-tying 16 three-point shots against the Orange. Although more teams were using the 2–3 zone, thereby acknowledging its effectiveness, the difference was that only Boeheim was married to it. It was automatic. When Syracuse was playing on television and Bill Raftery was at the mike, he liked to say: "The Cuse is in the 2–3 zone," adding in his excited, speeded-up voice while accentuating each word in his unique way, "with man-to-man principles."

However, as football analyst Lee Corso was fond of saying, "Not so fast, my friend." Syracuse showed signs of becoming the team that Boeheim had high hopes for in the preseason by putting together resounding wins over Miami and Pittsburgh, teams that came to town with a combined 23–5 record. With pain-in-the-butt Jamie Dixon gone, the Orange ended a five-game losing streak to the Panthers. On the Boeheim meter, after the nightmarish start that had many SU fans cringing, some who wanted the old man put out to pasture and the sooner the better now wanted Jimmie to be president, especially after the Cuse cruised to a 28-point lead over Pitt in the first half on its way to a 77–66 win whose score resembled the Panthers' 76–61 football win over Syracuse. There was a resurgence of hope in the land of the Orange—at least until the next game.

Interestingly, and unusually, Boeheim extended his postgame press conference to take issue with a column written by Bud Poliquin, who penned that the Orange, regardless of its two appearances in the previous four Final Fours, was in a three-year downward spiral. Boeheim responded by calling 2015–16, when SU lost 14 games but reached the Final Four, one of the five best seasons he'd ever had in his forty-one years at Syracuse. Clarifying his stance, Boeheim stated, "The Final Four in college basketball is the only thing that matters ... That's what's important." Boeheim, however, had a little different take in 2012 when he said in his postgame comments following SU's loss to Ohio State in the NCAA tournament, "I don't subscribe to the theory that you have to win this or that in the tournament to have a good year ... [The team] played great this year. They really have. A tremendous year." And back in 1979 when a much younger Boeheim told *Sports Illustrated*, "You can't judge a team by what it does in the NCAAs. Everybody loses ... but one [team]."

A bad loss at Virginia Tech was followed by a good payback win over Boston College during the up-down, up-down season. Then came a matchup of 2016 Final Four teams, with No. 9 North Carolina beating the Orange, 85–68, as Roy Williams joined Boeheim and seven others in the 800-win club. A two-touchdown underdog, Syracuse had an opportunity to get a possible season-changing win but couldn't pull off a mega upset. The game lacked the interest of past encounters because SU brought an unimpressive 11–7 record to Chapel Hill. After forty-one years, Boeheim finally found out how the have-nots have lived as the Orange—lacking execution, toughness, leadership, and heart as well as a good point guard, rebounding, and defense— lost at No. 15 Notre Dame, 84–66. It was a game, like so many others that season, that SU was never in. Boeheim had the look of despair as he watched the Fighting Irish take out four years of frustration in ripping apart his team. It continued the worst SU start since 1970 when Richard Nixon was in the White House and the Vietnam War was raging. Many Syracuse fans had already checked out.

When all seemed lost, suddenly and unexpectedly Syracuse, spurred on by the Dome court advantage, upset No. 6 Florida State, 82–72. The Orange improved to 13–9. Leading the charge was Andrew White (24 points, nine rebounds, and four steals), John Gillon (21 points including the last 13 of the game, career-high 11 assists), and Tyler Lydon (14 points, 11 rebounds, and a personal-best six blocks). The Cuse gave demanding Orange fans a glimpse of what Boeheim envisioned in the preseason. As the game winded down, Otto's Army taunted FSU with the Seminoles' famed pulsating "Wo, Wo, Wo,

Wo, Whoa; Wo, Wo, Wo, Wo, Whoa" tomahawk chop war chant. Unfortunately, the fans stormed the court, something a power program should not do, especially after beating a team that had only recently become relevant in college basketball. It was Boeheim's 998th on-court victory.

To many Syracuse fans, the countdown to 1,000 wins was two. The NCAA stripped SU of 101 wins and silenced the school from recognizing the vacated wins in any way, including in the media guide or in the Dome. In an interview with Bud Poliquin, Boeheim stated, "Look at the record book. We don't have them all, but we have won those games. That I can say … I've won 998 games, but I don't have 998 wins. Everybody knows I won [those games]. The NCAA knows that. They've taken them away."

In its next outing, down by 16 in the second half, Syracuse stormed back to capture its first road win of the season in a wild overtime victory over NC State. John Gillon's career and PNC Arena-high 43 points (10 of 13 from the floor, 9 of 10 from three-point range, and 14 of 14 from the foul line) powered the Orange. Gillon scored the last five points of regulation, including an off-balance three from the corner with 1.1 seconds left to send the game into overtime. He had nine assists to boot. Gillon's offensive performance was the best since Gerry McNamara poured in 43 points against BYU in the 2004 NCAA Tournament. Fellow transfer Andrew White III added 28 points, including the first nine points in the extra stanza. Tyler Lydon contributed 15 points as SU snapped a seven-game away losing streak to keep its flickering postseason hopes alive.

There was jubilation in Jimmieville as Boeheim vanquished No. 9 Virginia, 66–62, to bag his 1,000th win, the alternative facts from the NCAA notwithstanding. Behind by 12, the Orange, with an efficient offense and tenacious defense, again overtook the Cavaliers to improve to 15–9 and 7–4 in the ACC. It was reminiscent of the 16-point comeback that knocked Virginia out of the NCAA tournament the previous year, eerily by almost the same score, 68–62. About to be cremated two weeks earlier, the Cuse came back with a vengeance to win its fourth straight game, including two against Top 10 teams. In the second half, Syracuse shot a mind-boggling 73.7 percent from the field and 66.7 percent from beyond the arc to derail the Cavs and reinstate its position in postseason tournament discussion.

In the waning seconds of the contest, Matt Park, the Voice of the Orange, in defiance to the NCAA, blurted out: "Can Jim Boeheim get his one-thousandth win of his career? You bet your asterisk he can!" The fans screamed, "One thousand, one thousand, one thousand!" and held placards supporting 1,000 wins. Some accentuated their point with a picture of a screw before the NCAA and stated "NCAA Kiss My Asterisk" as they stormed the court. This time, however, because of Boeheim's monumental accomplishment of joining Krzyzewski as the only members of the men's Division I 1,000-win club, the court rush was warranted. The scene, similar to the good old days when the Dome rocked with regularity, qualified as another "Syracuse Moment."

The majestic triumph came 999 wins after Boeheim, on November 26, 1976, beat Harvard for his first win in the Tip-Off Classic in Springfield, Massachusetts, where forty years after defeating the Crimson, he was inducted into the Naismith Basketball Hall of Fame. In between those wins, Boeheim had been around the track a few times. When he registered his first win, Gerald Ford was president, *Rocky* was playing in theatres, the price of gas was 57 cents, and the Dow Jones was hovering around 1,000, ironically the number of victories he piled up in 41-plus seasons.

"I've been a part of 1,000 wins. We might not have that many on the record, but I've been here for 1,000 wins," Boeheim told ESPN. "That's a lot of wins." As an emotional Boeheim exited the court, he turned, triumphantly held both hands high, and waved his appreciation to the 27,553 in attendance. Whipping his fist-clenched arm indicated that this milestone was special.

Fifth-year transfers White and Gillon were key components in Syracuse's resurgence to relevance. Leaving the court, Gillon told Syracuse beat writer Donna Ditota, "We wanted big games like this ...

We wanted to play on the biggest stage in college basketball. And that is where we are."

Andy Katz, before the game and again following the game, ripped the NCAA for taking Boeheim's wins away. Jay Bilas, along with a big orange 1,000 poster he put up, mocked the NCAA by posting, "Jim Boeheim joins Pat Summitt, Coach K, and Tara VanDerveer as the only four D1 coaches to hand their opponents 1,000 losses!" CBS's Matt Norlander headlined, "No matter what the NCAA says, Jim Boeheim now has 1,000 wins, and everybody knows it." In his story defending the coach's quadruple-digit victory total, Norlander wrote, "In reality, he won those games." He called the NCAA sanctions "a hollow discipline, a puny calculation that's mocked by everyone outside the NCAA ... What is an undisputed fact is that Jim Boeheim had given opponents 1,000 losses."

"I think the people here feel we should not have lost those wins, and that's probably the way all fans would feel ... Obviously, there's some question about whether some of those, or all of those, should have been taken, but they have been," Boeheim said. "The fans are not going to accept that." A video showed a player from each of Boeheim's milestone wins congratulating their coach. Twitter, Facebook, and other social media outlets lit up in support of Boeheim. Support also came from Mike Krzyzewski, who gave Boeheim a congratulatory call for his 1,000th win. The New York State Legislature officially honored Boeheim, and in the US Congress, Representative John Katko congratulated Boeheim while again harshly criticizing the NCAA for its excessively harsh treatment of the fabled coach.

Those who had a few weeks earlier trashed Boeheim and his zone now praised the coach and wanted him to coach forever. Those who had resigned themselves to a losing, postseason-less year perked up. In his postgame comments, Boeheim acknowledged that by pointing out that when the team loses, several people say "I'm too old, the zones no good, [and things] along those lines, but when we win [there are hardly any critics]. What that tells me is that those people are just haters ... That's the way the world is now." The next day the *Syracuse Post-Standard* published a complete section commemorating Boeheim's 1,000th win. Later that summer, the 2017 edition of "Boeheim's Army" also disregarded the NCAA ruling by honoring the coach with a "1,000" insignia sewed over The Basketball Tournament logo on the upper-left front of its jersey.

That out of the way, Boeheim took his on-court 1,000–351 record to Clemson and added to it as the red-hot Orange grabbed its fifth consecutive win, 82–81, when freshman Tyus Battle buried a three-point shot as time expired. As Bill Raftery would say—onions! According to the NCAA, Boeheim reached 900 wins for the second time, but for most others counting, it was No. 1,001. Syracuse gained a much-needed road win to improve to 16–9 and 8–4 in the ACC, numbers almost unimaginable just three weeks earlier. But just when the momentum was picking up, the Orange fizzled as it lost at Pittsburgh, a 2–9 team in the ACC without departed coach and Boeheim-killer Jamie Dixon. Pitt's 80–75 win, its sixth in its last seven games against the Orange, may have put the dagger in Syracuse's NCAA aspirations. Gillon extended his consecutive free-throw streak to thirty-four, tying Brandon Triche's school record. In at once expressing his passion, frustration, and anger, a fan stated, "Syracuse basketball has cost me two marriages already!"

After five consecutive victories, SU lost its second straight game, a tough to stomach 76–72 overtime setback to No. 8 Louisville. With the scored tied at 58 and 3.6 seconds to go, the Orange had a chance to win in regulation, but Gillon, when driving to the basket, lost the ball without getting off a shot. Earlier in the game, he had made two foul shots to break the school's consecutive free-throw record. The Cuse fell behind by eight in overtime but gallantly fought back and, with the score 74–72, again had a chance to knot the game up with 2.7 seconds remaining, but Tyler Roberson missed two free throws and SU missed an opportunity to get another much-needed Top 10 win. Before the national anthem, there was a moment of silence for

Fab Melo, who a couple of days before had passed away, with his smiling face displayed on the video board.

With both teams on the NCAA bubble, Georgia Tech appeared to have sent Syracuse to the NIT when the Yellow Jackets beat the Orange, 71–65. Slicing a 13-point lead to two, 67–65, SU had the ball and a chance to tie or win. A very questionable illegal pick by Tyler Roberson with 16 seconds left didn't help. However, there was enough blame to go around for the failure to win a game that SU could have won.

Just when Syracuse seemed down for the count, the speedy Gillon raced down the court and banked a three-pointer from beyond the top of the key as the clock struck zero to sink Duke, 78–75. The game instantly became another Syracuse-Duke classic. Gillon's shot rivaled the game-winning shots launched by Pearl Washington against Boston College and Tyler Ennis against Pittsburgh, not just because the Orange took down the No.10 Blue Devils, but more so because it looked like it would propel the Orange into the NCAA tournament. Like "Comeback Cuse" and "Cardiac Cuse" teams of the past, the Orange, as it had done when coming from behind in five of its last nine games, overcame a nine-point deficit to even up its record with Duke at 3–3 since joining the ACC, 5–5 in the all-time series, and the Boeheim-Krzyzewski match-up at 4–4. The frenzied Cuse fans stormed the court, but because of the significance of the win and the opponent, it was also warranted. The victory broke Syracuse's three-game losing streak and stopped Duke's seven-game winning streak. It was the Orange's third Top-10 win. Krzyzewski's 1,065 wins and Boeheim's 1,001 on-court wins set a new record for combined victories for coaches facing each other (2,066), and it did so even with Boeheim's 900 NCAA victories (1,965). Along with 26 points, six assists, and zero turnovers in another heroic performance, Gillon extended his school consecutive free-throws made record to 43. "We go as John Gillon goes," stated Boeheim after the game.

Andrew White III, who played two years for the Jayhawks in the mayhem of famed Phog Allen Field House, told *Syracuse Post-Standard* columnist Bud Poliquin, "The roar I heard after John hit the shot was different from what I'd ever heard at Kansas. I felt like I'd seen it all up until then." Battle told Poliquin, "This is why I picked this school. Being here at Syracuse is a completely different experience. The students were filling the Dome two hours before the game. The fans are the best in the country, and the Dome is a special place." Experiencing the pandemonium reinforced to transfers Gillon and White and freshman star Battle why they chose Syracuse—to experience a passionate, in some ways unique, big-time basketball environment.

Played before the 81st 30,000-plus crowd in Carrier Dome history, nationally the largest college basketball crowd of the season, the dramatic finish that produced an epic win and an electric and deafening atmosphere inside the dome reminiscent of days gone by, qualified the event as another "Syracuse Moment." The nation watched it on ESPN. The victory was the tonic for a Syracuse community that had, by SU criteria, struggled to cope with a trying season. During his postgame press conference, Krzyzewski paid tribute to the Syracuse basketball legacy. "It's so good that Syracuse is in the league," he stated. "It's amazing to add not just the quality of play, but the history of the program, the culture. [Syracuse] is a valued, valued asset for the ACC."

Not being able to sustain success, the bipolar Orange got dumped by No. 7 Louisville, 88–68. In some ways, the game was a microcosm of the season. Pitino's great defense aside, as in some of its other losses, Syracuse was suicidal. As the Cardinals cruised to a 23-point lead in the first half, the remainder of the game for SU fans was like pulling out fingernails with a pair of pliers. The only positive takeaway was that Gillon extended his free-throw streak to 47 straight. Just as quickly as the Boeheim protesters got back in the Boeheim boat after the Duke win, they again jumped out after the Louisville loss.

Bowing to Louisville, the Orange made the Georgia Tech game a must-win, in a season of must-wins, if it hoped to make the NCAA tournament. Making a statement, Syracuse, in a high-stakes game, took the Engineers behind the woodshed, 90–61. It was a record-breaking day for SU's fifth-year transfers. Andrew White III shot the lights out, canning 8 of 9 three-pointers, to pour in a career-high 40 points that also matched Gene Waldron for the most points in the Carrier Dome and eclipsed Hakim Warrick (36) for the most points by a senior on Senior Day. "It was one of the best shooting performances that I've ever witnessed," stated Boeheim. "It was just surreal, and he was fantastic," stated losing coach Josh Pastner. John Gillon had 10 points and 10 assists but his school-record consecutive free-throw streak of 48, which also tied Virginia's Jeff Lamp for third highest in ACC history, was stopped. As if he was torpedoed from a battleship, Tyus sank three three-pointers in the first four minutes to bust through and around the Ramblin' Wreck defense en route to 22 points. Another 30,000-plus crowd ensured that Syracuse again finished second in the nation in attendance, averaging 23,142 fans a game, 320 less per contest than the Kentucky Wildcats attracted to Rupp Arena. The win enabled Syracuse to earn a bye in the ACC tournament and face Miami in the second round at the Barclays Center.

If the SU team that thwarted Georgia Tech showed up, the Cuse had a chance to beat North Carolina and everybody else. If the SU team that got spanked by St. John's showed up, the Orange could lose to Le Moyne or Onondaga Community College. It was that type of season. Boeheim had breathed oxygen into his team that in December was gasping for air and near dead. Remarkably the almost lifeless Orange responded with a little run that put SU on the verge of an NCAA tournament invitation. However, losing five of its last seven games, including in the first round of the ACC tournament to Miami, put the decision in the hands of the committee. For some reason though, Boeheim went off during the postgame press conference. He complained about playing the conference tournament in Greensboro, calling it of "no value, none." He also lobbied for SU to be in the NCAA tournament. The unfortunate rants drew national attention, with some in the media calling the aging but still fiery coach "caustic," "cranky," and "mouthy." Like Donald Trump spontaneously taking to Twitter to spout off on irrelevant topics, purposely going off task to lambast Greensboro was another instance of Boeheim using a microphone to unnecessarily create a controversy where none existed. The episode proved again that Boeheim was, as former teammate George Hicker stated, "quirky."

The Greensboro Grasshoppers minor-league baseball team mocked Boeheim by offering a "Jim Boeheim No-Value Night" promotion on April 11 where the team would give anyone with a valid New York State driver's license a free ticket and a $20 food and drink voucher. Soon thereafter, in a friendly response, the Syracuse Chiefs minor-league baseball team countered with an April 7 "Jim Boeheim Added-Value Night" promo, where, along with several other giveaways, anyone with a valid North Carolina identification would be admitted free. The team that drew the smaller crowd for its promotion would make a donation to the other team's charity of choice. Syracuse attracted the larger attendance—4,844 fans to 3,948— so the Chiefs had the last laugh.

Its NCAA hopes precariously hanging by a thread, Syracuse had to wait uncomfortably for four days to learn its situation. Nips66/@okmickey123, a Cuse super-duper fan, typed "Committee will let us in because we're America's team and the people of the world like to watch our team play our unique style and our coach run the show like the all-time great that he is … It's an insult that we're even in the discussion [of possibly being out]." That opinion, putting a premium on the Syracuse brand relative to television ratings, was contrary to Carmelo Anthony's "They hate us" rant from the previous year.

On March 12, although the temperature in Syracuse was 20 degrees with possible snow showers, the Orange and its fans probably had the air conditioning on because they were forced to sweat out Selection Sunday. When Syracuse was left out of the NCAA tournament, SU only had to look in the mirror for the reasons—several bad losses, poor road record, not enough total wins, ugly RPI, poor finish to the season, and then, to top it off, the untimely remarks Boeheim made about Greensboro that might have turned off some committee members. It was daylight saving time and the start of longer days, but it was also the end of meaningful games for the Orange.

Syracuse did receive a No. 1 seed—in the NIT. Playing in the NIT was not a reason for joy in Orange country, but drawing UNC–Greensboro (25–9), champions of the Southern Conference with a 25–9 record, as a first-round opponent created a buzz because of the spat between Boeheim and the city of Greensboro. The "Greensboro vs. Boeheim" T-shirts produced would have heightened interest even more had the game been played in Greensboro, a city that Boeheim declared had "no value." Once again, Syracuse and Boeheim proved their ability to grab national attention, sometimes good and sometimes not so good. After twenty inches of snow buried Central New York to postpone the game, Syracuse buried the Spartans, 90–77, to save Boeheim from eating Carolina crow. White, among his 34 points, canned seven three-pointers and with 109, broke the single-season school mark for three-pointers formerly held by Gerry McNamara, who had 108. Combined with the 40 points he fired in against Georgia Tech, White became the only person other than Dave Bing to register 40 points and 34 or more points in the same season. Battle made his 57th three-pointer to move up to fourth in school history behind Donté Greene (90), McNamara (85), and Malachi Richardson (79) for three-point shots made by a freshman.

Syracuse's season, however, ended with a disappointing 85–80 loss to Mississippi. Playing in the NIT and playing at home made the setback sting even more, especially after the preseason optimism voiced by Boeheim. A 19–15 mark might be acceptable at many schools, but in Cuse country, it was carted off to the dumpster. Boeheim had suffered three straight years of double-digit losses for the first time, including his most ever defeats (15) in 2016–17. Those clamoring for change argued that the Syracuse program, due to sanctions and subpar recruiting, had a downward trajectory. Others credited Boeheim for getting a team with four first-year Syracuse players and a sophomore to within one win of dancing, especially after losing two centers (Coleman and Chukwu) and a small forward (Moyer) to injuries. Lost in the shuffle was that Boeheim again passed Bobby Knight for second place all-time with 903 official wins, while his on-court win total reached 1,004. Tyler Lydon was selected 24th by the Denver Nuggets in the NBA draft, making it six consecutive years that Syracuse had a player selected in the first round, a streak surpassed only by Kentucky (8) and Duke (7).

As Amba Etta-Tawo, the Syracuse fifth-year football transfer from Maryland where he had a nondescript career, zoomed to an All-American season in the fall, White and Gillon proved that graduate one-and-done hoopers could also be great pickups. Despite being at SU for only one year, the fifth-year transfers etched their names in the school record book: White for the most three-pointers in a season (112), and Gillon for consecutive free throws (48). Each also enjoyed outstanding individual games, White with a 40-point game and Gillon a 43-point game. Gillon also heaved buzzer-beaters to tie NC State and defeat Duke, and his scoring down the stretch almost singlehandedly beat Florida State.

The fallout from being ousted from the NIT had barely settled when Mike Hopkins, Syracuse's longtime loyal, hardworking assistant coach and recruiter extraordinaire, informed Boeheim that he was offered the head coaching job at the University of Washington. As head coach-designate, Hopkins was penciled in to take over after Boeheim called it a career following the 2017–18 season. Surprisingly, Hopkins accepted the job. Only insiders know for sure how the change of plans occurred, but the way that it played out was perplexing and awkward.

Hopkins, who played for Boeheim, coached under him, and had been with him for twenty-five years, told blogger Adam Zagoria: "I [had] a great job. I work[ed] for one of the greatest coaches to ever coach the game…I would never have gotten the opportunity [to coach Team USA] if I hadn't worked at Syracuse University and worked for Jim Boeheim. I always [felt] like I [went] to the Harvard School of Basketball."

With Hopkins heading west to coach the Huskies, Boeheim agreed to a contract extension with an undetermined end date. And just like that, instead of Boeheim retiring at the end of the 2017–18 season as planned, the 73-year-old coach would continue to sit on the Syracuse bench, chin in the palm of his hand, periodically scowling and riding the refs, while trying to guide the Orange to more basketball wins.

The Boeheim fan club, citing stability and believing that the legendary coach could make Syracuse great again, loved it that the Hall of Famer would continue coaching the Orange. Those who had grown disgruntled with slo-mo Boeheim-ball and the aging and set-in-his-ways coach believed stability meant mediocrity. Blaming Boeheim for bad weather and rush hour traffic, they hated it that he would stay on for a few more years. They squawked that just like Bobby Knight, Willie Mays, Muhammad Ali, and Bobby Bowden had hung around too long, so had Jim Boeheim. Closer to home, they feared he would go out like Syracuse football coaching legend Ben Schwartzwalder, who took the Orange to the national championship in 1959 and seven big-time bowl games en route to a Hall of Fame career, only to witness his last team finish 2–9 and play its final game in front of about 13,000 people in Archbold Stadium. They felt it would have been better if Boeheim had exited the previous year after taking the Orange to a surprise Final Four. For better or for worse, depending on what side of the fence one stood in the Boeheim debate, Syracuse marched on.

Boeheim's enthusiasm for recruiting indicated that he was planning on coaching for another four or five years since he wanted to coach his youngest son, Buddy, a 6-foot-5 deadeye shooter who had announced that he was going to prep school before playing for his father in 2018–19. That also allowed Boeheim to continue his quest to win another national championship and give him reasonable time to win 1,000 official games. Asked hypothetically if Buddy wasn't playing well how he would justify putting and keeping him on the court, Boeheim jokingly told Jeff Goodman of *ESPN Insider* that he would say, "You are right, he shouldn't be playing, but his mother told me he needs to play."

2017–18

Before that, however, Boeheim faced another interesting situation. The Orange opened the 2017–18 season against Cornell, which meant that Boeheim would be coaching against his oldest son, Jimmy, a 6-foot-7, left-handed freshman forward for the Big Red. At 73, the oldest coach who also has the longest tenure at one school in NCAA basketball, Boeheim started his 42nd season with a 77–45 win over Cornell, the 38th straight time the Cuse defeated the Big Red. Jimmy Boeheim scored Cornell's first five points and finished with 11 total. The curtain also opened on the Tyus Battle Show. SU was counting heavily on its projected NBA first-round pick to carry the team. With Battle playing as expected, a vastly improved Frank Howard, Oshae Brissett demonstrating his immense potential early, a surprisingly good Marek Dolezaj, solid play from Paschal Chukwu and Bourama Sidibe, and strong defense and rebounding, unranked Syracuse swept it first six games, including a resume-padding win over Maryland when an injured Battle scored SU's last nine points to close the case. SU then clashed with No. 2 Kansas where the Jayhawks proved to be too much for the inexperienced Orange. Coincidentally, a few days later Washington, coached by former SU assistant Mike Hopkins, used the 2–3 zone to upset Kansas, the primary difference being that Devonte' Graham, who had back-to-back 35-point games, was red-hot against the Orange but ice-cold against the West Coast Huskies when he only scored three points. With the emergence of Matthew Moyer, dominant rebounding, and a defense that made UConn look lost, Syracuse rebounded with a comfortable 72–63 win over the East Coast Huskies.

After a cushy win over Colgate that matched UCLA's 52-year all-time high win streak over California, the Cuse beat previously unde-feated Georgetown, 86–79, in overtime in a game as exciting as the old-time wars against the hated Hoyas. It was another barnburner that left Orange fans drained, but happy. Coaching against former Georgetown great Patrick Ewing and with one of his early stars, Louis

Orr, as an assistant on the Georgetown bench, the elderly Boeheim had to not only feel old but age as he watched the highly emotional, hotly contested matchup. Ewing's perfect record as a head coach was officially closed. "[The contention] was a lot like it used to be," stated a relieved Boeheim. "There just wasn't any blood on the floor." Winning the last four, Boeheim improved to 10–3 in overtime games against Georgetown. SU won for the 50th time against 43 losses in one of college basketball's best rivalries.

SU got off to a 10–1 start, with Brissett producing points and rebounding numbers that matched the best freshmen in Orange history. However, for the first time in thirty-six years, the Orange lost to St. Bonaventure. It was also the first time the Bonnies had ever won in Syracuse. After beating Eastern Michigan, a spunky Syracuse team opened ACC play by strangling Virginia Tech, 68–56. Putting the clamps on one of the best offenses in the country, the Orange, with a hard-hat, lunch-bucket mentality, continued to capture the fancy of its fans. That is until Syracuse's slow-down, substandard offense resulted in four straight losses that had Boeheim bashers screaming and pulling out their hair. Included was a last-second 51–49 setback to Notre Dame that disappointed the 24,304 fans who, following sixty-six straight hours of snow, braved a miserable day when temperatures barely got above zero to make their way to the Dome. Former SU star Dennis DuVal had his jersey retired at halftime. If the "Sweet D" of yesteryear had his jersey on, the Orange would have won. As Brent Axe stated, "Only mailmen have SU fans beat in their dedication to trudge through the elements to watch their team."

Losses at No. 3 Virginia and in double overtime to No. 23 Florida State followed. A career-high 37-point game by Battle against the Seminoles was wasted. The sporadic Orange recovered with three straight wins before dropping two in a row, including an embarrassing 59–44 loss to Virginia, SU's lowest scoring night in Carrier Dome history. The Orange's inability to score had many of its followers switching channels. With a 1–4 ACC start, NIT talk ratcheted up.

Irked by his "who cares" response to a reporter's question about the team's early problems in conference play, some fans thrashed Boeheim while others thought the old ball coach was doing a commendable job keeping the Cuse competitive with a ragtag bunch of tenacious but one-dimensional role players who individually were up-one-game and down-the-next. SU's defense kept the Orange competitive in some games and from getting blown out worse than they did in others. On a day when Mike Hopkins's Washington Huskies upset No. 9 Arizona after recently beating No. 25 Arizona State and earlier Kansas, Boeheim's followers found it increasingly difficult to defend the poor play of Syracuse.

After a few games in hibernation, Battle, Howard, and Brissett awoke just in time to lead SU to a 78–73 win at Louisville. The trio played well again, especially Battle who had a regulation game-high of 34 points, in a 78–70 win over Wake Forest that improved Syracuse's record to 17–8, 6–6 in the ACC. In a game pitting NCAA hopefuls, Syracuse lost at home to NC State. With SU's chances for an NCAA berth looking bleak, the Orange regained hope with a 62–55 upset victory at Miami. The "must-win" was so satisfying that when they got off the plane, Boeheim and his team weren't bothered by the difference between the Miami heat and the Syracuse cold. The Cuse, with four freshmen among its seven on-court players, three of whom were on-and-off again injured and seemingly held together by duct tape, continued grinding through a season that for its fans was equal parts aggravation and elation.

With No. 10-ranked North Carolina in town, the Orange had a great opportunity to impress the NCAA tournament selection committee. The Tar Heels built an early double-digit lead and stayed comfortably in front for most of the game before the Cuse staged a frantic comeback to tie the contest, 74–74, with 1:39 to go, only to fall short, 78–74. With 32.6 seconds remaining, SU had the ball and was down two. The game was there for the taking, and the Tar Heels took it when the Orange turned the ball over and took an ill-advised shot. The damaging loss in front of college basketball's largest on-campus crowd of the season appeared to be the dagger that dashed

Syracuse's NCAA hopes. If it wasn't, then the 60–44 blowout loss at Duke seemed to be. The Orange defense held the No. 5-ranked high-scoring Blue Devils to 27 points below their scoring average, but Boeheim taught Krzyzewski too well because K's 2–3 zone held SU's almost nonexistent offense to its season-tying low point total. Whereas Battle, Howard, and Brissett had big games against North Carolina, the Big Three tanked against Duke. The game didn't have the big buildup of some past Syracuse-Duke games but, even in a down year, the city loves its Cuse because the Palace Theatre in downtown Syracuse showed the game.

With its NCAA lifeline at stake, Boston College was the iceberg and SU the RMS *Titanic* as the Eagles won easily, 85–70. The loss by a limited SU team to a mediocre BC team turned some enthusiastic supporters into cynics. The final regular-season home game against No. 18 Clemson presented Syracuse with an opportunity to get a signature win that had the possibility of putting the Orange back into the NCAA picture. It was fitting that in crunch time Marek Dolezaj, wearing No. 21, the jersey number retired that afternoon in honor of Lawrence Moten—the all-time leading scorer in SU and Big East history—calmly sank a free throw that clinched a crucial 55–52 win over the Tigers. Despite fifteen inches of snow that ravaged the city the day before, Syracuse still drew 28,670 fans, the largest on-campus crowd in the nation. Battle, with 17 points, joined Gerry McNamara, Billy Owens, Lawrence Moten, and Jonny Flynn as the only Orange sophomores to score 1,000 points.

Syracuse began ACC tournament play by beating Wake Forest, 73–64, improving to 20–12 on the season and giving Boeheim his 38th 20-win campaign and 33rd according to the NCAA. Still teetering on the tightrope between The Big Dance and falling into NIT purgatory, the Orange squared off against No. 12 North Carolina and was tarred and feathered, 78–59. The outmanned Cuse competed well, but the proud Syracuse program never was interested in participation trophies.

For the third straight year, SU was on the NCAA bubble. Based on a couple of quality road wins and its strong strength of schedule, Syracuse was the last team selected for the NCAA tournament. It was Boeheim's 33rd trip to the NCAA's and the program's 39th appearance in what has become college basketball's biggest show and America's biggest office pool. Similar to 2016, there was an immediate backlash from pundits around the country, including Doug Gottlieb, who called Syracuse's selection "laughable." Although Syracuse's selection was surprising to many, others criticized SU's inclusion as "baffling," "inexplicable," "a travesty," "a big joke," and "absolute garbage." Joe Ovies of 99.9 The Fan ESPN Radio in Raleigh, North Carolina, stated, "The FBI needs to subpoena the NCAA committee for selecting Syracuse." Rob Dauster from NBC Sports was a little kinder when he said, "The NCAA Committee got the perfect field, except for Syracuse."

One theory for the negative reaction is that Syracuse is a big-name program that gets the benefit of the doubt based on its brand, although some people apparently forgot that the Cuse was the first team out the previous year. "Syracuse is in because they sell tickets. Period," stated Charles P. Pierce. John Brickley (@ESPNBrick on Twitter) wrote, "Syracuse gets in because they have Jim Boeheim." Joe Dolan tweeted, "Syracuse could go 0–27 and make the Tournament somehow. What a clown show."

Slotted as a First Four play-in game, the Orange was dispatched to Dayton where, down seven with seven minutes to go, SU defeated Arizona State, 60–56. Syracuse danced its way from Dayton to Detroit and, once in Motown ala Martha and the Vandellas, Cuse fans were dancin' in the street after upsetting No. 6-seeded TCU, 57–52. Then, in what amounted to a home game for Michigan State, Battle scored 16 of his 17 points in the second half as the Cuse shocked the No. 3 Spartans, 55–53, making it March sadness for a Big 10 regular-season MSU team that finished with a 30–5 record. Howard contributed 13 points before fouling out, forcing Boeheim to end the game with three freshmen, a sophomore, and a walk-on, Braedon Bayer, who played the final 6:39 in the win-or-go-home game. On the day before as well as the day after St. Patty's Day, SU had a little luck of the Orange, but it was mostly its staples of determination, courage, and pride of the Orange that enabled the handful of wounded, battle-weary, wet-behind-the-ears warriors, who were playing their third game in five days, to fight on to a series of victories that again captured the admiration of people and headlines in newspapers across the country. It was a three-day party in the Motor City, and the Orange nation, like Lionel Richie, danced all night long. Cheering on the Orange were Detroit residents and former SU stars Derrick Coleman and Dave Bing, the former mayor of Motown who was asked by some why he had on a Syracuse shirt instead of one representing nearby Michigan State. "I went to Syracuse," he proudly told Matthew Gutierrez of *The Daily Orange.* Just the way it won the trio of games could arguably qualify as not just a "Syracuse Moment" but a "Syracuse Weekend." After snapping a personal five-game losing streak against Jamie Dixon, Boeheim extended his winning streak against Tom Izzo to five.

From the onset, Boeheim's lockdown defense locked in ASU, TCU, and MSU and threw away the key in holding three high-powered teams that had averaged 80-plus points per game to season-lows in the 50s. "No one plays zone like we do," stated Brissett, who scored 15 points and grabbed nine rebounds against the Spartans. "We're always moving, and we challenge every shot, so teams never get easy looks against us." That shouldn't surprise followers of Syracuse or college basketball. In Syracuse's last 15 NCAA tournament games, which included two Final Four runs, the Orange had surrendered a paltry 54.5 points a game. Also, as a double-digit seed, the Orange was 7–1.

In the Sweet 16, Syracuse faced a rematch with No. 2-seeded Duke. The game was played in Omaha, Nebraska, which is already home to a Syracuse, the namesake town of about 2,000 people located fifty miles south of Omaha that could almost fit into the Carrier Dome. The Syracuse-Duke game featured college basketball's two winningest coaches, Coach K with 1,099 victories and Coach B with 1,027/926 victories. It was a matchup of Boeheim's trademark 2–3 zone versus Krzyzewski's more or less copycat 2–3 zone. Syracuse had lost to Duke, 60–44, a month earlier and was a big underdog. However, ESPN's FiveThirtyEight, based on a composite of six computer ratings, tabulated that Boeheim was the best coach at upsetting teams in the NCAA tournament since it expanded to sixty-four teams in 1985, winning 54 times when SU was predicted to win only 44 times.

The contest pitted preseason No. 1 Duke against an Orange team that didn't receive a single vote in the preseason polls. Syracuse, a No. 11 seed, came up just short of trying to repeat its performance two years prior when as a No. 10 seed SU advanced to the Final Four. Trailing, 67–65, with seven seconds remaining, the Cuse, in a battle that caused Krzyzewski at the beginning of the second half to toss his jacket on the floor and at the end had him nervously squirming on the bench, pushed Duke to its limit before falling, 69–65. It was a winnable game even though Syracuse missed dunks, turned the ball over 16 times, was called for shot-clock violations, and committed other mental mistakes, all of which enabled the Blue Devils to hang on in a zone-centric war of wits between two of the most recognized coaches in college basketball. Whereas the Syracuse zone swallowed ASU, TCU, and MSU, the Dukies were able to crack Boeheim's celebrated 2–3 defense just enough to eke out the win.

Maligned by some all year, the overachieving Orange took advantage of getting into the Big Dance by making yet another improbable, magical, and miracle March run that made Syracuse basketball relevant again and enabled an up to then so-so season to end on a high note that made it another Syracuse odyssey to remember. Krzyzewski edged ahead of Boeheim, 6–5, in their personal competition, and Duke took a 7–5 lead in the series that had again become a big-time rivalry. Battle finished with 712 points, second best as a sophomore behind Bing in SU annals. Syracuse sports fans got a little solace the next day when the popular Orange lacrosse team beat Duke, 15–14, in another thrilling sports contest between the two schools.

Taurean Thompson transferred prior to the season, Geno Thorpe quit after six games, and Howard Washington was lost to a midyear season-ending injury, all of which left the Orange with only seven available scholarship players, only two of them guards. Of those seven, Bourama Sidibe and Paschal Chukwa played with tendinitis in their knees, and Matthew Moyer dealt with an injured ankle. Regardless, Boeheim, like a broken record, turned in yet another example of what was "one of his best coaching jobs ever" by getting the Cuse to its 20th unofficial and 19th official Sweet 16 and finishing with a much-better-than-expected 23–14 record. "I've never been any more proud of a team for what they done in these last ten days," he stated about a team that he got to play to its potential.

Heading into the 2018–19 season Syracuse got a big boost when Brissett decided against being a "one-and-done" and Battle opted against being a "two-and-through." With both returning, along with an infusion of talent including quality recruits Jalen Carey, Robert Braswell, and Buddy Boeheim, SU will be returning all five starters for the first time since 1999, insuring that Syracuse will start the season in the Top 25. With sanctions in the rearview mirror, if Syracuse plays to its standards, the Orange could be on the road to again becoming an elite program.

17

THE 2–3 ZONE

The 2–3 zone is to Syracuse what the Eiffel Tower is to France. Mention it anywhere and immediately Jim Boeheim and Syracuse basketball both come to mind. "The short history of our zone is we started out as a man-to-man team with some zone and over the years our zone got better but we still played man," Boeheim explained in his postgame press conference after Syracuse stifled Indiana's high-scoring offense in the 2013 Sweet 16. "The problem when you play man is you have to spend an hour on your man defense every day. When you play your preseason games, your non-conference games, if you're playing man, your zone isn't getting better. So finally it dawned on me, after about twenty-seven or twenty-eight years, that if we played zone all the time and didn't waste time playing man-to-man and put some wrinkles in the zone because we had more time to practice it, that our defense would be better."

The defense got better, and in some years, it was great. The 2–3 zone became Boeheim's calling card. Syracuse's zone defense had been time tested and proven effective. More specifically, the zonemaster took a relatively simple zone that he learned as a player at Syracuse and made it a part of his defense when he took over in 1976, before going exclusively to the 2–3 prior to the 2009–10 season following a preseason 82–79 exhibition loss to crosstown NCAA Division II Le Moyne College. "I made a crucial decision on the spot. From that point forward, my Syracuse teams would never spend one more minute playing man-to-man defense," Boeheim states in his book *Bleeding Orange*. Boeheim said he went exclusively to zone to make practices more efficient because he wouldn't have to waste time teaching man-to-man fundamentals such as switching, double-teaming, overplaying the passing lanes, and defending the pick-and-roll. Practicing zone also kept his team more focused and enabled his players to have fresher legs. In his book, Boeheim gives the major advantages of playing zone:

- It provides an advantage at tournament time because (most) teams haven't played against a very good zone team during the season.
- It helps to keep your players from getting into foul trouble.
- Psychologically, a zone, especially "the Syracuse Zone," can psyche the other team out, causing them all kinds of problems trying to figure it out.
- Playing strictly zone cuts back on planning time, whether it's preparation during practice or having to make defensive decisions during games.

Syracuse's defense was never your garden-variety zone. Boeheim continually modified and refined it over the years as the game changed, particularly extending it out further with the advent of the three-point shot. He frequently tweaked it from game to game, depending upon the opponent and situation. The result of all the changes was a very unique zone, perplexing to opponents.

Incorporating precise movements and predicated by reads, reactions, and rotations that included suddenly springing a changing variety of traps from all angles, Syracuse's precision zone flustered opponents into creating turnovers. At its best, the Orange stole the ball, deflected passes, and blocked shots at an astonishing rate. Mike Hopkins, Boeheim's chief assistant, pointed out that although people always talked about Syracuse's length, it was also the speed of the players that enabled the lanes that seemingly were open to quickly close. When played correctly, the 2–3 zone forced opponents to take shots that Syracuse wanted them to take, not shots that they wanted to take.

True, sometimes teams or certain players got hot, like Seton Hall in 2011 when an outside shooter who ordinarily shot 29 percent caught fire and shredded the zone. If the Orange and Pirates had played the very next night, Syracuse would have still come out in its patented zone and limit, or allow, if you want, the Hall and that same player or players who burned them the night before to take the exact same shots. And statistically, almost all of the time, that player and that team would not make those shots because those were low-percentage shots. Therefore almost 75 percent of the time Syracuse won.

When opponents ripped the zone, critics asked Boeheim, "Why didn't you switch to man-to-man or try something different?" When excellent man-to-man teams like Pittsburgh or Michigan State got smoked, which they did from time to time, critics rarely reamed Jamie Dixon or Tom Izzo or questioned them with, "Why didn't you go into a zone? Why didn't you try something different?" At least not as much as they blasted Boeheim.

Boeheim listened to the ongoing debate about his defense and stated, "If we lose, it's always that we shouldn't be playing the zone. If you lose with man-to-man, it's somehow better." When questioned why he strictly played zone, Boeheim's stock answer was, "That's the defense we play. That's who we are." In other words, the Orange would live and die with its customized 2–3 zone, tweaked when Boeheim thought it needed to be tweaked—whether it was from half to half or possession to possession. And history informs that about three-quarters of the time the Orange lived. Regardless, basketball traditionalists saw the zone as a gimmick or junk defense, something to go to temporarily to throw the other team off or, in certain situations, to change the tempo of the game—not something you relied on for virtually every minute of every game. Even Bobby Knight, perhaps the biggest basketball purist of them all and someone who certainly knew a little bit about the game, toward the end of his career became supportive of Syracuse's zone. On January 21, 2014, Knight told Rece Davis on ESPN radio's *Open Court*, "Boeheim has a very specific way to play the game. He's put an approach to basketball together, one that he specifically recruits for. First and foremost, he's been able to get the kind of talent to play the game that way. He picked a way to play and worked on it and stuck with it and has been successful with it better than anyone in college basketball. I think his specific style of play is the best system that's going in basketball and has been for some time. Defensively, they've been taught and taught well, and not overly taught. He has confidence in his defensive approach. Syracuse has been very, very successful playing that way for a long time. It helps if a school has something particular that they're known for. That helps in specifically recruiting for everything they play. And he's got that." On inbounds defense, Knight said he wished that thirty-five years ago he had done what Boeheim had done. Sometimes Knight solved the zone, and sometimes he was victimized by it. He overcame it to win the 1987 national championship, but he was also baffled by it because after that he lost four straight to Syracuse, including being pulverized, 102–78, in the preseason NIT in 1988.

The zone was especially effective when playing against teams that had never played against it before, such as in the NCAA tournament. Whereas outstanding coaches who had seen it multiple times—such as Jamie Dixon, Rick Pitino, and Jay Wright—figured out ways to bust the zone, most coaches seemed bewildered and their teams out of sync when facing the Orange. That's the way Boeheim wanted and expected them to feel, like a fish out of water. The master of the 2–3 had often said, "You can try to simulate the zone in practice with your players. But it's not the same thing as playing against our zone."

Even former SU player and assistant coach Louis Orr, who won Big East Coach of the Year in 2003 with Seton Hall and MAC Coach of the Year in 2009 with Bowling Green, struggled against his old school, going 2–5 against Boeheim. "People would say to me, 'You coached with him, and you can't figure out the 2–3 zone.' We tried to control tempo and tried to play inside out. If we had any success, and it was just a little, it was a big win for us. Syracuse is Syracuse," he stated.

When SU was in its element and the Orange played the zone the way Boeheim preached, the Syracuse defense was a tough nut to crack. It may have seemed like a simple zone to some, but it wasn't. Most opposing coaches said that. Former West Virginia and current Michigan coach John Beilein experienced futility in battling Boeheim. "I don't know how to beat it," he admitted to Mike Janela of the *Daily Orange* in 1995. "I'm 0–7 against Coach Boeheim, and I haven't found a way to beat him ... You can't beat it." Beilein finally solved the riddle in the 2013 NCAA tournament when his Wolverines beat the Orange, 61–56, and the following season when they won again, 68–65, in Ann Arbor. Georgetown's John Thompson III wasn't able to figure it out either, stating, "At the end of the day, you almost have to tell your guys to just play. Just go out and figure it out on your own. They adjust so well. You just have to let your players play," he said.

When Syracuse's defense was at its best during the 2013 NCAA tournament Thompson's Hall of Fame father, John Thompson Jr., perplexingly told Charles P. Pierce: "Everybody's talking about the 2–3 zone. That's not a [typical] 2–3 zone. The 2–3 zone has been with us since the dawn of time. It's the way [Syracuse's zone] slides and moves out there, like a damn amoeba. The only time it's a 2–3 zone is when they're waiting for you to bring the ball to it. Then it becomes something else." Adrian Autry, who played for Boeheim, explained what made the Syracuse zone different. "You don't see a zone that works and moves like our zone," he said. "The rotations, the bumps, the slides, the adjustments, the activity, and how we extend it. It's a unique zone."

Hall of Fame coach John Chaney, who understood zones since his match-up zone at Temple became synonymous with him almost to the extent the 2–3 was with Boeheim, simply called the Syracuse zone "devastating." Ex-Georgia Tech coach Bobby Cremins on national television stated, "Jimmy Boeheim is the best zone coach in the history of our game." Cincinnati coach Mick Cronin said, "Boeheim doesn't get enough credit for his defense. It's not a high school 2–3 zone. They make adjustments. They pick out what they're going to try to take away from you. Until you get in the game, you're not sure how they're going to play the 2–3 zone. They don't play it the same all the time. And they'll change within a game. If you start hurting them, they'll make adjustments. Scoring is my biggest concern against Syracuse. It's everybody's concern against Syracuse." Former coaches who became television analysts always explained and diagrammed ways to beat Syracuse's zone, but none of them were able to do it when they coached against the Orange. A reason may be because Boeheim's zone, paraphrasing Forrest Gump, was like a box of chocolates. You never knew what you're going to get (when you walked on to the court at any given time).

In his blog, Rick Pitino credited the 2–3 zone as a big reason why Boeheim had been a consistent winner and so successful over the course of his career. "Well, Jim will tell you from a scouting standpoint that he has not seen one zone offense with as much screening or ball movement as man-to-man. He's correct," stated Pitino. "Add the fact that he recruits players who possess great length to cover the bumps and make it difficult to attack inside. Syracuse also fast breaks well out of the zone, as they get excellent triangle rebounding." Pitino credited the 2–3 zone he picked up from apprenticing under Boeheim from 1976–78 with helping him reach the Final Four. "If it wasn't for being with him, two of my [five] Final Fours wouldn't have happened," he stated. "At Providence [in 1978], we pressed for 40 minutes, and then fell back into the 2–3 zone. Without [the 2–3 zone], we don't go to the Final Four last [1994] year." In its 2015 preseason basketball issue, *Lindy's* summed it up this way: "[Syracuse's] zone defense is always there to make Cuse the equivalent of a full day at the dentist."

Even with the advantages attributed to Syracuse's defense, a perceived disadvantage is that it is difficult to rebound out of the zone.

On Matt Park's radio show, Boeheim countered that criticism: "Part of the rebounding [problem] is they're long rebounds … that come out to the guard spots. That's where the guards have to come back in there. And, the facts are, you're going to get outrebounded a little bit when you play zone, but you get so many positives back. You force more turnovers, you force them to take shots they don't want to take. So, in the long run, you can get outrebounded, but you've benefited in so many areas because of your defense."

As Knight stated relative to Syracuse's dependence on the zone, "It helps if a school has something particular that they're known for. That helps in specifically recruiting for everything they play. And Boeheim has got that." The 2–3 zone was Boeheim's brand, like Coca-Cola, Hershey chocolate bars, and Mercedes-Benz.

Boeheim's philosophy had always been to play the percentages. In his mind, the chances to win with the zone were in his favor. The result was that the Orange was extremely consistent and always good to very good but rarely great. Syracuse fans who yearned for more Final Fours and national championships were willing to take more risks and perhaps even sacrifice a few wins during the season in the hope that the Cuse would more frequently peak in the NCAA tournament and win those possible championships. It was a never-ending debate.

In basketball, the proven results were wins and profits for the program, as attested by a March 2015 *Forbes* magazine article that stated basketball revenue at Syracuse was estimated at $30 million with a profit of approximately $16 million. Syracuse's team value was projected at $26.8 million, the sixth highest in the nation behind Louisville, Kansas, Kentucky, Arizona, and North Carolina. One month later, the *Wall Street Journal*, utilizing its own criteria, listed the value of the Syracuse basketball program at $202.9 million, seventh highest in the country behind Louisville, Arizona, Kansas, Ohio State, Wisconsin, and Kentucky. And pretty much that was because the 2–3 zone was Cuse's trump card. It produced a winning hand most of the time.

When Boeheim decided to go exclusively with the zone, from a basketball perspective, he took the road less traveled. At various junctures and due to various circumstances, he at times veered further off the path and paved out his own road. A few years later, because of his success, the clinics he put on and the videos he produced on how to utilize the zone—and because they couldn't figure out a way to beat it—more and more coaches started to incorporate the zone into their defensive scheme. Imitation is the highest form of flattery.

Recruiting

Recruiting is the bloodline of a program, and the ability to recruit is tantamount to having continued success. Against the odds, Boeheim was able to recruit. The media can create or perpetuate images. The country didn't need a weatherman to find out the temperature in upstate New York. All people needed to do was tune into a Syracuse game on television because the cameras invariably went outside the Carrier Dome to show the snow on the ground and inform viewers throughout the nation how cold it was in the Salt City, never mentioning the blustery weather, blizzards, and that the mercury also dropped below zero during games at Michigan, Marquette, and Minnesota—places that will never be confused with Miami, Malibu, or Mississippi. Nor did they note the cold climate that the Connecticut Huskies were accustomed to. The overworked emphasis on Syracuse weather was detrimental to SU recruiting and sometimes used against the Orange by other schools since most high school kids prefer the sun to the snow, the beach to blizzards, and tossing Frisbees to tobogganing in blustery conditions.

With the deck stacked against him, Boeheim overcame that Central New York stereotype by reeling in some pretty good ballplayers. He had an eye for recognizing raw talent and an ability for developing that talent beyond other people's expectations. He regularly spotted and lassoed athletes who could run, shoot, rebound, and play zone defense, and then annually blended them into coherent units. Boeheim brought to Syracuse some elite prep players, for sure, including stars such as Pearl Washington, Derrick Coleman, Billy Owens, Sherman Douglas, John Wallace, Carmelo Anthony, Jonny Flynn, Donté Greene, Fab Melo, Dion Waiters, Michael Carter-Williams, Tyler Ennis, Malachi Richardson, and Tyus Battle, but still not nearly as many blue-chippers as Dean Smith, Krzyzewski, Pitino, and, later, Calipari, who didn't seem to have their coaching ability slighted because of their penchant for annually attracting high school All-Americans. "Jim's a great recruiter because he's very sincere and very thorough," Pitino stated.

Boeheim has arguably done his best coaching when he lacked big-name stars. His first recruiting class included then relatively unknown players like Roosevelt Bouie and Louis Orr, yet the "Louie and Bouie Show" ran from 1976 to 1980 and produced a 100–18 record. Through the years, overachievers like Orr, Rudy Hackett, Marty Byrnes, Gerry McNamara, and Marek Dolezaj, "sleepers" like Bouie, Erich Sanderson, Dale Shackleford, and Oshae Brissett, unsung players like Marty Headd, Hal Cohen, Howard Triche, and Tyler Lydon, and projects like Rony Seikaly, Fab Melo, and Paschal Chukwu played pivotal roles as the Orange piled up winning seasons and postseason tournament berths. Toward the end, as the recruiting rules changed, Boeheim successfully changed his strategy to bring in fifth-year senior transfers like Andrew White III, John Gillon, and, for 2018, Elijah Hughes from East Carolina to bolster his lineup.

Other than Wallace, the 1996 Final Four team started out with a cast of players few people outside the Big East had ever heard of. In 2013 and 2016, Syracuse again started the season without nationally acknowledged stars on its roster, yet advanced to the Final Four. Former SU player and longtime assistant Mike Hopkins stated, "I think [Boeheim] thinks he can win with anybody. Any situation, he has an answer for. That's what I think makes him great."

However, Pitino also said he thought some of the players that Boeheim recruited were the reason for some of his perception problems. "Jim took players that seemed to be undisciplined from a recruiter's eye," he said. "He took players that nobody else wanted.

"Players can make a coach look good, or they can make a coach look bad. Jim took players regarded as headaches, and sometimes they didn't make him look good. Look at Derrick Coleman, Billy Owens, and Rony Seikaly. When they got to the next level, they had difficulties. But that's not a criticism of Jim," Pitino made clear. "It's a compliment because he could handle them. Players like 'Pearl' Washington and [Tony] 'Red' Bruin were not easy to deal with, but he dealt with them very well. Very few coaches could handle some of the players he's had and still win the number of games that he's won. That's to his credit."

Not unlike many other programs, some of Syracuse's players had problems on and off the court in college and/or later in the NBA. Rest assured, however, that if Boeheim hadn't landed them a few years earlier, coaches from coast-to-coast were lined up in the hopes of getting the opportunity to try and handle Pearl and Owens, regarded by many as the No. 1 and 2 high school seniors in the country when the Cuse corralled them in 1984 and 1989. The same with Bruin (1980), Coleman (1987), and Fab Melo (2011) when they were prep All-Americans out of New York City, Detroit, and Weston, Florida, respectively. On February 11, 2017, Melo, at the age of 26, passed away in his sleep from an apparent heart attack. "I'm very sorry to hear about the passing of Fab Melo," Boeheim tweeted. "He was a kind, genuine person who was committed to doing his best while he was at Syracuse. Our staff and his teammates were fortunate to have had the opportunity to know Fab. Our prayers go out to all of his loved ones."

18

BOEHEIM DEBATE CONTINUES: POINT-COUNTERPOINT

Even when his career was winding down and after he had just taken the Orange to two Final Fours in four years, Boeheim was still hearing the same complaints from people who wanted him to retire. With social media in full force, Boeheim became even more of a lightning rod, a polarizing figure for Internet debaters, almost all of whom claimed to be Syracuse fans. Those against him still stated that he lacked a sound coaching philosophy, played a playground offense, a lazy defense, and was incapable of making good in-game and especially end-of-game decisions and adjustments. They said he just threw the ball out and let the players freelance, that he had done less with more than any other coach in the country, that his 20-plus win seasons almost every year were due to playing easy teams, and that his reluctance to play good teams on the road didn't prepare Syracuse for the NCAA tournament. When the Orange didn't dance as far as they thought they should in the NCAA tournament, they canceled out any success the team may have had in the regular season. They complained that Boeheim had only won one national championship in 40-plus years, and they simply chalked that up to Carmelo Anthony, as if Calhoun could have won in 1999 without Richard Hamilton, in 2004 without Emeka Okafor, and in 2011 without Kemba Walker, or the Huskies could have been champions in 2014 under Kevin Ollie without Shabazz Napier. As if John Thompson could have won in 1984 without Patrick Ewing and Larry Brown in 1988 without Danny Manning, Rick Pitino in 1995 without his team of future pros and John Calipari in 2013 without his team of one-and-doners. Or going back further to Norm Sloan at NC State in 1974 without David Thompson and John Wooden at UCLA in the 1960s and 1970s without Kareem Abdul-Jabbar, Bill Walton, plus his other stars and the decade and a half assistance provided by Sam Gilbert, recognized as the program's sugar daddy. None were discredited for winning with a superstar the way that Boeheim was. The anti-Boeheim crowd shrugged its shoulders when the Orange opened most seasons with 10 or 15 non-conference wins and then went into "its February swoon," though that was the case with most schools who competed in tough leagues like the Big East and ACC where winning mid-season conference games was difficult.

Pro-Boeheim people pointed out that Boeheim's philosophy proved to be a winning one, that his motion offense attracted recruits because they enjoyed playing that running style that allowed them freedom to utilize their creativity and talent, that his zone statistically was usually among the best defenses in the nation every year and one that, toward the end of his career, slowly but surely more and more coaches began emulating. They pointed out that Boeheim was the winningest coach in the Big East conference, had the best road record in the Big East, and that the strength of the Big East and later the Atlantic Coast Conference provided plenty of tough competition that sufficiently prepared the Orange for the NCAA tournament. Contrary to the naysayers, considering that through 2018 Boeheim only had 20 McDonald's All-Americans compared to 74 at Duke, 72 at North Carolina, 63 at Kentucky, 43 at Kansas, and 35 at UCLA, Boeheim clearly got more out of less than any coach in the country. They reminded people that Boeheim had advanced to five Final Fours, nine unofficial and eight official Elite Eights, 19 unofficial and 18 official Sweet 16s, and that his 60 on-court NCAA tournament wins were fourth best all-time. They noted that from 2009–10 through 2012–13, the Orange had won 121 on-court games, the most SU wins in four consecutive seasons ever. Furthermore, that in 2017–18 Syracuse concluded its 48th consecutive on-court winning basketball season, the longest streak of continued Division I success in the country—and that most of that was under Boeheim's tutelage. On top of that, in the last quarter-century, Syracuse was one of only a handful of schools to have reached the NCAA championship game three or more times. SU is also tied for 11th with four other programs for advancing to the Final Four six times.

They noted furthermore that when Boeheim faced his toughest competition, such as when Syracuse reached the Elite Eight, Boeheim fared pretty well. When he advanced to the Final Four, he won the first game three out of five times, while winning once and losing twice in the national championship game. When the going got its toughest, Boeheim won most of the time. No matter the circumstances, Boeheim won. Krzyzewski, Pitino, Knight, and other coaching colleagues agreed—that's coaching and not coincidence.

In response to those who complained that it had been fifteen years since Carmelo Anthony led Syracuse to the top in 2003, they pointed out that North Carolina endured a twenty-five-year lapse from its 1957 national championship until Michael Jordan led the Tar Heels to the 1982 title, Kansas had to bide its time for thirty-six years from 1952 until Danny Manning took KU to the promised land again in 1988, that the Ohio State teams with Jerry Lucas and John Havlicek won back-to-back titles in 1960 and 1961, but the Buckeyes are still waiting to reach the summit again. They felt the Boeheim's detractors needed to understand just how difficult it was to win multiple national championships. Except for John Wooden's ten-year UCLA dynasty, only a handful of programs have won two or more national titles. Furthermore, the programs that are ranked higher than the Orange are mostly large state schools. Compared to other small private schools, in the sports world, Syracuse had very little company. Instead of knocking the Orange, they accentuated that Syracuse, for its accomplishments on the hardwood, was the envy of more than 300 Division I schools.

In short, Boeheim boosters said, if it's not broken, don't fix it. Those with little respect for the Hall of Famer and everything he had accomplished were not interested in and did not want to hear any of that. For them, if they saw Boeheim walking on water, their response would be: "See, I told you he couldn't swim."

The old-timers remembered the nation-leading 27-game losing streak that Syracuse endured prior to the Bing-led SU renaissance. They said the younger fans griped because they never experienced what bad basketball really was. They felt that Boeheim's Orangemen had been winning for so long that many people alive had become spoiled. They felt that anyone who criticized Boeheim for the underachieving teams of 1988, 1989, and 2016, to be fair, had to give him equal credit for the overachieving units of 1996, 2009, 2010, 2013, 2016, and 2018. Before the 2016 season, one Internet contributor wrote, "It's time for the old man to retire." To which another retorted, "No it isn't." It was a never-ending debate that went on throughout his career. And continues to go on.

Discussions and debates are also ongoing about Syracuse's status in the college basketball environment. Based on a combination of history, tradition, championships, prestige, and the ability to sign five-star recruits that usually end up in the NBA, most people would consider the blue blood programs to be Kentucky, North Carolina, Duke, and Kansas and maybe UCLA and Indiana, although the Bruins and Hoosiers have lost some of their luster and may no longer be top-tier. Blue bloods may not win the national championship every year, but they are expected to compete for it, and failure to do so is disappointing to their fan bases. Many people would include Syracuse a tier below in the elite category, along with Arizona, Louisville,

Connecticut, and Michigan State, meaning programs that have maintained a high level of success over a long period of time, are regularly ranked in the Top 25, and are routinely selected for the NCAA tournament. In any given year, the elite programs can and do beat the blue bloods and can be expected to compete for the national championship. Elite programs are respected nationally, just not as much as the blue bloods.

The case for Syracuse's inclusion among the elite is that the Orange was very good when it won two Helms national championships (1918, 1926) before the establishment of the NCAA tournament. After that, they added a national championship in 2003, six trips to the Final Four, and over four decades of sustained success that included numerous seasons in the Top 25 rankings and regular trips to the NCAA Tournament. With 1,985 on-court conquests, Syracuse ranks fifth in all-time wins, trailing only North Carolina, Kentucky, Kansas, and Duke. With 1,884 official victories, the Cuse is sixth, behind UCLA. Accustomed to winning, the program has enjoyed 48 consecutive on-court winning seasons, the longest active streak in Division I. However, the sanctions officially snapped that mark in 2004–05, reducing SU's run to 35 seasons.

Without question, Boeheim played the biggest part in the Orange's return to national prominence. With 1,027 on-court victories, Boeheim has won more than half of the school's triumphs. As a player, graduate assistant, assistant coach, and head coach, almost continuously since 1962, Boeheim has been associated with Syracuse for a half-century and more than 1,600 of the school's 2,882 games. Told by a reporter how many of SU's games he had been involved with, Boeheim laughed and responded, "Is that all? I thought I was here for the very first one." To put it bluntly, Boeheim has a vested interest in his alma mater. No wonder he bleeds Syracuse Orange and, like all coaches, wants every call to go his way.

EPILOGUE

Jim Boeheim is a basketball junkie, pure and simple. He lives and breathes basketball. Meetings, keeping up with opponents and recruits, and practice are not enough. He goes home and sometimes watches four or five basketball games on television. Boeheim doesn't just watch the games. He studies them, looking for something to gain a competitive edge. As a result, he's won more basketball games than almost everybody in the country. "I just like the game," he stated about his consumption with it.

Besides Dick Blackwell, his high school coach, Fred Lewis, his college coach, Roy Danforth, for whom he was an assistant, and John Egli, from whom he got some of his early ideas for the zone, Boeheim continually studies other coaches and picks up things here and there along the way. He learned some things about the motion offense from Bobby Knight, how to apply full-court pressure from John Wooden, and incorporated some of the things that North Carolina did. Plus he picked up numerous coaching nuggets from being Mike Krzyzewski's right-hand man and from working with professional athletes at the Olympic Games. Recognizing that some of the best coaching is done at the high school level, he even takes ideas from prep coaches to improve his coaching.

While Boeheim takes a little bit from this one and a little bit from that one, he doesn't copy anyone. Boeheim is his own man. He dances to the beat of his own drummer. Like Frank Sinatra, he does things his way, and his way is different from many other coaches. A few cases in point: Boeheim doesn't have shootarounds prior to a game, a standard practice among coaches. Against the grain, he creates a relaxed atmosphere with a professional culture within his college program, one with few restrictions. A delegator who gives his assistant coaches and staff members responsibilities and expects them to do their jobs, Boeheim allows his subordinates the liberty to use their knowledge and skills to have a sense of ownership in the program. "I don't tell them what to do every day," he explained. By allowing them to work without close supervision, he provides them with the experience they need to one day run a successful program of their own.

Generally, Boeheim's routine is to observe the start of practice, preferring to let his assistants take the players through their drills. He usually waits until the team begins scrimmaging or practicing game situations before he gets involved. During games, however, Boeheim assumes complete control. Possessing an extraordinary knack for making decisions, Boeheim relies solely on his judgment and experience. Becoming a micromanager, he rarely seeks input from his assistants, choosing to make all the game decisions himself. Unlike many head coaches, Boeheim's assistants do not sit next to him on the bench during games. He doesn't hang around with them either, even on road trips where his habit is to stay in his hotel room and read, which is why it is reasonable to believe that he was unaware of what others involved in his basketball operation were doing all the time.

Boeheim wants his athletes to graduate and get a great university experience, but, again taking a different approach from many of his peers, he doesn't overplay his importance by trying to be a father figure or their leader in life. He believes his primary responsibility is to be their coach and not a philosopher or policeman. He doesn't try to control his players off the court and watch them 24/7. Maintaining an NBA mentality, rather than monitoring their every move, Boeheim treats his players like adults and allows them their freedom, counsels them and then expects them to make the right decisions. When traveling to away games, he allows them a lot of leeway. Scoop Jardine told *Sports Illustrated,* "Half the time I didn't even see him. I saw him when it was time to see him." However, if players get into trouble, there are consequences. Never one to muzzle his players, Syracuse practices and the locker room are generally open, with players almost always assessable to the media, another rarity in many big-time programs. Boeheim believes that one of the key components of his success over the years is that he tries to be consistent with everything that he does and in doing so strives to improve all facets of the game every day. "We work on everything in order to get better," he said.

Assistant coach Mike Hopkins who played for Boeheim and had been a part of 644 of Boeheim's 1,027 on-court wins, including four that he head-coached in Boeheim's absence, said that a key to Boeheim's success was that Boeheim was able to make complex things simple and that he almost had a sixth sense for making decisions based on feel. Hopkins said that instead of focusing on an opponent's tendencies, Boeheim concentrated on Syracuse's strengths and style of play. The best example, of course, was Boeheim working on improving his zone regardless of the opponent. In a way, Boeheim's philosophy is similar to Alabama football coach Nick Saban, who emphasizes that an important element of his "process" is that the Crimson Tide plays to the program's standards, no matter who lines up across from his team.

Though it may be hard for some of the younger fans to believe, Boeheim in some ways has changed over the years. Roosevelt Bouie, who played on his first team, said that when Boeheim first became head coach that there were no chairs to sit on during practice, only 15-second water breaks, and that the players ran with bricks in their hands and the gym was quiet with no distractions. Several years later, Bouie watched a practice and found it interesting that there were several chairs on the sidelines, a bucket filled with Gatorade and sports drinks, a pack of gum on the table for each player in their favorite flavor, no bricks, and a lot of talking and laughing. "I think he's mellowed," he said, "but he still gets the job done."

Boeheim may have mellowed somewhat, but according to Hopkins, who had been around him for many years, Boeheim still had the competitive fire in his belly. "He'll have his moments when he has his tirades, but he's always been a great communicator. Sometimes he's yelling, and sometimes he's not. He knows how to push the buttons. He's a master at getting the guys to do what he wants them to do."

Old enough to be the grandfather of the players that he coaches, Boeheim realizes that society, in general, has changed and so have accepted norms. However, he doesn't buy into all of the changes. A relic who still reads the newspaper, Boeheim does not email, does not read blogs, and does not surf the Internet. He doesn't own a computer, but he does have a cell phone. Whereas in his era players listened to Elvis Presley and The Beatles on a record player and there was no social media to distract them during the day, he understands that current players are attached to their cell phones and into texting, tweeting, and listening to rap music. As he advances in his career, he understands that the dictatorial style of coaching that was in vogue when he played no longer works. Bouie said that back in his day when the coach told him to do something, he did it, but with many of today's youth that wasn't necessarily the case. He said Boeheim told him, "Now kids have a tendency to take things personally."

Despite the generational and cultural differences, Boeheim somehow manages to adjust and relate to the athletes who come from vastly different backgrounds than his. "I'm not friends with them, but I've met a lot of his players through the years. Almost all of them told me that they would run through a wall for him. [Longtime assistant coach] Bernie [Fine] has also told me that," stated the late Rick Dean, Boeheim's old teammate. "[Jim's] basic personality is the same. I think there are four things that it takes to be a coach: the ability to recruit, be a good practice coach, a good game coach, and the relationships that you have with your players. I think, based on his record, that Jimmy gets no worse than an A-minus in any of those four categories.

I think he gets high marks across the board, maybe higher in some areas than others. I just don't think you can sustain what he did for that many years and not be good in those areas," continued Dean. "I see Jimmy the same way he was as a player. His basic personality is the same. He's calm, collected, smart, analytical, and well prepared. From my experience in the military I learned that the man at the top is responsible {for the success of that organization], and Jimmy is at the top."

George Hicker added, "I think Jim has always been fair with his players. I think that every year by the end of March he has it figured out and has the best players on the court [for postseason play]. That's why he is able to keep winning."

Through the decades, Boeheim has changed in some ways, and in some ways, he hasn't. What remains a constant is that the Ws keep coming. As legendary Connecticut women's coach Geno Auriemma jokingly told Vickie Fulkerson of TheDay.com, "Jim Boeheim was in the room when [James] Naismith [the inventor of basketball] determined the basket was going to be ten-feet tall," then seriously added, "Syracuse has a long tradition ... I enjoy talking to [Boeheim]. I think he's got a different perspective on the coaching profession. He's somebody when I have a question, when I felt I needed to run something by someone, I would feel comfortable getting an honest opinion from him. He's very honest, very realistic. He gives you an honest assessment of his team, your team."

As many have said or alluded to, Jim is Jim. Except to only those in his close circle, whom Boeheim would sometimes show other dimensions of his personality, what you see is what you get. When it comes to winning basketball games, the result is pretty good, especially if someone is a Syracuse University basketball fan.

Like everyone else, Roy Danforth, the man Boeheim replaced, said that he couldn't foresee the level of success that Boeheim and Syracuse would achieve. "No, I couldn't imagine that. Not at all," he stated. "Jim has done a great job. He's had a great career. He is certainly deserving of all the accolades that he has received."

Jim Boeheim has endured. He has withstood the toughest test of all, the test of time. Loyal as the day is long, Boeheim, unlike some, never job-hopped. He is a nester, not a nomad. Despite all the moaning and groaning from near and far, Boeheim enjoys as much job security as anybody in big-time coaching can expect or hope for. If he ever had reason to look over his shoulder, it might have been in the early 1980s when the late Larry Costello was named head coach at Utica College, Syracuse's sister campus fifty miles to the east. A long basketball pass away, some speculated that Costello, from the Syracuse suburb of Minoa who had played professionally for the old Syracuse Nats and coached the Kareem Abdul-Jabbar-led Milwaukee Bucks to an NBA championship, was waiting in the wings in case Boeheim stumbled or took a misstep. However, Boeheim never did. He has survived NCAA problems in the early 1990s, cancer, the Bernie Fine fiasco, conference realignment, and NCAA problems in 2013 and 2015. He has not only survived, he has thrived. Boeheim is a Syracuse lifer. He is known throughout the basketball world, but he belongs to Syracuse.

C. R. Wysocki may have spoken for a lot of people when he stated his personal feeling about Boeheim in a May 14, 2016, letter to the editor of the *Syracuse Post-Standard*. "Jim, you truly don't know how much joy you have brought to anyone connected to the city of Syracuse and/or to Syracuse University in their lifetime, but also the pride that you have instilled in all Syracusans everywhere. You stayed the course through all of the criticisms; the compliments, the ups and the downs, and you remained true to the city, the Central New York area, and to your school. I (and I am sure the majority of Syracusans) just want to say thank you. One of life's amazing nuances is how people that you have no personal relationship with and, most likely, have never met face-to-face can have such an impact in a person's life and these three gentlemen (Joel Mareiniss, Pearl Washington, and Boeheim) certainly have influenced the lives of many in our community."

Boeheim, for sure, has and continues to do a lot for the community, much of it behind the scenes and without publicity. On at least a couple of occasions and maybe more, he has complied with requests from people to call a family member who was dying but hoped to speak with the coach before passing. After one such occasion, online commenter donnie4hof wrote, "Dang Jimmy. I try so hard not to like you, and then you go and do something like this. Very nice."

SU's national championship, six Final Fours, three Hall of Famers, 45 All-Americans, Dave Bing, "The Louie and Bouie Show," "Manley Field House is officially closed," Pearl's shot versus Boston College, Keith Smart's dagger from the corner, "The Cuse is in the house," Hakim Warrick's block, the six-overtime win over UConn, the 2–3 zone, and Jim Boeheim are all a part of Syracuse's basketball lexicon. To be clear, Boeheim is either responsible for, a part of, or connected in some way to almost all of that.

The lyrics as written by Paul Anka, Claude François, and Jacques Revaux for Sinatra's "My Way" in some ways seem like they could also apply to Jim Boeheim. With apologies, here they are modified to fit Boeheim:

> *And now the end is near*
> *I can see the finish line*
> *Not yet, but in due time*
> *I've won a lot, lost a few*
> *Experienced great highs and depressing lows*
> *And I did it my way*

> *To many it's just a game*
> *Played with a ball and a basket*
> *They don't understand*
> *It's in my blood, in my DNA*

> *Such a thrill playing at home*
> *Almost heaven in the Carrier Dome*
> *I've repped Syracuse U and the USA*
> *Doesn't get much better than that*
> *More importantly, I did it my way*

No excuses, I've taken it on the chin
Not fun because I like to win
I've made mistakes and I've taken the heat
Stayed the course, didn't skip a beat
Through it all I did it my way

Got to 1,000 but the NCAA said no
So still got a ways to go
Out recruiting, on the road again
More games to play, more games to win
Before I pack it in
Rest assured, I'll do it my way

Thought about pulling the plug
But the thought of coaching Buddy
I felt the tug
To keep doing my thing
For another shot at the championship ring
When it's all over, no matter the ending
Let it be clear, I did it my way

When my time is up
Underneath the court that bears my name
Is a resting place as good as any
When it's all said and done
Let it be said, I did it my way

For four-plus decades and counting, Boeheim has loomed over the city like no other figure. When he finally retires, whenever that will be, it will be a brave new world for Syracuse basketball. The first season should be pegged "One AB," the year "After Boeheim." For whoever it is, following in the footsteps of a legend will not be easy.

APPENDIX:

BOEHEIM IN THE COACHING RANKINGS

All-time Division I Coaches by Wins

1. Mike Krzyzewski   1,100
2. Jim Boeheim   1,027/926
3. Bob Knight   902
4. Dean Smith   879
5. Adolph Rupp   876
6. Jim Calhoun   873

Active Division I Coaches by Wins

1. Mike Krzyzewski   1,100
2. Jim Boeheim   1,027/926
3. Bob Huggins   845

Division I Coaches with 20-Win Seasons

1. Jim Boeheim   38/33
2. Mike Krzyzewski   34
3. Dean Smith   30
4. Bob Knight   29
4. Lute Olson   29

Division I Coaches by Number of NCAA Tournament Wins

1. Mike Krzyzewski   91
2. Roy Williams   72
3. Dean Smith   65
4. Jim Boeheim   60/56
5. Rick Pitino   54
6. Jim Calhoun   49
6. Mike Izzo   47
6. John Wooden   47
8. Lute Olson   46
9. Bob Knight   45

Division I Coaches by Number of Seasons with Current School

1. Jim Boeheim   42
2. Mike Krzyzewski   37

Coaches Fastest to 100 Wins

	Games	Seasons	Year
1. Doc Meanwell	109	7th	1918
2. Buck Freeman	110	5th	1932
3. Adolph Rupp	116	6th	1936
4. Jim Boeheim	117	4th	1980
4. Jerry Tarkanian	117	5th	1973

Coaches Fastest to 800 Wins

	Games	Seasons	Year
1. Adolph Rupp	972	37th	1969
2. Dean Smith	1,028	33rd	1994

3. Mike Krzyzewski	1,064	33rd	2008
4. Jim Boeheim	1,088	34th	2009

Active Division I Coaches by Total Games

1. Mike Krzyzewski   1,438
2. Jim Boeheim   1,398

Most Wins by School

Kentucky	2,263
Kansas	2,248
North Carolina	2,232
Duke	2,144
Syracuse	1,985/1,884
Temple	1,903
UCLA	1,849
Notre Dame	1,845
St. John's	1,817
Louisville	1,803
Indiana	1,801

Consecutive Winning Seasons Completed

1. Syracuse   48/35

Syracuse: Tournaments and Championships

NCAA Tournament Appearances (39): 1957, 1966, 1973, 1974, 1975, 1976, 1977, 1978, 1979, 1980, 1983, 1984, 1985, 1986, 1987, 1988, 1989, 1990, 1991, 1992, 1994, 1995, 1996, 1998, 1999, 2000, 2001, 2003, 2004, 2005, 2006, 2009, 2010, 2011, 2012, 2013, 2014, 2016, 2018
NCAA Tournament Record: (68–39/64–39)

NCAA Championships (1): 2003

Helms Foundation National Championships (2): 1917–18, 1925–26

NCAA Final Four Appearances (6): 1975, 1987, 1996, 2003, 2013, 2016

NCAA Elite Eight Appearances (10/9): 1957, 1966, 1975, 1987, 1989, 1996, 2003, 2012, 2013, 2016

NCAA Sweet 16 Appearances (20/19): 1975, 1977, 1979, 1980, 1984, 1987, 1989, 1990, 1994, 1996, 1998, 2000, 2003, 2004, 2009, 2010, 2013, 2016, 2018

NIT Appearances (13): 1946, 1950, 1964, 1967, 1971, 1972, 1981, 1982, 1997, 2002, 2007, 2008, 2017

NIT Record: 15–14

Big East Regular Season Championships (10): 1980 (tie), 1986 (tie), 1987 (tie), 1990 (tie), 1991, 1998 (BE 7), 2000 (tie), 2003 (West tie), 2010, 2012

Big East Tournament Championships (5): 1981, 1988, 1992, 2005, 2006

Naismith Memorial Basketball Hall of Fame (3): Vic Hanson (1960), Dave Bing (1990), and Jim Boeheim (2005)

Consensus All-Americans (10): Dave Bing (1966), Rony Seikaly (1988), Sherman Douglas (1989), Derrick Coleman (1990), Pearl Washington (1990), Billy Owens (1991), John Wallace (1996), Carmelo Anthony (2003), Hakim Warrick (2005), Wesley Johnson (2010)

All-Americans (45/23 individuals): Lewis Castle (1912, 1914), Joseph Schwarzer (1918), Leon Marcus (1919), Vic Hanson (1925, 1926, 1927), Billy Gabor (1946, 1947), John Kiley (1951), Vincent Cohen (1957), Dave Bing (1965, 1966), Vaughn Harper (1967), George Hicker (1967), Rick Dean (1967), Bill Smith (1971), Greg Kohls (1972), Dennis DuVal (1973, 1974), Rudy Hackett (1975), Jim Lee (1975), Roosevelt Bouie (1979, 1980), Louis Orr (1980), Danny Schayes (1981), Erich Santifer (1982, 1983), Leo Rautins (1983), Pearl Washington (1984, 1985, 1986), Rafael Addison (1984,

1985, 1986), Wendell Alexis (1986), Rony Seikaly (1987, 1988), Sherman Douglas (1987, 1988, 1989), Derrick Coleman (1987, 1988, 1989, 1990), Stephen Thompson (1989, 1990), Billy Owens (1990, 1991), Lawrence Moten (1993, 1994, 1995), John Wallace (1996), Etan Thomas (2000), Preston Shumpert (2001, 2002), Carmelo Anthony (2003), Hakim Warrick (2004, 2005), Gerry McNamara (2006), Demetris Nichols (2007), Jonny Flynn (2009), Wesley Johnson (2010), Andy Rautins (2010), Rick Jackson (2011), Kris Joseph (2012), C. J. Fair (2014), Tyler Ennis (2014), Rakeem Christmas (2015)

All-Americans Coached by Boeheim (44, 29 individuals): Bouie (1979, 1980), Orr (1980), Schayes (1981), Santifer (1982, 1983), Rautins (1983), Washington (1984, 1985, 1986), Addison (1984, 1985, 1986), Alexis (1986), Coleman (1987), Seikaly (1987, 1988), Douglas (1987, 1988, 1989), Thompson (1989, 1990), Owens (1990, 1991), Moten (1993, 1994, 1995), Wallace (1996), Thomas (2000), Shumpert (2001, 2002), Anthony (2003), Warrick (2004, 2005), McNamara (2006), Nichols (2007), Flynn (2009), Johnson (2010), Rautins (2010), Jackson (2011), Joseph (2012), Fair (2014), Ennis (2014), Christmas (2015)

Retired Jerseys (14): Vic Hanson (#8, 12/19/81), Dave Bing (#22, 12/19/81), Pearl Washington (#31, 3/2/96), Sherman Douglas (#20, 3/9/03), Wilmeth Sidat-Singh (#19, 2/26/05), Derrick Coleman (#44, 3/6/06), Rony Seikaly (#4, 1/13/07), Billy Owens (#30, 3/8/08), Billy Gabor (#17, 3/1/09), Carmelo Anthony (#15, 2/23/13), Roosevelt Bouie (#50, 2/21/15), Louis Orr (#55, 2/21/15), Dennis DuVal (#22, 1/6/2018), Lawrence Moten (#21, 3/3/2018)

All-Century Team: Rafael Addison (1982–86), Dave Bing (1963–66), Jim Boeheim (coach 1979–), Roosevelt Bouie (1976–80), Marty Byrnes (1974–78), Vincent Cohen (1953–56), Derrick Coleman (1986–90), Sherman Douglas (1985–89), Dennis DuVal (1971–74), Billy Gabor (1942–48), Rudy Hackett (1972–75), Vic Hanson (1924–27), Jason Hart (1996–00), Greg Kohls (1969–72), Jim Lee

(1972–75), Lawrence Moten (1991–95), Louis Orr (1976–80), Billy Owens (1988–91), Leo Rautins (1980–83), Danny Schayes (1977–81), Joseph Schwarzer (1915–18), Rony Seikaly (1984–88), Etan Thomas (1996–00), Stephen Thompson (1986–90), John Wallace (1992–96), Dwayne Washington (1983–86)

McDonald's All-Americans: Malachi Richardson (2015), DaJuan Coleman (2012), Rakeem Christmas (2011), Michael Carter-Williams (2011), Fab Melo (2010), Jonny Flynn (2007), Donte' Greene (2007), Eric Devendorf (2005), Carmelo Anthony (2002), Michael Lloyd (1992; started collegiate career at San Jacinto Junior College), John Wallace 1992, Adrian Autry (1990), Conrad McRae (1989), Billy Owens (1988), Derrick Coleman (1986), Stephen Thompson (1986), Rodney Walker (1985), Michael Brown (1984), Pearl Washington (1983), Tony Bruin (1979)

Sources: Syracuse Men's Basketball Media Guide 2017–18

Boeheim's Coaching Tree: Rick Pitino, Bernie Fine, Brendan Malone, Tim Welsh, Ralph Willard, Louis Orr, Tim O'Toole, Stephen Thompson, Wayne Morgan, Allen Griffin, Wendell Alexis, Adrian Autry, and Rick Callahan, as well as Scotty Hicks, Mike Hopkins, Troy Weaver, and Rob Murphy.

Syracuse Basketball: "Running with the Big Dogs"

Syracuse may not be in the top five of college basketball teams, but it doesn't take long to call the roll before coming to SU.

Syracuse #9: In March 2017, the Associated Press listed its Top 100 programs of all time since it began ranking teams in 1949. Giving points based on appearances in the AP poll and No. 1 rankings to determine elite programs and consistency, the AP designated Syracuse, with 581 points, as the No. 9 program behind Kentucky (1,111 points), North Carolina (1,098), Duke (1,032), UCLA (957), Kansas (857), Indiana (662), Louisville (627), and Arizona (595). The AP noted that Syracuse appeared in 47.7 percent of all the polls with seventeen No. 1 rankings since making its first appearance in December 1951. The Orange made the polls only seventeen times prior to

Boeheim being named coach in 1976, and since then, the Cuse has made over 500 appearances with at least one appearance every season since 1982–83. Syracuse's best full decade was the 1990s when the Orange was listed in 76.9 percent of all polls. Its worst decade was the 1960s when SU only made 2.02 percent of the polls.

Syracuse #3: In March 2018, according to Equity in Athletics data received by the Office of Postsecondary Education from the Department of Education website, Syracuse ranked third among colleges producing the most basketball revenue behind Duke and Louisville.

Syracuse #4: In March 2017, the US Department of Education released information regarding the money generated by college basketball programs. Syracuse basketball made $26.9 million, fourth behind Louisville ($45.6), Duke ($31), and Kentucky ($27.2).

Syracuse #7: In January 2016, the *Sporting News* listed its Top 15 college basketball programs since 2000–01. Syracuse was No. 7 behind Duke, Kansas, Kentucky, UConn, North Carolina, and Florida.

Syracuse #8: In September 2013, ESPN's Jeff Goodman came out with the College Basketball Future Power Program rankings. Syracuse was ranked eighth, behind Duke, Kentucky, Kansas, Louisville, Florida, Michigan State, and Arizona. Goodman stated, "Jim Boeheim has had it rolling in Syracuse for quite a while."

Syracuse #8: In August 2012, ESPN developed an intricate point system to try and determine the Top 50 college basketball programs in the last fifty years. Syracuse ranked eighth best in the country over the course of the last half-century, behind North Carolina, UCLA, Kentucky, Duke, Kansas, Louisville, and Indiana. ESPN stated Syracuse benefited from its "incredible consistency" over the long-term, placing in the top six for NCAA berths and winning percentage points, with no losing seasons since 1969.

Syracuse #1 in the Big East: On June 6, 2012, fourteen writers and television analysts on ESPN.com picked the best coaching job in the Big East. Based on several factors, the group tapped Syracuse as the best job in the conference, followed by Louisville, Connecticut, and Georgetown. The summation on Syracuse: "Take away the snow, and what's not to like about Syracuse? With a ready-made fan base, a home court that sets attendance records, and a rich tradition, the Orange are the class job of the league."

Syracuse #7: ESPN's Eamonn Brennan listed his top 10 most attractive men's coaching positions in the NCAA, with Syracuse ranked seventh, behind North Carolina, Kentucky, Kansas, UCLA, Indiana, and Duke. "Syracuse has a legendary coach who built a program that [has] dominated the Northeast ... Another attraction is the Carrier Dome."

Syracuse #9: NBC Sports' listing of the "10 Greatest Basketball Programs" of all time had Syracuse No. 9, trailing only Kentucky, North Carolina, Kansas, UCLA, Duke, Indiana, Louisville, and Arizona.

Syracuse #10: ESPN, in its 2007 list of the "Top 10 Best Basketball Programs in the Last 10 Years," had Syracuse No. 10, behind Duke, Michigan State, Connecticut, Florida, Kansas, North Carolina, Kentucky, Arizona, and Maryland.

Syracuse #9: *Triangle Hoops Journal*'s "Power Ranking of the Top 20 College Basketball Programs" of all time had Syracuse No. 9, behind Kentucky, UCLA, North Carolina, Duke, Kansas, Indiana, Louisville, and Michigan State

Syracuse #7: "Fan Vote Top 10" had Syracuse No. 7, behind North Carolina, Duke, UCLA, Kansas, Kentucky, and Indiana.

Syracuse #8: CBB's "Blue Bloods Top 10" all-time programs, based on NCAA appearances, Final Fours, total wins, and overall consistency, listed Syracuse No. 8, behind UCLA, Kentucky, North Carolina, Indiana, Kansas, Duke, and Louisville.

Syracuse #4: In January 2015, *National Geographic Traveler* magazine stated that Syracuse was one of the "Final Four" best cities for college basketball, along with Lawrence, Kansas, home of the Kansas Jayhawks; Chapel Hill, North Carolina, home of the North Carolina Tar Heels; and Spokane, Washington, home of the Gonzaga Bulldogs. Writer Katie Knorovsky stated, "The chill of upstate New York is no match for Orange Fever."

Syracuse #7: Through March 2016, Syracuse, with 14, was tied for seventh with Louisville and Connecticut for the most appearances in the NCAA tournament since the field was expanded to sixty-four in 1985. Ahead of that trio was Duke (23), North Carolina (21), Kansas (20), Kentucky (19), Arizona (16), and Michigan State (15).

Syracuse #12: In August 2015, *Sporting News* ranked the best college basketball alumni teams based on talent and current alumni playing in the NBA. Syracuse was No. 12 with forwards Carmelo Anthony (New York Knicks) and Jerami Grant (Philadelphia 76ers); guards Michael Carter-Williams (Milwaukee Bucks) and Dion Waiters (Oklahoma City Thunder); center Rakeem Christmas (Indiana Pacers); and sixth man Wes Johnson (Los Angeles Clippers).

Syracuse #9: In March 2016, college professor Ryan Brewer's annual study ranking college basketball's most valuable teams based on what their worth would be on the open market determined that Syracuse was the ninth most valuable program in the country. The top 10 most valuable college basketball programs were: Louisville ($301.3 million), Kansas, Kentucky, Indiana, Ohio State, Arizona, North Carolina, Wisconsin, Syracuse ($203.9 million), and Duke.

Syracuse #4: In March 2017, Businessinsider.com, using a calculated formula based on basketball revenue, found that the fair market value of Syracuse basketball players to the school was $1.01 million, which trailed only the $1.72 million of Louisville players, $1.16 million of Duke, and $1.02 million of Kentucky. The average fair market value of a Division I basketball player to the school was $170,098.

Ranking the Coaches

Boeheim #5: On August 2, 2012, *Athlon Sports* ranked the top college basketball coaches according to several multifaceted criteria. Boeheim came in fifth, behind Michigan's Tom Izzo, Duke's Mike Krzyzewski, Kentucky's John Calipari, and Kansas' Bill Self.

Boeheim #6: On September 17, 2013, an ESPN poll of journalists using similar criteria as the previous entry had Boeheim sixth, with the rest of the order the same except that Rick Pitino jumped to second behind Izzo, with Krzyzewski, Calipari, and Self following.

Boeheim vs. Calhoun #6: On September 3, 2015, the *New York*

Daily News named its Top 10 coaching rivalries in all of sports, professional and college. In a list dominated by college basketball, Boeheim vs. Calhoun came in at No. 6 behind Nick Saban vs. Urban Meyer, Rick Pitino vs. John Calipari, Gene Keady vs. Bob Knight, Bo Ryan vs. Tom Izzo, and Mike Krzyzewski vs. Roy Williams.

ABOUT THE AUTHOR

Dr. Donald F. Staffo has been a sports journalist for 40-plus years. He is the author of ten books and more than 2,150 articles that have been published in a variety of national, regional, and local publications. He covered University of Alabama football and basketball for the Associated Press for thirty years and was a newspaper columnist for more than twenty years.

He retired as professor and department chair emeritus after a 50-year career as an educator. He is the second person and the only living person to receive the American Alliance for Health, Physical Education, Recreation, and Dance's three highest national awards and be inducted into the National Association of Sport and Physical Education Hall of Fame. The recipient of five national, nine state, six distinguished alumni, two regional, and twelve institutional/local awards, he has received the highest awards from four of his five alma maters and has been inducted into five halls of fame, including NASPE, The Ohio State University College of Education and Human Ecology Hall of Fame, the SUNY Brockport Hall of Heritage, and the Greater Utica (NY) Sports Hall of Fame. He has received citations from the US Congress, the Alabama House of Representatives (2), Alabama Senate, the New York State Assembly (2), and the New York State Senate (2). He is the only person to be awarded the title professor and department chair emeritus in the 142-year history of Stillman College. He earned his PhD from The Ohio State University, MA from Western Kentucky University, BS from SUNY Brockport, and his AA from Fulton-Montgomery Community College.

ACKNOWLEDGMENTS

The author expresses his appreciation to all who participated in this project by sharing their thoughts, information, feelings, recollections, and opinions. A big thank you to John Pitarresi, a longtime Syracuse beat writer, for initially reading the manuscript, checking for accuracy, and making suggestions, to Richie Duffy, a former teammate and longtime friend of Jim Boeheim, who provided ongoing encouragement and helped connect me with numerous people, and to Don Cronson and Mike Cutillo, who provided several courtesy photographs and continuous support. Also, to the *Finger Lakes Times* and the Lyons Central School District for providing courtesy photos. Without their contributions this book would not have been possible.

Finally, to my wife Marilyn, who provided encouragement and the technical support that enabled me to complete this task and who persevered while I dedicated myself to this project. This book is dedicated to Marilyn, my daughters, Andrea and Deanna, and their families, to my deceased parents, Nicholas and Pauline Staffo, and to all fans of Syracuse University basketball.

INDEX